THE ANGLO-SAXON AGE

c. 400–1042

A HISTORY OF ENGLAND IN ELEVEN VOLUMES

General Editor: W. N. Medlicott

* *Already published*
Some of the titles listed above are provisional

THE ANGLO-SAXON AGE
c. 400−1042

by

D. J. V. FISHER

LONGMAN

LONGMAN GROUP LIMITED
London

*Associated companies, branches and representatives
throughout the world*

© Longman Group Limited 1973

First published 1973
ISBN 0 582 48277 1
Set in Linotype Baskerville
Printed in Great Britain at
The Aberdeen University Press

INTRODUCTORY NOTE

ONE of the effects of two world wars and of fifty years of ever-accelerating industrial and social revolution has been the growing interest of the citizen in the story of his land. From this story he seeks to learn the secret of his country's greatness and a way to better living in the future.

There seems, therefore, to be room for a rewriting of the history of England which will hold the interest of the general reader while it appeals at the same time to the student. This new presentation takes account of the recent discoveries of the archaeologist and the historian, without losing sight of the claims of history to take its place among the mental recreations of intelligent people for whom it has no professional concern.

The history will be completed in a series of eleven volumes. The volumes are of medium length, and are intended to provide a readable narrative of the whole course of the history of England and give proper weight to the different strands which form the pattern of the story. No attempt has been made to secure general uniformity of style or treatment. Each period has its special problems, each author his individual technique and mental approach; each volume is meant to stand by itself not only as an expression of the author's methods, tastes, and experience, but as a coherent picture of a phase in the history of the country.

There is, nevertheless, a unity of purpose in the series; the authors have been asked, while avoiding excessive detail, to give particular attention to the interaction of the various aspects of national life and achievement, so that each volume may present a convincing integration of those developments—political, constitutional, economic, social, religious, military, foreign, or cultural—which happen to be dominant at each period. Although considerations of space prevent minute investigation it should still be possible in a series of this length to deal fully with the essential themes.

A short bibliographical note is attached to each volume. This is not intended to supersede existing lists, but rather to call attention to recent works and to the standard bibliographies.

W. N. MEDLICOTT

CONTENTS

1*

MAPS

INTRODUCTION

THE END OF ROMAN BRITAIN

THE end of Roman Britain and the beginning of Anglo-Saxon England were not directly consecutive or datable events. For some decades before their final evacuation elements of the Roman garrison had from time to time been withdrawn from Britain either to support the pretensions of claimants to the Imperial throne or, at moments of crisis, to defend Roman frontiers on the Continent. When this happened Picts from the regions beyond the Firth of Forth, Scots from Ireland,[1] and Saxons from the eastern shores of the North Sea, ravaged the coasts of Britain and occasionally penetrated deep into the lowland zone. Until the end of the fourth century the Empire was strong enough to repair the damage done by these incursions and to reconstitute the garrison, though on a steadily reducing scale of numbers. But the troops taken to Gaul by Constantine III in 407 were never replaced and when, three years later, the last remnants of official Roman administration were driven out, the natives of Britain were left to fend for themselves.

From this point onwards until the arrival of the Augustinian mission in 597 any detailed reconstruction of the sequence of events is highly conjectural, but there is a fair measure of agreement about their outline. The native population fought with some measure of success against their traditional foes, of whom the Picts were the most formidable, and to assist them in their defence they invited Saxon warriors to settle in eastern England as federate troops. Before long the mercenaries turned against their paymasters and by the end of the fifth century the Saxons were firmly established in eastern England.

---

[1] Picti and Scotti were the names employed by Latin writers for the inhabitants of the lands north of the Forth, and of Ireland, respectively.

A British revival confined them within that area and in the middle of the sixth century Celts still occupied more than half of England. Thereafter, though the Germanic occupation of the rest of the lowland zone of Britain was not long delayed, much of the west and north was to remain unsubdued. Anglo-Saxon England never attained the territorial limits of the Roman province of Britannia and the Anglo-Saxon occupation of even its eastern and southern parts was a long-drawn-out process.[1]

Britain had not been totally immune from the disasters which afflicted the Roman Empire in the third century, but her insularity had protected her from the worst consequences of barbarian attack and internal disturbance and she shared in the benefits conferred by the reconstruction and reform effected by Diocletian and Constantine. About the beginning of the fourth century almost all the forts of northern Britain were extensively rebuilt and a considerable road-building programme demonstrated governmental interest in a flourishing economy. In 297–298 British craftsmen were sent to assist in the restoration of Autun after its destruction by the Bagaudae, bands of deserters, displaced persons and revolted peasantry who roamed destructively over Gaul. Both the towns and the countryside were more prosperous than ever before: Picts, Scots and Saxons were temporarily quiescent.

The golden age ended when in 342 Picts attacked the protected territories north of Hadrian's Wall and Saxons resumed their raiding on the east coast. The emperor Constans hurried to Britain and reorganized the military defences of the north and of the Saxon Shore.[2] Seven years later Constans was deposed by a military usurper, Magnentius, who, in the attempt to support his pretensions, drained Britain of troops. Magnentius was killed in 353, but the soldiers he had withdrawn were not replaced. Barbarian attacks are reported in 360 and 365, and in 367 Picts and Scots mounted a concerted assault by land and by sea which overran or outflanked Hadrian's Wall, defeated such forces as the Roman military commanders could

---

[1] S. S. Frere, *Britannia* (London, 1967) provides an excellent account of the period covered by this chapter.

[2] Because of its vulnerability to Saxon attack the coastline between the Wash and the Isle of Wight was known as the Saxon Shore. It was defended by forts and fortified harbours such as Burgh Castle, Reculver, Richborough and Porchester, whose garrisons in the fourth century formed a unified command under the count of the Saxon Shore. He shared responsibility for the defence of Britain with the duke of the Britains, whose headquarters were at York.

assemble, and penetrated deep into Britain. For two years the government lost control and the countryside was overrun by plundering barbarian bands. Then the emperor Valentinian despatched four regiments of the Roman field army under Count Theodosius to Britain and the barbarians, who wanted loot rather than land, quickly dispersed.

This achieved, Theodosius reorganized the military defences of Britain to insure against a repetition of the recent disaster. One reason for the Pictish success of 367 had been the treachery of the irregular troops quartered beyond Hadrian's Wall, whose responsibility it was to gather intelligence of barbarian movements: these troops were now removed and the outpost forts which had been overrun were abandoned. Instead, additional responsibility for frontier defence was handed over to the rulers of the native tribes who inhabited the region between the Wall and the Firths of Clyde and Forth, who in return received an increased measure of autonomy. The forts of the Wall now became less important and though restored were garrisoned by irregular militia instead of regular troops. Having experienced the vulnerability of a linear defence to mobile and amphibious attack Theodosius supplemented his frontier dispositions with defences further south; a number of forts in northern England were rebuilt more elaborately than those on the Wall and garrisoned with regular troops. To provide early warning of attack a new system of signal stations was built on the road to the south from Carlisle, and along the east coast from the mouth of the Tyne to Flamborough Head a chain of lookout and signal stations was constructed which as well as providing warning also served to coordinate naval action by fleets based on the estuaries of the Tyne, Tees, and Humber. In Wales, to discourage Scottic raids from Ireland, Caernarvon was rebuilt and naval bases established at Holyhead and in the Bristol Channel. On the south coast Porchester was replaced by a new base at Bitterne, near Southampton. Even more important for the future, Theodosius modernized the defences of almost all the towns in Britain by adding projecting towers to their existing walls which could carry defensive artillery so spaced that it could provide covering fire along the whole face of the walls; the towns were garrisoned by small detachments of regular troops. Protected by these defences the native inhabitants were able to defend themselves effectively for many years after the last remnants of the Roman army had left.

To restore the economy after barbarian raiding might appear a more formidable task than the military reconstruction, but the permanent damage done appears to have been slight. The towns had suffered little. Even the more vulnerable villas mostly escaped destruction. It is likely that the confusion caused by marauding bands permitted slaves and coloni to flee from their masters and a number of villas appear to have ceased to operate at this time, but such were exceptions. One effect of disruption which has been noticed was that small-scale pottery factories closed down and pottery production became concentrated in a few large centres, at Cranbeck in Yorkshire, the Nene Valley, the Oxford region and the New Forest; concurrently in the south crude homemade wares began to appear.

The Theodosian restoration though brilliantly conceived and executed only stabilized the situation temporarily. The Empire continued to suffer from the dual strain imposed on it by competing rivals for the Imperial throne and continuous barbarian pressure on the frontiers. Both factors affected Britain. Military usurpers to the throne denuded the island of troops to support their claims; the central government, in desperate straits, withdrew troops from Britain to defend Italy.

In 383 Magnus Maximus, the military governor of Britain, revolted against the emperor Gratian and crossed to Gaul, where he successfully maintained himself until his death at the hands of the emperor Theodosius five years later. The Wall continued to be held and the kingdoms to the north were still friendly, but the garrisons of the north-western parts of Britain and of North Wales had been taken by Maximus to Gaul. An attempt to compensate for their loss by establishing native kingdoms in Wales allied to Rome, on the model of the kingdoms north of Hadrian's Wall, was not immediately successful. By the end of the century Scots from Ireland were established in Caernarvonshire, and in Pembrokeshire,[1] Carmarthenshire and Gower; seaborne Pictish raids were also resumed. Between 396 and 398, Stilicho, the imperial military commander, organized punitive expeditions against Picts, Scots, and Saxons but their effects were more than counterbalanced by his further withdrawal of British troops in 401 to fight Alaric and his Visigoths. This

[1] It is possible that the recognition of the authority of a warrior-chief from the tribe of the Deisi, from southern Ireland, in Pembrokeshire was part of the policy of Maximus, whereby he proposed to transform erstwhile raiders into defenders of part of the exposed coastline of Wales.

withdrawal was on so considerable a scale that the commands of the duke of the Britains and the count of the Saxon Shore were henceforth quite ineffective.

The inhabitants of Britain remained fully conscious that their province formed part of the Empire, but they were by now even more aware of the dangers which threatened them as their dwindling garrison faced the impossible task of repulsing an increasing weight of barbarian attack. To some men the defence of the Empire was still paramount, to others the defence of Britain was their first priority. Even the attitude of the army was ambivalent for though transfer from Britain meant their promotion into the field army many of the soldiers had close ties with their garrison stations and did not wish to leave them. Their dilemma was underlined when, probably in 405, Niall of the Nine Hostages, high king of Ireland, ravaged the southern coast. The conflict between leaders representing different views of where Britain's interests lay may explain the obscure events of 406-7, when the army in Britain raised three usurpers to the Imperial title in quick succession. In 406 Marcus was declared emperor, only to be killed before the end of the year. His successor Gratian lasted only four months. These men may have received their support from the party which wished to concentrate all resources on local defence. Their policy appeared both timid and unrealistic when in December 406 hordes of Vandals, Alans, and Sueves crossed the Rhine and penetrated deep into Gaul. Even the isolationists might feel that if unchecked the barbarians might reach the Channel coast and pose an additional and immediate threat to Britain. The new crisis led such men to combine with those who were more conscious that Britain was part of the Empire and, feeling that defence was best secured by maintaining the integrity of Imperial frontiers, were prepared to contribute to its defence. Constantine III, Gratian's successor, secured general support for an offensive policy, crossed to Gaul in 407 with a British army and quickly restored the military situation; in 409 he secured control over Spain. In that year the emperor Honorius recognized him as prefect of the Gauls. Unwisely, Constantine then intervened in Italy and fell under suspicion of conspiring to overthrow Honorius; the barbarians in Gaul took up arms again and his British commander in Spain rebelled against him. In 411 he was compelled to surrender to Honorius and was soon after executed.

Meanwhile a devastating Saxon raid on Britain had again exposed the defencelessness of the island. Constantine's ambitious policy was thereby condemned. The ruling classes in Britain expelled his officials and attempted to re-establish relations with the legitimate emperor from whom they asked help. At the time Honorius could do nothing to assist but he wrote a letter authorizing the civitates (the partly self-governing areas of local administration into which Britain was divided) to undertake their own defence. There was no Imperial decision to abandon Britain, nor did the native population wish to secede from the Empire. It was for long hoped and expected that when better times returned the Roman connection would be reaffirmed.

Some contemporary historians believe that this hope was realized, partially and temporarily, by a Roman reoccupation effected between 417 and 429. They argue that the defeat of the tyrants in Gaul and the suppression of the Armorican rebellion made possible the restoration of imperial authority in Britain, and that the evidence of a document known as the *Notitia Dignitatum* translates possibility into near certainty.[1] The *Notitia* provides lists of the military commands of the Empire; though originally compiled after the separation of the eastern and western parts of the Empire in 395 it was subsequently kept up to date and even as late as 425 continued to include a section relating to Britain, which numbered among the military forces assigned to it a field army of 6,000 men under the command of an official styled the ' count ' of Britain. It was thought that the office of count, a military official with a local command, made its first appearance in 410, so that if the army of Britain included a comital contingent among its numbers, then it could only have arrived after the date traditionally accepted for the end of Roman rule. The subsequent identification of counts, with the same local authority as the count of Britain, in other parts of the Empire, perhaps as early as 395 and certainly before 410, has undermined the force of this argument, and it appears more likely that a small field army under a count was introduced and maintained for a time in Britain at the turn of the century to compensate for the reduction of garrison troops which had been proceeding for some time on a dangerous scale. The more general argument that the British lists would not have been retained had no Roman armies remained in

[1] A good discussion of the Notitia is C. E. Stevens ' The British section of the Notitia Dignitatum ', *Archaeological Journal*, XCVII (1941): it is discussed more generally by A. H. M. Jones, *The Later Roman Empire 284-602* (Oxford, 1964) vol. III, pp. 347-80.

Britain is countered by the contentions that either Rome did not recognize that Britain was irretrievably lost and kept the account of its military establishment because it might subsequently prove useful or, alternatively, that the retention of such out of date material is a normal characteristic of bureaucratic inertia. It might reasonably be thought that coin evidence would make a decisive contribution to the determination of a problem of this kind. But Britain drew most of its gold and silver coinage from the mints of Gaul which had ceased to function after 395, so that the absence of later coins in Britain is unreliable testimony on which to base conclusions.

There remains the literary evidence. A fifth-century Gallic chronicler asserted that ' in the reign of Honorius (*ob.* 423) Britain was for ever lost to the Roman name '. The sixth century Byzantine writer Procopius, after mentioning the defeat of the usurper Constantine in 411, continued: ' But in spite of this the Romans were never able to recover Britain, which from that time continued to be governed by usurpers.' Neither source is sufficiently well informed to inspire confidence but in the absence of better testimony it can only be concluded, albeit provisionally, that Britain was finally lost to Rome in 410.

Authority fell at first into the hands of the provisional council, the only body representing the civitates, but before long other changes occurred.

I

SUB-ROMAN BRITAIN: THE FIRST PHASE
OF SAXON OCCUPATION

1. The Evidence: Literary and Archaeological

THE principal literary source which purports to give an account of the years after the Roman withdrawal is a work entitled *De Excidio et Conquestu Britanniae*. Written by a British ecclesiastic in the middle of the sixth century its prime purpose was to exhort his readers to live better lives, and history was invoked principally to demonstrate the disasters which inevitably attended moral corruption. It contains demonstrable errors which may be partly attributable to its derivation from oral tradition, it lacks dates, is sparing of names of persons and places, and is replete with obscurities. Nevertheless the story it tells is, in outline, plausible and its author, Gildas, a man of some learning and intelligence, was contemporary with the latter part of it. Other writings provide information which serves to confirm or to complement or to correct parts of the ground which Gildas covered. A life of St. Germanus of Auxerre, composed in Gaul in about 480, illuminates conditions in the early part of the period. Also from Gaul are two probably contemporary but anonymous *Chronicles* which occasionally refer to events in Britain. Sixth-century Byzantium maintained contacts with Gaul, the channel through which some strange notions and a few valuable facts about Britain reached the historian Procopius.

Writing two hundred years after Gildas, Bede could find little to alter in the account given by his predecessor. Bede was a critical scholar in a position to know of such oral traditions relating to the conquest and settlement as were current in his day and having access to any written materials which might have survived; in particular his close contacts with abbot Albinus of St. Augustine's, Canterbury gave him opportunities to learn what was remembered about the conquest of Kent. That Bede was content in general to paraphrase Gildas must be accounted a strong argument in favour of the credibility of the British writer. He did, however, give the earlier narrative greater precision by contributing a few personal names and some dates, and he added an invaluable analysis of the continental homelands of the invaders and of their settlement areas in Britain which owes nothing to Gildas. Despite its derivative character, the great reputation of Bede and the clarity of his exposition ensured that his version of Gildas, more circumstantial than its model, is that which has passed into the common stock of historical beliefs about the Anglo-Saxon conquest; the consequences of Bede's editing of his sources will be considered later.

In the first half of the ninth century a British writer, Nennius, of whom nothing certain is known, put together a *Historia Brittonum;* its character is aptly described in the preface to one of the manuscripts of the work: ' I have heaped together all that I found, from the annals of the Romans, the writings of the Holy Fathers, the annals of the Irish and the Saxons, and the traditions of our old men.' Beginning at the Creation it proceeds through the history of early Britain to the Roman conquest and occupation of the island, thence to the struggle between the Britons and the Saxon invaders; after an interlude relating to the activities of Palladius and St. Patrick in Ireland comes a further instalment of the account of the British resistance to the Saxons, whose hero is Arthur, duke of Battles, who commanded the Britons in twelve engagements with the Saxons, culminating in a victory at an unidentified place called Mount Badon; this is followed by chapters on Ida, king of the Bernicians, and the genealogies of the royal families of Kent, East Anglia, Mercia and Deira; the work ends by returning to Ida and his successors, whose history it relates until the middle of the seventh century, interspersing its comment with fragments of information relating to British history. The *Historia Brittonum* is clearly a composite work of uneven historical value, and it has been a bone of contention among scholars for generations.[1]

Though much remains obscure there is now general agreement that Nennius's Arthur, though not mentioned by Gildas, was a genuinely historical figure, and that the latter section of the *Historia*

---

[1] A good account of Nennius and the problems associated with the so-called *Historia Brittonum* is L. Alcock, *Arthur's Britain; history and archaeology* (London, 1971), esp. pp. 31-2.

Brittonum, the so-called ' Northern British History ', is a primary
source for Northumbrian history in the sixth and seventh centuries.
Its account of the first phase of the Saxon settlement is of more dubious value; its central character is the British ruler Vortigern, whose
conflicts with his domestic enemies St. Germanus and Ambrosius
Aurelianus and whose dealings with the Saxons are described in a
manner which combines the probable, the possible and the fabulous
in proportions which so far have defied the skill of any editor to
disentangle. The *Historia Brittonum* cannot be ignored but its
statements cannot be accepted unless they receive independent corroboration. Another late compilation, the *Anglo-Saxon Chronicle,*
although not begun until the last decade of the ninth century,
incorporates much early material and is particularly important
because it preserves the English tradition of the manner in which
the kingdoms of Kent, Sussex and Wessex were founded. It gives a
date for every event it records, but there are no grounds for assuming
that the early dates are anything better than guesswork.

These are meagre materials from which to write history, but they
can be powerfully reinforced by evidence derived from archaeology
and place names.

According to Gildas the departure of the legions was followed by
a period of devastation, anarchy, and famine which ended with a
fruitless appeal for help to Aetius, ' thrice consul ', the Roman
commanding general in Gaul. Forced then to recognize that salvation
depended on their own efforts the Britons fought the invaders more
successfully: the attacks of Picts and Scots became less frequent, and
the Britons felt secure enough to indulge in civil wars. This was a
time of material prosperity but of moral corruption, when ' kings
were chosen for their exceptional cruelty and shortly after murdered
by their anointers '. It ended when Britain, weakened by civil war
and plague, was threatened by renewed Pictish attack, and ' all the
councillors together with the proud tyrant who at that time exercised
chief authority in the island ' invited Saxons to assist in the defence.

Three shiploads of Saxons were given lands in eastern Britain in
return for their military assistance and these were soon followed by
others who agreed to fight for their hosts on similar terms. The
Saxons were soon so numerous as to terrify the natives who had
invited them to settle. They entered into a confederacy with the
Picts whom they were supposed to fight and they demanded more

pay, threatening to devastate all the island unless their demands were met. Finally they revolted and ' the fire lit by the hands of the pagans . . . continued its burning course from the eastern to the western sea, without any opposition, and covered almost the whole surface of the doomed isle '. Many Britons were butchered, others were reduced to slavery, some fled overseas; others, ' remaining in their own country, led a miserable life with fearful and anxious hearts among the mountains, woods and steep rocks '. But this catastrophe was followed by a second British revival and the return of some, at least, of the mercenaries to their own country. Led by a Roman aristocrat, Ambrosius Aurelianus, the Britons succeeded in repelling their enemies. For some years afterwards the fortunes of war fluctuated until at the siege of Mons Badonicus the Britons won a great victory. There followed a period of more than forty years which extended until the time when Gildas wrote his tract. It was characterized by respite from war against the invaders but disturbed by the civil wars of contending kings. As the calamities of earlier years were forgotten and a ' generation succeeded acquainted only with the present peaceful state of things, all the bonds of peace and justice were so shattered and overturned that except in a very few people not a memory of them was to be found '. Gildas named five kings who ruled in Britain in his day and had little good of them to record. He warned his fellow countrymen that unless they repented of their evil ways further disasters must follow.

Before considering the conflicts of opinion which the obscurity of Gildas has generated it may be advantageous to take note of evidence provided by other literary authorities and by archaeological discoveries.

The *Life* of St. Germanus of Auxerre by Constantius shows that the final withdrawal of Roman troops in 407 was not followed by catastrophes on the scale of those of 367 and 383. If there was at first some confusion it was shortlived and the Britons successfully maintained themselves against their enemies. The Theodosian reorganization of urban defence and the policy of Magnus Maximus in strengthening the ties of friendship with the British kingdoms beyond the Wall and establishing British kingdoms in the west proved their value. The Byzantine historian Zosimus, who wrote in about 500, but is thought to have derived his material from an earlier writer, confirms that the people of Britain by their own efforts freed themselves from the attack of the barbarians. Though the danger from Picts and Saxons remained ever-present the Scottic raids from Ireland gradually ceased in the second quarter of the fifth century. The spread of Christianity in Ireland after the successful mission of St. Patrick transformed the old hostility between the inhabitants of Celtic Britain and those of Ireland into a close and friendly relationship both cultural and economic. When, shortly after the middle of the century, Scots from the northern Irish kingdom of Dalriada looked overseas for settlement they colonized the district of Argyll in Scotland, which also became known as the kingdom of Dalriada and was to enjoy a great future.

The *Life* shows that within Britain the conflict between the Romanizing and the insular parties continued for as long as the prospect of a resumption of direct Roman rule could be entertained. It was further embittered by the spread of the Pelagian heresy among those of the ruling classes who were hostile to Rome. Contact with Roman Gaul and particularly with the Gaulish Church was for long maintained. In answer to a British appeal for help in combating Pelagianism a council of Gallic bishops in 429 despatched Germanus, bishop of Auxerre, and Lupus, bishop of Troyes. It seems that there was at that time no field army in Britain but the fact that Germanus met on this visit ' a man of tribunician power ' suggests that Roman type garrison commanders were still to be found. The bishops triumphed in more than the business which they had been sent to accomplish. After a successful preaching tour followed by a great assembly in which the Catholic bishops confounded their Pelagian adversaries Germanus, who had formerly been a Roman general, led the British forces to a great victory over an army of Picts and Saxons. It is probable that Germanus paid a second visit to Britain in 446–7 accompanied by Severus bishop of Trier. At this time the Britons were still holding out against barbarian attack but on this visit the representative of local authority whom Germanus met was a certain Elaphius, described simply as ' the first man of the district '.

Though Honorius in 410 had written to the city-states of Britain, Gildas tells of wars between kings and mentioned ' the proud tyrant ' who invited Saxon federates to settle in Britain. Place names and the genealogies of native dynasties preserved in some *Lives* of saints and medieval Welsh compilations amply confirm that, particularly in the west and north, the government of the civitates by groups of magistrates was replaced by the rule of kings. Of those kings Vortigern, forerunner of the ruling dynasty of Powys, is the best authenticated. He was the dominant figure in Britain between about 425 and 450, the leader of the party hostile to Rome and in religion a Pelagian hostile to Germanus. Since he was powerful enough to transfer Cunedda, king of the Votadini, and his people from their lands north of Hadrian's Wall to north Wales, with the object of expelling an Irish colony which had established itself there, he must have exercised authority over a wide area. He probably, though this is not certain, established Saxon troops in eastern England to assist in repelling the Picts. Constantius made no mention of Vortigern by name, but his account of the mission of Germanus leaves little doubt about Vortigern's role in the story and both confirms and adds substance to the scanty outline of events provided by Gildas.

The impression of a gradual deterioration of civil and military institutions which the *Life* conveys finds confirmation in numismatic and archaeological evidence suggestive of a parallel decline in the level of economic and social life. From before the end of the fourth century the amount of money in circulation was decreasing and after 407 no new coins came into circulation. Existing coins continued to be used for a time but by 430 barter had universally taken the place of coinage as a medium of exchange. Some of the large pottery factories which had survived the troubles of 367–368 continued to produce wares for another forty or fifty years but mass-produced pottery gradually disappeared and its place was taken by handmade wares or by utensils of metal and glass for the wealthy or of wood and leather for the poor.

A few instances of the destruction of villas by marauding bands, as at Wraxall in Wiltshire, are well-evidenced but until at least as late as the end of the fourth century some owners, like those at Great Casterton in Rutland and Hucclecote in Gloucestershire, felt sufficient confidence in the future to lay new mosaic floors. St. Patrick's father was a villa proprietor, living admittedly in the far west of Britain, who continued to cultivate his estate until about 430 despite periodic visitations from raiders. In general the villas decayed and went out of cultivation gradually. Their buildings betray a steady process of decline; a bath wing converted to a corn dryer or fires lit on the floor of a living-room. When labour could neither be kept nor replaced, and as the countryside became increasingly insecure, villa owners took refuge within the walled towns.

Fields continued to be tilled only if their produce could be easily transported into the towns.

The fate of both villas and towns depended partly on their location, but almost everywhere towns sustained active life, though on a diminishing scale, well into the fifth century. Caistor-by-Norwich may have been deserted after a massacre, but other urban centres, such as Canterbury, continued to be occupied even after Germanic settlers had established themselves within the walls. At Verulamium excavation has traced the gradual decline of Romanized urban life, but even in the second half of the fifth century the aqueducts and fountains of the town still operated. In the central and western areas of England towns may have maintained themselves for many years. But the steady erosion of the level of economic activity was incompatible with the maintenance of genuinely urban activities. Even when no catastrophe intervened the towns everywhere stagnated, degenerating first into mere fortified centres protecting their surrounding territories, then gradually falling into ruins, inhabited by squatters rather than citizens. The conquering Germanic adventurers of the mid-fifth century came into contact with a civilization becoming steadily less sophisticated than that of a hundred years earlier.

It was also, in some respects, a different civilization. As Roman influence declined there was a revival of British craftmanship. Whereas at the turn of the century Christianity had been a minority cult confined to the upper class and urban population by the middle of the century it was firmly established.

Over much of Britain these changes were taking place, but archaeological evidence also points firmly to the view that Germanic settlement had begun earlier and extended over a considerably wider area than any literary sources indicate. Examination of the pottery in cemeteries in Yorkshire, Lincolnshire and East Anglia has revealed the existence of a substantial quantity of Roman pottery decorated according to Saxon taste and datable to the fourth century.[1] It must have been produced to satisfy the needs of people living in this area in the fourth century who liked their pottery decorated in barbaric fashion and for whom it was worth-while for commercial manufacturers to turn out a special line. Excavation of a great cemetery just outside Caistor-by-Norwich has produced the earliest types of

[1] J. N. L. Myres, *Anglo-Saxon Pottery and the Settlement of England* (Oxford, 1969) ch. 5.

Anglian pottery to be found in England and this suggests a settlement of Angles direct from Schleswig, which began before the end of the fourth century and is interpreted as evidence of considerable settlement of federate type, designed and permitted to assist in guarding the cantonal town, its provincial governors and its provincial treasury against the dangers of the time. There was nothing new in using barbarian troops to defend Roman frontiers: after the defeat of the attack of 367 a German chieftain, Fraomar, was sent to England to command a detachment of Alemanni from the middle Rhine which was serving somewhere in Britain. This may not have been an isolated instance of the use of German troops and it is possible that in late Roman times the garrisons of the east coast forts were largely Germanic in composition. If so, the distinctive type of Roman pottery with Saxon decoration may also have been manufactured to accord to the tastes of the Germanic federates. Another hypothesis has been advanced as a result of excavations carried out at Caistor-on-Sea and at Burgh Castle, just across the estuary from Caistor.[1] Whereas the fort at Burgh Castle yielded only ten of these distinctively Romano-Saxon pots the civilan seaport of Caistor produced fragments of more than sixty such pots. The inference made from these discoveries is that the demand for this pottery came primarily from the civilian population and that the population of Caistor-on-Sea and probably of other eastern ports already contained a considerable Germanic element in the late fourth and early fifth centuries.

Although most of the evidence for such settlement in England at an early date in the fifth century comes from East Anglia, it is not limited to that region. A large early cremation cemetery has been found on the marshy ground just outside the gates of the legionary fortress of York. Here, as at Caistor-by-Norwich, it is at least plausible that the earliest settlers were mercenaries introduced either by the Romans or by the Britons to provide protection against Pictish attack. Early cemeteries in Surrey, at Mitcham, Croydon, and Beddington, may well represent settlements established to protect the southern approaches to London. So much evidence of early Saxon settlement on the east coast has accumulated that the meaning of the term ' Saxon Shore ' has itself been questioned. It was for long assumed that the Saxon shore was so called because it was subject

[1] C. Green, *Sutton Hoo; The Excavation of a Royal Ship Burial* (London, 1963) pp. 117-18.

to Saxon attack and that the business of the count of the Saxon Shore and the coastal forts extending from the Wash to the Isle of Wight was to repel Saxon incursions. It has recently been suggested that the Saxon Shore was so designated because it was an area of Saxon settlement.[1] This historical revision has not found general acceptance, but that it could be formulated is an indication of the strength of the evidence for the Germanic occupation of much of eastern England in late Roman times. Nor is evidence lacking that federates might be stationed in inland areas. Historians were for long puzzled by the evidence pointing to a very early date for the first Germanic settlements in the Oxford region; it was difficult to see how they could have established themselves in central England and by what route they had arrived there. It seems possible that they indicate the establishment of barbarian troops, probably Franks, to protect the eastern approaches to the Cotswolds, the most prosperous region of late Roman Britain.

2. THE PROBLEM OF GILDAS

Sufficient has been said to demonstrate that the story told by Gildas is deficient in two major respects; his account of Britain in the four decades after the departure of the legions is very general and brief, and since he gives no indication of the degree of Germanic settlement in Britain which had taken place, largely under official sponsorship, in the late Roman and sub-Roman periods, he gives the impression that the settlement of mercenaries by ' the proud tyrant ' marked a turning point in British affairs to which a definite date might be assigned.

More controversially, some historians think that Gildas allows an impossibly short time for the events which he thought to have intervened between the failure of the appeal to Aetius and the arrival of the Saxons.[2] He said that the Britons appealed for help to the magister militum of Gaul, Aetius, described as ' thrice consul '. Aetius became consul for the third time in 446 and for the fourth time in 454. The appeal of the Britons must therefore be assigned to within these years. Thereafter, Gildas alleged, the Britons rallied, fought the Picts and Scots successfully, enjoyed a period of pros-

---

[1] A. D. White, *Litus Saxonicum* (Wisconsin, 1961).
[2] C. E. Stevens, ' Gildas Sapiens ', *E(nglish) H(istorical) R(eview)*, LVI (1941), remains indispensable for the discussion of this problem.

perity, made and unmade kings, and fell into moral degeneracy. Learning that Picts and Scots were planning a further assault, and with Britain weakened by plague, the proud tyrant invoked Saxon aid. Gildas gave no indication as to the span of years which elapsed between the unanswered appeal to Aetius and the enlistment of the Saxon mercenaries. But if the first of these events occurred in 446 at earliest and was followed by a British recovery and some years of prosperity the arrival of the Saxons and the subsequent rebellion could hardly have occurred until well into the second half of the fifth century. So late a date is incompatible with such other, admittedly fragmentary and dubious, literary evidence as exists, with later Anglo-Saxon traditions concerning the date of their settlement, and with the archaeological evidence already cited. An anonymous *Gallic Chronicle* under the year 442 states, ' Britain long troubled by various happenings and disasters passed under the authority of the Saxons '. This entry appears to record a decisive transfer of power to the Saxons rather than their first arrival; even if it was a record of their arrival it would still be too early to reconcile with Gildas. Anglo-Saxon tradition, retailed by Bede and supported by the Kentish king lists in the 'A' version of the *Anglo-Saxon Chronicle*, was of a settlement in the middle of the fifth century; the *Chronicle* records the establishment of the kingdom of Kent by Hengest, his brother Horsa and his son Aesc between 449 and 473. These facts suggest that the Saxon mercenaries were first settled in Britain some years before 446.

To resolve this dilemma it has been suggested that Gildas misplaced and misinterpreted the appeal to Aetius in his narrative. It is common ground that Gildas's knowledge of events remote from his own time was exiguous; a man who thought that both the Hadrianic and the Antonine Walls were built by Magnus Maximus could well be ignorant both of the date of Aetius's third consulship and of the circumstances in which the appeal to him was made. If the period of prosperity assigned by Gildas to the period after the failure of the appeal to Aetius is assigned instead to the years between 410 and 442 (and it is agreed that these were, comparatively at least, prosperous years) before the appeal, then his account would fall into line with other evidence; no further adjustment would be required to the later part of the story, of which Gildas had firsthand knowledge. It is argued that the sub-Roman decades witnessed a successful military defence of Britain against Pictish attack achieved by kings at the expense of a gradual running down of the machinery of Roman civil administration and the general standard of culture. Faced by the threat of renewed Pictish attack and fearful of Roman intervention from Gaul, King Vortigern invited Saxon federates to settle in eastern England among other Germanic inhabitants who could well have been established there for many years; a date about 430 has been suggested for this. The new arrivals received allowances and the promise of lands. They were speedily reinforced by others of their race, attracted by the wealth of Britain. Then, when what they regarded as adequate grants were not made to them they revolted against their paymasters and overran large areas of Britain (in about 441-442). Vortigern's policy had proved disastrous, but the Romanizing party still hoped for assistance from the Continent and some time between 446 and 454 they appealed for help to Aetius, the Roman commander in Gaul. ' The barbarians drive us into the sea, the sea throws us back on the barbarians and so two modes of death await us, we are either slain or drowned.' The appeal was un-answered and henceforth the Britons knew that they must fight alone. Initial disaster was followed by recovery. Under Ambrosius Aurelianus, a man ' born in the purple ', the leader of the pro-Roman party, the Saxons were checked. His successor Arthur, after protracted campaigning during which twelve battles were fought, in about the year 500, won an important victory at Mount Badon which confined the Saxons to the areas of their early settlement in the east. For more than forty years after the victory Britain enjoyed prosperity and peace, blemished by that moral backsliding and cor-ruption which for Gildas inevitably attended any improvement in the material conditions of life.

Revision of Gildas on these lines is plausible and on many grounds attractive, but it does not command universal acceptance. A natural reluctance to countenance the drastic surgery of excising an episode from one part of the body of a major source of information and transplanting it elsewhere, with the consequent transformation of its proportions, is reinforced by the suspicion that it may be unneces-sary. In so far as Gildas wrote history at all his theme was the ' fall and conquest ' of Britain, not the history of sub-Roman Britain. A longer preface to that part of the story covering the years after 410 might commend itself to posterity; Gildas may well have known that the years after 410 were comparatively prosperous and that there had long been a Germanic element in the population of eastern

England—but these things were irrelevant to his purpose. Until then, as the *Life* of Germanus testifies, there were still vestiges of Roman administration and civilization in Britain; more than the withdrawal of troops in 407, or the expulsion of Constantine III's administrators in 410, the failure of Aetius in 446 to respond to a desperate cry for help marked the end of the long pretence that Britain was still Roman. In retrospect this failure could be seen as a dividing line between a time when Germans settled in England as federates and the time when they established themselves as conquerors. The appeal to Aetius was so critical an episode in the story that Gildas was concerned to write that to alter its position in the narrative requires powerful justification.

Such justification would be removed if it were possible to refute the claim that an unrevised Gildas assigns too many happenings to the years between the appeal and the battle of Mount Badon. Some historians believe that this can be done.[1] They point out that the difficulty of accommodating a period of prosperity between the appeal of 446 and the arrival of the Saxon mercenaries derives entirely from Bede's attribution of the year 449 to the arrival of Hengest; from Bede it was adopted by the compilers of the *Anglo-Saxon Chronicle,* and from both authorities by most later writers. But there is in Gildas no indication of the time which elapsed between the two events; Bede's date was no more than an unjustified inference from Gildas and has no independent authority. There is, in fact, no compelling reason to believe that the Saxon mercenaries arrived until a decade or more after the appeal to Aetius. It is, moreover, unjustifiable to buttress the traditional date of reference to the strength of an Anglo-Saxon tradition that postulates a mid-fifth-century date for the ' coming ' of the Saxons. The annals of the *Anglo-Saxon Chronicle* to which appeal is made are not concerned to describe the coming of the Saxons but to record events which led to the establishment of kingdoms in south-east England. They begin with entries relating to battles fought by Hengest, Horsa, and Aesc between 449 and 473, continue with a series of entries relating to battles fought by Aelle and his three sons and continue further with the relations of battles fought by Cerdic and Cynric. This series of entries is not meant to imply the consecutive conquest of Kent, Sussex, and Wessex but the establishment of the three kingdoms at a

---

[1] Recently, D. P. Kirby, *The Making of Early England* (London, 1967), pp. 16-17, though he considers the available evidence to be too inconclusive to support a final judgment.

period which can only be broadly dated in the later years of the fifth century. It may be significant that though the *Chronicle* claims Aesc to be the son of Hengest, who according to Bede was the ancestor of the ruling dynasty of Kent, Kentish dynastic tradition makes no such connection but derives the name of the ruling family directly from Aesc who, according to the *Chronicle,* became king in Kent in 488. Between the unanswered appeal to Aetius and the establishment of the kingdoms of southern England something like forty years may have elapsed. This would allow time for victory over the Picts followed by a period of prosperity, a new threat countered by the recruitment of Saxon mercenaries and their rebellion, which was in turn followed by a period of uneasy equilibrium between the Britons under Ambrosius Aurelianus and Saxon adventurers led by men like Hengest who sought setlement in Britain.

The *Chronicle* record of an unbroken succession of Saxon victories is naturally one-sided, for no people deliberately keeps alive memories of defeat, and Gildas makes plain that the struggle was evenly matched. Fighting was mostly confined to the eastern part of Britain and though that part could never be entirely delivered from the invaders Arthur's victory at Mount Badon put a period to further expansion. By that time the whole of south-eastern and eastern England had definitely pased under Saxon rule. Events in Gaul could explain the intensification of Saxon pressure in the later years of the century. For decades Saxon warriors had been moving southwards into Frisia, Britain, and northern Gaul, where they settled on the coast near Boulogne and Bayeux. In 463 a body of Saxons under their king Eadwacer occupied Angers but were quickly driven out. But the development of Frankish power in Gaul thereafter barred further Saxon expansion southwards and encouraged them to seek compensation in Britain.

Acceptance of an unrevised Gildas implies that the Anglo-Saxon conquest, as opposed to Anglo-Saxon settlement, did not begin until well into the third quarter of the fifth century. In the present state of the evidence, which forbids dogmatism, the balance of argument appears to favour those scholars who believe that at the time of the British appeal to Aetius a substantial part of eastern Britain had already been forcibly occupied by Saxon warriors.

One instance of the way in which Bede embellished his model, by the attribution of a date to the arrival of the Saxon mercenaries, has already been discussed. In similar vein he gave to the British king who invited the Saxons to Britain, vaguely designated by Gildas as the ' proud tyrant ', the name Vortigern; this attribution is confirmed by independent evidence. More important, he first followed Gildas in assigning their settlement to the eastern part of Britain; then, almost in parenthesis, he added, ' their first leaders are said to have been Hengest and Horsa. Horsa was afterwards killed in battle by the Britons, and in the eastern part of Kent there is still a monument bearing his name '. It has been asserted that this famous passage, to be found in the chapter which assigns Vortigern's invitation to the year 449, by identifying the first Saxon leaders as Hengest and Horsa, associating Horsa with Kent and attributing that event to a specific year, has substantially contributed to the firmly held but unhistorical tradition of the arrival of the Saxons in Britain, giving to it a quite unreal precision as to both date and location. By describing Hengest and Horsa as the first leaders of the Saxons it hindered the acceptance of the fact that Germanic elements had been long settled in Britain by the middle of the fifth century and by associating Horsa with Kent it gave to the south-east a unique importance which it did not possess, ignoring the likelihood that federates introduced to fight the Picts would be established in some more northerly area of the east coast.

There is justice in the criticism, but it is easy to see how Bede could have been misled. Better informed than Gildas in that he knew that the third consulship of Aetius began in 446, his instinct for chronological precision led him to date Vortigern's invitation to the Saxons a few years later, while from Albinus he had learned the Kentish tradition about Hengest. As we have seen, Gildas probably misplaced the appeal to Aetius in his narrative and in consequence Bede, following Gildas, dated Vortigern's invitation to the Saxons which probably occurred in about 430, twenty years too late. There is good reason to believe in the historicity of Hengest who may well have arrived in Kent in about the middle of the fifth century; but it is clear that he was by no means the first Saxon leader, and the Kentish may not have been the most important foothold that the Saxons acquired in these years. The story of Hengest was only an episode in a prolonged drama enacted along the whole eastern seaboard of Britain; its importance should not be exaggerated. Yet having said so much, the last word rests with Bede. He repeated Gildas's general statement that the first Saxons were settled in the eastern part of the island; the subsequent details which have been criticized are prefaced by the cautionary phrase, 'it is said that'; later historians have tended to ignore Bede's own caveat.

3. THE CONTINENTAL HOMELANDS OF THE INVADERS AND THEIR SETTLEMENT AREAS IN ENGLAND

During the fifth century the continental enemies of Britain were described simply as the 'Saxons'; this usage was practised both by Roman writers and by Gildas. In the sixth century the Byzantine historian Procopius was, by implication, more specific when he remarked that the population of Britain consisted of three races, Angles, Frisians and Britons. Bede, in a section of his *Ecclesiastical History* which owes nothing to Gildas, was yet more precise; his careful definition of the peoples who invaded Britain together with the regions from which they derived and the regions of England in which they settled has necessarily formed the basis of all subsequent investigation of this matter. They came, he said,

> from three very powerful nations of the Germans, namely the Saxons, the Angles and the Jutes. From the stock of the Jutes are the people of Kent and the Victuarii, that is, the race which holds the Isle of Wight and that which in the province of the West-Saxons situated opposite that same Isle of Wight is to be called the nation of the Jutes. From the Saxons, that is from the region which is now called the land of the Old Saxons, came the East Saxons, the South Saxons and the West Saxons. Further, from the Angles, that is from the country which is called Angulus (Angeln in Schleswig) between the Jutes and the Saxons, are sprung the East Angles, the Middle Angles, the Mercians, the whole race of the Northumbrians,—that is, those people who live north of the river Humber—and the other peoples of the Angles.

Bede was almost certainly correct in locating the home of the Angles in modern Schleswig; his intimate acquaintance with members of the Northumbrian royal family put him in a good position to acquire knowledge of Anglian traditions current in his own time and his observations on this point receive substantial independent corroboration. In the first century Tacitus mentioned the Angles as one of seven small tribes who worshipped the goddess Nertha at an island sanctuary; they were a seaboard people though whether their sanctuary was located in the North Sea or the Baltic Sea he did not make clear. Ptolemy in the second century described them as an inland people inhabiting lands west of the Elbe, but his evidence is outweighed by the tradition preserved in the Old English poem

Widsith that Offa, king of Angeln, established the boundary of his kingdom on the river Fifeldor (thought to be the river Eider) and by King Alfred's statement in the preface to his translation of Orosius that ' before they came to this land ' the Angles lived on the islands east of the Jutland peninsula. Bede's assertion that the Anglian migration to England had been so heavy that even in his time Angeln was empty of people, finds a measure of support from recent archaeological work which has demonstrated that in this area which had been densely populated in the third and fourth centuries the number of cemeteries declined markedly in the fifth century.

The Saxons were not mentioned by Tacitus but Ptolemy located them in modern Holstein, south and west of the territory of the Angles, in part of the area where Tacitus had placed the Chauci. The Chauci had occupied the coastal region from the Elbe to the Ems: they were probably a combination of many small tribes who lacked political unity but shared the same culture. By the third century the Chauci had disappeared and the Saxons, spreading southwards, then occupied the territory from the mouth of the river Eider to the mouth of the river Weser and its hinterland. Like the Chauci, and later the Franks, the Saxons were slow to acquire political unity and even in the eighth century the Old Saxons were ruled by many tribal chiefs and submitted to a single war-leader only temporarily, in time of war. The Saxons who settled in England remained well aware of their affinity with the continental Saxons who retained their identity until their subjugation by Charlemagne in the eighth century. The Saxon lands were heavily populated and from the third century onwards their inhabitants supplemented their resources from the proceeds of piracy at the expense of the provincials of Gaul and Britain.

West of the Weser and extending as far as the Zuyder Zee Ptolemy placed the Frisians, mentioned by Procopius as one of the peoples who had inhabited Britain, but ignored by Bede. Once again archaeological discoveries have supplemented the deficiencies of the literary sources. The Frisian coastland was a marshy area for long sparsely inhabited by a people who built their houses on *terpen,* artificially raised mounds which provided protection against flooding. Excavation of the *terpen* has revealed that in the first half of the fifth century Frisia experienced a large-scale migration of Saxons; geographical conditions compelled the newcomers to build mounds for their dwelling-places and the civilization they reveal contrasts markedly with that of the native Frisians. But though the migration

2

of Saxons southwards into Frisia occurred on a significant scale the capacity of the *terpen* to accommodate new settlers could not go on indefinitely and further southward expansion was barred by the also expanding Frankish tribes. If land hunger was to be satisfied it could only be achieved by taking to the sea and crossing to Britain. The role attributed to the Frisians by Procopius is explicable by reference both to the Saxon migration into Frisia and the likelihood that whatever their original provenance many of those who settled in Britain in the fifth and sixth centuries came immediately from Frisia. For many of the stock of the original Anglian and Saxon lands Frisia was no more than an intermediate habitation before their descendants moved on again, to Britain. Of others it can safely be said that whether by origin Angle or Saxon it was very likely that they would arrive in Britain after a landfall of indeterminate duration on the Frisian coast: sailing in small open boats without sails and navigational aids the adventurers would seek to make their North Sea crossing as short as possible and so would hug the land until this was achieved. According to the poem *Beowulf* a Danish leader named Hengest fought in Frisia; if this Hengest were the man connected with the settlement of mercenaries in Kent (and no other Hengest is known) he would exemplify this kind of migration. Among the earliest leaders of the Germanic settlers in Northumbria, according to Nennius, were a son and nephew of Hengest. The grave goods of the earliest cemeteries in Northumbria are remarkably similar to those found in Frisian cemeteries; this coincidence offers further confirmation of the suggestion that after their migration from Schleswig some of the Angles, at any rate, moved into Frisia before moving on again to settle in Britain. The connection between Frisia and England is rendered certain by the linguistic similarities which, though common to both English and Frisian, distinguished them from both German and Scandinavian languages. It has been said with authority that ' English and Frisian are collateral branches of a common linguistic stock, and there can be little doubt that the differences between the later forms of the two languages arose after the period of the English migration to Britain '.[1]

This account of the homelands of the Angles and Saxons reveals that in the centuries prior to their descent on Britain the tribes of north-west Germany were continuously on the move; such movements probably contributed to the diminution of racial distinctions

---

[1] F. M. Stenton, *Anglo-Saxon England* (3rd edn, Oxford, 1971), p. 6.

among them. For this reason Bede's statement that each race settled in particular regions of Britain requires modification, thought it had a sound historical basis and an element of contemporary reality. It has been demonstrated that cruciform brooches are characteristic of the Anglian area of England and that saucer brooches characterize the Saxon area and that both types can be found in the continental homelands of the immigrants in the areas attributed by Bede to the Angles and Saxons respectively. Even so, this evidence itself argues strongly against any rigid demarcation of the boundaries of early settlement on racial lines, for though cruciform brooches predominate in the area north of the Wash they are not unusual in the southern area; conversely, early ' Saxon ' brooches have been found in districts which later appear as distinctively Anglian, notably in the Cambridge area. Since the linguistic peculiarities which characterize later Saxon and Anglian dialects cannot be observed until long after the migration period had ended they cannot be used as evidence of different racial origins; it is generally agreed that they were the product of political and geographical differences within England itself. Nor have attempts to designate some personal names as distinctively Anglian and others as distinctively Saxon met with approval. Indeed, it could be urged that the distinction Bede made between the Angles and the Saxons in the extract quoted from just one chapter of the *Ecclesiastical History* is not typical of his thinking. In general he used Angle and Saxon as terms which could be used interchangeably, as when he wrote of ' the tribe of Angles or Saxons ' who were invited to Britain by Vortigern. If there ever had been substance in the notion of an Anglian Northumbria Bede's near contemporaries took a perverse delight in standing it on its head by describing Northumbria as Saxonia, as did abbot Adomnan of Iona and Bede's own abbot Hwaetbert. It seems probable that the differences between the Angles and the Saxons had been diminishing for many years before the conquest and that the circumstances of a seaborne migration further reduced them.

The first racial group mentioned by Bede was the Jutes, said by him to have colonized Kent, the Isle of Wight and southern Hampshire; they present the greatest difficulty to the historian.[1] Bede's

---

[1] Of the considerable literature devoted to this problem among the most important contributions are, J. E. A. Jolliffe, *Pre-Fuedal England: The Jutes* (Oxford, 1933); C. F. C. Hawkes, ' The Jutes of Kent ', *Dark Age Britain*, ed. D. B. Harden (London, 1956); S. C. Hawkes, ' Early-Saxon Kent ', *Archaeological Journal*, cxxvi (1941); Myres, *op. cit.* ch. 6.

assertion that they were the northern neighbours of the Angles would place them in the Jutland peninsula, but until recently few contemporary scholars would have accepted his attribution. The name Jutland is derived not from *Jutae* but from the Scandinavian *Jótar,* who occupied this region after it had been vacated by its previous inhabitants. Nor do the burial customs of the Jutes suggest Jutland as their home. Cremation was chiefly practised by Germanic tribes remote from Roman influence. It rapidly became obsolete among the Saxons but was very common among the earliest Anglian invaders, and might have been expected to be still more usual among the Jutes—yet cremation cemeteries are almost unknown in fifth-century Kent. Conversely, such literary references as there are to the Jutes point to their association with the Saxons rather than to the Angles. Yet while the field systems of Kent contrast strikingly with the field systems of both the so-called Anglian and the Saxon areas they bear a close resemblance to the field patterns of the Ripuarian Franks of the middle Rhine and the study of early Kentish grave goods, particularly from female graves, has revealed their close resemblance to the contents of continental Frankish graves. From these facts the conclusions have been drawn that wherever their original homeland may have been the Jutes' route to Britain was by way of the middle Rhine, that by the time of their arrival they were indistinguishable from Franks, and that their settlement in Kent was a byproduct of the more important Frankish expansion into Gaul. That Kent was Frankish finds support in a letter of Pope Gregory I (590-604) to the Frankish kings Theuderic and Theudeberht in which he refers to the Kentings as ' your subjects '.

Some scholars, principally archaeologists, while accepting the argument in its general lines, have been influenced by the diversity of cultures which they find in Kent to suggest modifications to it. They have argued that in Kent there is early evidence of at least two principal cultures and some minor groups. One of these cultures is represented by settlements in the northern coastal area and resembles other Anglo-Saxon settlements of the early period; the other is characterized by the strong Frankish affinities which have already been mentioned and reveals in its metal work and jewellery techniques more advanced and a level of artistic achievement far higher than those of the fifth-century Angles and Saxons. Since the Frankish goods found in Kent reflect styles and techniques which had become obsolete in Gaul by the beginning of the sixth century there is no reason to argue that they antedate the artefacts of the poorer Anglo-Saxon culture. They suggest accordingly that the preponderant element in the population of fifth-century Kent consisted of Franks, mercenaries or immigrants to Britain, who had arrived before the Roman military strength in Gaul had collapsed; but that Jutes and Saxons settled in smaller numbers at about the same time after having crossed the North Sea from Frisia in the manner ascribed to many others of the Angles and Saxons. Though the culture of Kent was of diverse origins its inhabitants were described as Jutes because the ruling dynasty of Aesc, which had established itself before the end of the fifth century, was of Jutish-Saxon stock. Other archaeologists, while accepting a Frankish predominance in Kent, are disposed to believe that it did not occur until the sixth century and suggest that the settlers came rather from the lower than the middle Rhine area.

It may fairly be remarked that if Kent was settled by Franks it is odd that though Augustine's Gaulish interpreters could make themselves understood in Kent the language of Kent bears no traces of having been influenced by the language spoken by the Franks. Though the cultural resemblances between the Ripuarian Franks and the Kentings are striking they are no more remarkable than the similarities between Kentings and East Anglians who were certainly not Franks. Nor is there any early tradition of Frankish settlement in Kent. The claim of Frankish kings to exercise some degree of authority in Britain cannot be traced further back than the late sixth century and for it two alternative explanations have been offered, neither of which has its basis in conditions during the migration period. It has been suggested that the subjection, in the middle of the sixth century, of the *Euthiones,* a Jutish people living on the northern frontier of the Franks, gave rise to claims by later Frankish kings to authority over all the Jutes, including those in Kent. Alternatively, an explanation offered by Procopius may be preferred; testifying to the annual migration of the inhabitants of Britain to Gaul he commented that ' by these means they [the Franks] are winning over the island '.

The problem of the Jutes is far from resolution, but recently the greatest living expert on Anglo-Saxon pottery has concluded a rigorous examination of the available material by declaring that the closest parallels to the pottery of Kent come from Jutland.[1] In the

---

[1] Myres, *op cit.,* p. 95.

face of such evidence it would appear unwise to reject out of hand Bede's categoric assertion that the Jutes came thence. It can plausibly be argued that Jutland was the original home of the Jutes, that, like other northern peoples and often intermingled with them, they migrated southwards, that some of them settled on the lands bordering the Franks; and that others, whether directly or by way of Frisia, settled in south-east England, where their leaders established themselves as rulers of all the racially mixed peoples who at that time inhabited Kent.

Bede's further remarks about the Kentings, whether or not they should properly be called Jutes, namely, that they colonized the southern shores of Hampshire and the Isle of Wight, though at first sight improbable, are certainly true. West of Pevensey as far as Selsey Bill the kingdom of Sussex was early established, but further west the grave finds provide abundant evidence of secondary settlement from Kent. In the ninth century Bishop Asser, the biographer of King Alfred, recorded that Alfred's maternal grandfather was of Jutish origin, descended from Stuf and Wihtgar. He describes these two men, who figure prominently in the early history of Wessex, as nephews of Cerdic, traditionally the founder of the West Saxon royal dynasty. Cerdic and his men were Saxons; that his nephews were Jutes may be yet another pointer to the affinity between ' Jutes ' and Saxons. As late as the twelfth century the reference of Florence of Worcester to the New Forest, ' which in the tongue of the English is called Ytene ' (Jutish), reveals the vitality of the memory that southern Hampshire was settled by this elusive people.

In general it appears that Bede's account of the various races who settled in England is validly based but that he made the distinctions between them, and between the regions of England in which they settled, sharper than they were. Like Gildas he ignored the evidence of heavy Germanic settlement in England before the departure of the Romans.

Bede described the settlement areas of the English in terms applicable to his own day, although in the late fifth century Mercia, Wessex, and Northumbria were terms without meaning; for this reason his remarks on that topic, though incidentally illuminating, are less helpful to the student of the earliest period of the migration than is his account of the origins of the invaders. In the present state of knowledge it is impossible to achieve precision, but the best evidence for determining the extent and density of early Germanic settlement is provided by cemeteries and place names. The pagan Anglo-Saxons commonly cremated their dead in shallow graves unmarked by mounds or commemorative stones. Large numbers of such burials have been recorded, almost all of them in the eastern and southern parts of the lowland zone of Britain. No sites have been found to the north of the Yorkshire wolds and none west of the Pennines, while penetration of central England appears to have been almost confined to the river valleys. The greatest concentration of burials is to be found in Kent, southern Sussex, the Oxford region, along the upper and middle reaches of the rivers that run into the Wash, in the valley of the upper Trent, and the east Riding of Yorkshire; but they have been mapped in smaller numbers in most of the area east and south of a line drawn from York to Portland except in areas known to have been marshy or heavily forested. Some of these early cemeteries reveal an intense Germanic female culture which argues heavy settlement, not only of warriors but also of their womenfolk.

Place name scholars were, until recently satisfied that the archaeological evidence found confirmation in place names. It was thought that one group of place names with the Old English ending *-ingas* was of indubitably early date.[1] Sometimes this ending is found compounded with a first element denoting a natural feature, as in Epping, ' dwellers in the upland ' and Avening, ' dwellers by the Avon '; this usage, to denote the settlers in a particular region, continued to be practised late in the Anglo-Saxon period and therefore such names cannot be used as evidence of early settlement though some of them may well date from the invasion period. But some *-ingas* terminations are prefixed by personal names of such great antiquity that they had gone out of use before written records were kept; of this type are Hastings, ' the descendants or dependants of Haesta ', Cannings, ' the people of Cana ', and Reading, ' the people of Raeda '. They were originally folk names which, when the folk concerned had settled in a particular place, became place names. They were held to reflect the social organization typical of the migration period, antedating the establishment of kingdoms, when the typical social unit was the band of a war-leader. Where such concentrations of place names are found, not only in particular concentrations as in Sussex, Kent,

---

[1] A. H. Smith, ' Place names and the Anglo-Saxon settlement ', P(*roceedings of the*) B(*ritish*) A(*cademy*), XLII (1956).

Essex and East Anglia, but in lesser numbers almost everywhere in south and east England, they were deemed to be evidence of early settlement. The suggestion has, however, been made that these -*ingas* names should be assigned to a later phase of Anglo-Saxon history, to the time of territorial expansion and social consolidation.[1] Yet, in general, this group of names corresponds well with the distribution of pagan cemeteries, although in some areas, notably the Oxford and Cambridge districts there are many cemeteries but comparatively few -*ingas* place names. This disparity of evidence has been explained on the hypothesis that early settlers in both these regions were particularly exposed in times when political and military fortunes fluctuated. British reoccupation of an area once settled by the invaders might terminate the use of their Germanic place names while leaving untouched the cemeteries in which they had cremated their dead. Conversely, both Essex and western Sussex are rich in -*ingas* names but apparently poor in cemeteries; it has been suggested that the peoples who settled in these areas never in England practised the ordinary Teutonic methods of burial, whether by cremation or inhumation, with weapons and other gear. Within this area of early settlement the density of Germanic population is attested by the virtual disappearance of all traces of pre-Saxon nomenclature. Only the large and medium sized rivers, Roman towns and major geographical features retain their Celtic names.

By the year 500 Germanic peoples were securely entrenched and in control of most of the coastal areas of south-east and eastern England and had penetrated far inland up some of the rivers which run into the North Sea. They had occupied Kent, Sussex, and southern Hampshire; Essex, East Anglia, Lindsey, and the east Riding of Yorkshire; and inland, the region of the upper Thames and the territory which lay between this area and the Cambridgeshire fens. Occasionally the migrating invaders may have been substantial tribal units but the -*ingas* place names suggest that often they were no more than small groups of people united for military and later for economic advantage in their dependence on a leader. The hesitancy of the conquest may have been due as much to the smallness and independence of the migrants as to the efficiency of

---

[1] By J. M. Dodgson, ' The significance of the distribution of the English place-names in -*ingas, inga* in south-east England ', *Medieval Archaeology*, X (1966).

British resistance. But Bede's statement that Aelle, king of the south Saxons, who lived towards the end of the fifth century, was the first king to establish authority over all the English peoples south of the Humber, though not to be taken literally, suggests that at a quite early date the originally independent followings of minor leaders in southern Britain merged into a larger grouping under a distinguished warrior. Whether it had been formed in response to the aggressive initiatives of Arthur or in order to increase the offensive capabilities of the newcomers is not known; nor did Aelle's confederacy survive, but the tendency for small groups to amalgamate was thus early exhibited.

In 550 the invaders were still confined within the territories they had occupied fifty years earlier; they may have endured some losses. The battle at Mount Badon had been a great British victory. When Gildas wrote most of Britain was still ruled by British kings, and prosperous, though the kings were constantly at war with one another. Procopius provides corroboration of some aspects of the picture of Britain in the mid-sixth century as painted by Gildas. After mentioning that the population of Britain comprised three peoples, Britons, Angles, and Frisians, he remarked that each race was so fertile that every year it sent large numbers of men, women, and children to the land of the Franks. It was long ago established that a substantial migration of Britons to Armorica (Brittany) began in the late fifth century and was renewed in the late sixth century; but it would be harder to believe that Angles and Frisians returned in large numbers to the Continent if it were not confirmed by a continental tradition, first recorded in the ninth century, that Angles from Britain were settled in Thuringia by the Frankish ruler Theuderich in the fourth decade of the sixth century. If Britons fled to escape the invaders the Germanic reverse migration is only explicable on the assumption that the British kingdoms were subsequently strong enough successfully to resist Saxon efforts to acquire further territory for settlement. The kings of Kent between Aesc and Aethelberht, and of Sussex after Aelle are no more than names; no West-Saxon advance out of Hampshire is recorded until 552.

But the Britons failed to take advantage of their reprieve. About the middle of the sixth century the Anglo-Saxon advance was resumed and made rapid headway against a disorganized opposition.

2*

2

THE SECOND PHASE:
THE CHARACTER OF CONQUEST

WHEN Gildas wrote *De Excidio* Britain was at peace. Within a few years of his death the invaders had broken out from the beach heads within which they had been contained for fifty years and were pressing hard against the British kingdoms. In the south-west the Saxons reached the Severn by 577 and though further progress was spasmodic they pushed forward their frontier by tactical bounds through Somerset and Devon as far as the river Tamar. The kingdom of Bernicia was established north of the Tyne in the second half of the sixth century and in the second decade of the seventh century a Bernician king defeated a British army at Chester on the Irish Sea. Lack of literary evidence makes the reconstruction of the stages by which midland England was colonized by Angles and Saxons almost totally conjectural, but by the middle of the seventh century the recently formed kingdom of Mercia already threatened to become the strongest power in Britain. Why the assault on the Britons was renewed at this time is unknown, but the fact is indisputable.

1. THE MAKING AND EXPANSION OF WESSEX

The *Anglo-Saxon Chronicle* provides the basis for the traditional account of the establishment of the West Saxon kingdom.[1] It relates how, under the leadership of Cerdic and his son Cynric, the West Saxons landed on the shores of Southampton Water in the last decade of the fifth century and subsequently pressed northwards into

[1] G. J. Copley, *The Conquest of Wessex in the Sixth Century* (London, 1954), gives a good account of the origins of Wessex; it accepts the main lines of the Chronicle account, complementing it with evidence from place names and archaeological studies.

Wiltshire and the area of the middle and upper Thames, then west-wards into Gloucestershire and Somersetshire. The *Chronicle* account suggests that sporadic fighting continued in the areas of early settlement during the first half of the sixth century and dates the first advance in 552, when Cynric defeated the Britons at Salisbury. Four years later Cynric and his son Ceawlin again defeated the Britons at Barbury Hill near Swindon; in 568 Ceawlin and Cutha defeated King Aethelberht of Kent; in 571 after a battle at ' Bedcanford ' (unidentified), Cutha secured four towns, Limbury, Aylesbury, Bensington, and Eynsham, which controlled the area between the middle Thames and the Saxon settlements in Bedford-shire, which had probably been lost to the Britons after the battle at Mount Badon. The defeat of three British kings at Dyrham in 577 by Cuthwine and Ceawlin gave the Saxons Gloucester, Cirencester, and Bath, opened the valley of the Severn to Saxon colonization, and separated the Britons of the north-west from those living north of the river Severn. In 586 Ceawlin and Cuthwine fought against the Britons at Fethanlaeg, identified by Sir Frank Stenton as Stoke Lyme in north-east Oxfordshire, in a campaign which though yielding considerable booty was ultimately unsuccessful; Cuthwine was killed and Ceawlin returned in anger to his own land. The *Chronicle* describes the stages by which Cerdic and his descendants created the West Saxon kingdom.

For a variety of reasons the truth of this account has been challenged. It is incomplete in that it makes no mention of the earlier Jutish settlement in southern Hampshire which is well attested by both literary and archaeological evidence. Many of its statements appear incompatible with other known facts; that fighting on any scale took place in southern England in the first half of the sixth century conflicts with Gildas's contemporary statement that this was a period of peace; the northern migration from Hampshire is put in question by a disturbing lack of early cemeteries and place names in northern Hampshire and Wiltshire; that Cynric, who fought with Cerdic in 495, lived until 560 is improbable. Furthermore, there is strong evidence to support the view that the West Saxon kingdom originated in the Thames Valley, which has yielded impressive evidence of heavy and early Saxon settlement. In the face of these difficulties it has been argued that the *Chronicle* version of the origins of the kingdom of Wessex cannot command acceptance. None of these objections has lacked an answer.

The fact of Jutish settlement in south Hampshire is undeniable and memories of it were still current in Wessex in the last decade of the ninth century when the *Chronicle* was written; but it might legitimately have been regarded as an irrelevance or have been deliberately omitted from a compilation designed to glorify the West Saxon royal dynasty. There is no conflict with Gildas if it is recognized that the group of *Chronicle* entries after 514 relating to battles fought against the Britons are duplicates of earlier annals from 495. If it is further admitted that the *Chronicle* chronology for the first half of the sixth century is sheer guesswork, no more than an attempt by its authors to give firmness to traditions of the conquest about which they knew very little, the problems posed by the dates it assigns to the early leaders of the West Saxons offer no serious obstacles to the acceptance of the general outlines of its narrative. Nor need the *Chronicle* be held to imply Cerdic's leadership of a substantial folk-migration northwards from Hampshire. The paucity of pagan Saxon cemeteries and of early place names in north Hampshire and in Wiltshire makes such a migration implausible, though recent excavation at King's Worthy in Hampshire has revealed a large cemetery used from between about A.D. 500 to 600 whose grave goods show close affinities to those from Kentish and South Saxon graves and there is also a significant group of early place names in south Berkshire. It is worth remembering, too, that the route attributed to Cerdic passed through country for the most part unattractive to settlers who would therefore leave behind them few evidences of their passage, a region characterized not only by the absence of Saxon cemeteries but also by a paucity of evidence of British settlement. All that is claimed for Cerdic is that he was the leader of a small war band, in character no different from many others which established themselves in British territory. Champions of the historicity of the *Chronicle* account argue that though in its present form it dates from late in the ninth century, the preservation of archaic case-endings, and the presence of very early forms of personal and place names, reveal that it incorporated much earlier material. There is nothing intrinsically improbable in its account of Cerdic's movements and the places associated with Cerdic's name suggest that he and his band followed the line of an ancient trackway from Southampton Water to Charford-on-Avon, thence by the most natural route through Sarum and Barbury to the Thames Valley, where they made contact with other Saxons long-settled to the south of the Upper Thames. The name Cerdic, generally regarded as derived from the Celtic Ceretic, is too unusual to have been invented. In this view the *Chronicle* relates the story of the leader of a small war band who travelled from the Solent to the Thames, whose descendant Ceawlin either imposed his control over or was accepted as king by the much larger group of cognate Saxons of the Thames Valley; its concern is with the early history of the West Saxon ruling dynasty rather than with the origins of the West Saxon kingdom.

Despite its apparent success in reconciling discordant evidence this interpretation of the course of events is still questioned. It has recently been suggested[1] that the early entries in the *Chronicle* relating to Cerdic and Cynric are misdated by half a century and that their arrival in the Solent should not be placed before 550— thus disposing of the problem of where they and their followers settled for the first fifty years after their landfall, and with it the necessity of qualifying Gildas's assertion that fifty years of peace followed the battle of Mount Badon. Passing quickly through the Jutish area of southern Hampshire Cynric's victory over the Britons at Old Sarum gave him control over the area of modern Wiltshire. At about this time another Saxon people who had been living in the valley of the Upper Thames since at least the beginning of the sixth century were, under their king Ceawlin and his kinsmen Cutha, Cuthwine, and Cuthwulf, expanding the area under their control at the expense of the Britons living to the north and west. It is argued that the two groups led by Cynric and Ceawlin sometimes cooperated against the Britons, but that eventually Ceawlin attempted to absorb the Wiltshire Saxons into his kingdom. His attempt was unsuccessful and for another century the two peoples retained their separate identities, until the Wiltshire Saxons were subjugated by Caedwalla, a descendant of Ceawlin. On this hypothesis the story that Ceawlin was descended from Cerdic is a fiction, invented late in the seventh century to camouflage the reality of conquest.

Though there is doubt whether the fusion of the Wiltshire and the Thames Valley Saxons was effected by Ceawlin or by Caedwalla there is general agreement that historic Wessex emerged out of the amalgamation of two originally distinct peoples. This conclusion

[1] D. P. Kirby, ' Problems of early West-Saxon history ', *E.H.R.*, LXXX (1965).

derives additional support from recent discussion[1] concerning the nature of the great earthwork of Wansdyke, which bisects the kingdom of Wessex from east to west. It used to be thought that Wansdyke was a sub-Roman work, probably built on the initiative of the southern British *civitates* against the threat of the expanding Saxon communities of the Upper Thames. It is now suggested by some authorities that Wansdyke is not a single work but was constructed in two parts, both of later date than was generally supposed —east Wansdyke in the late sixth century and west Wansdyke as an extension made about forty years later and devised as a frontier demarcation between Wessex and Mercia. Other archaeologists, though convinced that the Dyke is a single work, are satisfied that it is a late sixth-century construction. In either event if the revised date finds acceptance it is necessary to envisage a political situation in which the northern and southern halves of the later West Saxon kingdom were in different hands until late in the sixth century. By those who believe Ceawlin to have been the son of Cynric, it is suggested that after his successful advance from Wiltshire to the Thames Valley he was eventually defeated at Fethenlaeg (584) and subsequently withdrew into Wiltshire leaving the Thames Valley area in revolt; Wansdyke might then have been built by Ceawlin and the Wiltshire Saxons to guard against attack from the north. Those who believe that Ceawlin ruled the Thames Valley Saxons, a people quite separate from those of Wiltshire, suggest that the Wiltshire Saxons built the dyke as protection from Ceawlin's aggressive intentions.

At this stage of the debate it appears that the balance of argument favours those who believe that Ceawlin was a Cerdicing who, by virtue of his military prowess, succeeded in imposing his leadership on the Saxons of the Upper Thames and there established the centre of his kingdom. The subsequent history of westward advance is certainly more explicable if it is assumed that, despite the subsequent feuding of members of its ruling family, the West Saxons had become a single people by the end of the sixth century. Yet the unresolved differences of opinion concerning the origins of the West Saxon kingdom provide a good illustration both of the uncertainties which still surround some of the crucial problems of Anglo-Saxon

[1] See especially A. and C. Fox, ' Wansdyke reconsidered ', *Archaeological Journal*, CXV (1958), and J. N. L. Myres, ' Wansdyke and the origin of Wessex ', in *Essays in British History Presented to Sir Keith Feiling*, ed. H. R. Trevor-Roper (London, 1964).

history even at this comparatively late date and of the dependence of the historian on scholars in other disciplines in resolving them.

The battle of Dyrham (577) had opened up the west, and pagan cemetery finds indicate that by the beginning of the seventh century the West Saxons had penetrated into north Somerset as far as the Mendips and into eastern Somerset as far as the Fosse way.[1] In the south, in Dorset, the only evidence of Saxon advance is found on the coast at Hardown Hill. It seems that the Saxons made no attempt to penetrate Dorset by land and were content to leave the thin soils of that shire in British hands. At that time the Celtic kingdom of Dumnonia (comprising present-day Devon and Cornwall) remained intact, though not for long. In 614 the West Saxon rulers Cynegils and Cwichelm defeated the Britons at Beandun, which has been convincingly identified with Bindon overlooking Axmouth, in east Devon; this victory extended the West Saxon frontier ten miles into Dumnonia.

Further westward expansion was, by comparison, slow and spasmodic, perhaps as much made necessary by the success of continuing Mercian pressure on the original homelands of the West Saxons in the Upper Thames Valley as to a conscious desire for expansion. A battle fought at Cirencester in 628 between the Mercian Penda and Cynegils and Cwichelm, kings of Wessex, though followed by an agreement left the Severn valley, the fruits of the West Saxon victory at Dyrham, in Mercian hands. Ten years later Dorchester-on-Thames was still the principal residence of West Saxon kings and it became the seat of their first bishop; but increasing concern for the south-west is shown by the establishment of a second bishopric at Winchester early in his reign by King Cenwalh (641-672), which before long became the ecclesiastical centre of his kingdom. In 648 Cenwalh's grant of a huge apanage of three thousand hides near Ashdown to his kinsman Cuthred, Cwichelm's son, possibly served the double purpose of recognizing a cousin's rights to participate in kingship while at the same time creating a defensive march against Mercian aggression; this area was attacked by Wulfhere of Mercia in 661 and it is recorded that Cuthred died in that year, though whether in battle defending his territory is not stated. Shortly before this Cenwalh, perhaps taking advantage of the uncertainties which prevailed in Mercia for a brief span after Penda's death, had felt

---

[1] This account is based on W. G. Hoskins, *The Westward Expansion of Wessex* (Leicester, 1960).

strong enough to resume the attack on the Britons. A victory in 658 at Peonnan, recently identified as Pinhoe, seven miles north-west of Exeter, pushed the frontier forward to the Exe, an advance confirmed and extended by battles fought by Cenwahl in 661 and by King Centwine in 682, when ' he put the Britons to flight as far as the sea '. Confirmation of Saxon encroachment into Devon is found in Willibald's *Life of St. Boniface* which states that at about this time Boniface entered a monastery at Exeter. Meanwhile, further east the battle at Badbury Rings (665) transformed what had been a British salient in Dorset into an enclave; West Saxon kings made grants to religious houses in this area but the high proportion of British place names in Dorset, higher than in Devon, and some evidence pointing to a survival of a Celtic upper class into the eighth century suggest that in Dorset the British were left relatively undisturbed.

Despite victories over the Britons this was not a glorious epoch in West Saxon history, but the consequence of these battles in combination with Mercian expansion in the Thames Valley was that by the time of Caedwalla (685-688) and Ine (688-725) the centre of gravity of the West Saxon kingdom had moved from the middle Thames to the lands beyond Selwood.

These kings were strong enough to prevent further losses to Mercia and in 710 Ine renewed the assault on Dumnonia. The result of this battle, fought probably some distance west of the river Tamar, is unknown; but in 721 or 722 the Saxons were defeated in Cornwall, on the estuary of the river Hayle. The final conquest of Dumnonia was to be a protracted business. Two battles between the West Saxons and the Britons are recorded during the reign of King Cuthred (740-756), and his successor Cynewulf (757-786) was said to have ' often fought great battles against the Britons '. The Britons seem to have held their own until after the end of the century. The end of their independence came as a consequence of the revival of West Saxon power under King Egbert (802-839). In 815 he harried Cornwall from east to west, yet ten years later the Britons were strong enough to attack eastwards beyond the Tamar and the *Chronicle* records that ' in this year [825] there was a battle at Galford between the Britons and the men of Devon '. In 838 the Britons of Cornwall, having allied with the Danes, were defeated by Egbert at Hingston Down; throughout the ninth century, Cornwall retained her native kings but now they existed under the domination of the kings of

Wessex. The last episode in the story of the English conquest of Britain was accomplished.

2. THE KINGDOM OF NORTHUMBRIA

One of the main approaches for the early settlers had been the river Humber and its tributaries. They moved northwards into eastern Yorkshire and southwards into Lincolnshire and up the valley of the Trent, where they established themselves in south Nottinghamshire and Leicestershire as soon as they had emerged from the marshes of the lower river. There is no early literary tradition of settlement in these areas but Nennius claimed that the first Teutonic leaders in Northumbria were a son and nephew of that Hengest whose exploits in Frisia are recounted in the poem *Beowulf* and whose association with the settlement of Kent is traditional. The vague implication of a connection between Northumbria and Frisia in the migration period receives some corroboration from the remarkable similarity between the grave goods of the earliest cemeteries in Yorkshire and those of Frisia. By the end of the fifth century the chalk hills of the Yorkshire Wolds and the Vale of York had been heavily settled by Germanic immigrants who soon established what became known as the kingdom of Deira. Expansion to the south and west was barred by the British kingdom of Elmet, which occupied the valleys of the rivers Aire and Wharfe between the Vale of York and the Pennines, while the inhospitable countryside beyond the Tees discouraged advance northwards. Nothing is known of the process which created the kingdom of Deira, but its first king known to history, Aelle, reigned in the second half of the sixth century.[1]

At about the same time another Northumbrian kingdom, Bernicia, was established north of the Tyne; its capital was the coastal fortress of Bamburgh and its first king was Ida. Early settlement in Bernicia was concentrated in two coastal areas, the estuary of the Tyne and the country between the rivers Coquet and Tweed. Since there is a marked absence of pagan cemeteries between the Tees and the Tyne it is improbable that Bernicia was colonized by a landward movement from the south. The newcomers could conceivably, but improbably in view of the lateness of the settlement, have been a new

---

[1] Valuable suggestions for revising the accepted dating of some events in early Northumbrian history will be found in D. P. Kirby, ' Bede and Northumbrian chronology ', *E.H.R.*, LXXVIII (1963).

wave of invaders from the Continent. Local tradition, preserved in the twelfth-century compilation *Symeon of Durham*, believed that settlement had been achieved from the south; more important, Bernician kings even at the end of the seventh century still called themselves *Humbrenses*. In all probability the earliest arrivals in Bernicia came from Deira by sea.

Though more recently settled than Deira the new kingdom of Bernicia was the spearhead of Germanic advance to the west and north. Progress at first was slow and for fifty years the Bernicians could do no more than maintain themselves precariously against strong British kingdoms. West of the Pennines in the area of modern Cumberland and extending over the northern shores of the Solway Firth was the kingdom of Rheged. Further north, the most important of the British kingdoms, Strathclyde, controlled much of south-west Scotland from its capital at Dumbarton on the northern shore of the Firth of Clyde. Since the middle of the fifth century modern Argyll had been occupied by immigrants from Dalriada in northern Ireland, who had established a kingdom which was also called Dalriada; it had steadily increased in power and under Aedan mac Gabrain (*c.* 574-608) was pressing east and south against Britons and Bernicians and northwards against the Picts who inhabited Scotland north of the Firths of Forth and Clyde. In the sixth century the Picts had been divided into two nations separated from each other by the central Highlands but they had recently combined under the rule of a single king. Over most of this area a desolate countryside supported a sparse population, so that fluctuations in political boundaries were frequent and unlikely to be subject to detailed record. English settlement across the Pennines and into Scotland was achieved by infiltration as much as by conquest. Edging along the river valleys into the interior they sometimes encountered strong resistance from the Britons and at times were in danger of expulsion from the lands they had won. Some idea of the nature of the Bernician conquest can be gleaned from the writings of Taliesin, a poet at the court of Urien and his son Owain, kings of Rheged; from another contemporary British poet, Aneirin, whose *Gododdin*[1] described a British attack on the newcomers which was defeated at Catterick; and from the stories gathered later by Nennius. They indicate a long struggle in which neither side was consistently vic-

[1] Recently edited by K. H. Jackson, *The Gododdin: The Oldest Scottish Poem* (Edinburgh, 1969).

torious. The British kingdoms were weakened by disunity. They fought not only the Angles but one another; the record of a battle fought at Dumbarton indicates hostility between the kings of Strathclyde and Rheged. But they were yet powerful enough to stage offensive as well as defensive operations. According to Nennius, Ida's son Theodric was on one occasion besieged for three days on Holy Island by a British confederacy led by Urien, king of Rheged, and the siege was raised only after Urien had been assassinated by a rival chief, Morcant. Hussa, the fifth of Ida's successors, suffered attack by four British kings. Not until the time of Aethelfrith (593-616) did the situation radically alter in favour of the invaders.

Bernicia and Deira may have been united under Aethelric of Bernicia after the death of Aelle of Deira in 588; at the latest they were united by Aethelric's successor Aethelfrith, who married Aelle's daughter. Under Aethelfrith the boundaries of the new Northumbrian kingdom were dramatically enlarged. His most notable victory was won in 603 against the Dalriadans at an unidentified place in Bernician territory called Degsastan, perhaps Dawston, in Liddesdale. It eliminated the Dalriadan threat to the Scottish lowlands, nor, wrote Bede, ' from that time to the present day has any king of Scots in Britain dared to make war against the English '. The victory also made easier the path of Bernician colonizers to the north; though there is no positive evidence of Bernician settlement in lands north of the Tweed until the second quarter of the century the fact that the English St. Cuthbert was born (in 625 or 631) in Tweeddale or on the southern slopes of the Lammermoors suggests that this area had by then been in English occupation for some time. Aethelfrith's other great battle was his victory over the Britons of north Wales at Chester between 613 and 616. According to Welsh tradition Cadran, king of Gwynedd, was sheltering Edwin, the son of Aelle of Deira, who was planning to recover his father's kingdom; if true, this would provide an adequate explanation for Aethelfrith's campaign, which, culminating on the shores of the Irish Sea took him far from the seat of his power. The place names of Cumberland reveal no substantial English settlement in the early sixth century so that Aethelfrith's army must have fought this engagement after risking an extended march through hostile country. The victories of Degsastan and Chester justify Bede's summing up of Aethelfrith's reign : ' He above all others laid waste the nations of the Britons for none before him had rendered their lands either habitable for the

English by the extermination of the nations or tributary to them by their conquest.'

The battle of Chester proved to be only a temporary setback to Edwin. He wandered as an exile first to Mercia then to the court of Raedwald, king of the East Angles, at that time the most powerful ruler in southern England. Raedwald not only refused to deliver Edwin into Aethelfrith's hands but also, doubtless apprehensive of the increasing power of Northumbria, led an army to the north. Aethelfrith was killed in a battle against Raedwald's army fought on the river Idle on the frontier of Deira in 616. His numerous sons fled into exile and Edwin succeeded to both Deira and Bernicia. As well as dominating the kings of southern England and introducing Christianity to his own kingdom Edwin (616-632) maintained pressure on the Britons. Bede wrote: ' Like no other king before him, he held under his sway the whole realm of Britain, not only English kingdoms but those ruled over by the Britons as well. He even brought the islands of Anglesey and Man under his power.' Nothing is known of events in the northern parts of his kingdom but of its westward extension there is no doubt. Having conquered the British kingdom of Elmet and expelled its king, Certic, he invaded the territories of Cadwallon, king of Gwynedd. Cadwallon was besieged in Priestholme and forced for a time to seek refuge in Ireland. But British resistance was still unbroken and in 632 Cadwallon in alliance with Penda of Mercia defeated and killed King Edwin at the battle of Hatfield.

The next two years were critical. Edwin's kingdom broke into its component parts, Deira falling to Osric, a cousin of Edwin's, and Bernicia to Eanfrith, son of Aethelfrith. Both were killed within a year, Osric in battle, Eanfrith by treachery. Cadwallon and Penda systematically ravaged Northumbria with the intention of destroying its power for ever and all the male members of Edwin's family were eliminated. Northumbria was saved when, late in 633, Oswald, another of Aethelfrith's sons, at the head of a small force surprised Cadwallon at Heavenfield, near Hexham. Cadwallon was killed and his army suffered heavy casualties. The battle was decisive. All Northumbria regarded Oswald as a deliverer and accepted him as king. Henceforth the Britons of north Wales were reduced to the defensive. No British king of comparable stature succeeded Cadwallon and no hope remained of driving the English out of the territories they had occupied since Aethelfrith's time.

Oswald was king in Northumbria from 633 until 641. During the early years of his reign the capture of Edinburgh from the Britons of Manau Gododdin opened the way for the occupation of Lothian. Northumbrian dominion over north-western England was confirmed by the marriage of his brother Oswiu to Riemmelth of Rheged, and by his encroachments on the territories of the Strathclyde Britons. Oswald's ambition was not confined to the north and west; while engaged on a campaign against Mercia he was defeated and killed at Oswestry by a combined British and Mercian army. This proved to be only a temporary setback. Under Oswald's brother Oswiu (641-670) the offensive against Picts and Scots was resumed. No details of these operations are recorded but Bede states that Oswiu ' tamed for the most part the nations of the Picts and Scots who held the northern part of Britain and made them tributary '. His reign marked the highwater mark of Northumbrian power and the limits of its territorial expansion. Oswiu's son and successor, Ecgfrith (670-685), was decisively defeated in 685 by the Picts, who thereby regained their independence, which subsequently they never lost; English expansion northwards was permanently halted.

Thereafter the consolidation of Pictish power north of the Firths of Clyde and Forth and the increasing strength of the kingdom of the Mercians combined with internecine troubles to force Northumbria on to the defensive. Only one further advance was effected, when King Eadberht (737-758) annexed the plain of Kyle from Strathclyde. A few years later he allied with Angus, king of the Picts, in an attack on Dumbarton, but immediately afterwards his army was destroyed. By the middle of the eighth century the territorial limits of the Northumbrian kingdom had become stabilized, and so remained until its destruction by the Danes.

3. THE MIDLANDS

Between the Thames and the Humber, between the Severn and the heavily settled lands of Middle Anglia, lay the area which later became the kingdom of Mercia. At about the middle of the sixth century this large area of midland England contained two enclaves of Germanic settlement, one in the valley of the middle and upper Trent, the other in the valley of the Warwickshire Avon. The Trent settlement formed the nucleus of Mercia, that of the Avon produced the kingdom of the Hwicce, which subsequently was incorporated into Mercia. During the course of the next decades small groups of pioneers pushed forwards from existing settlements and established themselves over all the midland shires. By the middle of the seventh century the rulers of the Trent valley people had established their dominion over all the lesser folk groups, and the Britons had everywhere been driven back across the Severn. No history, no tradition even, of the process by which this was achieved has survived. The rulers of Mercia suddenly intervene on the political scene of the mid-seventh century, decisively, but without warning.

4. The Character of Conquest and Settlement

By the end of the sixth century most of southern Britain except Devon, Cornwall, and Wales was subject to Anglo-Saxon political control and the British dynasties and aristocracies were destroyed. The conquest of Britain had been a gradual and protracted process, spanning two centuries, prepared for by substantial previous settlement and achieved in two phases separated by a half century of peace. Generalizations about its character are likely to be no more than partially true.[1] In the first phase England east and south of a line drawn from Flamborough Head to the Solent was occupied. Gildas testifies that this conquest was characterized by the slaughter, enslavement or flight of the native inhabitants. The slaughter was emphasized in the Anglo-Saxon traditions of the fighting in Kent and Sussex; sometimes, as at Pevensey, whole communities were massacred, ' there was not even one Briton left there '. Flight too was remembered, ' the Britons forsook Kent and fled to London in great terror ' and ' the Welsh fled from the English like fire '; and the large-scale British migration to Armorica is well-evidenced. The *Laws* of Aethelberht of Kent which reveal three classes of half-free *laets* who may well be of British stock, the fact that Wilfrid is said to have freed no fewer than two hundred and fifty slaves when he received the great estate of Selsey in Sussex, proves that the fate of many of the natives was not extermination but slavery. Conquest was preceded by battles, often hard-fought, and the very ability of the native population to defend themselves contributed to their heavy losses. In this area of primary occupation the concentration of

---

[1] For contrasting views see R. Lennard, ' From Roman Britain to Anglo-Saxon England ', *Wirtschaft und Kultur* (Festschrift zum 70. Geburstag von Alfons Dopsch, Leipzig, 1938), and H. P. R. Finberg, ' Continuity or cataclysm ' and ' Roman and Saxon Withington ', *Lucerna* (London, 1964).

Germanic place names and of early cemeteries argues for an intensity of Germanic settlement which makes credible Bede's assertion that the migration to England had left Angeln uninhabited even in his own time. Yet the *Chronicle* annal for 571 is a reminder that even in this area there remained not only a substantial subject population but also British enclaves which remained unsubdued for a long period.

The early conquests were achieved by independent war bands each under its own leader, though circumstances quickly compelled them to form larger groupings. The greatest of such confederacies was certainly that which accepted the leadership of Aelle, king of the South Saxons, who brought under his command many of the war bands established in southern England. It was ephemeral, but some of the smaller federations created by intertribal conquest or by the natural attraction exerted by particularly able and distinguished leaders achieved greater permanence. By the middle of the sixth century the kingdoms of Kent, Sussex, Essex, East Anglia, and Deira were becoming recognizable. These kingdoms remained confined within their original limits. The second phase of conquest was achieved by war-leaders whose origins sometimes lay within the older settled territories but who operated independently of the rulers of the older kingdoms.

In the south and north this second phase was characterized by a far greater degree of political direction than had hitherto been apparent. Over the Celtic kingdoms of the north and west victories could only be won by leaders who themselves disposed of substantial military resources. The drive west across the Pennines and north into Pictland was directed by Bernician kings; the Celtic rulers of the lower Severn region and the kingdom of Dumnonia were defeated by the kings of Wessex. These were not the large-scale migrations of land hungry peasants but conquests directed towards political dominance and the acquisition of permanent tribute; the best lands were occupied, but neither necessity nor interest demanded more. In Bernicia the conquerors remained an aristocracy living on the tribute paid by the subjected natives; in Wessex the *Laws* of Ine show that even considerable landed estates remained in native hands; in both areas the high proportion of Celtic place and river names provides confirmation of the continued existence of a substantial British element in the population. There were pitched battles, and sometimes the slaughter, as at Chester and at *Beandun*, was heavy, but their sequel was neither the extermination nor the expulsion of the defeated. In western Wessex, particularly, the bitterness of conquest was not increased, as elsewhere, by religious differences. The acceptance of Christianity by West Saxon kings quickly established a bridge between the conquerors and the natives, especially when the piety of those kings led them to make extensive grants of land to old religious foundations. There is evidence, too, of intermarriage between Anglo-Saxons and Britons. Oswiu, king of Northumbria, married a princess from Rheged. Not only does the name of the traditional founder of the ruling dynasty of Wessex, Cerdic, derive from the Celtic Ceretic but the names of Caedbeth king of Lindsey and Caedwalla, king of Wessex, contain the same Celtic element. Nor was political cooperation between Anglo-Saxon and Briton out of the question; early kings of Mercia allied with Welsh kings in their mutual fear of the power of the Northumbrians. In central England, it is likely that opportunities for peaceful coexistence were better than elsewhere; here there was abundant forest and swamp land, not too difficult to clear and drain, and potentially highly attractive to the new settlers. It could support a far higher level of population than inhabited it in the fifth and sixth centuries and accordingly offered the possibility for native and newcomer to live peacefully together.

Such conclusions appear at first sight to contradict both the philological and the place name evidence. The strongest argument against a high degree of British survival appeared to be that the language spoken by the Britons had almost no influence on the language spoken in Anglo-Saxon England; not more than sixteen nouns were taken from Romano-British into Anglo-Saxon. Yet it is becoming increasingly apparent that often the native Britons understood Anglo-Saxon and that the two languages came into close contact. The best opinion now holds that the disappearance of the British language was the result not of the elimination of Britons but of the total political and economic dominance achieved by the Anglo-Saxons over a subject population.[1]

Of place names it has been said that:

> When one turns to habitation-names, names of villages and homesteads, these are rarely found to contain Brittonic elements even in Devon, Somerset, Gloucestershire and the shires adjacent to Wales.

[1] K. H. Jackson, *Language and History in Early Britain* (Edinburgh, 1953), pp. 241-6.

. . . In the whole of Lancashire, for example, less than sixty place-names containing Brittonic elements have been noted, and by origin as well as by usage most of them were strictly English place names.

This scholar's conclusion was that

those who seek to prove a very considerable British survival in England must find support for their thesis in evidence other than that provided by place names.[1]

If habitation names are unhelpful in the resolution of this problem the analysis of other categories of name has proved more rewarding.

As a general principle it may be stated that the persistence of names is directly related to the number of people who use them for identificatory purposes. For this reason the names of large rivers, hills and other topographical features, and of large towns are very conservative; conversely, field names, the names of small streams, and other minor names lack permanence because, being current among only a small number of people, they can easily be forgotten, changed, or replaced. Operating from this principle an analysis of the river names of Anglo-Saxon England has yielded results bearing on the problems of Anglo-Saxon settlement and British survival more precise than any hitherto provided by other types of historical material.[2] A map based on this evidence records three main areas of English settlement. In the eastern area only the large rivers retain their Celtic names, together with the names of major topographical features and of a few large towns; this area appears to correspond with the region of primary settlement effected before 550, in which the density of Germanic settlement was such that they renamed even the lesser waterways. In the central area of England the names not only of the large but also of a substantial number of medium-sized and small rivers are British, together with more names of lesser topographical significance than in the eastern area; this central zone would correspond with the territories absorbed by Wessex, Mercia and Northumbria in the century between 550 and 650. In much of western England—the north-eastern shires of Cumberland, Westmorland and Lancashire, the Welsh March, Dorset and Devon—even small streams have British names and British names of all kinds abound; this area was the last to be dominated by the English.

[1] F. T. Wainwright, *Archaeology and Place Names and History* (London, 1962), pp. 60-4.
[2] Jackson. *op cit.* pp. 219-23.

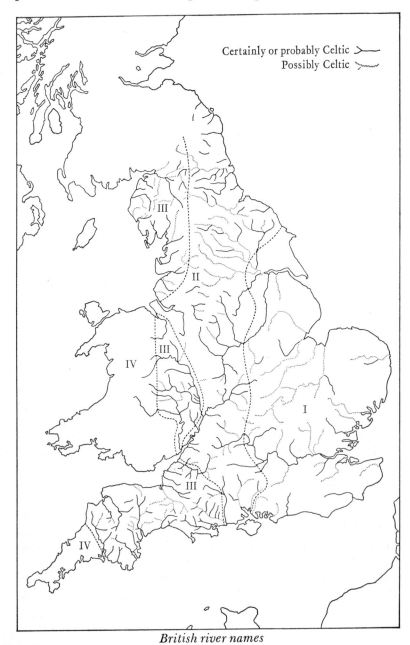

Certainly or probably Celtic
Possibly Celtic

British river names
(From Loyn: Anglo-Saxon England and the Norman Conquest)

Farther west still, in Wales and Cornwall, all categories of name are overwhelmingly Celtic. The evidence of river names confirms what on other grounds would be suspected; that the degree of survival of the native inhabitants increased as the pace of conquest diminished and that in the north and west the native element in the population of England remained much larger than in the areas of primary settlement.

The survival of a substantial British population does not necessarily imply the survival of Romano-British institutions and culture, nor, if they were obliterated, was this necessarily the consequence of the barbarity of the invaders. As we have seen, many of the characteristics of Roman Britain had disappeared during the long period which elapsed after the departure of the Roman army and before the Germanic conquests. Though Gildas lamented the destruction of the twenty-eight cities of Roman Britain they had long been in decline; significantly, he said nothing of Roman villas because they had disappeared before his lifetime. Vestigial survivals of Roman administration may be seen in ' the man of tribunician power ' whose daughter was healed by Germanus, and even much later, in the seventh century, the missionary Paulinus encountered a ' prefect ' in Lincoln; but it seems that before the middle of the fifth century the Britons had reverted to the tribal organization which had preceded the coming of the Romans. There is no evidence that Roman administrative boundaries or Roman law influenced the territorial limits or the social organization of the newly emerged kingdoms.

As Roman cultural influences weakened there was a revival of Celtic art forms in jewellery and domestic ornament. During most of the Roman period Christianity had been one cult among many, its dominance confined to certain areas and social classes; in the sub-Roman decades Christianity became much more widely diffused, as the influence of pagan cults diminished and as Christian influences penetrated the highland zone and the peasantry were converted. On this view of fifth-century development the gulf that exists between Roman Britain and Anglo-Saxon England could have been created during the sub-Roman phase of British history, rather than as the consequence of Germanic invasion. In Britain Roman civilization had been imposed from above on a primitive society and in an alien environment. As soon as this pressure was relaxed the Britons readopted forms of political association and ways of life more natural to them. Their prolonged resistance to the invaders was bought at the price of a continuous decline in governmental sophistication and the general level of civilization.

How far and in what respects the political and social organization of the newcomers differed from that of the native Britons is a difficult question to answer. Much of what has been written about the north German tribes in the fifth century is little better than conjecture. Tacitus described Germany and the Germans but his work is not free from the suspicion that it is less a neutral record of observed fact than a tract written with ulterior motives and designed for consumption in Rome. Even if it be admitted that he knew something about the tribes who lived near the Roman frontiers in the first century A.D. it would make him a dubious guide to the Germans of three hundred years later who had, in the meantime, been involved in continuous movement; it is improbable that their institutions and customs had not changed significantly since his time. Many of the peoples who invaded Britain had not been in contact with Roman influences or subject to Roman observation. Later Roman historians have little to add to Tacitus and by the middle of the sixth century it was possible for Procopius to believe that the whole country north of Hadrian's Wall was inhabited only by snakes and wild beasts and that any man who travelled there would die at once from the pestilential atmosphere; there is little reason to believe that late Roman writers were much better informed about conditions in northern Germany. The Germans were themselves illiterate and could leave no written remains which might cast light on their way of life in the migration period, though some poetry of a much later age contains traditions which may be used with caution. Gildas has something to say about Celtic Britain in his time but nothing about the invaders.

Literary deficiencies are not compensated for by archaeological materials. Roman building was largely in stone and despite depredations left its mark on the countryside; Saxon building was in timber and has left no traces. The chronology of events in Roman Britain largely depends on coins and inscriptions, which are lacking for the Anglo-Saxon period because the invaders saw no use for them. The materials which have been excavated came mostly from cemeteries, not habitation sites. The jewellery, pottery, and weapons which furnish the graves make it possible to trace the movements of peoples and to identify the territories they occupied both on the Continent and in England; they provide some evidence of the religious beliefs and the way of life of the immigrants; the distribution of early cemeteries provides evidence of the kind of country they preferred for their settlements. Archaeological evidence is sometimes confirmed and sometimes complemented by that of place names. But there remain vital questions to which the available materials provide no answer; there is no way of establishing a firm chronology of events and our knowledge of the customs and political arrangements of the Angles and Saxons can only be inferred from the practices which they can be seen to follow in England in the early seventh century when written materials again become available.

A few elementary facts emerge from the evidence. The Anglo-Saxons came as war bands under military leaders; it is generally believed that these companies were small in number and uncoordinated in their activities, but it is possible that there may have been some larger tribal groups which arrived under the leadership of kings. They were agriculturalists concerned to find lands for cultivation and settlement, and sufficiently skilled to adapt their farming practices to the nature of the terrain. Their economic and administrative arrangements were of a nature which made towns unnecessary. In religion they were pagan. In many respects the society of the Anglo-Saxons may have resembled that of the Romano-Britons, with the important exception that the latter were Christians. The poet Taliesin gives the impression that there was little difference between the sub-Roman kingdoms and the kingdoms established by the Germanic conquerors. Both were ruled by kings who surrounded themselves with bands of aristocratic warriors whose preoccupation was fighting and whose prime virtues were valour and loyalty. The poem *Gododdin,* written in about 600, tells how an élite force of Celtic warriors fought against the Anglo-Saxons at Catterick. Wearing their gold collars they prepared for the battle by feasting and drinking from gold cups; they fought to the death; only one man, the poet himself, survived the encounter. Such a company Beowulf might have led to battle.

In one important respect, at least, it could, until recently, be confidently asserted that the Germans effected a dramatic break with the past; Romano-British agricultural practices were thought to have been radically different from those of the Anglo-Saxons. From the evidence of Romano-British sites it used to be thought that their agrarian economy was primarily pastoral, concentrated on upland

The Anglo-Saxon Age

areas and directed from either the ranch-type villas of the wealthy or isolated peasant farmsteads; when they grew cereals they cultivated small rectangular fields with a light plough. By contrast, it seemed, the Anglo-Saxons preferred to settle in nucleated villages located in river valleys, following a farming pattern based on cereal production in large open fields broken up by the heavy plough and divided into strips. These conclusions were based on the findings from Roman sites readily identifiable as such because the evidence for their occupation had not been overlaid by later Anglo-Saxon settlement. Recent research has substantially modified this simple picture in a number of important respects. There remains agreement that throughout the Roman period a pastoral economy continued to dominate the highland zone and that its typical unit of cultivation was the isolated farmstead. Elsewhere, the importance of arable farming in late Roman Britain is now strongly emphasized. The needs of the garrison together with those of an expanding population, itself fostered by the Roman peace, provided a stimulus to cereal production. In the areas of lighter soil mixed farming became usual though the isolated farmhouse remained the characteristic unit of exploitation. But over much of lowland Britain there was a valleywards movement and a concentration on cereal cultivation both by villa owners and by settlements of peasants living in nucleated villages. Aerial photographs have revealed the existence of large nucleated villages in regions as far apart as the Fens and Wessex while in other areas unified tracts of fields have been detected which are thought to be too large to have been worked as a single farm. Although by comparison with the large and luxurious villas of the Cotswolds the corn-growing villas of East Anglia and the Midlands were small and poor they were an important element in late Roman agriculture in Britain. Evidence has also been found for the use of a heavy plough indistinguishable from that used in later times on rich and heavy soils. The importance of arable farming in late Roman Britain is demonstrated by its capacity to export corn in considerable quantities. As late as A.D. 359 Julian, in an emergency, increased the regular export of corn to the Rhineland by an additional 600 bargeloads.

Corn-growing on a large scale, the use of the heavy plough, and peasant settlement in nucleated villages were all characteristic of the last phase of Romano-British agriculture, which in these respects resembles that of the Anglo-Saxons. What has not so far been convincingly revealed is the practice of strip-farming in the open fields. At Brading in the Isle of Wight a large area of 'Celtic' fields has been identified close to a villa where a heavy mouldboard plough was discovered. It is likely that the use of the heavy plough caused fields to be enlarged but that its use was restricted to villa owners, while the peasants continued to use their more primitive equipment on their small fields. How far the more advanced forms of cultivation were disrupted when the villas were deserted it is impossible to say, but what is known blurs the old sharp distinctions between Roman and Anglo-Saxon agriculture and emphasizes the importance of the changes which occurred in the last period of Romano-British history.

Still more recently the thesis of a break in agrarian continuity has been questioned from another angle. It has been argued that the distinctive feature of Anglo-Saxon farming, namely the cultivation of open fields divided into strips allocated among the inhabitants of the nucleated village, was not a primitive and traditional habit of cultivation imported into England by the Angles and Saxons from northern Germany and naturally practised by them in their newly acquired lands.[1] Studies in early Germanic field systems on the Continent have been employed to support the contention that at the time of their settlement the invaders were accustomed to unitary holdings in their fields and that the characteristic strips came into being only gradually as the population increase caused holdings to be split up, the area of cultivated land to be enlarged, and holdings to be reallocated.

In general, historians are increasingly taking the view that patterns of agriculture are determined more by the facts of physical geography and by farming techniques and implements than by differences of race. In the west and north the maintenance of a pastoral or mixed agriculture was imposed by the character of the terrain; when they settled in these areas the Saxons adapted themselves to living in isolated upland farmsteads just as easily as in the lowland zone of intense primary settlement they lived in nucleated villages. In neither area did the new political masters change dramatically the long established methods of land use.

Over much of eastern and southern England the population consisted largely of new settlers of Germanic race; as the conquest extended westwards it is likely that victorious kings rewarded their

---

[1] See J. Thirsk, ' The common fields ', *P(ast and) P(resent)*, 29 (1964), the rejoinder by J. Z. Titow, *P.P.*, 32 (1965), and Miss Thirsk again, *P.P.*, 33 (1966).

subordinates with grants of land but that the natives who had previously tilled the soil continued to do so. For them the new dispensation would mean little more than a change in masters, though the form their servitude took, whether in tribute, labour service, or both, would depend on the nature of agrarian exploitation in each locality. The circumstances of the conquest of Kent, the west Midlands, and Bernicia were so different that the sequel to conquest permits few generalizations. The degree of continuity with the past varied from region to region. Only one thing is clear, that ultimately the invaders established their political and social dominance over the whole of England.

3

THE CONVERSION OF THE ANGLES
AND SAXONS

Long before territorial expansion had reached its limits some of the pagan conquerors had accepted the religion of the con-quered.[1] Yet there was no continuity of Christian practice in lowland Britain nor did the subject population play any direct part in the work of conversion. Christianity was brought back to Britain by the activities of missionaries from Ireland and from Rome. The Irish mission stemmed from the work of Christian teachers in the sub-Roman period of British history; the Roman mission owed everything to the initiative of Pope Gregory the Great.

1. CHRISTIANITY IN LATE ROMAN AND SUB-ROMAN BRITAIN

Christianity may have been introduced into Britain as early as the second century but little can be learned about its progress until the fourth century. In 314 three British bishops, a priest, and a deacon attended the Council of Arles; an unspecified number of bishops were at Sardica in 347 and in 359 three of the British bishops present at the Council of Rimini had their expenses paid out of public funds by reason of their poverty. The distribution of archaeo-logical evidence shows that the Christian Church was by this time firmly entrenched in the lowland zone of Britain and in a secondary area along and behind Hadrian's Wall, that there were Christians in most large towns, and that the urban aristocracy sometimes built

---

[1] Important recent contributions to the subject of this chapter will be found in *Christianity in Britain 300-700*, ed. M. W. Barley and R. P. C. Hanson (Leices-ter, 1968).

churches in their country villas. But the contrast between the splendid wall-paintings of the villa at Lullingstone (Kent) and the mosaics at Hinton St. Mary (Dorset) and the unremarkable relics of urban Christianity which have survived suggests that except for the wealthy villa owners Christian communities were poor. Pagan cults continued to flourish and between 360 and 380 new temples were built at Lydney (Gloucestershire) and Maiden Castle (Dorset) and repairs were carried out in others.

Evidence of the vitality of the Christian communities becomes richer towards the end of the fourth century and in the early years of the fifth. Negatively, the coin series at many pagan temples suffered a reduction in volume, the temple theatre at Verulamium was abandoned, and one temple was converted to industrial use. Positively, the activities of Ninian, Dubricius, and Patrick show Christianity extending its influence from the lowlands into the highland zone of Britain and even beyond. A Briton, Pelagius, was at the centre of one of the most hotly contested disputes which threatened the orthodoxy of the Christian Church in the west. In Britain particularly, his teaching on free will gained him strong support from some members of the ruling class.[1] Utterly opposed to Augustine's view that the frailty of man's nature made him completely dependent for salvation on God's favour (or Grace) Pelagius insisted that man determined his own destiny by the exercise of his own unaided will. This was congenial doctrine to those in Britain who were struggling, without help from Rome, to defend their island from barbarian attack. By the 420s Pelagianism had acquired such a hold that the British catholic bishops appealed to the Continent for help, and it was to combat the Pelagian heresy that St. Germanus and Bishop Lupus of Troyes were sent to Britain. The interest aroused by the controversy attracted a huge crowd to listen to the debate. But other events connected with this visit, particularly the incident which tells how Germanus baptized the British forces before his battle against the Picts and taught them to shout 'Alleluia' when they attacked, suggests that the peasantry were, even now, largely unconverted. For some years longer the Church in Britain, now restored to orthodoxy, maintained contacts with the Church in the west; St. Germanus probably made a second visit in the 440s, accompanied by Severus, bishop of Trier. When in 455 Pope Leo

[1] J. N. L. Myres, ' Pelagianism and the end of Roman rule in Britain ', *Journal of Roman Studies*, L-LI (1960-1).

altered the arrangements for fixing the date of Easter his modification was accepted in Britain; when the next change in such arrangements was made, forty years later, contacts with the continental Church had been broken.

In the last phase of its existence the Church of lowland Britain exhibited a vigorous internal life. The interest in and bitterness aroused by the Pelagian controversy shows that it could not be accused of tepidity; more constructively, in this period it showed the will to evangelize the populations of the highland zone, hitherto largely unaffected by Christian activities.

Nevertheless, it appears that in eastern Britain Christianity was extinguished by the invaders, or withered away. The conquerors were unlikely to be impressed by the virtues of a religion which appeared unable to preserve its practitioners from defeat, nor is there any hint that the Britons where they survived, showed any disposition, at any rate for a long time, to convert their new masters. The stone churches which the Romans had built gradually decayed. They were for long reminders of the old religion, and in Canterbury King Aethelberht was to give his queen and her Frankish bishop the old church of St. Martin's for the exercise of their faith; other old churches were restored to Christian use after Aethelberht's conversion. But their permanence is evidence of the skill of their Romano-British builders and the durability of the materials they used, not of the continuity of Christian faith and practice inherited by the native population.[1] A Christian church needs ordained priests to administer its sacraments and it seems impossible that the supply of priests could have been maintained during the lengthy period that elapsed between Anglo-Saxon conquest and the Roman mission. It is sometimes suggested that the mass conversions and baptisms recorded by the early missionaries in Kent and Deira are inexplicable unless a substantial element of the population retained memories of Christian beliefs; such argument is unconvincing. That the acceptance of the king's religion by his people had little relationship to genuine conversion was demonstrated frequently in the half century after Augustine's arrival, when peoples followed their kings back to paganism as readily as they had embraced Christianity. Christianity was in origin an urban religion, yet London, the greatest city of

[1] A different view is expressed on this and a number of related matters by H. G. Richardson and G. O. Sayles in *Law and Legislation from Aethelberht to Magna Carta* (Edinburgh, 1966), pp. 161-2. The whole of Appendix I, ' Kent under Aethelberht ', contains much that is stimulating, still more that is controversial.

Roman Britain, was to be for long one of the most obdurate and best attested strongholds of paganism.

2. CELTIC CHRISTIANITY

In sharp contrast, Christianity was by this time firmly established in the highland zone of Britain and in Ireland.[1] In Wales Dubricius had begun his missionary work in the south-east, where Roman influences were strongest; his disciples extended it over the whole country. By the beginning of the fifth century there was a Christian community in Galloway, whose first bishop was Ninian. According to Bede he was a Briton regularly instructed in Roman practice who built a stone church at Whithorn (Candida Casa) from which he ministered to his own people and evangelized among the southern Picts. Any inference connected with the life of St. Patrick suffers from the uncertainty which surrounds it, but if, as is usually accepted, he lived in the middle of the fifth century, a letter written by him to Coroticus, king of Strathclyde, would confirm that Strathclyde was at least nominally Christian at that time. A marauding expedition made to Ireland by subjects and allies of Coroticus had attacked a Christian congregation during a religious service, killing some of its members and carrying others into captivity. Scots and apostate Picts were the principal offenders but Patrick also appealed to the subjects of Coroticus to have no intercourse with him until he restored the captives. Further afield it seems that Christianity had been introduced into southern Ireland in the fourth century through the influence of traders from Gaul and Britain; in 431 Pope Celestine sent Palladius to the Christian community there to act as their bishop and to undertake systematic evangelization. The mission quickly terminated with the death of Palladius in the following year, but it is generally believed that his task was assumed and completed by Patrick, a native of the incompletely Romanized region of north-west England.

In all essentials of organization and doctrine the expanding Church remained thoroughly Roman. As the fourth century evidence shows, the British Church, like the Church everywere else in the Empire, modelled its organization on that of the civil government;

[1] See C. Thomas, *Britain and Ireland in Early Christian Times A.D. 400-800* (London, 1971). K. Hughes, *The Church in Early Irish Society* (London, 1966) is excellent.

its bishops were established in the principal towns, which were centres both of civic and religious administration. In the recently converted areas Ninian and Patrick were bishops, and the evidence of Gildas shows unequivocally that in the sixth century the British Church retained its episcopal organization. Yet the highland zone of Britain had few towns and during these years of expansion Britain was falling back into a congeries of tribal kingdoms. In this area and in Ireland diocesan organization was retained, but adapted to conform to the requirements of the tribal kingdoms. In doctrine, too, the orthodoxy of the Celtic Church was unquestioned and was later to be attested even by its opponents, St. Wilfrid and Bede, though with the passage of time the increasing isolation of the Celts fostered local practices which differed from those of the other Roman churches.

In one important respect Celtic Christianity differed from that of late-Roman Britain, in which monasticism had not been a force to be reckoned with. During the fourth century the establishment of monastic communities, at Tours under St. Martin, at Marseilles by Cassian, and at Lérins by Honoratus, initiated a movement which exercised a powerful attraction on the minds of the faithful in Gaul. Bishop Lupus of Troyes who visited Britain with Germanus had connections with Lérins and the contacts which British clergy maintained with the Gallic Church would have ensured the introduction of monasticism in Britain had time allowed. Such a development was stillborn as a result of the Germanic conquest. But there was no break in the contacts between Gaul, the Mediterranean world, and the Celtic West, and in all the Celtic lands monasticism rapidly took root. In the time of Gildas the British Church was still administered by bishops but the monastic order was increasing its influence; at the end of the century though Augustine treated with British bishops, the great Welsh monastery at Bangor contained two thousand monks ruled by seven abbots. Similar developments in Ireland, though geographically more remote, were to have a greater influence on the history of the Church in England.

Patrick had insisted that he was a bishop and he created a Church governed by bishops; but monasticism found in Ireland a particularly receptive soil. It may have owed something to the British Church in Wales, for contacts between Wales and Ireland are a well-evidenced characteristic of these years. David, Gildas, and a third Briton were reputed to have given a mass to the Irish Church and tradition maintains that Gildas undertook a missionary tour in Ireland; Irish ecclesiastics came to St. Cadroc's monastery at Llancarvan and Cadroc is said to have visited not only Ireland and Scotland but Cornwall and Brittany as well. St. Samson visited Ireland and was given a monastery by its abbot, whom he had cured of an illness: on his return to Britain he sent his uncle to govern the Irish monastery. Much may fairly be attributed to the strength of an ascetic movement which gained ground in the sixth century and found its aspirations satisfied by a rigorous monastic discipline. But more important than any other factor in explaining the expansion of Irish monasticism is the character of Irish society which provided a particularly favourable environment for it. In Ireland property was the possession of the family not of individuals; it could be given away only with the consent of the whole family. The pious aristocrat who wished to endow a church without infringing family right could only do so by persuading his whole kindred to adopt the religious life and to use the family lands to endow a monastery. In this way the monastic property continued to belong to the family, which also provided abbots for the monastery. This happened frequently and at first there appeared to be no conflict between bishops and monasteries because monastic churches may often have been founded in places where bishops had acquired little influence. But rapidly the greater monasteries, Durrow, Bangor, and Clonmacnois, established colonies, sometimes on land hitherto unappropriated, sometimes overseas, and sometimes other foundations joined a larger and more distinguished federation. The organization that emerged from these changes was very different from that of the Patrician age. Whereas the bishop had exercised jurisdiction over a tribe the abbot of the mother house of a monastic confederation (*paruchia*) ruled daughter houses which might be a hundred miles or more distant from it. The head of the monastery was its abbot, often in priests' not bishops' orders; bishops lived in monasteries where they fulfilled the functions of their order, but the abbot's authority was supreme; the abbot of the mother house appointed the superiors of the daughter-houses. During the seventh century the monastic federations became more important than the tribal bishoprics. Often bishops adopted the monastic way of life and in the seventh century episcopal churches attempted to build up their dioceses on extra-territorial principles.

In other respects Irish monasticism developed in ways not unique to Ireland, but more intensely than elsewhere. One distinctive feature, inherited from the peculiar character of early Irish society, was its respect for learning and scholarship. Pre-Christian Ireland had schools of law and literature which provided systematic training for the lawyers and poets attached to the royal courts; this tradition of scholarship, put to Christian uses, was for long carefully sustained in the scriptoria of Irish monasteries, from which it was to be diffused into England, Gaul, and even farther afield. The range of Irish influence was itself the product of a force which can be everywhere identified but which operated in Ireland more spectacularly than elsewhere; the urge to pilgrimage and to self-imposed perpetual exile. Columbanus in Gaul and Fursa in England both sought solitude; that disciples flocked to them and monasteries were founded for them were unsought consequences of the respect felt for their sanctity. In other Irishmen the urge to exile was combined with a sense of pressing obligation to convert the heathen. For these reasons Irish influences operated powerfully over much of western Europe in the seventh and eighth centuries.

Though the distinction between the spiritual functions of the bishop and the jurisdictional authority of the abbot characterized the whole monastic body in Ireland, and though zeal for learning and for pilgrimage was widespread, there was still room for infinite variety of practice within Irish monasticism. The history of the Church in Britain was to be particularly affected by the practice of Iona, where in about 565 Columba, an Irishman of royal birth, having left the monastery which he had founded at Durrow, established himself with twelve companions. Iona's situation was admirably suited as a centre for missionary work in north Britain. Columba converted Brude, king of the northern Picts, and when, after Brude's death, the two Pictish kingdoms were united the sphere of his activities extended over all the Pictish lands as well as over the Scottic kingdom of Dalriada. By the time of Columba's death in 597 monasteries modelled on the Irish pattern and subject to Iona were established over all the country north of the Forth and the Clyde. Bede commented that Iona ' held for a long time pre-eminence over all the monasteries of the northern Irish and over the monasteries of the Picts, and was their superior in ruling their communities '. Organizationally, the supremacy of the abbot called for comment: ' it has as its ruler an abbot who is in priest's order, to whose authority contrary to normal practice, the whole province must be subject, following the practice of that first leader who was not a bishop, but a presbyter and monk '. Adomnan, abbot of Iona and Columba's biographer, tells a story in which a bishop who lived in the community, reluctant to ordain a man to the priesthood, performed the ceremony after the abbot had assumed responsibility for it. Although organizationally Iona was a typical Irish monastery there was a considerable gulf between the savage rigour of the rule imposed on his monks by Columba's contemporary Columbanus and the moderate ascetism and benevolent authoritarianism of Columba. At Iona the monks worked in the fields but were not driven to exhaustion; their diet was sparse but adequate, and as varied as local resources allowed. Columba was accessible to all, both monks and laymen. He and his monks were frequently absent from their monastery while they engaged on preaching tours. Iona was Irish monasticism in its most attractive guise; it was from Iona that Christianity came to Northumbria.

The history of Celtic Christianity within Britain in the sixth century may well have been less impressive. Lack of evidence makes discussion of the condition of the Church in the north-British kingdoms almost totally conjectural; but for Wales and those parts of western England not conquered by the Anglo-Saxons, Gildas is a contemporary source, though one not given to seeing the brighter side of any phenomenon on which he commented. The secular Church in his day was thoroughly worldly. Episcopal appointments were often bought by wealthy men from kings. If Gildas can be taken literally, bishops often lived with their wives, for he exhorts the bishop to be the husband of one wife and to rule his house well, having his children in subjection with all chastity. By contrast with the secular Church the monastic order was well disciplined and growing in importance, and what Gildas says of them goes some way to justify the description of this period as the 'Age of the Saints'; they included among their number Illtud, Samson, and David. One characteristic of the Celtic Church, whether reformed or degraded, Gildas exemplified to the full: a detestation of the barbarian invaders whether Pictish, Scottic, or Anglo-Saxon, and especially the latter. The British Christians appear to have made no attempt to convert their heathen conquerors. Between the two races there existed bitter hostility and suspicion. The heaviest ecclesiastical penalties were imposed on fellow-countrymen who cooperated with the invaders. At the Synod of the Grove of Victory it was enacted that: ' He who acts as guide to the barbarians, let him do penance for thirteen years, that is, if there does not ensue a slaughter of Christian folk and the shedding of blood and lamentable capture. . . . When these follow, let the man abandon his arms and spend the rest of his life in penance.'

The loss to Christendom of the areas of Roman Christianity in lowland Britain was in part compensated for by the conversion of the Britons of the highland zone, the Scots of Ireland, and the Picts of Scotland. Orthodox churches existed in all these areas; they had been further enriched by a rigorous monastic life and by frequent contacts between the various regions; but they would have no dealings with the Angles and Saxons.

3. Anglo-Saxon Paganism

In the areas of England where they settled the Anglo-Saxon conquerors followed the religious practices they had observed in their homelands. Information on this subject is notoriously scanty because Christian writers were reluctant to describe the pagan beliefs and practices which ecclesiastical legislation was trying to suppress. Nonetheless the evidence of place names reveals clearly that paganism was widespread in England; the names of heathen gods Tuw, Thunor, and Woden form the first element in a considerable number of early place names and their frequent association with a second element such as *leah* (wood or clearing in a wood) and *beorg* (mound) gives some indication of the sites favoured for heathen sanctuaries. More numerous are a group of place names containing the words *hearh* (hill sanctuary) and *weoh* (shrine) which preserve the memory of cult centres unconnected with the name of any particular god; they are found combined sometimes with a personal name in the genitive case suggesting that they were privately owned and sometimes with a genitive plural indicating that they were tribal sanctuaries. Such place names are widely distributed over the whole of midland and southern England; their notable absence in East Anglia, Lincolnshire, and the territory north of the Humber is probably explicable by the paucity of pre-Conquest charters, which provide the main body of such evidence, for these areas. The heathenism of East Anglia is attested by Bede.

Though widespread there is no evidence that this ' religion ' was centralized in its organization, and the piecemeal character of the settlement would explain the diversity of religious practice. In the first century, when Tacitus described the Anglii as one of a group of seven tribes who worshipped Nerthus, the cult of that goddess, who periodically perambulated the villages in a sacred chariot, was a unifying influence; in the eighth century the sacred oak of Geismar in Hesse, felled by Boniface, was the centre of a widespread cult. But in England the pagan cults were localized and there is no evidence that even the small independent kingdoms of the early post-migration period had any specially holy place or any particular god for whom the folk felt an exclusive veneration and though there was a professional priesthood there is no evidence of an ecclesiastical hierarchy. In these conditions it must often have seemed a simple matter to admit the Christian God into the pagan pantheon. Raedwald, king of East Anglia, visited his overlord Aethelberht, king of Kent, and there accepted Christianity; on returning to his people he set up an altar dedicated to Christ in the same temple which housed an altar used for pagan sacrifices. Of the qualities of the gods little is known and it would be dangerous to attribute to them the characteristics that they bear in the Scandinavian mythology of much later date.

In addition to the gods whose cults are indicated by place names Bede's *De Temporum Ratione* reveals the worship of other divinities, side by side with the continuing practice of older fertility rites. In this work he explained the names of the months of the heathen year and described the practices which characterized them. The year began on 25 December; the second month was called *Sol-monath*, in which cakes were offered to the gods; the third month was *Rhed-monath* because of sacrifices to the goddess Rheda; in the fourth month sacrifices were made to Eostre. The fifth and eighth months derived their names from the agricultural pursuits which were dominant in those seasons and the sixth and seventh months were together called *Litha*, which means moon. September was *Halegmonath*, holy month, or month of offerings in gratitude for the harvest. The tenth month took its name from the first full moon of winter. The eleventh month *Blot-monath* was the month of sacrifices, when the cattle that could not be fed during the winter months were killed off and eaten. The last period of the year, *Guili* (Yule) covered both the last and the first month of the year. Sacrifices to the gods were necessary to avert their unpredictable displeasure with men, to bring success in war and good harvests.

The world of the Anglo-Saxons was peopled with evil spirits and monsters whose maleficent activities plague mankind. Belief in their reality is testified by place name evidence in most of the counties of England. St. Guthlac had to fight against the demons of the fen country. *Beowulf* describes the victory of its hero over a savage monster, Grendel, and of the revenge sought by the monster's mother, herself a monster who lived in a cave a day's swimming distance beneath the surface of a dark lake. Beowulf slew this monster too, but fifty years later was fatally wounded in defending his land from the attacks of a dragon incensed by the plunder of a treasure which it had been guarding for three hundred years. The poem was recited for the entertainment of a Christian audience, but it entertained not because it created a world of fantasy but because it portrayed on a heroic scale what was felt to be reality.

The intervention of gods and demons in their daily lives was a fact taken for granted by the Germanic immigrants, but what they believed to happen to them after death we do not know and it is probable that beliefs were both varied and in process of change. Complexity of belief is suggested by the variety of practice revealed in their burial customs; bodies could be cremated or buried, with or without elaborate furnishings of grave goods. The practice of including weapons, jewellery, clothes, and food appropriate to the social status of the dead man or woman implies a belief in some kind of life after death but even so broad a generalization as this finds little support in literary sources. The zealous worship of the gods was to Coifi the high priest of Northumbria a guarantee of benefits on earth—and his disposition to desert them the consequence of his feeling that assiduous service had been inadequately rewarded. The Northumbrian nobleman who spoke after Coifi asserted that ' the life of man appears for a little time but what follows on what has gone before of that we surely know nothing ', and none disputed his statement. Though the warrior spent his life fighting and sudden death was no remote contingency for him, Beowulf does not contemplate an after-life when he says, ' Each of us must expect an end to life in this world; let him who may win glory before death, for that is best at the last for the dead warrior '.

To add the Christian God to the variety of other gods already worshipped was comparatively simple and apparently expedient, but to destroy all heathen temples and idols was a far more difficult task. More difficult still would it be to eradicate the beliefs of the common people in the virtue of magical spells and charms which were used to ensure good crops and to provide protection against the powers of evil which surrounded men, and to enforce the prohibition of the worship of trees, walls, and stones. The sequel demonstrated the tenacity of traditional practice. On the death of Aethelberht of Kent a pagan reaction threatened to destroy all that Augustine and his companions had achieved. Aethelberht's son Eadbald 'abandoned his baptismal faith and lived by heathen customs, so that he had his father's widow as wife '. Though he subsequently repented it was not until the reign of his son Eorcenberht (640-646) that the idols in Kent were destroyed and half a century later King Wihtred found it necessary to impose penalties on those of his subjects who sacrificed to devils. In Essex, Mellitus was driven out of his church in London, and the kingdom remained pagan for forty years afterwards. The defeat of King Edwin in 632 was followed by a shortlived relapse into paganism in Northumbria; East Anglia, whose king Eorpwald had accepted Christianity at the persuasion of Edwin, relapsed when Eorpwald was shortly afterwards killed. In 747 it still seemed necessary to the churchmen assembled at the Synod of Clovesho to instruct priests to take measures against the belief in sorcery, incantation, and other heathen practices.

Yet despite its widespread diffusion and tenacity, especially in the south-east, perhaps the most remarkable feature of English heathenism was its tolerance of the new religion and indifference to the fate of the old. In both Kent and Northumbria the question of acceptance was a matter of discussion, not of acrimonious dispute, and the newly converted kings did not enforce the compulsory baptism of their subjects. Penda of Mercia, though himself undisposed to forsake his gods, allowed his son Peada to adopt the new religion and permitted missionaries to work in both Middle Anglia and Mercia. There were no martyrs among the early Christian missionaries of England, which contrasts markedly with the history of the missionary activity of the English themselves on the Continent in the eighth century. It was partly a consequence of the incoherence of heathen belief, organization, and practice in England. Perhaps even more it was because the Christian missionaries of the eighth century appeared to the heathen Frisians and Saxons as agents of a Frankish power which wished to subjugate and enslave them, with the result that paganism became identified with the cause of tribal independence. The missions to England were in no way compromised by any connection with a hostile secular power; whether Celtic or Roman their motives were exclusively religious.

4. THE CONVERSION—THE ROMAN MISSION

If at first it appears that the Christian West was lukewarm in its concern to convert the new inhabitants of the lost Roman province the explanation lies largely in the difficulties it was itself facing in the one and a half centuries between A.D. 450 and 600. The British Christians of the fifth century had appealed successfully to Gaul for assistance, but in the second half of that century northern Gaul was overrun by heathen Franks and it was not until early in the sixth century that Clovis was baptized. After his death his kingdom was divided between his sons, and civil war between the branches of the royal family created conditions unfavourable to an interest outside the Frankish lands; the Gallic Church was itself soon to be in need of radical reform. Apart from its initiative in sending Palladius to Ireland the Roman Church had never been an active missionary force in the west, and in any event faced desperately pressing problems in Italy.

The decision to send Augustine to recover England for Christendom was taken by Pope Gregory the Great, and it marked a new departure in Roman policy taken at a time when the burden of maintaining traditional commitments seemed to prohibit the assumption of additional obligations. Upon Gregory fell the tasks of administering the city of Rome in a period of chronic, and sometimes acute, crisis. He defended the city against siege by the barbarian Lombards; he coped with plague; he supervised the papal estates in Italy, which provided for the material necessities not only of large numbers of ecclesiastics and laymen but for the work of administration; he negotiated with the Byzantine emperor and with the barbarian kings of western Europe. In addition he exercised devotedly his pastoral charge of the whole Church, writing books for the edification of the faithful, corresponding regularly with the ecclesiastical dignitaries of the whole Christian world and issuing direction, encouragement, and reproof as seemed appropriate. In such circumstances it is astonishing that Gregory had the strength not only to initiate Augustine's mission but also to sustain it in times of difficulty and discouragement, and to guide Augustine in his subsequent conduct of the established mission. It was well under way when the second phase of Anglo-Saxon conquest was still gathering momentum.

Northumbrian tradition, which may well rest on a basis of fact, preserved the belief that even before he became pope Gregory was concerned to convert the English. The *Life* of Gregory, written by a monk of Whitby between 680 and 714, tells us that Gregory saw some Englishmen in Rome and on learning that they were heathen he begged Pope Benedict I (574-578) to allow him to undertake a mission to England. Permission was granted but after having travelled for three days messengers recalled him to Rome whose population had protested against his departure. The first indisputable evidence of Gregory's interest is a letter written by him in September 595 to Candidus, a priest sent from Rome to manage the papal patrimony in Gaul; since the money from Gaul was not current in Italy, Candidus was instructed to use it to relieve the needs of the poor and to buy English boys who might then be placed in monasteries, possibly with the idea that they would then be trained as missionaries. A letter written to Syagrius, bishop of Autun, in 599 says that Augustine's mission had been despatched after long thought.

It does not seem likely that Gregory had any great knowledge of affairs in Britain, but in several letters he expressed the belief that a Christian mission would be welcome there. Writing to Theuderich and Theodeberht, kings of the Franks, in 596 he said that he had heard that the English eagerly desired conversion, and both in this letter and in a letter written later to Queen Bertha he was disposed to blame the Frankish clergy and the Frankish queen for dilatoriness in seizing the opportunities that had offered themselves. Certainly the prospects for the Church were favourable at this time. Contact between south-east England and the continent had never ceased entirely and the marriage of Aethelberht, king of Kent (560-618), to the Christian Frankish princess Bertha was both evidence of and opportunity for closer relations. She had come to Kent attended by a bishop, Liudhard, and with the guarantee of freedom to worship in Christian fashion; she had been assigned a church in Canterbury which had survived from Roman times. King Aethelberht and the Kentish court were thus familiar with the external forms of the Christian religion, though had the missionaries been sure of their reception it would be difficult to explain the fears and doubts which Augustine and his companions certainly felt.

There is a singular contrast between the dearth of information concerning the emergence of the Anglo-Saxon kingdoms and the admirably documented account of the Augustinian mission which Bede constructed in his *Ecclesiastical History*. Bede's veracity has been closely questioned in recent years but the result of the discussion so far has been to confirm his reliability on most important issues and to explain such errors as have been demonstrated in terms of the inevitable limitations of even the most omniscient of eighth-century scholars. His account is based on twenty-eight papal letters which had been copied for his use from the papal registers and a series of answers (*Responsiones*) purporting to have been made by Gregory to questions asked by Augustine; it is the authenticity of the *Responsiones* which has principally been under attack and the provisional judgment is that while certain answers are of later composition for most of them Gregory was indirectly if not immediately responsible.[1]

Having determined to despatch a mission Gregory chose as its leader Augustine, the provost of Gregory's own monastery on the Coelian Hill in Rome. They set out early in 596 but by the time they had reached southern Gaul their misgivings caused them to send Augustine to Rome to seek permission for them to return. Gregory encouraged Augustine and in a letter to his companions ordered them to proceed on their journey and to obey Augustine in all things. To ease their journey he wrote at the same time a series of commendatory letters to the ecclesiastics of the regions which the party traversed and to the rulers of the Franks. The group of forty men, which included Frankish interpreters, landed in Thanet early in 597 and though Aethelberht was not prepared immediately to commit himself to the new religion he gave its missionaries freedom to preach and provided them with a lodging in Canterbury. Augustine's success was immediate and by the middle of the following year Pope Gregory was able to tell the bishop of Alexandria that ten thousand Englishmen had been baptized on Christmas Day 597. Bede implies that King Aethelberht was among the first converts and Canterbury

---

[1] The authenticity of the *Responsiones* was queried by H. S. Brechter, *Die Quellen zur Angelsachsenmission Gregors des Grossen* (Münster in Westf. 1941). His arguments were countered by M. Deanesley and P. Grosjean, ' The Canterbury edition of the answers of pope Gregory I to St. Augustine ', *J(ournal of) E(cclesiastical) H(istory)*, X (1959), which was in turn questioned by R. A. Markus, ' The chronology of the Gregorian mission to England: Bede's narrative and Gregory's correspondence ', *J.E.H.*, XIV (1963). An important contribution to the debate has recently been made by P. Meyvaert, ' Bede's text of the *Libellus Responsionum* of Gregory the Great ', *England before the Norman Conquest*, ed. P. Clemoes and K. Hughes (Cambridge, 1971).

tradition holds 1 July 597 to be the date of his baptism; but it has been suggested that it did not occur until 601 at earliest and that even then Aethelberht was never a genuine convert.[1] The reason for preferring the later date is that no mention of the event occurs in any of Gregory's letters until that year, and then only by implication; but it can be argued that the king's acceptance of the new religion was so much a prerequisite for the large-scale conversions that had by then taken place that it would not call for special mention, nor is there anything in the letter of 601 to suggest that the baptism had only recently taken place. Grounds for suggesting that Aethelberht's conversion was only skin-deep are his second marriage to a pagan princess and the heathenism of his son Eadbald; if justified, such doubts would explain the later misfortunes of the Church in Kent, but they had no immediate consequences for the mission.

Augustine was the abbot of a band of monks but this was insufficient basis on which to establish a permanent organization for the new Church. With papal approval he crossed to Gaul and was there consecrated bishop. On his return he sent two members of the mission, Laurence and Peter, to Gregory to report progress and seek further instructions. Illness and pressing business prevented a speedy answer, but the letters written in 601 in their detail and comprehensiveness reveal the deep concern felt by Gregory for the success of the mission. They were brought by Laurence and Peter who were accompanied by reinforcements, of whom the most important were Mellitus, Justus, Paulinus, and Rufinianus; they also bore with them a pallium for Augustine and ecclesiastical furniture of all kinds, vessels, vestments, relics, and service books. At the same time Gregory wrote to the bishop of Arles instructing him to assist the Augustinian mission to the best of his ability.

In a letter to Augustine Gregory outlined the organization which he hoped to see established in Britain. A metropolitan see was to be founded in London and twelve bishops were to be ordained who would be under the jurisdiction of the archbishop. Augustine was instructed to send a bishop to York, with authority to consecrate twelve more bishops; provided that the new bishop was well received there Gregory declared his intention of sending a pallium to him. The archbishop of York was to be subject to Augustine during his lifetime but afterwards whichever of the two metropolitans was senior in ordination was to have precedence. It is possible that

[1] Richardson and Sayles, *op. cit.* pp. 162-4.

Gregory's plan reflected his awareness that the fundamental political frontier in late sixth-century England was the river Humber, but it is more likely that Gregory was attempting to base his ecclesiastical organization on what was remembered of Roman political organization, when London and York were the two chief cities of Britain. Certainly his choice of London for the southern archbishopric shows little awareness of political realities at that time; this instruction was not and could not be carried out. Augustine depended for his success on support from the great Aethelberht whose capital was Canterbury, while London was the chief city of a mere under-king, and though its ruler was the nephew of King Aethelberht it was situated in an area where paganism was strongly entrenched. Augustine accordingly remained at Canterbury. Nor were Gregory's plans for the northern province fulfilled; it was not until 735 that York was established as an archbishopric, nor did it ever receive its complement of bishops.

Having outlined his plan for the Church in the newly converted territories Gregory continued: ' We will further that your fraternity shall have subject to you not only those bishops which you have made yourself or such as the bishop of York shall have ordained, but further, all the bishops of Britain.' It was in accordance with this directive that between 601 and 604 Augustine attempted unsuccessfully to assert his authority over the British Church in Wales. A conference between Augustine and the Welsh leaders revealed a difference in the manner of computing Easter and other usages contrary to those of Rome. According to Bede ' these Britons confessed that the way of righteousness which Augustine preached was true but that they could not abjure their old customs without the consent and permission of their own people '. A second conference was arranged which also proved fruitless. Augustine's pride has sometimes been blamed for his failure, and some support for this reading of his character comes from an undated letter to him from Gregory which while congratulating him on his successes warned him against self-glorification; but it is also clear that Gregory underestimated the magnitude of the difficulties which faced the Roman party. The Welsh ecclesiastics could see no justification for Augustine's claim to exercise authority over them and harboured a deep suspicion of his intentions; in their isolation they had developed traditions different from those of Rome which they felt it their sacred duty to preserve, nor would they welcome a Roman emissary who came to them under the sponsorship of the greatest English king in southern Britain.

Despite this setback the success of the mission seemed assured. In 604 the see of Rochester was established, with Justus as its first bishop. In the same year, after the conversion of Saeberht king of the East Saxons, a bishopric was established in London, his capital city, for Mellitus. Raedwald, king of the East Angles, also accepted baptism at Aethelberht's court, though his acceptance of Christianity was only nominal. At Canterbury, Augustine established the seat of his bishopric in an old Roman church which he restored and dedicated in the name of the Holy Saviour (Christ Church). One of his main tasks was to train a native clergy to assist in the work of conversion and pastoral care, which Pope Gregory did not regard as normally compatible with the observance of a strict monastic rule. Accordingly, the way of life followed by Augustine and his household was communal but not monastic and for the needs of a monastic community he established before his death a monastery whose church was dedicated to St. Peter and St. Paul, soon to be better known as St. Augustine's, a mile from the city. Elsewhere in Kent we are told that the Christians built new churches and repaired old ones, fallen into disuse since the departure of the Romans. These successes were largely due to the skilful and sympathetic direction of Pope Gregory; in a letter to Mellitus he said that he had pondered over ' the cause of the English ' for a long time, and as a result countermanded instructions he had previously sent to King Aethelberht. The king had been told to set himself against the worship of idols and overthrow the buildings of their temples; now Gregory decided that only the idols should be destroyed and the temples consecrated to Christian worship, and though pagan sacrifices must be abjured religious feasts on dedication and saints days should take their place. In this spirit the Christian festival of Easter was named after the heathen goddess Eostre and Christmas was celebrated on the day of the old midwinter feast. Example and persuasion were combined with an understanding of the spiritual needs of a primitive people; force and violent change were proscribed.

The deaths of Pope Gregory in 604 and of Augustine at some date between 604 and 609 deprived the mission of its impetus, An attempt by Archbishop Laurence, who had been consecrated by Augustine as his successor during his lifetime to persuade the Irish and British clergy to adopt Roman practices proved abortive. A letter he and

his fellow bishops wrote to the bishops and abbots of Ireland reveals
that the hostility of the British Church to Rome was matched by that
of the Irish; with pained surprise Laurence reported that a visiting
Irish bishop not only refused to eat with his community but even to
take his meal in the same house as them. Contact with Rome was,
however, maintained and in 610 Mellitus went there to discuss the
needs of the Church with Pope Boniface IV and was present at a
synod of Italian bishops. That royal support was essential to survival
was speedily revealed when Aethelberht died in 616. His son Eadbald
who succeeded him was pagan and his rule gave his subjects the
opportunity to revert to heathenism; in Essex on the death of Saeberht the same thing happened. Mellitus was driven from London
and for a time both he and Justus of Rochester took refuge in Gaul,
and Laurence prepared to follow them. At this critical juncture
Eadbald changed his mind so that Laurence remained in Canterbury and soon Justus was restored to Rochester; but Essex remained
obstinately heathen despite the defeat of its kings in battle.

Kentish Christianity was saved, and favourable political circumstances enabled it to undertake one belated missionary enterprise. In
625 Aethelberg, the sister of Eadbald, married Edwin, king of Northumbria, it having been agreed that she should be free to practise
her religion and that Edwin himself would adopt it if his counsellors approved. Aethelberg was accompanied to the north by Paulinus,
one of the reinforcements who had arrived in England in 601, who
was ordained bishop before setting out. According to Bede, Paulinus
laboured earnestly for some months while Edwin was reluctant to
make a decisive move despite receiving exhortatory letters from Pope
Boniface V. When Aethelberg was safely delivered of a daughter
Edwin gave thanks to his gods though Paulinus attributed the easy
labour to his own prayers. The king then promised to accept Christianity if Christ gave him victory in his imminent war with the king
of the West Saxons and, in earnest of his pledge, allowed his daughter to be baptized. Even after his triumphant return he continued to
hesitate, but being at last persuaded, he resolved to summon a council of the notables of the kingdom so that if they too agreed they
should all be baptized together.

The discussion in the assembly showed that the king's attitude was
the decisive factor. The first speaker was Coifi, chief of the king's
priests, who immediately testified to the futility of the old religion.
No one spoke in its defence, and when Coifi's request that Paulinus

should tell more about the God he worshipped was satisfied the chief priest himself asked that the useless heathen temples and altars be destroyed. Defying the laws that a priest must never ride except on a mare nor carry weapons, Coifi rode on the king's stallion, girt with a sword and carrying a spear in his hand, to the temple at Goodmanham, twelve miles from York; throwing his lance into the building he commanded those present to set fire to it and all its courts. Edwin and all the nobility of his kingdom were baptized at York on Easter Eve in a wood church dedicated to St. Peter which had been built for the occasion. York was to be the bishop's seat and immediately after his baptism Edwin started to build a bigger church of stone.

For the next six years Paulinus was spectacularly successful, his work being greatly assisted by Edwin's dominant position in the north. At this time Lindsey was under his overlordship and by 627 Paulinus had established a church in Lincoln, in which he consecrated Honorius, the new archbishop of Canterbury. His mission also prospered in Bernicia and on one occasion he spent five weeks at the royal vill of Yeavering in Glendale, teaching and baptizing the folk who flocked to him from the surrounding countryside; in this northerly area it is likely that some of his hearers were Christian Celts. In Deira his centre was the royal vill of Catterick, and he built a church at Campodunum near Leeds, also a royal vill: this is the only local church to be mentioned in Bede ' because at the very beginning of the newborn church oratories and places of baptism could not be built '. Edwin's influence over Eorpwald, king of East Anglia, the son of that Raedwald who had housed both heathen and Christian altars in his temple, led to another attempt to convert the East Angles, but the death of Eorpwald rendered it stillborn.

Learning of the success of the northern mission Pope Honorius decided that it was now time to implement Pope Gregory's plan for the establishment of a second archbishopric in Britain. He sent pallia to Paulinus and to Honorius of Canterbury with the instructions than when either of them died his successor should be consecrated by the survivor. Even before Honorius's letter had been written Edwin was dead and the work of the northern mission was in ruins. Paulinus fled to Kent, taking with him Aethelberg and a number of royal children; since the see of Rochester was at that time vacant he was appointed its bishop and there remained until his death. Only the deacon James remained behind in Northumbria.

For long afterwards he continued to preach and baptize, but despite his determination the immediate future of Christianity in the north was to be little affected by his work. The decisive importance of continued royal support for the success of a missionary enterprise had again been revealed, and was shortly to be demonstrated once more.

5. THE CONVERSION—AIDAN: FELIX AND BIRINUS

Edwin, king of Northumbria, had been defeated and killed at Hatfield Chase in 632 by a coalition of forces led by Cadwallon, the Christian king of Gwynedd and the heathen Penda of Mercia. His kingdom fell apart into its constituent elements, Deira and Bernicia, both of which were ruled for a short time by kings who relapsed into paganism; both were killed by Cadwallon who devastated the whole of Northumbria. But before the end of 633 Cadwallon was himself killed and Oswald, a son of King Aethelfrith, became king of Northumbria.[1]

Since the death of his father, Oswald had been in exile and part of the time he had spent at Iona where he had received baptism. One of his earliest acts as king was to send to Iona asking for a bishop to serve his people.[2] The first choice for the work proved unsuccessful and after further deliberation at Iona Aidan was consecrated and sent in his place. He established himself at Lindisfarne, near Bamburgh, with a company of monks, and worked in Northumbria until his death seventeen years later. In most respects the monasticism introduced by Aidan from Iona was typically Irish. The community subjected itself to a strictly ascetic régime; Aidan himself travelled widely and constantly in his huge diocese, generally on foot, so that he might readily converse with all he met, both rich and poor. He brought as well the customs of the Celtic Church relating to the method of calculating Easter and the Celtic tonsure. But an important difference between Lindisfarne and the Irish model was that though Lindisfarne was a fully monastic community it did not contain monks in episcopal orders. Aidan was both the bishop of the Northumbrians and the abbot of Lindisfarne, the sole source both of order and of jurisdiction.

Much of the great success which the mission enjoyed was due to

[1] *Supra*, p. 42.
[2] See D. A. Bullough, ' Columba, Adomnan, and the Achievement of Iona ', *Scottish Historical Review*, XLIII and XLIV (1964, 1965).

the continuing favour of King Oswald; Bede relates anecdotes which reveal their mutual respect and affection. On occasion the king acted as interpreter for the bishop since Aidan's knowledge of English was imperfect, and he was a generous benefactor who gave estates on which churches and monasteries were built. From Ireland and Iona came a steady stream of reinforcements who helped in the work of preaching. But, most of all, Aidan's influence is to be explained by the perfection of the example he set, for ' he taught nothing which he did not practise ', says Bede. He could speak his mind to king and nobles without arousing their hostility; he cared as much for the poor as for the mighty. Bede who, in general, was highly critical of the Celtic Church, saw in him an example which the slothful churchmen of his own day would do well to imitate; the only flaw he could find was his adherence to the false mode of computing Easter. Aidan for his part felt no hostility to the Romans; with Oswald's help he reconstructed Paulinus's church in York. Conversely, Honorius, archbishop of Canterbury, and Felix, bishop of Dunwich, held Aidan in high esteem.

Already in Aidan's lifetime monastic communities were founded in Northumbria, for men and women, and sometimes for both men and women; Melrose and Gateshead were the earliest houses for men while Heiu, the first Northumbrian woman to become a nun, founded a house for men and women at Hartlepool. The most illustrious of all was Whitby, a double monastery in which monks and nuns lived under the rule of abbess Hild, which became a training centre for bishops. Hild was particularly close to Aidan who had been instrumental in persuading her to follow her vocation in England rather than in Gaul where she had intended to go.

The success of the mission was not prejudiced by Oswald's defeat and death at the hands of Penda of Mercia, for Oswine in Deira and Oswiu in Bernicia continued to support it. Soon after the death of Oswine in 651 Northumbria was again united under Oswiu and reached the highwater mark of its power and influence, so that though Aidan died in 651 his successors at Lindisfarne, Finan (651-661) and Colman (661-664), were able to take advantage of this fact to extend their influence as far south as the Thames. Penda's son Peada, appointed by his father king of the Middle Angles, married Oswiu's daughter in 653, after having been baptized by Finan and undertaking to promote the conversion of his people. On his return to Middle Anglia he was accompanied by four missionaries who preached in Middle

Anglia and in Mercia. In the same year, following the conversion of Sigeberht, king of the East Saxons, during the course of a visit to Oswiu's court Cedd, one of the Middle Anglian missionaries, was sent with one companion to evangelize Essex. In Mercia Diuma, and in Essex Cedd, were consecrated bishops by Finan, though neither had permanent seats; both owed obedience to Lindisfarne.

While Aidan's zeal was achieving success in Northumbria both East Anglia and Wessex received missions; the initiative in these came directly neither from the north nor from Canterbury, though close links were to be quickly established between Bishop Felix of the East Angles and Archbishop Honorius of Canterbury.

Earlier attempts to convert the East Anglians had failed. Raedwald's acceptance of Christianity was followed by apostasy. Under the influence of Edwin of Northumbria, Raedwald's son, Eorpwald, made a second attempt to Christianize his people, but he was soon killed in battle and heathenism again triumphed for the space of three years. Eorpwald's brother Sigeberht became king of the East Angles in about 630; he had been converted while a political exile in Gaul and on his accession determined to bring his people into conformity with what he had seen there. In this he was aided by Felix, a Burgundian who came to East Anglia through the good offices of archbishop Honorius; for him a seat was established at Dunwich which was to be the centre of his work for the remaining seventeen years of his life. Soon after the arrival of Felix there came to East Anglia an Irish monk, Fursa, with a few companions. They preached successfully and endowments were given them for the establishment of a monastery at Burgh Castle near Yarmouth. Gallic bishop and Irish monk worked in different parts of the country, and continued their work after the death of Sigeberht in battle. His successor, Anna, was also a good Christian, whose four daughters all achieved fame for their sanctity of life.

Birinus came to Wessex in about 633, having obtained permission from Pope Honorius to work among the heathen Anglo-Saxons in those parts of Britain into which no teacher had yet penetrated; he had been consecrated bishop in Italy. Landing in southern England and finding its inhabitants still pagan he decided to begin his work there rather than to penetrate into more remote regions. King Cynegils of Wessex was converted, his overlord Oswald, king of Northumbria, acting as his godfather at baptism. Cynegils and

Oswald jointly established an episcopal see for Birinus in Dorchester where he was eventually buried after about twenty years of successful preaching and founding churches, though it is doubtful whether his activities extended beyond the Thames Valley. Cynegil's son, Cenwahl, who succeeded his father as king, was a heathen but he was for a time driven out of the kingdom by Penda of Mercia. After spending three years of exile at the court of Anna, king of the East Angles, where he accepted baptism, he was restored to his kingdom and received as his bishop Agilbert, a Frank by birth who had spent a long time in southern Ireland. Agilbert worked in Wessex for some years, but in about 660 abandoned his see. Bede's explanation of this is that Cenwahl, tired of Agilbert's outlandish speech, introduced into his kingdom another bishop, Wine, who spoke Saxon and assigned to him an episcopal seat in the city of Winchester; Agilbert, offended by this partition of his diocese, then returned to Gaul and became bishop of Paris. This version of events is misleading in that Agilbert did not go to Gaul and become bishop of Paris until after the Synod of Whitby, which he attended as the senior representative of the Roman party. After leaving Wessex Agilbert went to Northumbria, and it has been plausibly suggested that his departure from Wessex was the consequence of Mercian territorial expansion which deprived the bishop of Dorchester of both his flock and his endowments; since Cenwahl had by this time established Wine at Winchester Agilbert could go with a clear conscience. That Agilbert's ignorance of Saxon caused a breach between king and bishop seems unlikely because a few years later Cenwahl invited him to return, and, when Agilbert declined, accepted his Frankish nephew as substitute. Wine, recently installed at Winchester, proved to be as unsatisfactory a bishop as Agilbert and having been driven out by Cenwahl, probably in 666, he bought for himself the bishopric of London from Wulfhere, king of Mercia. For some time Wessex was left without a bishop until the arrival of Agilbert's nephew Hlothere; he was consecrated bishop of the West Saxons by Archbishop Theodore and exercised his office for six years (670-676).

6. THE VICISSITUDES OF THE MISSIONS: THE CONFLICT OF CELTIC AND ROMAN OBSERVANCES

The vicissitudes of the Christian missions in the sixty years which followed the arrival of Augustine had mirrored the personal attitudes of kings and the fluctuations in the political fortunes of the various English kingdoms over which they ruled. The early successes of the Kentish mission depended on the support which it received from Aethelberht at a time when Kent was the most powerful kingdom in Britain; stagnation set in when Aethelberht's superiority was first challenged then assumed by Raedwald of East Anglia; the triumph of Celtic Christianity in the north, its recovery in Essex and its infiltration into the Midlands was a pendant to the supremacy of the Christian kings of Northumbria. The attitudes of lesser kings determined the variable fortunes of the Church within their territories, but were themselves often strongly influenced by the rulers of the greater kingdoms.

In addition to the ending of Kentish political supremacy after Aethelberht's death another reason why, even after Eadbald's change of heart, the Roman mission failed to extend the area of its influence in southern England was that during the second quarter of the seventh century the growing power of the obstinately pagan Penda of Mercia—the slayer of Edwin and Oswald of Northumbria, and of Sigeberht and Anna, the Christian kings of the East Angles—was a formidable barrier to the progress of Christianity, and at times even threatened its continued existence.

To these primary facts two others may be added. Augustine may have been proud and authoritarian but he possessed qualities of leadership which were necessary at the inception of a missionary enterprise. His associates and successors were doubtless admirable men, but the flight of Mellitus and Justus to Gaul, the projected flight thither of Archbishop Laurence, and the subsequent return from Deira to Kent of Paulinus in circumstances which allowed James the Deacon to remain there, suggests that they were not of the stuff of which martyrs are made. The archbishops of Canterbury during the sixty years after Augustine's death are little more than names. More important, and probably a contributory cause of the apparent irresolution of the leaders of the Kentish Church, was the noticeable relaxation of papal concern with England during this period. It had, as we have seen, been a crucial factor in Augustine's success.

That general oversight of the Church's activities which characterized the pontificate of Gregory the Great became increasingly difficult to sustain during the middle decades of the seventh century and contacts between Canterbury and Rome became less frequent.

In 610 Mellitus had been present at a council held in Rome; Justus, archbishop of Canterbury, received a pallium from Pope Boniface V in 624; Pope Honorius (625-640) sent pallia to both Archbishop Honorius of Canterbury and to Paulinus of York and a letter of felicitation to King Edwin; in 635 Birinus was sent from Rome to England and when Paulinus returned to Kent he was given the see of Rochester, vacated by the death of its bishop Romanus when on a mission to Rome. But, increasingly, popes were preoccupied with their opposition to Imperial attempts to resolve their political problems by means of theological formulations of the faith designed to satisfy their dissident provinces. In 653 Pope Martin I was accused of complicity in a rebellion against the emperor; he was arrested, taken to Constantinople, declared deposed and exiled to the Chersonese were he died, worn out by his privations. His successor, Eugenius I, threatened with similar treatment, avoided it by dying. By comparison with these immediate crises the welfare of Gregory's remote plantation must have appeared of little account. Accordingly, and in striking contrast both to the Celtic mission in north Britain and the Midlands and to the Anglo-Saxon missionary effort on the Continent in the next century. Augustine's successors never received the continuing support which would have been necessary to maintain the momentum of conversion and to provide encouragement for those already working in the field.

Even in those parts of southern England where Christianity appeared to be firmly established it was still an aristocratic religion, patronized by kings and their courts but with only shallow roots in the countryside. Royal support might ensure that only Essex relapsed into paganism during the plague of 664 but it could not perform the evangelizing work of bishops and priests. The canons of the synod of Hertford and still more the *Penitential* of Archbishop Theodore are a striking commentary on the condition of Christianity in England eighty years after Augustine's mission. The *Penitential* begins with a chapter declaring that any bishop or ordained person who is a confirmed drunkard shall either change his habits or be deprived; a monk who vomits as a consequence of drunkenness must do penance for thirty days, a priest or deacon for forty days. There follows a section of twenty-two clauses detailing penalties for fornication and other offences which, if not blatantly superfluous, is evidence for the persistence of bestial sexual practices. Other sections of the *Penitential* deal with more normal sins; theft, murder, heresy, and so on, including instructions on the amends appropriate in cases of heathen sacrifices of different kinds.

The conversion of Penda's son, Paeda, and of his other son and successor, Wulfhere, were events of fundamental importance in the history of the Church in England. For the first time the Midlands were opened up to missionaries, and Mercian influence over the lesser kingdoms on its borders was exercised to promote their efforts. All England except Sussex and the Isle of Wight was now nominally Christian. Yet the Mercian mission came from Northumbria; it constituted a further blow to Roman influence and a further extension of that of Lindisfarne.

Christianity was secure, but in its organization it did not remotely resemble the plan envisaged by Gregory the Great in his letter of 601. The southern archbishopric was still in being, but its seat remained at Canterbury not London; far from having twelve suffragans subject to his jurisdiction, Honorius, the fourth successor to Augustine and archbishop of Canterbury from 627 to 653, exercised authority only over the bishops of Rochester and the East Angles. Birinus and Agilbert had been consecrated abroad and though followers of the Roman practices acted without reference to Canterbury, while Cedd in Essex and the bishop soon to be made for Mercia looked to Lindisfarne as their superior. On the death of Archbishop Honorius the consecration of his successor, Deusdedit, was attended by only one bishop, Ithamar of Rochester, despite the presence of two other bishops in southern England at the time. Apart from the fact that he was the first native Saxon to become an archbishop, that he did not attend the synod of Whitby, and that he consecrated Ithamar's successor at Rochester, nothing is known of Deusdedit and it seems likely that outside Kent his authority was unrecognized. There was still no archbishop at York; the mission of Aidan had been spectacularly successful, but it had brought in train the ecclesiastical leadership of Lindisfarne.

The result of the eclipse of Canterbury, the success of Aidan, and the assumption of missionary roles by churchmen acting independently of Canterbury was that the organization of the English Church now mirrored political realities. Instead of a tidy hierarchical structure there were ' tribal ' churches within autonomous kingdoms, of which that of Northumbria was by far the most influential. Between the practices of the Church in Kent, East Anglia, and

Wessex, and those of the other kingdoms there were important divergences; no ecclesiastical authority within England was universally recognized as supreme.

7. THE RESOLUTION OF THE CONFLICT: THE SYNOD OF WHITBY

In the early days of the English mission differences in practice between Roman and Celtic Churches, and the importance attached to them by their adherents, had been exposed when Augustine met the Welsh bishops. The conversion of the north and the Midlands from Iona greatly enlarged the territory in which Celtic observances obtained, and with the physical barrier to confrontation which had hitherto been constituted by heathen Mercia now removed by the conversion of Paeda and Wulfhere, it might seem that the days of the ' Roman ' Church were numbered.

Yet imperceptibly during the preceding fifty years the Roman party had been steadily gaining strength and the hostility of the Irish bishop who visited Canterbury during the archiepiscopate of Laurence had become quite untypical. The divergent practices of the Celtic Church were the result not of opposition to Rome but of isolation from it. In Wales they had become the heritage of a conquered race obstinately maintained against their conquerors, but to the Christians of Ireland, north Britain, and western Wessex now no longer isolated, Celtic practices, though cherished by virtue of their association with the saints who had effected their conversion, had to justify themselves in purely religious terms.

In Ireland, about the year 630, a number of southern abbots met at Durrow and decided to adopt the Roman Easter, and shortly afterwards delegates from a southern Irish synod went to Rome. The delegates kept Easter in Rome and met Christians of many races, all of whom affirmed that the Roman Easter was observed in their various lands; they returned to Ireland convinced that it was wrong for the Irish and the British to differ from the rest of the Christian world. From this time the southern Irish conformed to Roman practice though the northern Irish continued in their traditional ways. In Northumbria itself a Roman party supported by the queen, Alchfrith the king's son, and a number of churchmen was in being soon after the middle of the century, and an Irishman, Ronan, had already engaged in dispute with Finan of Lindisfarne. The gradual change of opinion which occurred was assisted by the fact that in the seventh century in the Anglo-Saxon parts of Britain and in Ireland there was in general a far greater awareness of the common missionary purpose of the Church than of external differences that divided them. The close relationship between King Oswald and Aidan had in no way inhibited Oswald's support for the conversion of Wessex by a bishop from Rome. In western Wessex the Irishman Maelduibh established a monastery at Malmesbury, and in East Anglia the Irishman Fursa worked in the same kingdom as Bishop Felix from Burgundy. At Lindisfarne, when Wilfrid became dissatisfied and expressed his wish to visit Rome and see the practices followed there, the authorities of the monastery far from dissuading him commended his purpose and gave him every assistance. He first went to Kent, where he met another Northumbrian, Benedict Biscop, with whom he travelled to Rome. Contacts between the Christian kingdoms of England and Ireland were thus frequent and easy, and as Christianity became securely established the advantages of the Roman organization became more apparent. The Celtic Church had adapted itself to a tribal structure of society, and, though in some ways modified in its transplantation to England, its organization was still that of a missionary church with too little emphasis on the need for pastoral work in the villages by priests permanently established; and it was unsuited to the political conditions which increasingly obtained in England in the seventh century. Some of its cherished practices were loved because they had been inherited from the age of the conversion and were associated with the memory of Columba and other saints rather than because their intrinsic value could be demonstrated.

A critical situation was created in Northumbria when King Oswiu married Eanflaed, the daughter of King Edwin, who had been brought up in the Roman observance in Kent. The differing ways of calculating the Easter festival meant that it was possible for the king to be celebrating the Easter feast while the queen was still keeping the Lenten fast. It is also possible that Oswiu anticipated political difficulties, for the secular champion of the Roman cause in Northumbria was his own son Alchfrith, underking of Deira, and had religious differences been allowed to develop the consequence might well have been a revival of Deiran particularism. To resolve the problems created by the practice of divergent customs within a single kingdom King Oswiu summoned a conference of the bishops and clergy of his realm under his presidency; it assembled at Whitby, the double monastery ruled by Abbess Hild.

At Whitby the practices of the Celtic Church were championed by Colman, bishop of Lindisfarne, and Cedd, bishop of the East Angles; the leader of the Romanizing party was Agilbert, former bishop of the West Saxons, assisted by two priests, James the Deacon, who had remained heroically in Northumbria after the departure of Paulinus, and Wilfred, who by favour of Alchfrith had recently supplanted Aidan's pupil Eata as abbot of Ripon. The debate centred on the method of computing Easter and on King Oswiu's instructions was opened by Colman. Wilfrid, the spokesman of the Roman party answered him. Colman appealed to Columba, Wilfrid to the practice of the whole Church outside north Britain and northern Ireland, and to the authority of the descendant of St. Peter, to whom the Lord had given the keys of the kingdom of Heaven. Oswiu took up this last point and asking Colman whether Peter was indeed the doorkeeper of heaven elicited his agreement. Then Oswiu ' smiling a little ', said that since one day he would himself be seeking admission to those gates he could not contend with St. Peter and would obey his commands in all things. All present agreed; ' abandoning their former imperfect usage they hastened to change over to those things which they had learned to be better '.

The synod of Whitby marked the end of the Celtic ascendancy, the triumph of the Roman Easter and of Roman organization, and it prepared the way for a unified English Church in free communication with the Latin Christianity of western Europe; in these crucial respects it proved decisive. Yet it would be wrong to dramatize either the antecedents of the synod, its conduct, or its immediate consequences. As we have seen, the pro-Roman forces in the Church had for some time been gaining strength. The so-called debate which prefaced the decision, in which Wilfrid's biographer Eddius assigns to him a leading role, was little more than a formality which political prudence enjoined upon King Oswiu; he had summoned the synod for the purpose of terminating a thoroughly inconvenient state of affairs within his kingdom and its verdict was predetermined.

Nor did the synod result in a complete submergence of Celtic influences in the English Church or of Celtic ecclesiastics. Colman relinquished Lindisfarne and returned to Iona, thence to cross to Ireland where he founded a monastery at Mayo. His successor as bishop was Tuda, who had been trained and consecrated bishop in southern Ireland and conformed to the Roman observance; but Tuda died shortly after his appointment. After an interval Eata, who after his departure from Ripon had returned to Melrose, became bishop of Lindisfarne; he had by this time accepted the decision of the Whitby conference, but in the light of his past history his Celtic sympathies cannot be questioned. Cedd, too, a leader of the Celtic party at Whitby, similarly accepted its verdict and returned to his work among the East Saxons. The motive which directed the actions of King Oswiu and these ecclesiastical leaders was to minimize as far as possible the disruptive consequences of the decision which had been taken. The triumph of Wilfrid, the champion of the Romanizing party was shortlived, for having been appointed bishop he insisted on travelling to Gaul for his consecration; on his return he found that Chad, a brother of Cedd and also a pupil of Aidan, had been appointed bishop in York. For a time Wilfrid retired to his monastery at Ripon and until the arrival of Archbishop Theodore his influence in Northumbria was less than his influence over King Wulfhere of Mercia. Nor, as we shall see, did the ascetic and missionary tradition of Aidan wither in the years after Whitby.

Still less did Oswiu's protestation of obedience to the successor of St. Peter imply any recognition of papal headship of the Church in his kingdom. He had manipulated the assembly to produce the result which he wanted; after the synod his authority over his Church and his bishops remained unimpaired. Finally, it must be remembered that the synod of Whitby was primarily a Northumbrian assembly; it does not seem likely that Archbishop Deusdedit attended it, and despite Oswiu's influence in southern England there was no reason why, for example, Wulfhere of Mercia should automatically follow the Northumbrian lead.

Far from heralding a period of rapid advance the synod of Whitby was followed by five years of almost unrelieved misfortune.

The attempt is sometimes made to compare the contributions made by the Roman and the Celtic missions to the conversion of England. Augustine worked in that region of England where paganism was most strongly established, favoured only briefly by the political superiority of a Kentish king whose immediate successor revised his father's policy and whose archiepiscopal successors received little consistent support. Aidan was encouraged by the king of a dominant Northumbria and backed by the unstinted resources of Iona and Ireland. The circumstances in which the two missions operated were so different as to defy useful comparison.

4

THE CONSOLIDATION OF THE CHURCH

THE acceptance of Christianity by Wulfhere, king of Mercia, had removed one of the remaining obstacles to the expansion of the Church's activity and the adoption of Roman practices by the Northumbrian king ended the danger of religious disunity. But during the sixty years after the synod of Whitby the eclipse of Northumbrian supremacy and the inability of any of the southern kingdoms to assume a comparable hegemony generated a political instability and its attendant constant warfare which made the work of ecclesiastical leaders far harder than in the days when they could depend on the powerful support of kings whose influence was felt over all England. That despite an unfavourable political climate this period could in retrospect be regarded as a golden age for the Church is tribute to the supreme talent of a papally appointed archbishop of Canterbury, Theodore of Tarsus.

1. POLITICAL EQUILIBRIUM

Once Wulfhere had asserted his authority over the lands ruled by his father the central geographical position of Mercia, the weakness of the kingdoms on its boundaries, the increasing preoccupation of Oswiu of Northumbria in northern affairs, and his own energy, determined the course of events in southern England. In 661 he harried on Ashdown and inflicted so heavy a defeat on Cenwahl of Wessex that he was able to detach part of Hampshire and the Isle of Wight from Wessex and give them to Aethelwalh, king of Sussex. The West Saxons, compelled to counter continuous Mercian pressure on the original nucleus of their kingdom, halted their drive westwards. Wulfhere also took the offensive against the Welsh who had taken advantage of the interregnum in Mercia to raid as far east as Lichfield. He slew Cynddlan, a Welsh prince of Powys, and destroyed his palace at Pengwrn (probably Shrewsbury). Bede's account of the measures taken to counter the revival of paganism among the East-Saxons after the outbreak of plague in the middle-'sixties testifies to the extension of Mercian influence into Essex: Wulfhere sent his bishop, Jaruman, to call the province back to Christianity. Subsequently he sold to Wine, recently driven out of his West Saxon bishopric by King Cenwahl, the bishopric of London. When Frithuwald, sub-king in Surrey, granted an estate to Chertsey Abbey he did so ' with the consent of Wulfhere, king of Mercia '. For the last part of his reign Wulfhere dominated the whole of England south of the Humber except Kent and East Anglia, and these apparent exceptions may simply reflect absence of evidence rather than lack of authority. In the north, against Northumbria, Wulfhere asserted his authority over the kingdom of Lindsey. Fifty hides of land at Barrow in that province were given by Wulhere to Chad to found a monastery; after Chad's death Archbishop Theodore ordained Wynfrith bishop over the provinces of the Marchmen, the Middle English, and Lindsey, ' over all which ', Bede says, ' king Wulfhere held sway '. But his success in Lindsey was premature, for when in 674 he led a Mercian invasion of Northumbria he was defeated and Lindsey was once again lost to Northumbria for four years; but Eddi's statement that Wulfhere had led ' all the southern peoples ' against Northumbria is evidence of the authority Wulfhere had held.

The effects of the defeat of 674 were only temporary, for in 678 Wulfhere's brother and successor Aethelred (675-704) defeated King Ecgfrith of Northumbria and recovered Lindsey. This minor kingdom, for so long the disputed prize in the fluctuating fortunes of Mercian-Northumbrian rivalry, was now finally incorporated into Mercia; its royal dynasty can be traced until the end of the next century but its kings never again aspired to independence. The annexation of Lindsey was not an isolated success. In the early years of his reign, with his western frontier secured by the subordinate kingdoms of the Hwicce and Magonsaetan, with Ecgfrith of Northumbria engaged in campaigns against the Picts, and Wessex after the death of Cenred (672) distracted by rival claimants for the kingship, Aethelred's freedom of action was unrestricted. In 676 he ravaged

Kent, and after the death of its king Eadric, in about 687, succeeded for a time in reducing the kingdom to a client relationship under kings drawn from the East Saxon royal house who maintained themselves with his support. Confirmation of the expulsion of the West Saxons from their territories north of the middle Thames was the transformation of their first bishopric at Dorchester into a Mercian see at some time between 675 and 685, and from Aethelred's grants to the monasteries of Abingdon and Malmesbury it appears that he controlled a considerable area of land south of the Thames. These acquisitions of authority and territory could not be consolidated; Mercian expansion was checked by strong kings in Wessex and the accession of Wihtred in Kent. In 685 Caedwalla, a royal exile, secured mastery of the kingdom of Wessex, within three years he had annexed the Isle of Wight, the kingdom of Sussex, and the district of Surrey and, for a brief period, was acknowledged as king in Kent. His successor, Ine (688-726), retained his predecessor's conquests for a time. The men of Kent were compelled to pay heavy compensation for their murder of Caedwalla's brother Mul; a reference to Eorconwald, bishop of London, as ' my bishop ' suggests that for a brief period Ine exercised authority there; and he certainly recovered territories on the south bank of the middle Thames. In 710 Nunna, king of Sussex, joined him in an attack on Dumnonia. But Ine's power in Kent was shortlived and before the end of his reign Surrey and Sussex had freed themselves from their subordination and offered refuge to exiles from Ine's wrath; the joint confirmation by Sigehere, king of Essex, and Cenred of Mercia (704-709) of the purchase of Fulham by Bishop Waldhere, Eorconwald's successor, shows that London had once again fallen within the sphere of Mercian influence. Meanwhile, in Mercia, Aethelred retired to the monstery of Bardney in 704; his successor Cenred, son of Wulfhere, after a brief reign troubled by Welsh attacks, left England to become a monk at Rome. He was succeeded by Ceolred, a son of Aethelred, who ruled until 716. Ceolred left an unsavoury reputation as a despoiler of monasteries, but it is worth noting that he fought Ine of Wessex at Woodborough in Wiltshire in 715, which suggests that the Mercians were by this time again capable of taking the offensive.

During the half century that elapsed after Oswiu's death the kings of Northumbria displayed no interest in the affairs of southern England, nor after 678, did Mercian kings again aspire to intervene in Northumbria; within southern England the successes of Wulfhere and Aethelred of Mercia and of Caedwalla and Ine of Wessex proved ephemeral. The balance of power between Northumbria, Mercia and Wessex fluctuated so rapidly that none of their kings could properly be styled ' bretwalda '. This period came to an end with the accession of Aethelbald to the Mercian kingdom in 716.

2. THE CHURCH AFTER WHITBY: THEODORE OF TARSUS

For the English Church the five years after the synod of Whitby was a period of increasing disorganization and demoralization. By 669 the only bishops in England were Chad in Northumbria, whose orders, conferred by Celtic bishops, were only dubiously valid; Wine who had recently bought the see of London from King Wulfhere of Mercia; and Wilfrid, now at Ripon but exercising his episcopal office only locally. Deusdedit, archbishop of Canterbury, had died in 664 and Wighard his designated successor, died in 667, before his consecration. Damian, ordained to Rochester in 655, had been dead for some time and no successor had been appointed. Cedd, bishop of the East Saxons, died during the plague which ravaged western Europe in 663-664, and his people relapsed into paganism. Jaruman, the only Mercian bishop, was sent by King Wulfhere to repair the damage in Essex, but he died soon afterwards and had not been replaced. Nothing is known of the East Anglian see between Bede's notice of the ordination of Bertgils by Archbishop Honorius in 652 and the ordination of Bisi by Theodore in 669. Agilbert had left Wessex when King Cenwalh appointed Wine to a second bishopric in his kingdom and Wine's subsequent departure left the West Saxons without a bishop. Shortage of bishops was a crucial weakness, for priests were trained in episcopal households, only bishops could confer ecclesiastical orders and confirm candidates in their baptismal vows; and because so few priests had been trained and so few local churches established, bishops bore the burden of preaching, of instructing candidates for baptism, and administering that rite. On their zeal almost everything depended; without bishops the Church's ministry could not be maintained.

The most favourable circumstance was that the dangers implicit in the situation were fully recognized in England. In this crisis Oswiu of Northumbria and Egbert king of Kent had jointly chosen Wighard to succeed Deusdedit at Canterbury and sent him to Rome for consecration. When news reached them that Wighard had died of the plague they turned directly for help to Pope Vitalian, leaving the choice of a suitable archbishop in his hands. Despite other pressing problems Vitalian faced up to the difficult task of finding an archbishop for a Church until recently torn by dissension and subsequently weakened by a succession of catastrophes. He needed a man who, by the strength of his personality could influence kings and direct the churchmen subject to him; capable of decision and firmness yet able to implement the decisions of Whitby with such moderation as would ensure their willing acceptance by all. The success of his nominee would depend on his ability alone, for Rome could not guarantee continued support.

Vitalian's first choice was an African, Hadrian, abbot of a monastery near Naples. Hadrian asked to be excused but suggested a man who might be fitting; this suggestion was rejected on the grounds of the physical infirmity of the person designated, but his second proposal, Theodore, a monk from Tarsus in Asia Minor, was conditionally accepted. The condition imposed was that Abbot Hadrian should accompany Theodore in order to ensure that he brought nothing ' after the manner of the Greeks, contrary to the true faith into the Church now subject to him '—the fear being, that far from being too rigorous, Theodore might introduce divergent practices from the East into England which would further complicate existing problems. A delay of four months ensued while Theodore's hair could grow so that it might receive the Roman tonsure and he was then ordained bishop, in March 668. Accompanied by Abbot Hadrian and by Benedict Biscop he set out for England. He was delayed in Gaul for some months by a political misunderstanding but put the delay to good use by staying for a time with Agilbert, now bishop of Paris, a man well qualified to brief him in the difficulties he would shortly encounter. Eventually allowed to proceed on his journey, Theodore was met by Raedfrith, reeve of King Egbert of Kent, who escorted him through northern France. He reached Canterbury in May 669.

Theodore's prime concern was the restoration of the authority of the archbishops of Canterbury over the whole Church; from unity would stem first organization then reform. Before the end already effected important changes. He ordained Putta to the long vacant see of Rochester and Bisi as bishop to the East Anglians. More important, he deposed Chad from his Northumbrian bishopric and restored Wilfrid as bishop of York; this demonstration of authority was balanced by a display of tact when Chad was re-ordained and sent to Lichfield to serve King Wulfhere and the Mercians. Neither Chad nor the kings of Northumbria and Mercia made any objection to these dispositions which testify not only to Chad's humility but to Theodore's diplomatic skill and to the general desire for the re-establishment of ecclesiastical order.

The means by which Theodore achieved his objective were three-fold. It was necessary above all that the number of bishoprics in England should be increased; that bishops should meet regularly in synods which would legislate to ensure a uniform and reformed prac-tice in the Church; and that the efforts of the bishops should be supplemented by means of an increased supply of adequately trained priests. These aims Theodore kept steadily before him, implementing them as opportunity offered.

In 672 Theodore convened at Hertford the first general council of the English Church, and by so doing he brought it into line with the practices of the churches of the Continent and with the law of the Church. Though only four bishops attended the synod Wilfrid of York was represented by legates and it legislated for the whole English Church. It defined those matters in which Celtic practice differed from that of Rome and ordered their uniform observance in the Roman sense, finally confirming the decision of Whitby for all England. The decrees of the synod relating to discipline and orga-nization similarly reflected the adoption of Roman territorial or-ganization and the rejection of the itinerant bishop and priest of the Celtic observance; no bishop should invade the parish of another; no cleric should leave his bishop without permission nor be received by another bishop without commendatory letters; no one should exer-cise priestly functions without the approval of the bishop in whose parish he was. That the synod was seen as a permanent element in ecclesiastical organization is proved by a decree deciding that the bishops should meet twice a year if possible, but annually at least. The ninth decree of the Council gave notice of a serious problem which faced Theodore—' that more bishops be added as the number of the faithful shall be increased; but for the present we say no more about this matter '. That more bishops were needed was obvious, but existing bishops were reluctant to suffer any diminution of their over-large dioceses and a further practical problem was that bishoprics could only be founded as kings made grants of lands and privileges adequate for the endowment of a bishop and his household.

Despite this hesitant declaration, when Bisi of the East Angles became so ill that he could not execute his office two bishops were appointed in his place, with their sees at Dunwich and Elmham. Theodore's next opportunity came as the result of a quarrel between Wilfrid of York and King Ecgfrith of Northumbria which culminated in 677 when Wilfrid was deprived of his bishopric and expelled from the kingdom.[1] The archbishop might have been expected to support Wilfrid since the king had expelled his bishop without any pretence that he had failed to carry out the obligations of his office. On the other hand it was certain that Wilfrid would not voluntarily agree to the division of his huge bishopric, despite its obvious desirability. Theodore acquiesced in Ecgfrith's arbitrariness in part because he could do nothing effective to counter it and partly because it gave him the opportunity of creating more bishops for the north. Before the end of 677 Bosa, a monk of Whitby, had succeeded to York, Eata, prior of Lindisfarne, was made bishop of the Bernicians with his see at either Lindisfarne or Hexham; Lindsey, at this time part of Northumbria, received its own bishop, Eadhaed. A few years later further bishoprics were created. Tunberht was ordained bishop for Hexham, leaving Eata at Lindisfarne; Abercorn, on the Firth of Forth, was established to serve the Pictish territories subject to Northumbria; and when Lindsey was recovered by the Mercians its former bishop Eadhaed was translated to a bishopric at Ripon. In the great kingdom of Mercia only one bishopric had been established at the time of Theodore's arrival, but after King Aethelred's reconquest of Lindsey in 678 the separate bishopric established in the previous year was retained, although a new bishop had to be found for it. It is probable that hostility to the subdivision of the Mercian see explains the deposition of Bishop Wynfrith of Lichfield by Theodore, who appointed Saxulf, abbot and founder of Mede hamstede, in his place. Soon afterwards new dioceses were established in the western part of the kingdom, at Worcester and at Hereford. For a time a bishop's see was established in Leicester for the Middle Angles and a bishop of Dorchester-on-Thames makes a fleeting appearance in two charters of this period. A byproduct of Wilfrid's quarrel with Ecgfrith was his mission to the still pagan South Saxons and the temporary establishment of a bishopric at Selsey (*c.* 681-685).

[1] The career of Wilfrid in the context of Northumbrian politics is discussed *infra*, p. 143.

Not all of Theodore's new bishoprics achieved permanence. Abercorn was abandoned after Ecgfrith's defeat by the Picts in 685, Ripon disappears from the records in the 690s, Leicester was not permanently established until 737, and Dorchester had no continuous existence. Nor was any progress made in providing more bishops for Wessex. Agilbert's nephew, Hlothere, was consecrated to the see of Winchester in 670 by Theodore and was succeeded in 676 by Haeddi, a close friend of the archbishop, but the political confusion of the next twenty years delayed the division of the West Saxon see until the first decade of the eighth century. Despite these limitations the central and critical fact remains that during his primacy Theodore had significantly increased the number of bishops and thereby reduced the English dioceses to units of a manageable size.

Similarly, the intention of holding an annual synod of the whole Church was too ambitious to be realized. After Hertford in 672 the next recorded national assembly met at Hatfield in 679 to declare the orthodoxy of the English Church and its abhorrence of the Monothelite heresy. Even so, the primacy of the church of Canterbury was now explicitly accepted by all and was underlined by Theodore's deposition of Wynfrith of Lichfield in 675 and of Tunberht of Hexham in 685.

Though he proved to be a highly competent administrator Theodore's reputation before his promotion to Canterbury had been as one of the most distinguished scholars of his age, and his companion Hadrian was similarly famous. They knew that the restoration of order was their immediate task and that the longer term need of the Church was for an ample supply of trained clergy to supplement the efforts of the bishops by providing a permanent and stable ministry in the countryside. Episcopal households were the principal source of such clergy and the increase in the number of bishops would automatically go some way towards meeting the need. Yet the pastoral preoccupations of bishops necessarily confined their concern for learning, which was almost equally necessary for a healthy church. With Theodore's active encouragement Hadrian at St. Augustine's, Canterbury, and later, Benedict Biscop at Wearmouth and Jarrow, added a new dimension to English monasticism by popularizing the rule of St. Benedict and combining with it a concern for ecclesiastical learning. At Canterbury a centre of excellence was created in which the quality of scholarship was so high that it attracted scholars from all England and Ireland and established standards which other houses emulated. To Canterbury came Oftor, formerly a pupil of Hild at Whitby, and Aldhelm, who had previously been instructed in the Irish learning at Malmesbury. All knowledge useful to churchmen was studied there—the texts of the scriptures, the science needed to calculate the dates of the Christian festivals, church music and the canon law; not only Latin but Greek also was taught. From 669 until 671 Benedict Biscop was in charge at St. Augustine's until Hadrian had learned sufficient English to be made abbot. On his release and after a fourth visit to Rome Biscop returned to his native Northumbria, where his new foundations at first Wearmouth then Jarrow, like St. Augustine's at Canterbury but unlike others in northern England, from the beginning were conceived of as being genuinely monastic. The first duty of their inmates was the recitation of the *opus dei*; being free of pastoral commitments his monks could devote time to the study of the scriptures and of those arts useful to the Church. One of the first monks of Jarrow was Bede, the greatest teacher of the early middle ages and a witness to the importance of the new monasticism.

The influence of abbot Hadrian and Benedict Biscop was widespread but, however admirable, their discipline and observance could not be imposed generally even by archbishop Theodore. The council of Hatfield decreed that bishops might not intervene in the affairs of the monasteries within their dioceses and this constituted a serious limitation on their authority. Since the early days of the Church in England the extension of Christian influences had depended first on the bishops and secondly on the communities of monks or clerics which were established by them or by pious kings and laymen. Such communities were styled ' monasteries ' or ' minsters ' though these terms did not necessarily imply that their inhabitants lived strictly cloistered and contemplative lives. Many had certainly been founded in the belief that salvation could best be attained by withdrawal from the world and subjection to a discipline of prayer, solitude, and physical privation. Some combined this belief with the recognition of an obligation to evangelize among the unconverted. In others, often founded by bishops, the community was conceived as an offshoot of the episcopal household designed to reconcile the advantages of communal living and spiritual discipline with the need to provide for the spiritual needs of the adjacent countryside, performing the functions of a parish church though for the population of an area far larger than that of the later parish. St. Augustine's under Hadrian and Wearmouth under Biscop were distinctive in their combination of a strict monastic régime with a strong emphasis on intellectual pursuits which left no time for pastoral activity; at these houses the basis of observance was the Rule of St. Benedict; Wilfrid's foundations were also strongly influenced by that Rule but showed no particular concern with scholarly activities. Some monasteries were founded with no intention of their becoming religious centres of any kind, when landowners succeeded in securing recognition of their households as monasteries and benefited from the large exemptions from public burdens which monasteries enjoyed.

From the beginning the 'monastery' was the characteristic institutional form assumed by Christianity in England. In the early stages of his mission Augustine had founded the monastery of St. Peter and St. Paul at Canterbury. By the end of the seventh century Kent was served by the two bishoprics of Canterbury and Rochester and by a number of royally endowed minsters, of which the first we know was the double monastery at Lyminge, near Lympne, established by King Eadbald for Aethelberg and her chaplain Paulinus on their return to Kent from Deira in 633. Later communities were Folkestone founded by Eadbald for his daughter Eanswyth, and the great houses of Minster-in-Sheppy and Minster-in-Thanet similarly established by Kentish kings for female relations. As well as these large double monasteries there were minsters at Dover and Reculver, both of them houses of clerics. In northern England Aidan brought monks from Iona and established his church and monastery at Lindisfarne; under the influence of Lindisfarne monasteries proliferated in Northumbria and the kingdoms converted from Lindisfarne. King Oswiu, in thanks for his victory on the Winwaed, founded twelve monasteries and assigned estates for their endowment; Saxulf, a rich thegn of the Middle Angles, founded Medehamstede and the father of St. Willibrord founded a monastery at the mouth of the Humber. The advance of Christianity into western Wessex was marked by Aldhelm's establishment of monasteries at Bradford-on-Avon and Frome, and the same phenomenon can be seen in Mercia.

Almost the only characteristic shared by the monasteries was that the founder of a house assumed direct lordship over it and all its properties; he determined the rule of life within it or the absence of

4*

rule. At Lindisfarne no specific rule was laid down until St. Cuthbert devised a compound of Benedictine and Columban practice for its monks; Benedict Biscop created a rule for his houses which he based on that of St. Benedict but which embraced customs that seemed good to him drawn from the many monasteries that he had visited. Wilfrid, Cedd, and Aldhelm, controlled all the houses of their foundation, with subordinates exercising local authority under their direction; and when great monasteries like Medehamstede sent out colonies the newly created daughter-houses remained subordinate to the abbot of Medehamstede; but, in general, each house was a rule unto itself.

One of the most remarkable forms assumed by early monasticism was the double monastery; this was not a single mixed community, but two communities one of men the other of women, under the rule of an abbess. Double monasteries had a long history in the east, but in the west were peculiarly Frankish institutions, which served as models for those of England. Bede mentions that when Eorconberht became king of Kent in 640 his daughter was a nun at Faremoutiers. 'For at that time because not many minsters had been built in England, many were wont to seek the grace of the monastic life in the minsters of the Franks or Gauls; moreover, they used to send their daughters to be taught and presented to the holy bridegroom there, and chiefly to Brie, and to Chelles and to the monastery of Andely.' Three successive abbesses of Faremoutiers were Anglo-Saxon princesses, including a daughter of Anna, king of the East Angles, and his stepdaughter. It is not surprising that double monasteries, when introduced into England from Gaul, achieved speedy popularity; they included some of the most distinguished communities of the seventh and eighth centuries and almost always they were, like Lyminge and Folkestone, founded for a queen or a princess. This popularity was not confined to Kent. In Northumbria they were numerous and included Whitby, one of the houses established by King Oswiu after the victory on the Winwaed. In Middle Anglia Ely was originally a double monastery, as were Much Wenlock in Shropshire and Wimborne in Wessex. In the double monasteries as in male communities the way of life was determined by the founder and showed no uniformity of practice; there appear to have been no communities designed exclusively for women.

The control of the founder over his community was communicated by him to his heirs. Even so ardent a reformer as Wilfrid took infinite pains to ensure that his nephew succeeded him as abbot of Ripon; the monastery founded by St. Willibrord's father was still owned by his descendant Alcuin a century later. Benedict Biscop was much exercised in mind to ensure that the claims of blood should not prevail over the claims of fitness when the time came for his successor to be appointed and for this reason obtained a privilege from Pope Agatho securing his monastery from all outside intervention and vesting the election of the abbot in the community of monks.

Monasticism, in England as in Ireland, was clearly powerfully influenced by the character of the society in which it worked; the proprietary monastery and the double monastery were natural products of that society and could not be easily uprooted. Theodore disliked the double monastery but he had to accept it and he would have been powerless to impose his will on kings and noble patrons of other monasteries even if he had so wished. St. Augustine's and Jarrow were models of monastic observance but not even Theodore could secure the general adoption of their excellencies.

So considerable was Theodore's achievement as organizer and as teacher that there is risk of overlooking the personal, as distinct from the official, qualities which made so important a contribution to his success in resolving some of the major problems which confronted him on his arrival. It had appeared likely in 669 that he might encounter opposition from elements both of the defeated 'Celtic' and from the victorious 'Roman' parties. In the sequel this never materialized. In his treatment of Chad he showed a respect for goodness as strong as his determination to preserve strict orthodoxy and to demonstrate his primacy. In many respects Theodore showed himself sympathetic to certain aspects of Celtic observance and through his influence the Church adopted some of them, in particular the Celtic practice of private penance. A significant number of his appointments to bishoprics were men who, though they accepted Whitby, had been trained in the Celtic tradition. Conversely, with the unwitting assistance of Northumbrian kings, he showed himself well able to cope with the Roman champion Wilfrid, who though zealous for reform was also autocratic and unsympathetic to any measure which might diminish his authority in Northumbria.

Theodore's success in reconciling the adversaries of Whitby was crowned in 684 when, in a synod summoned by Ecgfrith and presided over by the archbishop, Cuthbert was consecrated bishop. Cuthbert had entered the monastic life at Melrose, which at that time was ruled by Abbot Eata.[1] He accompanied Eata to Ripon and when, having been given by Alchfrith of Deira the choice of adopting Roman practices or leaving Ripon, Eata returned to Melrose, Cuthbert followed his master; and again, when Eata became bishop of Lindisfarne Cuthbert accompanied him and became prior there. Both at Melrose and Lindisfarne he was concerned both with the discipline of the monastery and with preaching in the surrounding villages, taking particular care to visit the most inaccessible places ' which others were afraid to visit, and whose poverty and ignorance prevented the approach of teachers '. Occasionally he was away for a whole month at a time. After some years at Lindisfarne he retired to Farne Island, about nine miles away, and lived in a cell which he himself dug out and surrounded with an earth wall so that he could only see the sky. His life was one of extreme austerity: he changed his clothes once a year and used to walk into the waves up to his neck and then kneel on the shore to pray; he depended on the monks of Lindisfarne for food. In his ascetism, humility, and evangelistic zeal Cuthbert was typical of his Celtic teachers. But this is not the whole picture. Though he left Ripon with Eata both of them subsequently accepted the Roman reckoning of Easter, and as prior of Lindisfarne he devised a rule for his monks which was a moderate compound of Benedictine and Columban practice. Now, in 684, he reluctantly acquiesced in the demands of the archbishop and synod that he should leave the beloved solitude of Farne and accept the burden of the episcopate. Appointed bishop of Hexham he exchanged sees with Eata, and at Lindisfarne he remained until his death in 687. Though the records of his brief tenure of office are meagre they reveal him travelling the countryside at the head of a seemly retinue, preaching and confirming in the villages and ordaining priests. He fully recognized the importance of maintaining ecclesiastical order. With death imminent he withdrew again to Farne Island and his last message to the monks of Lindisfarne exhorted them to ' have no communion with those who depart from the unity of the Catholic peace, either in not celebrating Easter at the proper date or in evil living '. In Cuthbert were combined the best qualities of Celtic and of Roman

---

[1] An early anonymous life of the saint together with Bede's prose life are edited and translated by B. Colgrave, *Two Lives of St. Cuthbert* (Cambridge, 1940).

Christianity; his elevation to the episcopate epitomized their fusion in the Theodoran Church.

Theodore's achievement should be assessed against the political background of his time which was, as we have seen, a period of political confusion in which no kingdom was dominant and in which both intertribal and internecine wars were as prevalent as at any time before or after. Southern England was particularly disturbed. Wessex after Cenwahl's death was shared by a number of lesser kings for about ten years until in 685 Caedwalla secured mastery there; this was followed by West Saxon attacks on Sussex by first Caedwalla then by Ine. Mercians attacked Kent, and in 676 ravaged Rochester, which was so poverty stricken that no one wanted its bishopric. Political chaos of this sort hampered the work of ecclesiastical organization and made Theodore's task one which called for the utmost diplomacy; lacking any basis of political power his effectiveness rested entirely on the influence of his personality. On one occasion at least it proved sufficient, when Theodore successfully made peace between Ecgfrith of Northumbria and King Aethelred of Mercia after a battle in which Aelfwine, Ecgfrith's brother, had been killed. Bede recorded, ' Though occasion seemed to have been given for a more violent war and more lasting enmity between the kings and their fierce peoples. Theodore . . . completely extinguished the dangerous fire that was flaring up. . . . And this peace treaty lasted for a long time between these kings and their kingdoms.'

Any account of Theodore's activities must necessarily emphasize his dealings with the great men of his time, both in the Church and in the English kingdoms, and in so doing will underline the statesmanlike qualities of farsightedness and moderation with which he pursued his objective of establishing the English Church on a secure organizational basis. But in his appreciation of Chad and Cuthbert Theodore showed a generosity of mind, a breadth of sympathy and a love of goodness which goes beyond the supple awareness of the diplomat of the desirability of reconciling conflicting ideas. A sound organization was the prerequisite of an effective Christian ministry, not an end in itself. In his *Penitential* Theodore revealed his concern to raise the standards of behaviour among priests and laymen; combining discipline with exhortation, it also reveals a lively awareness of the difficulties which ordinary folk experienced in trying to live Christian lives in a time of exceptional difficulty. When he authorized the husband or wife whose partner had deserted or been carried off into captivity to remarry after five years, and the wife of a man condemned to penal slavery to remarry after one year he was courageously and sympathetically applying the spirit of Christian teaching to the harsh circumstances of contemporary life.

Already sixty-eight years of age when he landed in England and unfamiliar save at second-hand with the background and problems of the church he had been sent to rule, Theodore found ecclesiastical morale at a low ebb and suffering from lack of leadership, such bishops as it had on bad terms with one another; political conditions were unfavourable to the establishment of unity in the Church. Within twenty years a complete transformation had been effected. Bede summarized Theodore's achievement: 'And this was the first among the archbishops whom the whole church of the English agreed to obey.' He died in 690, having established a claim to be regarded as one of the greatest, if not the greatest of all the medieval archbishops of Canterbury.

Though by the time of Theodore's death much had been accomplished his purpose was far from complete fulfilment. Some immediate problems remained incompletely resolved: there was still only one bishop in Wessex; Bishop Wilfrid still aspired to recover his authority over the whole Northumbrian church; St. Cuthbert's dying exhortation is a reminder that on the periphery of England Celtic observances were still followed by the Britons of the south-west and of Wales, by the northern Irish, and by the Picts. Other obstacles required decades for their removal. Parts of England had only recently been evangelized and everywhere heathen practices were deeply rooted in the habits of the common people; in 747 the synod of Clovesho condemned those who practised divinations, auguries, incantations and the like and in 786 the papal legates sent to enquire into the state of the Church demanded that 'if anything has remained of the rites of the pagans it is to be plucked out'. It was to take a long time before this situation could be remedied and for the present there were too few priests and too few churches for even substantial villages to enjoy a permanent ministry. In his account of St. Cuthbert Bede tells us that 'It was then the custom of the English people that when a cleric or priest came into a village, all flocked at his command ready to hear the word', and though his *Letter* to Archbishop Egbert implies that the number of village churches had increased since that time there were still too few priests in Northumbria.

It is very necessary that you appoint several assistants for yourself in the sacred work, by ordaining priests and instituting teachers, who may devote themselves to preaching the word of God in the various villages and to celebrating the holy mysteries and especially to performing the rites of baptism, wherever opportunity arises.

That a similar situation obtained in Wessex is shown by the *Life* of St. Boniface which mentions the occasional visits of ' priests or clerics, travelling about, as is the custom in these parts ' to preach to the people of the town in which Boniface lived as a child. The Mercian church, in the last of the English kingdoms to be converted, may fairly be assumed to have fully shared the deficiencies of the others. Over much of England the people depended for preaching and for the administration of the sacraments on the occasional visits of priests despatched for the purpose from the nearest minster. Theodore's *Penitential* allowed a bishop to confirm and a priest to say mass in a field if it should be necessary. One hundred years later the biographer of St. Willibald indicated the absence of permanent village churches when she mentioned incidentally that ' on the estates of the nobles and good men of the Saxon race it is a custom to have a cross, which is dedicated to our Lord and held in great reverence, erected in some prominent spot for the convenience of those who wish to pray daily before it.' To all these problems Theodore's successors addressed themselves undramatically but with conspicuous success. More spectacularly, even before England was fully converted English churchmen were actively concerning themselves with the evangelization of their pagan kinsmen on the Continent.

3. The Consolidation of Theodore's Achievement

With so much to be done, Berhtwald (692-731), Theodore's successor at Canterbury, must have resented the distraction which inevitably resulted when, after Theodore's death, Wilfred once again revived his claim to authority over the whole Northumbrian Church. Wilfrid was supported by successive popes but was totally unacceptable to Aldfrith king of Northumbria; Berhtwald, though well aware that Wilfrid's success would involve the reversal of Theodore's policy of increasing the number of bishops in the north, was continuously pressed from Rome to secure justice for the bishop. For six years, 699-705, in councils of the English Church over which he presided Berhtwald attempted to arrive at a compromise which would be acceptable to all parties in the dispute. It was a thankless task for Berhtwald's only weapon in dealing with the Northumbrian king whose power over his church was absolute was persuasion, while Wilfrid had repeatedly shown as conspicuous a capacity for alienating first Ecgfrith then Aldfrith as he showed in captivating first Wulfhere then Aethelred of Mercia. In Wilfrid's biography, written by his priest Eddius, the bishop appears as a wronged hero; to later observers he appears more like the first of the great ' prince-bishops ' of the Church.[1] Familiar with the sophistication of Gaul and Rome, he was convinced of the need and desirability of making ecclesiastical authority awe-inspiring by its impressive display; churches must be large, vestments richly adorned, and gospel books elaborately decorated with gold leaf and precious stones. Wilfrid's zeal is unquestioned, but he was certain that the Church's welfare was best secured when it was under his control and direction; his courage in the face of danger, demonstrated in his missionary enterprises in Frisia and in Sussex, readily degenerated into a haughty and abrupt refusal to consider any abatement of what he considered was due to him. He was an aristocrat by origin and to the fingertips, well endowed for leadership in perilous times but lacking the ability to cooperate in the humdrum task of reorganization which was, at the time, the Church's greatest need. It would have been a misfortune if Wilfrid had achieved his purpose; but the bishop's resolution was no match for the king's physical power. After many vicissitudes and after King Aldfrith's death a settlement was reached. Wilfrid was restored to Ripon and Hexham, and disturbed ecclesiastical politics no more. He died five years later in a monastery which he had founded at Oundle; and with his death Ripon ceased to be the seat of a bishop.

In coping with their long term problems the ecclesiastical leaders of the post-Theodoran generation were favoured by circumstance. They were a remarkable group of men bearing witness to the vigorous intellectual and spiritual life of Canterbury and the great northern monasteries. Berhtwald had been abbot of Reculver; he was ' a man trained in knowledge of the scriptures and deeply learned in ecclesias-

---

[1] *The Life of Bishop Wilfrid by Eddius Stephanus*, ed. and trans. B. Colgrave, (Cambridge, 1927), is fiercely partisan but it is an essential source of information both for the bishop and for Northumbrian history in the seventh and early eighth centuries.

tical as well as in monastic discipline, yet not to be compared with his predecessor '—a comment offered not in disparagement of the new archbishop but a measure of the respect in which Theodore was held. Among the bishops he ordained was Tobias, ' a man skilled in the Latin, Greek and Saxon languages and of much erudition otherwise '. Haeddi, bishop of Winchester until 705, had a reputation for sanctity and miracles were said to be performed at his grave. Daniel, his successor at Winchester, was fully instructed in ecclesiastical matters and knowledge of the scriptures, a correspondent of Bede, a counsellor of Boniface and a good diocesan until physical infirmity limited his ability to move around his diocese. Aldhelm in the newly created see of Sherborne was distinguished not only as a man of letters but as an exemplary diocesan, and after his death in 709 his successor Forthere, who was still alive when Bede wrote, was also reputed to be ' very learned in the Holy Scriptures '. We know little of the Mercian bishops of this period, but in the north three successive bishops of York were pupils of Hild at Whitby; Bosa, John of Beverley and Wilfrid II were all men of enviable reputation, while Acca, bishop of Hexham, was a pupil of Wilfrid. When a new bishopric was established in the north at Whithorn it was filled by Pecthelm, a pupil of Aldhelm, who was a friend and informant of Bede to whom Boniface referred for advice on matters of ecclesiastical law. At St. Augustine's the tradition of Hadrian was sustained by Albinus who possessed some knowledge of Greek and knew Latin no less well than English, his mother-tongue. At Wearmouth-Jarrow the hopes of Benedict Biscop were realized by Abbot Ceolfrith and Bede.

The efforts of churchmen were the more effective because they were supported by kings of singular piety. Aethelred of Mercia consistently befriended Wilfrid in his times of adversity and offered him opportunities for exercising his evangelizing abilities in Middle Anglia: he retired from his kingship to become abbot of Bardney in Lincolnshire. His successor Cenred abandoned his kingdom and ended his life in the monastic habit at Rome; Aethelbald of Mercia acquired subsequently an unsavoury reputation as the target of Boniface's strictures on his personal morals but as an exile in the days before he ascended the throne he was the intimate friend of Guthlac, the hermit of Crowland. In Northumbria King Ecgfrith though the enemy of Wilfrid was equally the friend of Cuthbert and Benedict Biscop, and his brother Aldfrith who succceeded him was 'a man most learned in the scriptures', who won Bede's approval despite his enmity for Bishop Wilfrid. Caedwalla king of Wessex terminated his stormy career by going on pilgrimage to Rome, and his successor Ine followed him thirty-seven years later. Royal support was shown not only by gifts of lands on which to found new monasteries but by the conferment of other benefits. The *Laws* of Wihtred king of Kent begin by stating that the Church shall be free of taxation, and a Kentish council declared that the monasteries founded by the king or his ancestors should be free from secular lordship—each community free to choose its own head subject only to the bishop's consent. In the *Laws* of Ine church-scot, a levy in kind from all freeholdings, was made compulsory; it had to be paid by Martinmas and any defaulter was penalized by the payment of sixty shillings to the king and a twelvefold payment of the original obligation to the Church.

With such leadership and such support the objectives of Archbishop Theodore were steadily advanced. During the archiepiscopate of Berhtwald the South Saxons received a bishop of their own though after two incumbents the see was left vacant and authority over them reverted to the bishops of Winchester. But in 705 on Haeddi's death the West Saxon bishopric was permanently divided when Aldhelm was established in a see at Sherborne, and in about 731 the loss of Abercorn after Ecgberht's defeat at Dunnichen Moss was compensated for when Pecthelm became the first bishop of Whithorn. In 737 the see of Leicester was finally detached from Lichfield. The southern sees were now of such moderate size as to be susceptible to adequate supervision by a vigorous bishop; but there were still too few bishoprics in the north and Bede insisted that more were necessary even after the establishment of Whithorn.[1] Bede urged that Bishop Egbert should take steps towards implementing the Gregorian plan by creating more sees and applying to Rome for metropolitan status for the Church of York. In 735 York became a separate archbishopric though no more subordinate bishoprics came into existence. As a consequence of this move England henceforth was divided into two ecclesiastical provinces. The separation facilitated the tendency of Northumbria to withdraw from the affairs of southern England but its intention was simply to improve the organization of the Church in the north.

[1] The condition of the Northumbrian church is discussed *infra* pp. 149-51.

The authority of Canterbury over southern England was never questioned during these years, and was strikingly demonstrated by a letter of Waldhere bishop of London to Archbishop Berhtwald which may be attributed to the years 704-705. In the letter Waldhere asked permission from Berhtwald to attend a meeting between the kings of Essex and Wessex to which he had been summoned; he needed permission because in a synod held in the previous year it had been agreed that there should be no intercourse with the West Saxons until they had obeyed the archbishop's decree touching the consecration of bishops. He completed the letter by adding that he had recently refused to attend a Mercian council because he did not know the archbishop's views on the matter to be discussed. For some unknown reason Berhtwald had been consecrated in Gaul, but the consecration of Tatwine (731-734) was attended by bishops from Kent, Essex, Wessex, and Mercia, and increasingly bishops sought consecration from their archbishop.

Not the least important of the consequences of Wilfrid's difficulties with his kings was that he established abiding friendships with both Wulfhere and later Aethelred of Mercia, who, under his influence, quickly adopted Roman practices. By degrees the remaining centres of Celtic observance were persuaded to accept the Roman orthodoxy. In the south-west the West Saxon advance was not a simple matter of fighting followed by subjection of the native population— Cenwalh made generous land grants to old established Celtic monasteries in the areas newly subjected to him[1]; Aldhelm was a pupil of Maelduibh at Malmesbury before attending the school at Canterbury and Ine's *Laws* reveal a disposition to reconcile his British subjects to West Saxon rule. It was in this atmosphere that Aldhelm, while still abbot of Malmesbury, wrote a book exposing the errors of the Celts and ' through the reading of the book many of the Britons who were subject to the West Saxons were led by him to the celebration of the Lord's Easter '. In about 704 the northern Irish were persuaded of the superiority of Roman practice by Adomnan, abbot of Iona, who witnessed it at the Northumbrian court while on a mission there. His attempt to convert his monks of Iona to his newly discovered beliefs was unsuccessful, but in 716 they were convinced by Egbert, an Englishman who had spent most of his life in Ireland. Soon after 710 the Pictish King Nechtan wrote to Abbot

[1] Finberg, *op. cit.* ' Sherborne, Glastonbury and the Expansion of Wessex ', esp. pp. 94-102.

Ceolfrith of Jarrow asking him for a letter containing the arguments he might use to confute those among his people who were opposed to the Roman Easter and tonsure; a letter was composed for this purpose, almost certainly by Bede, which achieved its purpose and Nechtan ordered all his subjects to conform. The only Christian people who remained intransigent were the Welsh who were not won over till 768.

Concurrently with these events, throughout England old monasteries were obtaining additions to their endowments and new communities were coming into existence through the munificence of kings and bishops and lay noblemen. Wimborne was founded as a double minster by two sisters of King Ine, Aldhelm founded monasteries at Frome and Stratford on Avon; in Mercia Wilfrid was particularly active in the ten years which followed his second expulsion from Northumbria and Guthlac's hermitage at Crowland was reputed to have become soon after his death a great community; and there was a host of other houses. Some of these new monastic communities were founded with the intention of involvement in pastoral work. Already between 675 and 691 Frithuric, a Mercian ealdorman, had given land at Breedon in Leicestershire to Medehamstede to provide for a minster and a priest. But monasteries continued to be the property of their founders, some of them small and undistinguished, while others both in southern England and Northumbria were ecclesiastical foundations only in name.

Very gradually it seems that the efforts of the communities of clergy in the minsters or monasteries were being supplemented in the countryside by the establishment of local churches served by a resident priest. A tentative beginning had been made in the seventh century, for the *Life* of St. Cuthbert tells how the saint had a vision in which he stayed in a *parrochia* belonging to the abbess of Whitby, and it is recorded that John of Beverley, bishop of York (705-718), consecrated village churches for two thegns Puch and Addi. By 747 it appears that it was quite normal for priests to be allocated to specific localities by bishops, for in that year they were admonished to fulfil their duties diligently. Bede's letter to Egbert, while evidence that many large villages still lacked a church and permanent priest, suggests that the situation had improved since the days of Bishop Cuthbert. Only a start had been so far made and the completion of a parish system would not be achieved until after the Norman Conquest, but the process by which thegns built churches and established priests on their estates was to continue steadily for the next century and a half and was of immense importance: through these priests the work of conversion was so consolidated that even the conquest of much of England by heathen Danes could not destroy what they had achieved.

5

THE EARLY KINGDOMS

CONCURRENTLY with the processes of conquest, settlement and conversion, and in part explaining why conquest took so long to complete, were developments within the society of the invaders. The war bands had developed into tribal kingdoms which took time to consolidate. The more powerful kingdoms absorbed the lesser but were themselves often distracted by internal tensions. The larger kingdoms fought one another in contention for a hegemony which to their rulers was as important as further expansion westwards. Christian Welsh kings allied with pagan Mercian kings in mutual fear of the power of Christian Northumbrians. The military efforts of the conquerors were never exclusively directed towards the subjection of the Britons.

1. THE CREATION OF KINGDOMS

By about the middle of the sixth century the Anglian peoples settled in Yorkshire had been fused to form the kingdom of Deira and from it a war band had detached itself and established a foothold further north in Bamburgh, which was soon to form the kingdom of Bernicia. At about the same time a prince with strong south-Swedish connections led a new invasion into the sparsely populated areas of south-east Suffolk. Early settlement in East Anglia had been reinforced during the fifth century by new immigrants, mainly Anglian and probably direct from Schleswig, and was concentrated on the north of the region. The descendants of the Swedish prince welded all the settlers of East Anglia into a single kingdom. By the end of the century the Saxons of Wiltshire and the Thames Valley had probably been merged into Wessex and the small kingdoms of Lindsey, Essex, Kent, Sussex, and Wight were clearly visible. Of the creation of the kingdoms nothing can be said with certainty, and only the last of them to appear, Mercia, of which nothing is known until the second quarter of the seventh century, provides indications of the manner in which they might have come into existence.

The English Midlands appear to have been settled originally by a large number of independent groups each under its own leader. Since some of their names, *Pecsaetan* (dwellers in the Peak), *Gyrwe* (dwellers in the Fens) and so on, are derived from physical features, they may not always have been tribal units but simply groups of adventurers brought together by the need to cooperate in their pioneering enterprises. One of these groups, the *Mierce,* men of the March or frontier (though whether the frontier was between English and Britons or between southern English and northern English is debatable), which had settled in the valley of the upper Trent, gradually established its dominion over many of the other groups. Before the middle of the seventh century Midland England had become the kingdom of Mercia. When Penda fought the Northumbrians on the Winwaed in 655 he led a confederacy of thirty sub-kings, many of whom must have once been independent rulers of satellite territories. They supplied military contingents to their over-lord in time of war and paid tribute to him. An eighth-century document, the *Tribal Hidage,* provides a list of the folk groups which by then had been incorporated into the Mercian kingdom.[1] Each was by then assessed for taxation at a round number of hides; the small Middle Anglian *Feppingas* were rated at 300 hides; the group occupying the lands of the old Celtic kingdom of Elmet (the *Elmetsaetan*) was rated at 600 hides, while the large group of *Wreocensaetan* (dwellers around the Wrekin) was rated at 7,000 hides. Some of the larger groupings absorbed into Mercia may well themselves have been the product of earlier amalgamations.

Such knowledge as we have concerning the nature of early Anglo-Saxon settlement suggests that the obscure developments which culminated in the emergence of the Mercian kingdom were not unique. They assume that the territory of the future kingdom was already subjected to the new settlers. This condition was satisfied in south-eastern and eastern England by the mid-sixth century; it

[1] Recently discussed by C. Hart, ' The Tribal Hidage ', *T(ransactions of the)* *R(oyal) H(istorical) S(ociety)*, fifth series, XXI (1971).

had been achieved by the slow process of concurrent conquest and settlement by the early war bands. In Mercia, if the absence of recorded military engagements indicates the penetration by peasant communities into hitherto sparsely populated areas of extensive forest and wasteland, a similar domination was achieved by peaceful means a century later. The nuclei of the West Saxon and Deiran kingdoms may well have been formed by the fusion of lesser groupings, but their subsequent development was different. Everywhere pioneers edged forward, creating new frontiers as they did so; but in western and northern areas the boundaries of Wessex and Northumbria were both secured and suddenly extended by battles which at a single stroke brought new territories and their native populations under Anglo-Saxon control and opened up new lands for settlement. Their advancing frontiers reflected royal military initiative and the facts of physical geography. Within these kingdoms, the lesser units of administration must have been determined as much by kings as by the pattern of early Anglo-Saxon settlement.

As soon as the kingdoms came into existence the further process of absorption of the lesser by the greater can be seen in operation. Out of the confused conditions of the period of conquest seven major kingdoms emerged, known to historians as the Heptarchy. In fact the predominance first of Northumbria, then of Mercia, and finally of Wessex makes Heptarchy a misleading description of the distribution of power and the nature of political evolution in England between the beginning of the seventh century and the coming of the Danes. Kent after Aethelberht, East Anglia after Raedwald, and Essex and Sussex from an even earlier date, were never comparable in strength with the larger and later kingdoms created by the second phase of conquest. Even before 600 the territory of the Middle Saxons had been taken over by the East Saxons, whose kings were themselves by then clients of the kings of Kent and later of the kings of the East Angles and of the West Saxons. From the middle of the seventh century Essex was little more than a dependency of Mercia and when, a century later, Aethelbald incorporated London and Middlesex into Mercia nothing politically significant was left. Lindsey, unable to maintain its independence, was for much of the seventh century disputed between Northumbria and Mercia until Northumbrian preoccupations in northern England left Mercian dominance unchallenged. The expansion of the Mercian kingdom resulted in

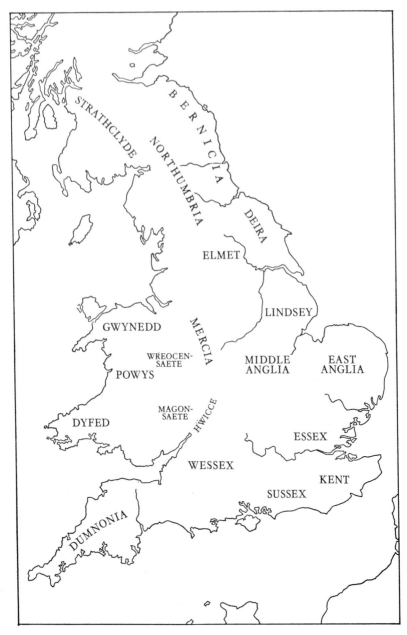

Political divisions of southern Britain. c. 600

the subordination of the kingdoms of the Hwicce (in the lower Severn valley) and the Magonsaetan (in modern Herefordshire), and of the Middle Angles in the east. The South Saxons, threatened by Wessex, sought to secure their independence by alliance with the rulers of Mercia; Caedwalla of Wessex ruled Sussex briefly, but the Mercian supremacy ultimately resulted in the relegation of the South Saxon kings first to the status of sub-kings then of ealdorman of the Mercian kingdom; they never recovered their independence and in the ninth century Sussex was incorporated into Wessex. Even Kent fell victim to the pressure of the newer and larger kingdoms. Caedwalla invaded Kent in 688 and established himself there as king for a brief period, but in the following year the Kentishmen restored their royal line to the throne. In the next century Kent was subjected to Mercia and ultimately accepted the lordship of the kings of Wessex as the only alternative. Sometimes absorption was easily achieved. The small kingdom of Wight was incorporated into Wessex by Caedwalla after a savage campaign; justifying himself on the ground that its inhabitants were pagan he ' endeavoured to wipe out all the natives by merciless slaughter and to replace them by inhabitants of his own kingdom '; the two brothers of its king who had fled for safety to the mainland were captured, baptized, and immediately executed. Wight subsequently created no problems for West Saxon kings. Sometimes, as the history of Deira and Kent reveals, the smaller kingdoms bitterly resented subjection.

If one theme of Northumbrian history is the extension of the territorial limits of the kingdom at British expense another is the struggle of its generally Bernician kings to maintain its territorial integrity against the disruptive tendencies of its two elements, Deira and Bernicia. On Aethelfrith's death Northumbria remained united for a time under its new king, Edwin, a son of Aelle of Deira; but after the battle of Hatfield his kingdom broke into two. One of Aethelfrith's sons, Eanfrith, ruled Bernicia; a cousin of Edwin's Osric, became king in Deira. The deaths of both within a year at the hands of Cadwallon permitted the reunification of the kingdom under Oswald, another of Aethelfrith's sons, after his victory over Cadwallon at Heavenfield. But Oswald's defeat by Penda at Oswestry in 641 was again followed by division. Bernicia passed to Oswald's brother Oswiu, and Deira to Oswine, son of that Osric who had been killed by Cadwallon. It was probably to obtain support in Deira that Oswiu married Eanflaed, daughter of King Edwin, but this proving insufficient he attacked Oswine and procured his death by treachery. Continued Deiran antipathy for Bernician rule found expression in their choice of Aethelwald, a son of Oswald as their king and his acceptance of a client relationship to Penda of Mercia as protection against Oswiu. Oswiu's victory over Penda at the river Winwaed not only established him as the most powerful king in England; it also put an end to Deiran particularism; but it had taken a long time. The resistance of Kent to Mercian domination in the eighth century similarly found expression whenever opportunity offered.

2. The Conflict for Hegemony: The Bretwaldaship

Despite their internal problems it seems that from the earliest period of conquest the ruler of one of the kingdoms aspired to a superiority over the others.[1] At first, the kingdoms of the south-east, Sussex, Kent, and East Anglia achieved most prominence by virtue of their density of population and their wealth, but the expansion of the new kingdoms abutting on British held lands inevitably relegated the older kingdoms to positions of secondary importance. The process by which the lesser kingdoms were absorbed into the larger produced a situation in which almost the whole of England was divided between Northumbria, Mercia, and Wessex, whose kings contended for supremacy. East Anglia, though for a time subjected to Mercia, maintained its independence by virtue of its size and wealth, and the protection afforded by the rivers and swamps which made its frontier; but after Raedwald it was never a match for the greater kingdoms and remained out of the main stream of events until its destruction by the Danes.

Bede goes out of his way to remark that Aethelberht of Kent was the third king who governed all the southern provinces of the English; he adds that Aethelberht's predecessors in this respect were Aelle, the founder of the South Saxon kingdom, and Ceawlin king of the West Saxons; and that his successors were Raedwald of the East Angles and Edwin, Oswald and Oswiu, all kings of the Northumbrians. His list covers about a century and since in another place he states that Aethelbald of Mercia ruled all the kingdoms to the south of the Humber it could be properly extended to include both him and his successor, Offa. The *Anglo-Saxon Chronicle,* omitting

[1] E. John, *Orbis Britanniae* (Leicester, 1966) pp. 1-63 is important for this subject.

the Mercian kings, perhaps deliberately, states that Egbert of Wessex was the eighth *Bretwalda*. Whether this term was merely a flattering epithet applied loosely to those kings whose military prowess and consequent territorial dominion impressed their contemporaries or whether it implied a formal claim to rule over all southern Britain and retained a memory of the time when Britannia was a diocese of the Roman Empire subject to a single authority, is debatable. The fact remains that from the end of the sixth century the ruler of one of the kingdoms exercised a measure of hegemony over the others. That authority reflected political realities; it was not transmitted hereditarily but was the sequel to successful war and it passed to whichever king could, in an age of continuous warfare, impose his will on other kings.

The implications of hegemony varied with circumstance. When Aelle was *Bretwalda* it cannot have meant much more than that he was the acknowledged leader of the southern English during that early period of conquest when the success of the invaders was still uncertain. In his time only a part of England had been subjected and it is difficult to believe that he was anything more than the foremost military leader of his age. Similarly, no matter how far from solved the problems connected with Ceawlin may be, it is perfectly clear that though he was powerful enough once to defeat Aethelberht of Kent his authority was very restricted territorially, and at no time extended far north of the river Thames.

Aethelberht's kingdom of Kent though small was both richer and more sophisticated than the territories ruled by Aelle and Ceawlin. Geographically the part of Britain closest to the Continent, it appears to have been enjoying a level of civilization as high as that of Merovingian Gaul with which contacts were maintained. English moneyers have been identified at Quentovic[1] in the sixth century and diplomatic contacts were maintained with the Frankish court, culminating in the marriage of Bertha, daughter of the Frankish king, to King Aethelberht and her sojourn in England accompanied by a Frankish bishop. In obedience to Pope Gregory's instructions Augustine acquired Frankish interpreters to assist him in his mission to the English, which reveals that Franks and Kentishmen understood one another's speech. Bede's account of the mission provides

---

[1] Quentovic, on the river Canche near modern Etaples, was in the sixth, seventh, and eighth centuries the most important point of departure from Gaul into England and from England to Gaul. In the ninth century it was superseded by Wissant.

confirmation that though pagan the Kentings were not barbarians; they treated Augustine with a combination of courtesy and circumspection. Some idea of the degree of Aethelberht's authority over other kingdoms can be inferred from the events of his reign; they give a measure of support to Bede's assertion that ' he had extended the frontiers of his empire as far as the boundary of the great river Humber '. When Augustine wanted to confer with the British bishops, with Aethelberht's help a meeting-place was chosen on the borders of the kingdoms of the Hwicce and of the West Saxons, which suggests that the Kentish king could ensure the safe conduct of a protégé far to the west of the boundaries of his own kingdom. The East Saxons, whose king had married Aethelberht's sister, were so much under Kentish authority at this time that it was Aethelberht who ordered the building of the church of St. Paul in London, the East Saxon capital. Aethelberht's influence induced Raedwald, king of the East Angles, temporarily to accept baptism. But even during his lifetime Aethelberht's position was being challenged by Raedwald who was named by Bede as the fifth ruler to exercise dominion over all the southern English.

The East Anglian bretwaldaship though transitory and at first sight inexplicable has become more comprehensible since the excavation of the famous ship-burial at Sutton Hoo on the river Deben close to the royal hall at Rendlesham.[1] Buried beneath a huge mound was uncovered the skeleton of a ship about 85 feet long and 14 feet wide. The ship contained no body but in its centre was a treasure chamber containing, in addition to what have been conjecturally identified as a royal standard and a ceremonial whetstone, the remains of a helmet, a coat of mail, a shield, a sword, a great silver dish, two silver spoons, a purse, coins, a bronze hanging bowl, and other articles. Many questions arising from this discovery remain controversial—it is, for example, almost certain that the grave commemorates an East Anglian king, but which king is uncertain. If the date of the burial is, as used to be thought from the coin evidence, 650-660, some time after the conversion of the East Anglians, it is odd that a Christian king should be buried with all the trappings

[1] The essential work for the study of Sutton Hoo is R. L. S. Bruce-Mitford. *The Sutton Hoo Ship Burial: a handbook* (rev. edn, London, 1968). Bibliographies appeared in *Speculum*, XXIX (1954) and XXXIII (1958). Recent contributions are C. F. C. Hawkes, ' Sutton Hoo: twenty-five years after ', *Antiquity*, XXXVIII (1964), and J. N. L. O'Loughlin, ' Sutton Hoo—the evidence of the documents ', *Medieval Archaeology*, VIII (1964). A good general treatment is Green *op. cit.*

necessary for his voyage through the underworld; and the grave contains no body. Some problems would be resolved if a recent suggestion that the dating of the coins should be revised to *c.* 625 finds acceptance; in which case the person commemorated might well be King Raedwald. Irrespective of these difficulties the evidence of the grave goods underlines the undeniable fact that the East Anglian kingdom at this time was immensely rich, that its ascendancy might well have rested partly in its control of the sea and that it enjoyed wideranging contacts, albeit not necessarily direct, with a much wider world. The grave contained objects from Byzantium,[1] Egypt, Gaul, and especially Sweden. The form of ship-burial, a distinctly Swedish tradition, and the parallels between some of the war gear and objects found in Swedish burials of the same time are particularly striking. The wealth and early cohesion of the East Anglian kingdom at a time when other kingdoms were still in the process of consolidation explains how a formidable warrior king like Raedwald could temporarily impose his will over much of England. Nor were his interventions confined to the lands south of the Humber. He received the exiled Edwin of Deira at his court, rejected Aethelfrith's attempts to bribe him into killing the exile and having defeated and killed Aethelfrith in battle placed Edwin on the Northumbrian throne. Raedwald was the first and the last East Anglian bretwalda.

The accession of Edwin to Northumbria in 616 initiated a period of nearly one hundred years during much of which, despite the separatist tendencies of Deira and Bernicia, the unity of the Northumbrian kingdom established by King Aethelfrith was generally maintained and Northumbrian kings exercised a measure of authority over all England. For a time their power delayed the developing distinction between the lands to the north and to the south of the river Humber. The range of Edwin's power is unambiguous, comprehending both new conquests from the Britons and a supremacy over all the other English kingdoms save Kent, the daughter of whose king he married. After his conversion to Christianity Edwin used his influence over Eorpwald, son and successor to Raedwald, to secure his baptism at the Northumbrian court. Evidence of Northumbrian authority over Lindsey is provided by the activity of Paulinus in Lincoln soon after Edwin's conversion, while shortly before, he had led an army into Wessex and slain five 'kings' in a punitive attack on persons who had conspired to assassinate him. Edwin's success

[1] The silver dish bears the assay mark of the Byzantine Emperor Anastasius I.

and the threat it posed to Britons and English alike led to the coalition of Cadwallon, king of Gwynedd, and the Mercian Penda, which defeated and killed him.

The emergence of Penda introduced a new factor into the internal politics of the Anglo-Saxon kingdoms. Until his time the disparate English settlements in the Midlands had been surrounded by kingdoms which had earlier achieved a measure of unity, and by the Britons of Wales. Presumably they had acknowledged the supremacy of Aethelberht and Raedwald, while their independence of Northumbria is suggested by the fact that the daughter of the first Mercian king known to history married Edwin while he was a refugee from Aethelfrith of Northumbria. But in 628 the *Chronicle* records that 'Cynegils [king of Wessex] and Cwichelm fought against Penda at Cirencester and afterwards came to terms'. At the time of the battle Penda, though a member of the Mercian royal house, was not king, but by his victory he took from the West Saxons the territory along the lower Severn which Ceawlin had won in 577. This conquest fused with the Saxon settlements of the middle Severn, became the under-kingdom of the Hwicce. Five years later, Penda allied with Cadwallon of Gwynedd and defeated King Edwin of Northumbria. The Welsh alliance, designed to check the increasing power of Northumbria, proved doubly profitable to the Mercians when the death of Cadwallon at Oswald's hands relieved Penda of any threat from the Britons of Gwynedd.

Oswald's victory reasserted both the unity of Northumbria under the Bernician dynasty and the supremacy of Northumbria over England. Bede says that he ruled within the same bounds as Edwin and exercised a similar lordship in southern Britain. Adomnan, abbot of Iona, described him as *imperator* of all Britain. His interest in and authority over Wessex is evidenced by his presence at Dorchester for the baptism of King Cynegils, whose daughter he married, and by his joint grant with Cynegils of Dorchester-on-Thames to Bishop Birinus. Whether this concern was motivated by fear of Penda's increasing power, by a determination to secure revenge for the defeat of 633, or was merely the natural expression of a desire to reassert authority south of the Humber is uncertain; but the location of Penda's victory over Oswald, near Oswestry, shows that it was the Northumbrian king who had taken the offensive in 643. Despite Bede's general assertion and the evidence of his influence in Wessex the extent and efficacy of Oswald's power south of the Humber must have been limited by that of Penda, whose victory starkly exposed the tenuous basis on which it rested. Penda's policy during these years, if the actions of any of these tribal kings can be so dignified, was twofold; negatively, to maintain the independence of his kingdom from Northumbrian domination and positively to expand the area under his rule by advances into the east Midlands and the south. In 645 he drove Cenwalh, king of Wessex, from his kingdom, compelling him for a time to seek refuge with Anna, king of the east Angles, and before the end of his reign he had incorporated the Middle Angles into his kingdom. But Northumbria remained Penda's principal concern and he made at least two destructive forays into Bernicia, in one of which he almost succeeded in setting fire to Bamburgh. Oswiu of Bernicia's attempts to reunite the Northumbrian kingdom eventually determined Penda to destroy the whole nation from the highest to the lowest. The extent of his influence was demonstrated by the number of allies whom he collected; thirty sub-kings accompanied him in the campaign of 654, their number including Aethelwald, king of Deira, Aethelhere, king of the East Angles, and Cadafael, king of Gwynedd. In the ensuing battle on the river Winwaed Penda was defeated and killed by the much smaller army of Oswiu.

Despite their continuous warring with one another a feature of these years is the frequency of intermarriage between members of the rival dynasties. Whether such marriages were motivated by considerations of external policy, or to minimize the dangers of increasing the number of families with an interest in the kingship which marriage within the kingdom might generate, or whether the prime concern was to ensure that the distinctive qualities of the blood-royal should not be diluted, is uncertain. The fact remains that marriage connections did not noticeably mitigate political animosities and that a knowledge of family relationships would provide a dangerous basis on which to construct any framework of political alliances. These facts are well demonstrated by the events of the middle years of the seventh century. Not only was one of Oswiu's sons, Ecgfrith, a hostage at Penda's court, but the connections between the two families could hardly have been closer. Alchfrith, another son of Oswiu, was married to Penda's daughter Cyneburh; Alhflaed, Oswiu's daughter, was married to Penda's son, Paeda. Alchfrith and Paeda were not only brothers-in-law but allies in their religious activities, and Paeda was sufficiently well regarded by his father to be given rule over the Middle Angles. Yet these relationships did not deflect Penda from his resolve to destroy Oswiu, and he found an ally in Aethelwald of Deira, Oswiu's nephew. After his father's defeat Paeda was murdered in circumstances which appeared to implicate his wife.

The battle on the Winwaed left Oswiu of Northumbria without a rival. For two years Mercia was dismembered, the area north of the Trent being ruled directly by Oswiu and the southern area by Penda's son Paeda, as a client of Oswiu. After Paeda's murder in 656 his kingdom was annexed to Northumbria and governed by officials appointed by Oswiu. Mercian subjection was ended when, in 657, a group of nobles rebelled against Oswiu's rule. They brought out of hiding a young son of Penda, Wulfhere by name, expelled the Northumbrians and established Wulfhere as king. Wulfhere quickly established his position and as he grew stronger Oswiu's authority south of the Humber diminished. After the synod of Whitby and the death of Archbishop Deusdedit, the decision to send Wighard to Rome to secure papal approval as his successor, made after joint deliberation between Egbert, king of Kent, and the Northumbrian king, argues that until that time at any rate Oswiu's influence in southern England remained considerable. But from the death of Oswiu until the middle years of the reign of Aethelbald of Mercia (716-757) no king was pre-eminent in England.

A narrative account of these years emphasizes the fluctuating fortunes of each kingdom, whose destiny was determined more by the military capacities of its ruler than by any other factor; an unpredictable defeat in battle could appear to nullify the work of twenty years. Northumbria was made by three kings of exceptional quality, Edwin, Oswald, and Oswiu; as Mercia was to be made by Penda, Aethelbald, and Offa; and Wessex by Egbert and Alfred. The circumstances in which all except Alfred obtained their kingdoms reveal the triumph of dominant personalities over unfavourable circumstances; all had to fight to secure acceptance in their own kingdoms before they could begin to assert their authority over others.

Part of the explanation of this situation lies in the notions of kingship widely held by the Anglo-Saxons. The early Anglo-Saxon king lists give a misleading impression of the nature of early kingship; they conceal the fact that it was by no means the rule for a kingdom to be governed by a single king; and being lists of kings rather than tables of family descent they do not accurately represent the blood relationship of kings to their successors. Among the Anglo-Saxons kingship was a personal, not an hereditary, office, and any male member of the royal kindred was eligible. After the death of Cenwald of Wessex in 672 all his successors for more than fifty years came from different branches of the royal house and each of them was faced by relatives with rival claims. Caedwalla, who fought his way to kingship soon after 685, was a member of a branch of the royal family which had not hitherto produced a ruler over Wessex; during his predecessor's reign he had lived as an exile. His successor Ine derived from yet another branch of the royal house and at least twice in his reign was threatened by the claims of kinsmen. On his death the kingdom passed to Aethelheard, whose connections with previous kings are quite unknown. In origin Penda was probably a landless member of the Mercian royal house whose position in the Midlands was secured by military success. His first appearance in history is recorded in 628 when he defeated the West Saxons, but he did not become king of the Mercians until after his alliance with Cadwallon and their victory over Edwin in 632. Mercia passed without division to the sons and grandsons of Penda until the death of Ceolred in 716, but Ceolred's successor, Aethelbald, was the grandson of a brother of Penda, who, during Ceolred's reign, had been driven into exile. On his death the kingdom passed to Offa, but only after a civil war.

The joint interest of the ruling family in the kingship is further revealed by the frequency with which kingdoms were shared. According to the *Chronicle* Hengest and Horsa were joint kings of Kent, and when Horsa died Aesc, Hengest's son, took his place. Cerdic and Cynric were joint kings of the West Saxons; Cwichelm was both son and joint ruler with Cynegils. King Edwin of Northumbria was believed to have killed five West Saxon kings in a single battle and, according to Bede, after the death of Cenwalh in 672 his kingdom was for ten years shared by a number of under-kings. Kent, after Eadric's death in 686, was shared for a few years by a number of kinglets and on Wihtred's death in 725 he was succeeded by three sons. The division of a kingdom between brothers is also to be found in Essex when Sigehere and Sebbi succeeded King Swithelm and to Sebbi succeeded his two sons Sigeheard and Swaefred. Among the Hwicce the brothers Eanfrith and Eanhere ruled as joint kings under the overlordship of Aethelbald of Mercia. In Northumbria at the time of the synod of Whitby Oswiu's son Alchfrith ruled as under-king of Deira.

There are thus many examples of father and son ruling as joint kings, of sons succeeding their father and sharing his inheritance and of members of the ruling house, none of whose ancestors had been kings, acquiring kingdoms through their martial ability. The principle which conceived of kingship as the property of the whole family rather than of an individual, and which admitted the divisibility of kingship, obviously encouraged conflict between members of the royal house. The continued prosperity of a kingdom depended on the success of its king in transmitting an undivided inheritance to a son or brother of full age, able to defend it. On this depended the pre-eminence of Northumbria in the seventh century. The success of Mercia in the eighth century was the direct consequence of the longevity and ruthlessness of its kings, Aethelbald and his cousin Offa. The triumph of Wessex in the ninth century was in large part due to the unusual solidarity of its ruling dynasty, which triumphed over circumstances which in other kingdoms might well have led to protracted civil wars. Conversely, the eclipse of Northumbria in the eighth century was the consequence of internal feuding between rival members of the royal family, and Mercian power did not long survive the deposition in 823 of Ceolwulf I, the last member of its ruling dynasty.

3. Social Structure of the Kingdoms

Concerning the social structure of the early kingdoms and the manner in which they regulated their affairs it is unwise to dogmatize. The scanty evidence relating to these matters is to be found mainly in the laws of the kingdoms of Kent and Wessex (no laws from other kingdoms have survived), which may occasionally be clothed in flesh and blood by vivid accounts of incidents related by poets and prose-writers whose concern was primarily to entertain not to instruct.

The *Laws* of Aethelberht of Kent reveal a complex society made up of noblemen, commoners, freedmen, and slaves. The value (*wergild*) put on the life of a nobleman (*eorl*) was 300 shillings—this was the amount the killer of a nobleman must pay to the kinsfolk of the murdered man if he wished to buy off the vendetta which would otherwise ensue; the value of a commoner's (*ceorl's*) life was 100 shillings; the freedman (*laet*) was worth 80, 60 or 40 shillings; the cost of killing a slave depended partly on the category in which he was placed and partly on the status of the owner, to whom the blood-price had to be paid. The penalty for any offence varied according to the status of the injured party; for lying with a maiden belonging to the king the price was fifty shillings; with a nobleman's serving-woman it was twenty shillings; with a ceorl's serving-woman it was six shillings. Class differences are clear. Yet, though ceorls obviously owned slaves, there is no evidence of the dependence of ceorl upon eorl. The murder of a ceorl might be compensated for by the payment of his wergild by the murderer to the ceorl's kindred, but in addition a fine of fifty shillings must be paid to the king. If a freeman was convicted of having stolen from another freeman he must not only pay threefold compensation to the injured person, but also a fine to the king which might amount to the whole of his goods. The Kentish ceorl's protector was the king; he knew no other lord.

But the *Laws* show equally clearly that no man lived in isolation; he was a member of a kindred-group.[1] If he were killed custom required his kindred to avenge his death or to secure monetary compensation for it. Conversely, the kindred of a guilty person helped to pay the monetary penalties imposed on him, although one clause in Aethelberht's law which debars a murderer's kinsfolk from contributing towards the wergild of a murdered man shows that already, in the interests of justice, a beginning had been made towards regulating and limiting the operation of the principle that a man could be regarded simply as a member of a kindred group. Aethelberht's laws consist largely of a tariff of damages payable for injuries, ranging from the fifty shillings payable for knocking out an eye to the thirty sceattas for knocking of the nail of the big toe; if the kinsfolk of the guilty party wished to avoid reprisals from the kinsfolk of the injured they had to offer payment of the appropriate sum. Another aspect of the protective role of the kindred appears in the code of Hlothere and Eadric, kings of Kent late in the seventh century, which devolved responsibility for the care of a fatherless child to the father's kindred. Without kinsfolk a man's position in the courts was seriously pre-judiced, for a man accused of wrongdoing normally answered the charge against him by swearing an oath declaring his innocence

---

[1] L. Lancaster, ' Kinship in Anglo-Saxon Society ', *British Journal of Sociology*, IX (1958), is an important study.

which had to be supported by the oaths of other men, their number dependent on the seriousness of the charge and their social status, who swore that their principal's oath was unperjured; the oath-helpers were normally provided by the accused man's kindred. The kindred group, which gave protection to and accepted collective responsibility for its members, was a basic element in Anglo-Saxon society.

Freedom involved obligations. The ceorl contributed to the maintenance of the king's household by paying a food rent (*feorm*) to his king. Originally the king had travelled about his kingdom enjoying the hospitality of his subjects; later, each household rendered its contribution to a conveniently situated royal estate where it was received by the king's reeve. Miscellaneous burdens such as cartage services, work on royal villages, the provision of hospitality to royal officers and servants engaged on the king's business were additional to the payment of the food rent. To support his status the Kentish ceorl might be expected to own about two hundred acres of arable land (a *sulung* or ploughland) supplemented by rights of pasturage in forest and marshland.

The *Laws* of successive Kentish kings in the seventh century show them adjusting or adding to the customary law of their people in the presence of the greatest of their subjects. Additionally, since public burdens were assessed on localities, the detailed allocation of taxation was effected in local assemblies which also regulated the interests of their communities in the woods and marshes and settled their disputes without control from above.

The late seventh century laws of Ine of Wessex go some way towards supporting the notion that English society was everywhere based on the free peasant community of the Kentish type. They also complicate the picture. Supplementing the Kentish evidence is evidence of the ceorl's obligation to military service; complementing it are numerous clauses relating to wergilds and compensation. There is also an important clause which ruled that if ceorls failed to enclose their portion of the common meadow or other shareland so that their cattle trampled on the crops of their neighbours they must make reparation for the damage done; critically important as evidence for the existence of open-field cultivation it also reveals the king and his advisors making provision to deal with a problem which in a later age would naturally have fallen within the jurisdiction of the manorial court. In some important respects the status of the West Saxon ceorl was less elevated than that of his equivalent in Kent. It is no longer generally believed that the wergild of the Kentish ceorl was substantially greater than that of ceorls in other English kingdoms but his economic position was more secure; in Wessex, as in the rest of England before the Danish invasions, the notional unit of land possessed by a peasant family was one hide, a unit of assessment to taxation which in area varied from 120 acres in Cambridgeshire to as little as 40 or 60 acres in parts of Wessex but in any event substantially smaller than the Kentish sulung. Nevertheless, Ine's laws leave no doubt as to the presence of free peasants in Wesssex, who owned their land, paid taxes to the king, served in the army when called upon and attended popular courts.

On the other hand, in other clauses of the *Laws* the importance of the noble element (*gesithcund*) in West Saxon society appears prominently. Whereas the wergild of the Kentish nobleman was three times that of the ceorl, in Wessex there were various degrees of nobility, among them a highly privileged class whose wergild was six times that of the ceorl. There were noblemen whose households included both slaves and freemen. The ruling that if dependants became embroiled with the law their lord had no right to the fines imposed, ' because he would not previously at home restrain them from wrongdoing ' argues his possession of disciplinary powers over them which he had failed to exercise. The man who moved to another district without permission of his lord and was subsequently discovered must both return and pay his lord sixty shillings in compensation. The evidence for a dependent tenantry is unequivocal: ' If anyone covenants for a yardland or more at a fixed rent, and ploughs it, if the lord wishes to increase for him the rent of the land by demanding service as well, he need not accept it, if he does not give him a dwelling; and he is to forfeit the crops '. Once again the ruling is that of the king and his council but the tenure described closely resembles that of the *gebur* of eleventh-century texts[1] and the villein of Domesday Book. The size of the holding was a yardland or virgate, both land and seed corn were provided by the lord; the tenant might refuse his lord's demand for both rent in kind and labour service, but only at the cost of losing his tenement and the crops on it. If the tenant had accepted a house from the lord as well as land, it appears that he was not free to refuse his lord's demand for services as well as rent. If this interpretation is correct the peasant

[1] See p. 327 *supra*.

holding a yardland and a house from his lord was effectively tied to his holding and the land on which he was required to work could only have been his lord's domain. Already the manorial estate had come into existence. According to some authorities the king and his counsellors were already regulating the size of the domain in relation to the amount of tenanted land. A chapter in the *Laws* laid down that if a nobleman wished to relinquish an estate he must show a proportion of *gesettland* at the time of his departure. *Gesettland* may mean no more than land which is sown, in which event the king's concern would have been simply to avoid having a derelict estate left on his hands by a life tenant; but the term *gesettland* may equally well mean land settled by tenants, who would pay both taxes to the king and rent to their lord, in which event the king's objects might have been both fiscal, to avoid a reduction in the tax-paying capacity of the estate; and, if the land in question had been recently colonized, to prevent an area still subject to attack being deprived of its potential defenders. Ine's *Laws* reveal not only lords, but degrees of lordship. Not only were some peasants dependent on lords, but there were men of noble status who recognized lords intermediate between themselves and the king. It is agreed that different circumstances of original settlement produced differing social and tenurial structures; there is general agreement that later Anglo-Saxon England had become a land of lordly estates cultivated by the labours of a dependent peasantry; there is less unanimity concerning the chronology and the forces which produced this result. Until recently it had been generally accepted that the manor evolved out of the free peasant community; it is now suggested by some scholars that the lordly estate was the typical unit of agrarian organization in England from the earliest period of Anglo-Saxon settlement.[1] Less than a century separated the *Laws* of Aethelberht of Kent from the *Laws* of Ine of Wessex; they have many features in common; nevertheless, it is argued, the general tenor of the West Saxon code, with its emphasis on lordship and dependent tenure, implies a society which from its origins was organized on principles which cannot be reconciled with the concept of free peasant communities bound together by the ties of kindred and acknowledging no lord but the king.

Historians convinced that the starting point in the development of Anglo-Saxon agrarian society must be a free land-owning peasantry

[1] The importance of T. H. Aston, ' The origins of the manor in England ', *T.R.H.S.*, VII (1958) bears no relation to its length. If its conclusions are accepted it compels a substantial modification of many long-cherished beliefs.

The Anglo-Saxon Age

explain the growth of manorial lordship as the long term consequence of the granting away of royal rights to favoured subjects. Britain was conquered by kings and princes at the head of bands of warriors and they were followed by others who came to settle. Continuous warfare against both natives and other groups of their own stock ensured the continuance of a military caste, the king's companions. The king was supported by the renders of his subjects; he, in turn, fed and clothed his retainers, rewarding them for their services with magnificent weapons and armour, bracelets and treasure, and eventually with grants of land. The reputation of a king depended on his generosity; so did his power, for generosity attracted young men to him from far and wide. But when a king granted land to a subordinate he could only give away what he owned—not the land itself, for that belonged to peasant communities, but the royal interest in it. The alienation of royal rights generally consisted of a transference of the food rents from king to subject; it might comprehend other services, and sometimes it included the profits which had previously accrued to the king from the justice done in local courts. In itself the transfer of obligation was in no way detrimental to the freedom of the peasant community. But at the best of times the ceorl's life was a harsh struggle for existence in which he had small opportunity to amass reserves to tide him over catastrophes; he and his family might be reduced to starvation by a short sequence of bad harvests, by disease which killed his livestock, or by the destruction wrought by marauding bands. Such disasters would affect not only single peasants but all the inhabitants of the place affected. The peasant, overtaken by misfortune, might well find himself unable to pay the dues he owed his lord—and lords, themselves dependent on territorially restricted estates, were both more liable to increase the dues demanded and less able than the king to abate their dues in bad times. In such circumstances peasants found it easier to provide labour than food rents; lords, who had been creating domains for themselves, were willing to accept it. In this way the payment of food rents by the inhabitants of a village to a nobleman was replaced by a system by which each landholder supplied labour service to his lord's domain. In theory the change amounted to no more than the substitution of one form of rent for another; in practice,

> it seems to have formed part of a wider revolution in which the individual tenants surrendered their holdings to the lord of the village

and received them back at his hands, acknowledging themselves to be his men, and placing themselves under his protection. When this step had been taken by the whole or the greater part of the village community, the manorial economy was brought within sight.[1]

Another step may have been taken when, having granted away his judicial profits and thus no longer possessing a financial interest in this group of his subjects, the king allowed lords to exercise jurisdiction over them directly, in private courts. To economic dependence was then added judicial dependence. The process so described operated from the earliest times, but the impact of the taxation, demands for military service, and the wholesale destruction which attended Alfred's wars against the Danes made freedom intolerably burdensome and accelerated what had hitherto been no more than a drift towards subordination; the similar circumstances of Aethelred's wars a century later were a further turn of the screw.

The evolutionary explanation of the depression of a once free peasantry into servitude has much to commend it, especially if the reservations which accompany it are borne in mind. It purports only to describe the central course of social development in Anglo-Saxon England and recognizes that communities existed from the earliest times whose inhabitants worked for a lord in return for his protection. It recognizes that, though the peasant class as a whole suffered a loss of status, individual peasants could rise above the general fortunes of their class and achieve prosperity.

Critics of this traditional hypothesis rest their alternative explanation on two main grounds, supporting them by reference to a number of lesser difficulties which the traditional teaching appears to involve. They acknowledge the existence of communities of free peasants, but deny their predominance. Negatively, they argue that if the drift into servitude did not become a flood until the second half of the ninth century only two hundred years is allowed for the transformation of a free peasantry into a society based on lordship; it could have happened, but it is unlikely. Positively, they urge the strength of the tie between lord and man which can be traced in Germanic society from a time long anterior to the English settlement. The very circumstances of a migration overseas must in many instances have removed men from their kindreds and strengthened the bonds which attached them to their leaders; the conquest was achieved by bands of warriors and their dependants, not by kindred groups. More

[1] Stenton, *op. cit.*, p. 472.

5*

specifically, the evidence of the group of early place names formed by the combination of a personal name with the element *-ingas* supplies proof of settlement made by the dependants and followers of individual leaders under lordly direction. As soon as written evidence becomes available, in the *Laws* of Ine, the same form of territorial organization, under lords, is found in Wessex. It can only be concluded that from the time of the conquest the lord's estate had been the typical unit of agrarian organization. There is little evidence in Ine's *Laws* for the existence of large numbers of free peasants owning a hide of land; nor is it easy to reconcile the mutually exclusive notions of peasants who owned whole hides (even in areas where the acreage of the hide was small) with peasants who lived on so narrow a margin of subsistence that they were compelled in consequence to seek protection—peasant families in the thirteenth century with no better techniques or equipment were fortunate if they farmed a quarter of a hide. While agreeing that convention and policy compelled kings to reward service by grants of land the critics argue that more was granted away than royal rights and services; they contend that when royal charters purport to grant land they mean exactly what they say, and support the argument by pointing out that when the king wished merely to grant royal rights the drafters of his charters were well able to devise formulae which made the fact plain. Their interpretation is fortified by the consideration that the typical recipient of royal favour, whether lay nobleman or religious community, could hardly have lived on the proceeds of royal rights over the five, ten, or even twenty hides which was the normal order of a royal gift. The early creation of manorial estates was often made easier by the substantial contribution made to the dependent peasantry by the subjected native population, who, in many cases, must have been numerous. The Kentish and West Saxon laws are much concerned with them; some of them were used as household slaves but more would have continued to live on the land under subjection to their new masters. The number of the unfree was under constant recruitment from Englishmen taken captive during the incessant intertribal warfare and from men reduced to slavery as punishment for crime. Whatever their original status they gradually became merged into a single category of dependent peasants. For these reasons, it is believed by some scholars that manors came into existence at the time of the earliest conquests and proliferated thereafter.

It must be emphasized again that these two divergent views of the way in which early English society was organized and developed are not totally exclusive. Each recognizes that both elements, free peasant communities and lordly estates, were to be found in England. The disagreement lies in their estimate as to which form of organization predominated. It is impossible to deny the importance of the free element, for without it the prominence given in all codes of law, until and including the reign of Alfred, to the rates at which kindreds might exact or pay reparation for injuries done to and by their kinsfolk becomes meaningless; in these clauses the codes assume that society consists of a network of kindred groups. An original freedom still left its marks on the structure of society, even on the eve of the Norman Conquest, in the persistence of a substantial class of freeman, in the vitality of the communal courts, and in the way in which lordly rights were regulated by law. Yet it is equally difficult to deny the importance and prevalence of lordship.

It may not be unreasonable to suggest that the differing circumstances of the two phases of conquest contributed to the patterns of social organization. In eastern and much of southern England where conquest was followed by a dense settlement of Germanic peasants it is likely that large numbers of free peasant communities established themselves. During the second phase of conquest large areas of British held land were quickly subjugated by conquerors motivated less by land hunger than by the desire for tribute and domination; war-leaders acquired extensive tracts of land on which they could settle their dependents on varying conditions according to their social status and their usefulness to him; land which could be made available to newcomers in return for agreed rents and services; and a subjugated peasantry in no position to bargain. Such conditions were clearly favourable to the creation of lordly estates. Yet just as there may well have been early estates organized as manors in eastern England it is equally true that the colonizing and pioneering activities which produced the predominantly free communities of that area may have been reproduced many times in western Wessex, Mercia, and Northumbria.

Whatever may have been the chronology of the process by which the nobility became transformed into landlords there is no doubt that from long before the Anglo-Saxon settlement the strength of

the kindred bond among the Germanic peoples was being undermined by the tie which bound men to their lords. The earliest
accounts of Germanic society describe chiefs attended by retinues of
wellborn young men who formed the nucleus of their war bands.
Having left their kindred, the protection of the lord and the com-
panionship of the other members of his *comitatus* created new bonds
of loyalty which took precedence over all other obligations. The lord
was expected to reward his followers generously; in return, loyalty
to him was regarded as the highest virtue and to desert him the
greatest infamy. The killing of a lord had to be avenged at all costs;
no one could be more wretched than the man who had lost his lord;
a man must not desert his lord when he suffered misfortune. These
conventions were transplanted to Britain during the migrations and
were recurrent themes in Anglo-Saxon poetry;[1] their power over
men's actions is amply vouched for in historical record. In 625
Lilla, a thegn of King Edwin, sacrificed himself to save his lord from
an assassin's dagger; the retainers of Bishop Wilfrid were prepared
to fight to the death to protect their lord from the heathen South
Saxons; while the future kings, Oswald of Northumbria and Aethelbald of Mercia, were exiles they were accompanied by their men.
Among such retainers the claims of kindred were still recognized—
Bede mentions the Northumbrian gesith who told his prisoner, ' now
you ought to die because all my brothers and kinsmen were killed
in the battle '—but they were, if necessary, subordinated to the
superior claims of lordship.

A striking demonstration of the overriding claims of lordship is
provided in the *Chronicle* account of the conflict between King
Cynewulf of Wessex and his rival Cyneheard. In 786 Cynewulf was
killed by Cyneheard in a surprise attack on the hall where he was
visiting his mistress. He had been attended by only a small retinue,
which included kinsmen of some of Cyneheard's supporters. Cyneheard's offer of freedom to his supporters' kinsmen was refused and
they fought him till all were killed. Next day the situation was
reversed. Cyneheard was attacked by a superior force which included
kinsmen of his followers; he offered his attackers their own choice
of money and land if they would accept him as king and told them
that among his adherents were kinsmen of theirs who would not
desert him. 'And then they replied that no kinsman was dearer to

---

[1] In *Beowulf, The Wanderer, The Battle of Maldon,* to name only the most
obvious examples.

them that their Lord, and they would never follow his slayer '. The attackers, in their turn, offered to allow their kinsmen with Cyneheard to depart unharmed. The offer was refused and in the ensuing battle Cyneheard and all but one of his companions were killed. A hundred years earlier archbishop Theodore's *Penitential* had treated killing at the command of a lord as a less heinous sin than killing in the course of a vendetta; about a century later the priority of claims of lordship over those of kinship was explicitly commanded in the *Laws* of King Alfred.

The equivalence of the Anglo-Saxon term *gesith* with the Latin *comes* (companion) strongly suggests that in all the English kingdoms, except perhaps Kent, the basis of nobility had been membership of the retinue of a victorious chief; the king's companions and their descendants were *gesithcund* (noble), distinguished from other freemen by their high wergild. But society was not static. As kingdoms became larger and kings fewer the rulers of once independent territories, some of whom could lay claim to distinction by birth, were compelled, or deemed it prudent, to accept dependence on one of the greater kings; they became indistinguishable from the nobility of service. Among the gesithcund class were men who, by virtue of the value the king put on their services, as military subordinates, as his representations in recently subjected territories, or as officers within his kingdom, acquired additional distinction. It became normal for men of gesithcund status to attach themselves not only to kings but to the greatest of their servants. Ine's *Laws* reveal a hierarchy of noble ranks; some nobles are landless, some are dependents of other lords, but others have acquired the rank of king's thegn or ealdorman.

Within the wellborn elements of society withdrawal from the kindred and attachment to a great lord was generally a matter of individual will and involved no loss of status. But from an early time humbler men were bound to lords in a dependence less honourable, and the combination of economic insecurity and political forces increased their numbers continuously. Poverty drove men to accept dependence in return for the security that the protection of a great man afforded. The increasing size of kingdoms involved not only the subjection of rulers but of their subjects as well, for they had to pay tribute and send contingents to royal armies. Slowly but steadily kings increased the range of activities with which they concerned themselves. These developments made necessary the intervention of officials, backed by royal authority, between kings and their subjects and rewarded for their services with grants of land. And from early in the seventh century the laws of Wihtred and Ine show kings improving the efficacy of their justice by limiting the kindred's power of protecting its members—in Kent a ceorl who wished to clear himself at the altar was not allowed to find support for his oath from the ranks of kinsmen but must secure oaths from three men of his own class; in Wessex a man who wished to clear himself of a charge of homicide was required, irrespective of his status, to include one man of high rank among his oath-helpers. Soon lords would assume responsibilities for their dependants which previously had been borne by the kindred; they accepted the responsibility for producing their men in court and paying the fines imposed for their misdoings. The development of private jurisdiction by royal grant contributed significantly to the enlargement of lordly authority. Early royal charters granting to subjects the profits of justice imposed on their men are ambiguous in their wording; they may be read as merely endowing the lord with the fines imposed in public courts; but by the end of the eighth century charters are found which free estates from the burden of public assemblies, by implication implying the existence of private courts. The protection of a kindred would avail little against a lord possessed of jurisdictional authority. It would be wrong to infer that dependence was always resented; still more wrong to infer that the ties of kindred were entirely superseded. The prelude to the story of Cynewulf and Cyneheard mentions a swineherd who exacted vengeance on the killer of his lord, an ealdorman; tenth-century legislation was still much concerned with regulating the conduct of the vendetta and in northern England one eleventh-century vendetta took toll of three generations. Nevertheless, the general tendency within Anglo-Saxon society was for ties of lordship, powerful from the beginning, to be extended and strengthened, with the attendant consequence that the kindred became progressively less important.

3. Governmental Institutions

Concerning the governmental and administrative arrangements of the early kingdoms very little is known, but enough has been written about pagan Germanic kingdoms on the Continent to show that the practices of different peoples varied so widely that analogies from them cannot safely be used to describe the character of the early Anglo-Saxon kingdoms in Britain. Certainly they were small and required little in the way of institutions. Their law was customary not royal, transmitted orally rather than in writing, and knowledge of it reposed in the body of the folk and was declared in the assembly of the folk by men specially learned in it. No sophisticated arrangements were needed to provide for the maintenance of the king and his retinue: they lived on the renders of their own estates and on the food farms paid by their subjects. The principal function of kings was to lead their people in war.

By the end of the sixth century, in Kent at any rate, the role of the king had become more complex.[1] Aethelberht's authority rested on his victories in battle, but he was a great deal more than a war-lord surrounded by military companions whose time was devoted to the pursuits of fighting his enemies, hunting, and quaffing mead in his hall. His court, though essentially that of a warrior king, must have discussed matters other than war. He maintained contact with the Frankish court and with subordinate kings in Britain; when Augustine landed he ordered that the mission ' should be provided with all things necessary until he had decided what to do about them ', and shortly afterwards arranged for Augustine to preach to him and his gesiths. Aethelberht's *Laws,* innovatory in their clauses relating to the new Church, its officials and its property, are in general a written statement of custom which reveals a king concerned with the internal problems of his kingdom. To some it has appeared that the Kentish king merely reproduced on a higher level the status of a nobleman because, though his wergild was higher and the cost of injuring a man under his protection or of infringing his peace was more than that imposed for similar offences committed against other men, the difference was only in degree. This view takes too little account of the ways in which the king was unique. On occasion he ' called his people to him ' and offences committed at such times were visited with double penalties and compensation to the king. Though the misdemeanors of freemen were primarily the concern of the kindred of the injured man, the king, who was the protector of all free men, must also be compensated. The *Laws* show a king who already governed his people, and the fact of causing part of

---

[1] J. W. Wallace-Hadrill, *Early Anglo-Saxon and Germanic Kingship* (Oxford, 1971) is indispensable; D. A. Binchy, *Celtic and Anglo-Saxon Kingship* (Oxford, 1970) is also valuable.

the customary law to be written down associated him more clearly than before with its administration and enforcement.

A century later the *Laws* of Ine declare that the king and his advisers ' have been taking counsel for the salvation of our souls and the security of our realm, in order that just law and just decrees may be established and ensured throughout our nation '. The salvation of souls involved the protection of the Church and payment of its dues; the security of the realm involved both provision for its defence and further measures to promote internal peace, from the regulation of agrarian routine to the treatment of a trader, as well as the normal tables of compensations for offences. It might fairly be inferred from Aethelberht's laws that the king had officials who collected his fines and assisted in arranging compositions between kindreds. In Ine's *Laws* specific reference is made to royal officials styled *ealdormen* who presided over courts; if a man exacted redress for an injury without first seeking a verdict in the court he must give up twice the value of what he had taken and pay thirty shillings to the king. In the range of its concern with the affairs of his subjects Ine's code anticipated those of the tenth century.

In both Wihtred's Kent and Ine's Wessex the king was associated in law-making with his counsellors. In Kent the assembly met at Barham and the notables, of whom Berhtwald of Canterbury and Gefmund, bishop of Rochester, are specifically mentioned, ' with the consent of all drew up these decrees, and added them to the legal usages of the people of Kent '; in Wessex Ine referred to the advice and instruction of his father, Cenred, of his two bishops and the participation in counsel ' of all my ealdormen and the chief counsellors of my people and with a great concourse of the servants of God as well '. Ine styled himself ' King by God's gift '. Such phrases suggest that Anglo-Saxon kingship was a form of limited monarchy of a specifically Christian type; they raise questions concerning the degree of a king's authority within his kingdom and the extent to which conversion to Christianity had affected the quality of kingship.

There can be little doubt that both custom and prudence contributed to the emphasis placed by Anglo-Saxon kings on the element of participation in the discussion and decision of vital matters. Aethelberht brought his gesiths to listen to Augustine's preaching; accounts of Edwin's acceptance of Christianity give the impression that though the course of the debate had been carefully stage-managed in advance it would have been unwise for him to act without prior discussion; and the same impression is given of accounts of the synod of Whitby. Yet royal initiative was often crucial in determining the decisions reached. The Kentish people followed Aethelberht to Christianity and subsequently under his son Eadbald relapsed into paganism. Edwin's decision to accept Christianity had been made before the issues were formally discussed, and when Oswald restored Christianity to Northumbria its teachers came from Iona, where the king had stayed during his exile, not from Canterbury whence the original mission had come. At Whitby the assembly accepted Oswiu's decision to accept the Roman method of calculating the date of Easter.

From the time of their conversion to Christianity churchmen figured prominently among the royal counsellors; their influence over kings was often considerable, but in early England kings never became puppets manipulated by their bishops. The fact of conversion did not transform the nature of kings overnight and kingship throughout the years between Aethelberht and Alfred combined elements from its pagan past and from its Christian present. Aethelberht and Edwin had good reason to hesitate before deciding to adopt a new God; paganism was deeply rooted in their countries and their authority in their kingdoms was unchallenged. If the new religion was to make converts of kings it had to take care not to pitch its demands too high, to demonstrate the greater power of the new God over the old, and to convince them that the change was advantageous. Popes and churchmen knew that the extension of Christianity could be achieved only through the cooperation of kings who would impose order within their kingdoms, protect churchmen and the Church's property, and be prepared to fight to extend the territorial range of the Church's activities. Pope Gregory the Great assured Aethelberht that Christianity would assure him of a place in heaven and made his name glorious to posterity, and encouraged him to use his royal power to the fullest extent for the promotion of Christianity; he told Childeberht, king of the Franks, that ' the royal office takes precedence of any other man's '. In similar vein Pope Vitalian encouraged Oswiu to extend his authority in Britain, quoting from Isaiah, ' I have given thee for a covenant of the people, to establish the earth and possess the scattered heritages ', and later in the same letter writing, ' Hasten then, your Highness, to fulfil our desire and dedicate the whole of your island to Christ our God '. The Church encouraged kings to extend their authority

within their kingdoms and to extend the boundaries of their kingdoms by conquering their still heathen neighbours, and by so doing
made Christianity attractive to rulers. Warrior kings were not told
that warfare was sinful, but encouraged to make war for Christian
purposes; against the heathen and the heretic it was praiseworthy.
Bede had no censure for Aethelfrith, who slaughtered hundreds of
the heretical Welsh monks of Bangor, but was convinced of the
sinfulness of King Ecgfrith's attacks on the Catholic Irish of Meath.

In their writings churchmen depicted what the good king should
be like. The Church taught that kingship was an office and that
its holders had obligations, primarily of a religious character; that
function was to ' labour day and night to bring about the conversion
of all your subjects to the Catholic and apostolic faith '. They
would be most effective if they paid heed to their ecclesiastical
advisors: Pope Gregory exhorted Aethelberht, ' so whatever counsel
he [Augustine] gives you, listen to it gladly, follow it earnestly and
keep it carefully in mind '. Since the preaching of the faith required
men and ecclesiastical establishments the king should himself give
generously and encourage others to give for this purpose, and he
must protect ecclesiastical endowments from attack. Of the more
general attributes of a Christian king much less was written, though
Aidan taught the Northumbrian kings who were his friends that
the good king took care not only of his warrior companions but of
the poor as well. Irish churchmen contributed the notion that the
future of a country was embodied in the person of its king—that a
good king could expect victory and prosperity but the sinful king
would bring defeat and disaster on his people. During the early years
of his reign when Ecgfrith followed righteousness his rule was uniformly victorious; God visited his sinful attack against the Irish by
permitting him to be defeated and killed at Nechtanesmere. By their
teaching and through their personal friendship churchmen often
exercised a considerable influence over kings; the affection felt by
Oswald for Aidan was not singular; Ecgfrith begged Cuthbert to
be his bishop and the notorious Aethelbald of Mercia valued the
friendship of the holy hermit Guthlac. The generous benefactions
of kings reveal their desire to secure and retain ecclesiastical favour.
But churchmen were most influential when they were most
restrained; kings would tolerate straight speaking and admonition,
thereby displaying their respect for ecclesiastical opinion, but they
would not brook interference in matters they regarded as theirs to

determine. Theodore's success depended on his diplomatic management of kings and of his awareness of how much he could profitably
ask of them; Wilfrid's career demonstrated that importunity and
the zeal which gave to the mandate of St. Peter a greater authority
in Northumbria than the will of the king might deprive a church-
man of any influence at all.

Despite the value of the support that the Church could offer to
kingship seventh- and eighth-century kings were aware that the
loyalty their people owed them rested on much older beliefs which
could hardly be reconciled with the Church's teaching. Ine styled
himself ' King by God's gift '; Aethelbald of Mercia, ' King by God's
grace ', but they knew that to most of their people they were kings
by virtue of their descent. The pagan Germans believed their kings
to be descended from the gods and from them inherited a super-
natural force; the royal blood alone possessed this magical virtue
and its possession was an essential attribute of kings. Any member of
the royal family was therefore eligible for kingship, but without it a
ruler's authority was illegitimate and unlikely long to maintain a hold
on his subjects. These beliefs were still held in England in the eighth
century, when the rulers of the English kingdoms demonstrated
their pride in the antiquity of their lineages by having their pedigrees
recorded.[1] Of English kings only the kings of Mercia could certainly
prove descent from a royal ancestor who had ruled in Germany
before the migration, yet most of the genealogies claimed Woden
as the founder of their dynasties. Wise kings possessed, or if they did
not possess, fabricated, a royal lineage because they recognized that
this still constituted their strongest claim on their subject's loyalty.
This was no flamboyant protestation of pagan origins—in fact the
ancestral paganism may well have been forgotten; what was crucial
was that a king should be the descendant of kings. Alcuin, at the
end of the eighth century, lamented the disorders which he witnessed
in England but he knew what had created them, ' scarce one of the
ancient royal kindreds survives, and by so much as their lineage is
uncertain by so much is their power enfeebled '.

Within such a society churchmen acquired influence over kings,
but their only weapons were persuasion, exhortation, threats of the
wrath to come, and the force of personal example. If kings refused
to listen or to take notice there was no element in the kingdom to

---

[1] K. Sisam, 'Anglo-Saxon royal genealogies ', *P.B.A.* XXXIX (1953), and H. R.
Loyn, *Anglo-Saxon England and the Norman Conquest* (London, 1962). ch. 5.

whom they could look for effective support; Rome was a long way distant, unable ever to do more than encourage or console. For these reasons the teachings of churchmen on the nature of kingship, its rights and its obligations made themselves felt very slowly. They created an ideal of what a king ought to be and how he should behave; but in general kings took from them those elements of their teaching which emphasized royal power rather than royal obligations.

It is unfortunate that no legislation survives from between the code of Ine to that of Alfred; Offa certainly promulgated laws, to which Alfred referred in the Preface to his own *Laws*, but they have not come down to us. Yet too great an emphasis on the occasions when new law was promulgated might well obscure the essential informality of the king's court, which possessed simultaneously the attributes of a domestic, a social, a military, and a political group. Basically it was the household of the king and his family, and those servants necessary to satisfy their needs. Because the king was a great lord his court was also a social centre which attracted other great men with their retinues, and men who sought to make their way in the world through service to him. Because kings were constantly at war their courts never lost the primitive attributes characteristic of war-leaders surrounded by their military companions and subordinates. Only occasionally was the king's court the place where the political business of his kingdom predominated. Normally the nucleus of his court consisted of his family and a few intimates; but since by general agreement certain kinds of business were best dealt with in a large public assembly the tribal kings occasionally summoned to their presence, to a more formal meeting, the most important men of their kingdoms both lay and ecclesiastical. The size of such assemblies depended on the size of the kingdom, on the king's will, and his sense of the difficulty and importance of the issues requiring resolution; in some degree their membership was affected by where the king happened to be, for the king was constantly travelling and local notables would naturally attend on him when he was in their district. The occasions when new law was made, though the most important, were also the least characteristic manifestations of the king's court.

Evidence for the existence of governmental institutions at a more local level than the kingdoms is fragmentary, but enough can be discovered to show that within each kingdom there were a number of territorial units which had their origins in the age of settlement.[1] The *Tribal Hidage* of the Mercian kings, previously referred to in another context, provides the clearest evidence for the transformation of areas of primitive settlement into units of royal administration. The inhabitants of these areas had become subjects of the Mercian king and their territories provinces of the Mercian kingdom; now assessed to tribute at a round number of hundreds of hides they must have possessed some assembly capable of apportioning the burden among their constituent villages. Within the kingdom of Kent were regions, styled lathes, whose populations determined locally their fiscal responsibilities to the king, regulated their common interests in the forests and marsh and settled their disputes in courts which met at a royal vill within the lathe. In Sussex similar divisions were styled rapes. Bede frequently referred to regions and provinces in the Northumbrian kingdom. Such subdivisions of the kingdom are hardest to find in Wessex, probably because they were overlaid at an early date by other units of local government, but even there a late seventh-century charter alludes to a province of Sonning and there are strong grounds for believing that the ' six hundreds of Basingstock' and the ' seven hundreds of Cirencester' which were still living memories in the thirteenth century were originally provinces of the West Saxon kingdom. How soon it became necessary to subdivide the provinces into smaller units is unknown and since the size of provinces varied considerably the need may not have been felt everywhere at the same time; but if a province were to be divided, the evidence of the Tribal Hidage, with its provinces uniformly assessed at round numbers of hundreds of hides, suggests that it would have happened by creating from it units each of one hundred hides. Though the midland hundreds of the tenth century were certainly not created in this way, this does not disprove the likelihood that the early West Saxon hundreds originated in the subdivision of provinces into units of one hundred hides; and since, by contrast with the regularity of the new tenth-century Mercian hundreds the hundreds of Wessex were, by the tenth century assessed at widely differing number of hides, it is likely that the process had begun well before the time of King Alfred.

In Wessex, by the ninth century, districts described as shires had come into being; they were units of judicial and military administration whose court was presided over, and whose military levies were

[1] *Supra* pp. 109-10.

led, by royal officials styled ealdormen. These districts were broadly identical with the shires which still exist today in southern England; they may have come into being partly by the unification of provinces into larger units and in more westerly areas, by the allocation of recently conquered territories as apanages to members of the royal family. When this happened is entirely conjectural. Ine's Law mentioned ealdormen who held *scirs* but this cannot be used as evidence for the existence of the later West Saxon shires in the seventh century because the word *scir* could be used of any administrative area irrespective of its nature and also in the abstract sense of ' office '. Outside Wessex there is no evidence for the existence of the shire; there were royal officials styled ealdormen in Mercia but, judging from their numbers, they could not have been responsible for areas as large as shires.

6

THE KINGDOM OF NORTHUMBRIA

FROM the reign of King Ecgfrith (670-685) onwards Northumbrian kings were increasingly preoccupied with maintaining the security of their northern frontier against the Picts, and after the death of King Aldfrith (685-704) the threat of external pressure was compounded by internal dissensions. As the strength of the Mercian kingdom reached its zenith Northumbrian weakness ensured that not only its inclination but also its capacity to maintain hegemony over the south would not revive. In 735 the elevation of York into an archbishopric broke the unity of the English Church maintained since the days of Archbishop Theodore, and confirmed Northumbria's increasing isolation from southern England. For these reasons the history of Northumbria from the end of the seventh century until the destruction of the kingdom by the Danes diverges steadily from the history of the southern kingdoms and requires separate consideration; Bede took it for granted that the Humber constituted a natural frontier between the northern and the southern English. For the Northumbrian kingdom this period of nearly two centuries was one of steady political disintegration. For the Northumbrian church the enfeeblement of royal power created acute problems with which its leaders grappled with some measure of success; a byproduct of their activities was a remarkable efflorescence of intellectual and artistic life which produced some of the greatest masterpieces of the Middle Ages.

1. NORTHUMBRIA ON THE DEFENSIVE

During the seventh century the capacity of Northumbrian kings to exercise authority over the southern English kingdoms had owed much to the pacific disposition of their northern neighbours, the Picts. The personal friendships established by Oswald and his brothers during their exile, and the common bonds forged by the activities of Irish missionaries among both Picts and Northumbrians, appear to have reconciled the Picts to Northumbrian domination. This fortunate circumstance ended during the reign of King Ecgfrith (671-685); it was his misfortune to find himself compelled to campaign on two widely separated fronts.

In 672, when Ecgfrith attended archbishop Theodore's synod at Hertford, his authority in the south appeared to be unchallenged. But in 673-674 he was compelled to undertake an expedition against the Picts; in 674 Wulfhere of Mercia led an invasion of Northumbria. Ecgfrith defeated both Picts and Mercians; Picts, Scots and Strathclyde Britons again accepted his overlordship, and the Mercian kingdom for a brief period was laid under tribute. Neither victory yielded lasting results. In 678 the Mercians, now ruled by Aethelred, Wulfhere's brother and successor, fought the Northumbrians again near the Trent. No details of the battle are preserved, save that Ecgfrith's brother was killed and that peace was restored through the mediation of Archbishop Theodore, but soon afterwards Lindsey passed finally under the control of Mercia. Henceforth Northumbrian kings ceased to attempt to exert control over central England. The permanent political significance of the apparently indecisive fighting of 678 was probably due to continuing troubles in the north. In 684 Ecgfrith sent a fleet to Ireland, though whether with the object of extending his authority over the Scots of Ireland or of cutting off Irish assistance to his rebellious subjects in Pictland is uncertain. So far as is known this force achieved nothing, but Ecgfrith followed up his naval enterprise in the next year by leading an army into Pictland. At Nechtanesmere (Dunnichen Moss) near Forfar the Northumbrians sustained a crushing defeat and Ecgfrith was killed in the battle. 'After this time', wrote Bede, ' the hope and strength of the English began to ebb and fall away. For the Scots recovered their land which the English had held; the Irish who were in Britain and some part of the Britons also recovered their liberty.' As a result of the battle Pictish dependence on Northumbria was terminated for ever. The recently established bishopric at Abercorn was now too vulnerable to Pictish attack to be maintained; its bishop returned to Whitby and the see was abandoned.

Despite the increasing pressure of external problems there is no suggestion that Ecgfrith's authority within his kingdom was challenged. The best recorded events of his reign are those recounting his dealings with Bishop Wilfrid, which reveal him in complete control of the situation. On his restoration to York by Archbishop Theobald in 669 Wilfrid had become the only bishop in Northumbria and a great figure at Ecgfrith's court. Acquiring great influence over Queen Aethelthryth he persuaded her to leave the king and enter the monastery at Coldingham. The hostility of the king thus aroused was compounded when Wilfrid antagonized Ecgfrith's new queen. In 677 Wilfrid was deprived of his bishopric and of his property and driven from the kingdom. After making a leisurely journey to Rome he appealed to Pope Agatho and in 679 in a council held at the Lateran it was decided that he should be restored to his see. He returned home, bringing with him the council's award, which he placed before a Northumbrian council; the council not only rejected the award but imprisoned Wilfrid for several months and then drove him into exile, where he remained until after Ecgfrith's death.

It cannot be convincingly argued that the bitterness between the king and Bishop Wilfrid adversely affected the Northumbrian church, for it is difficult to believe that had Wilfrid retained supreme authority the fruitful fusion of Roman and Irish traditions could have been effected as easily as proved possible under the bishops appointed by Ecgfrith and Archbishop Theodore. These men in their piety and zeal were model diocesans yet they appear to have experienced no difficulty in maintaining good relations with the king. Cuthbert and Wilfrid were contemporaries, yet their personalities could hardly be more contrasted. Bede appeared to be in no doubt as to which of the two had served the Church better. His admiration for Cuthbert was unbounded, but his references to Wilfrid are noticeably lukewarm; he castigated Ecgfrith's attack on Meath as an unnecessary assault on a people to whom the English owed much, but he made no criticism of Ecgfrith's treatment of Bishop Wilfrid.

With Benedict Biscop, too, Ecgfrith lived on the best of terms, and by his liberality made Biscop's great work possible. In 674 he gave Biscop fifty hides of land at the mouth of the Wear on which to found a monastery dedicated to St. Peter, a grant which he subsequently augmented. Eight years later Ecgfrith granted a further forty hides on which to found its sister house at Jarrow, dedicated to St. Paul.

The disaster at Nechthanesmere was partially redeemed by Aldfrith (685-704), Ecgberht's successor. He successfully concentrated
his efforts on re-establishing his northern frontier. Bede said that ' he
ably restored the shattered state of the kingdom although within narrower bounds '. His later judgment ' that from this time the strength
of the kingdom began to ebb and fall away ' was informed by hindsight and is at variance with his expressed statement that the debili-
tating practice of alienating royal lands for the foundation of pseudomonasteries which absorbed the endowments which should have
supported the military caste did not begin until after Aldfrith's
death. Aldfrith combined statesmanlike qualities with a reputation
as a man of letters. He corresponded with Aldhelm of Malmesbury;
Adomnan, who learned to approve Roman customs while a guest
at the Northumbrian court, gave the king a copy of his book on the
Holy Places which Aldfrith caused to be copied so that other men
might read it; he gave Benedict Biscop an estate of eight hides of
land in return for a treatise on cosmography which Benedict had
brought from Rome.

Despite his wide circle of ecclesiastical friends he was as determined as Ecgfrith to yield no ground to the revived claims of Bishop
Wilfrid. In 686 Archbishop Theodore's mediation had restored him
to Ripon, but when on the archbishop's death he renewed his claim
to authority over the whole Northumbrian church he was expelled
from Northumbria. After a long exile in Mercia Wilfrid again referred his case to Rome. Pope Sergius instructed an English synod to
hear Wilfrid's complaint, but it would concede no more than that
Wilfrid might return to his monastery at Ripon without exercise of
episcopal functions. A personal appeal by Wilfrid to Rome achieved
no more than an instruction from the new pope, John, to Archbishop
Berhtwald to hold another synod in which the issue might be determined, and letters to the kings of Northumbria and Mercia asking
them to bear in mind the decrees of previous popes on Wilfrid's
behalf. King Aethelred needed no urging but king Aldfrith remained
adamant.

2. The Disintegration of the Kingdom

After Aldfrith's death the kingdom was held for two months by
Eadwulf, a nobleman unconnected with the ruling dynasty, of
whom nothing more is known than that his hostility to Wilfrid was

as great as that of his predecessor. He was succeeded by Aldfrith's son, Osred, a child of eight years of age. His reputation has suffered because, with his contemporary Ceolred of Mercia, he was castigated by Archbishop Boniface for initiating the attack on the privileges of the Northumbrian and Mercian churches and indulging in a life of vice. A Northumbrian poem written about one hundred years later repeated Boniface's charge of moral laxness and added that he was continually in conflict with the great men of his kingdom, killing many and forcing others of them to seek refuge in monasteries. Even so, Osred must have been well served by his counsellors. His accession made possible a compromise which satisfied Bishop Wilfrid, and during his reign a victory over the Picts stabilized the northern frontier of the kingdom on the river Carron. It is possible that Osred was made the unique scapegoat for developments which neither he nor his successors could control. Nothing is known of the circumstances of his death except that he was killed in 716.

Cenred (716-718) and Osric (718-729) are merely names in the chronicles, but Ceolwulf (729-737) is famous as the king to whom Bede dedicated the *Ecclesiastical History*. In a letter to Archbishop Egbert of York Bede had suggested that the king would be a ready helper in the work of ecclesiastical reform; he was to be disappointed, for though pious and well-intentioned Ceolwulf was an ineffective ruler. As early as 731 he had been taken captive, humiliatingly tonsured and sent back to his kingdom. Already Bede looked to the future with anxiety when he wrote: ' Both the beginning and the course of his reign have been filled with so many and so great disturbances that we cannot yet know what to write about them or guess how they will end.' In 737 Ceolwulf relinquished his kingdom and retired into a monastery.

Temporarily decline was checked by the son of Ceolwulf's father's brother, Eadberht (737-758). After the failure of an early campaign against the Picts which had to be abandoned when Aethelbald of Mercia invaded Northumbria in his absence, Eadberht attacked the British kingdom of Strathclyde and in 750 he annexed the plain of Kyle. In 756, now in alliance with the Picts, he attacked the British capital of Dumbarton and imposed terms on them, only to suffer a serious defeat nine days later. Within Northumbria it was doubtless a help to him that throughout his reign his brother Egbert was archbishop of York; even so there are hints that his rule there was not trouble free. In 756 a rising on behalf of Offa, son of Aldfrith, was suppressed without difficulty, but when two years later Eadberht followed Ceolwulf's example and retired into a monastery his son and successor, Oswulf, was killed by his own bodyguard within a year. In retrospect, by comparison with what came after, Eadberht's could be regarded as a glorious reign, but this achievement can easily be rated too highly. It was later claimed for him that his reputation and good works earned for him the friendship of Pippin the Short, king of the Franks, who sent him royal gifts, but little weight can be placed on that statement since the same source also claimed for Eadberht a superiority over the kings of the English, the Picts, and the Britons which he certainly did not exercise.

The sequel was depressing. To Oswulf succeeded Aethelwald ' Moll ' (759-765) a noble of non-royal blood who could probably count on the loyalty of the men of his own region but few others. He held the kingdom for six years until he was defeated and driven out of the kingdom by Alhred (765-774), who could claim some relationship with the Bernician royal house. Alhred is known to history as a supporter of the missions to the Continent—in 767 Aluberht was consecrated bishop for the Continental Saxons at York; a Northumbrian synod summoned by Alhred supported the mission of S. Willehad to Bremen and in 773 he wrote to Lull of Mainz commending to him his kinsmen and friends. This letter, which asked Lull to befriend Alhred's embassies to Charlemagne, confirms the existence of Northumbrian contacts with the Frankish court which anticipated Alcuin's residence there. But as a king in difficult times Alhred was inadequate and in 774 he was deposed ' by the counsel and consent of all his people '. To him succeeded Aethelred (774-779), son of Aethelwald Moll, who maintained himself with difficulty for five years in the face of opposition which he savagely crushed; the only incidents recorded in his reign relate that ' ealdorman Eadwulf, seized guilefully by treachery was, after a short space of time, killed, buried and forgotten ', and three years later that ' three ealdormen Ealdwulf, Cyneberht and Ecga were treacherously killed by order of King Aethelred '. It is not surprising that in 779 Aethelred was expelled and the throne taken by Aelfwald (779-788), grandson of Eadberht; he was accounted a just and pious king during whose reign a papal legation visited Northumbria, but he was no more capable of imposing order than his immediate predecessors and he, too, was assassinated by a member of his own court. For a few months Aelfwald's nephew Osred was nominally king but he was driven from his kingdom when Aethelred returned from exile and recovered the kingdom. The second phase of Aethelred's rule resembled the earlier, characterized by the elimination of his political enemies. Aelfwald's son was tonsured and subsequently killed; Osred, returning from exile, was also killed, and an ealdorman Eardwulf having been captured and brought to Ripon for execution was saved allegedly only by a miracle. Aethelred's insecurity was exposed by his marriage in 792 to Aelflaed, daughter of Offa of Mercia, a measure doubtless intended to secure Mercian support. In his reign internal discord was made worse by external attack: in 793 Viking raiders sacked Lindisfarne and in the following year ravaged Northumbria; this fleet was severely mauled by both the weather and the Northumbrians, but such assaults underlined the need for strong rule. It was not forthcoming. Aethelred was murdered in 796 and for a period of less than a month a magnate named Osbald who had been elevated to the throne by a noble faction within the kingdom maintained himself until he was deserted ' by the whole company of the royal household and the nobles ', put to flight and banished from the kingdom.

A greater stability within the kingdom was eventually achieved when Eardwulf, a son of the magnate of the same name who had miraculously survived King Aethelred's murderous intentions, was recalled from exile and made king. Although an enemy of Aethelred, he had not been involved in the conspiracy against him and he may have secured more general support than most of his predecessors. He was strong enough in 801 to invade Mercia on the grounds that King Cenwulf had been providing refuge for his enemies, and the peace which was subsequently negotiated was made on equal terms. But in 808 Eardwulf was expelled from his kingdom. He went first to the court of Charlemagne, and thence to Rome. He returned to England accompanied by papal envoys and by representatives of the emperor, to be again received as king by the Northumbrians. The remaining years of his reign passed without recorded incident and Eardwulf was succeeded by his son, Eanred, who successfully maintained himself on the throne for more than thirty years.

Since the Northumbrian annals used by the compiler of the *Anglo-Saxon Chronicle* and later by *Symeon of Durham* came to an end in 806 no consecutive account of Northumbrian history in the ninth century can be written. In 829 king Eanred made a formal submission to Egbert of Wessex. In 844 Raedwulf, who had recently come to power after expelling Eardwulf's grandson Aethelred, was killed with one of his ealdormen while fighting a viking band, and Aethelred recovered his throne. In 848 or 849 he was succeeded by Osbert who was rejected by his people in 866 in favour of Aelle, another aspirant of non-royal lineage.

It was while Osbert and Aelle were fighting one another that a Danish army occupied York (866). Four months delay ensued before the rivals composed their differences. In the following March the Northumbrian force broke into the city, only to be defeated with the slaughter of both Osbert and Aelle and eight of their ealdormen. The Danes imposed Egbert, a puppet king, on the throne, who ruled for five years until driven out by the Northumbrians. He fled to Mercia with the archbishop of York. The Northumbrians then chose Ricsige for their king; he maintained himself until in 874 Halfdan led his army to Northumbria again. The Danes established themselves for a time near the mouth of the Tyne whence they mounted expeditions against both the Picts and the Britons of Strathclyde, but in 876 they withdrew southwards and the rank and file of the army settled in the area of modern Yorkshire.

The weakness of Northumbria after the death of Aldfrith had been the product of internal forces; weak rulers had been unable to maintain themselves when challenged, whether by rival claimants of royal blood or merely by ambitious magnates. Northumbria covered a huge territorial area, much of it broken country which lent itself to the propagation of local separatist movements; it had in the past only been held together by powerful military leaders. After Aldfrith's death this prerequisite of strength was lacking. Surprisingly, neither the Picts nor the Mercians, preoccupied with southern England, took more than an intermittent interest in the affairs of the Northumbrian kingdom. Even so, unable to exercise effective control over the whole, its kings seem generally to have restricted their activities to the southern regions of their kingdom; York and Catterick were their chief residences and even before the Danish settlement it seems probable that local magnates north of the Tees and west of the Pennines were enjoying virtual independence.

In the last decades of the ninth century the Danes occupied Yorkshire; the still English lands between the Tees and the Forth were ruled by Eadwulf of Bamburgh, a friend of King Alfred; elsewhere,

in Cumberland, Westmorland and Lancashire independent rulers
maintained themselves until, early in the next century they were
dislodged by Norse settlers, mainly from Ireland, who came in
sufficient numbers to impose their own distinctive nomenclature on
the area. By this time too, the whole plain around Solway Firth had
been incorporated into the kingdom of Strathclyde. Northumbria
was now nothing more than a geographical expression.

3. THE NORTHUMBRIAN CHURCH

The Northumbrian episcopate in the first quarter of the eighth
century included some distinguished figures, but in an atmosphere
of degenerating political order it would be reasonable to suppose
that they and their successors found it difficult to consolidate what
their predecessors had achieved and carry their work further. In a
famous letter written to Bishop Egbert in 734 Bede outlined the
deficiencies of the Church in his own time and suggested how they
might be remedied.

He said that Northumbria needed more bishops and more priests,
for ' many villages and hamlets of our people are situated in inaccessible mountains and dense woodlands, where there is never seen for
years at a time a bishop to exhibit any ministry or celestial grace.
Nor is it only a bishop who is lacking in such places to confirm the
baptized by the laying on of hands; there is not even a teacher to
teach the truth of the faith and the difference between good and evil
conduct.' Some of such few bishops as existed failed to preach regularly and neglected their duties; some priests were ignorant of Latin
and for this reason Bede had often given them English translations
of the Creed and the Lord's Prayer. Not only were shortcomings
obvious but some elements within the Church were a scandal. Since
the death of King Aldfrith large numbers of secular magnates had
secured grants of land under the pretext of founding monasteries; in
them they lived with their wives and children, absolved from secular
obligation and unconcerned with divine. So much land had been
given for the foundation of such pseudomonasteries that there was
now no land available for the endowment of new sees. An equally
important consequence of such ill-advised liberality was that the
king's resources were no longer adequate for him to reward the sons
of nobles and veteran thegns with estates; the kingdom might, in
consequence, be left defenceless against hostile attack. The pious

generosity of kings had gone so far that in the end the Church itself had suffered from their lack of discrimination.

Much of Bede's criticism was soundly based but it is wise to bear in mind the exaggeration to which even so judicious and scholarly a man might be prone when he adopted a homilectic tone. That the Church needed more bishops and more parish priests is indisputable; even so there were more and better bishops in Northumbria than at any time in the past, and probably more priests. The rate of advance did not satisfy Bede, but there had been no backsliding. He himself in the *Ecclesiastical History* listed the Northumbrian bishops of 731: Wilfrid at York, Aethelwold at Lindisfarne, Acca at Hexham, and Pecthelm at Whithorn. Wilfrid was a pupil of Hild's Whitby; Aethelwold was associated by tradition with the binding of the Lindisfarne Gospels, though nothing else is known of him; Acca was a learned and cultured pupil of Wilfrid and an exemplary diocesan; Pecthelm was a pupil of Aldhelm and the friend of Bede himself. It is hard to believe that any of these men did less than their duty. Similarly the adjuration to Egbert in the *Letter* may seem superfluous: ' I urge you, holy father, to restrain yourself with pontifical dignity from idle conversations disparagement and the other pollutions of an unbridled tongue.'

Conversely, there can be no doubt as to the justice of Bede's strictures on the vast number of Northumbrian monasteries under lay control, nor that even communities which had formerly enjoyed good reputations could become lax under the rule of an over-indulgent abbot or abbess; Coldingham, which in the second half of the seventh century was ruled by St. Aebbe and visited by St. Cuthbert, was degenerate by the beginning of the eighth. Nor can Bede's ascription of the monastic decline to the years after the death of King Aldfrith be safely impugned. Yet it must be recognized that from the beginning the abuses he described were implicit in the institution of the proprietary monastery, and that it was to provide against this risk that zealous abbots like Benedict Biscop sought the privilege of election of the abbot by the monastic community. Bede himself tells us enough about Jarrow in his own time to make it abundantly clear that there, at least, there had been no decline in the high standards of observance established by its founder. And if, in general, the condition of monasteries had degenerated there were still to be found in the north, even among the small houses most prone to decay, a few which maintained high standards. Craike was situated some twelve miles from York and had been founded and was ruled by a nobleman, Eanmund, who had been driven to follow the monastic life by King Osred, the son and successor of King Aldfrith. Provided with a teacher by Bishop Eadfrid of Lindisfarne it became a model house, and so it continued throughout the eighth century according to Aethelwulf's poem *De Abbatibus*, written between 802 and 820, which recounts the history of its abbots.[1]

Bede's object in writing to Egbert was to stimulate him to action; to contrast the fervour of the age of conversion and the subsequent labours of St. Cuthbert and Abbot Benedict with the tepidity of his own day, and to paint a gloomy picture of the contemporary Church was a means to that end. But though unduly harsh in blaming his contemporaries for existing deficiencies Bede's analysis of what was needed to achieve further progress was clearsighted. He urged Bishop Egbert to strive for the fulfilment of Pope Gregory's original design for the north. He should secure the elevation of York into an archbishopric and increase the number of bishops in his province; only in this way could a sufficient supply of priests be provided for country districts. He anticipated the problem of an inadequate episcopate by suggesting that, if necessary, bishops' sees could be created within existing monasteries and their endowments increased by annexing to them the properties of communities deemed disreputable. He also urged that since bishops ' are in the habit of saying that what is done in the various monasteries does not belong to the charge of kings, nor to the jurisdiction of secular rulers, but solely to your episcopal enquiry and investigation ', Egbert should carefully oversee the affairs of the monasteries to ensure that abbots and abbesses were suitable persons to rule, and to support the disciplinary efforts of pious rulers against contumacious monks and nuns.

Little of this programme was immediately implemented, save the erection of York into an archbishopric in the following year. But under King Eadberht, when Northumbria recovered some of its old glory, it is possible that attempts were made to suppress some of the more disreputable pseudomonasteries. Pope Paul wrote to him asking that he should restore to an Abbot Forthred three monasteries which an abbess had recently given him but which the king had taken and granted to one of his nobles. It looks as if Eadberht was acting on the warning given by Bede against the danger that excessive monastic endowments might jeopardize the safety of the kingdom. Archbishop

---

[1] Aethelwulf: *De Abbatibus*, ed. A. Campbell (Oxford, 1967).

6

Egbert was certainly aware of the king's action, which despite its justification nevertheless evoked a protest from the pope.

Between 704 and the accession of King Eadberht it is probable that the conditions for the close cooperation of kings and ecclesiastics were less favourable than they had been before, or were subsequently to become. Under Eadberht internal order was maintained and successful campaigns were fought in the north in 750 and 756 against the Britons of Strathclyde. Eadberht's archbishop was Bede's correspondent, his brother Egbert, who had been taught by Bede at Jarrow. He now established in his household at York what was quickly to become the most distinguished school in northern Europe. A kinsman, Aethelberht, was appointed master of the school and when he in turn was promoted into the archbishopric Alcuin succeeded to that office. Aethelberht was a great collector of books and the library at York and the teaching available there attracted pupils from a wide area. In this way Egbert responded to Bede's plea for an educated clergy.

The year after Pope Paul's letter Eadberht resigned his kingdom and withdrew into a monastery, and from this time onward until the destruction of Northumbria by the Danes the integrity of the kingdom was continuously menaced by civil commotions. Even so there is little clear evidence of decline in the Church. The succession of archbishops of York continued to be adequate and the school of York increased its fame. During the reign of Alhred (765-774) a Northumbrian synod sanctioned the mission of Willehad to the Frisians and both Alhred and Archbishop Aethelberht corresponded with Lull, the archbishop of Mainz, evidence of the continued interest taken by Northumbrians in the continental missions. In 786, George of Ostia, one of the two papal legates sent to England, visited Northumbria and appears to have been well satisfied, both with his reception and with what he saw. Some things needed amendment but this was understandable ' because as you know, since the time of Augustine, no Roman priest has been sent hither save ourselves '. News of the sack of Lindisfarne in 793 moved Alcuin, by that time resident at Charlemagne's court, to write a famous letter in which he described the calamity as divine retribution for the sins of Northumbrian kings and magnates; this kind of historical explanation was the common form of the age and it is more significant to notice that the letters he addressed at about the same time to Wearmouth, Jarrow, Lindisfarne, and York were exhortatory rather than condemnatory, warnings of dangers to be avoided and of virtues to be pursued rather than accusations of over-indulgence and neglect of duty.

For the ninth century the evidence is still more fragmentary than for the earlier period but it is worth remarking that Lindisfarne recovered from its devastation and that some of its later bishops were men of good reputation. Bishop Ecgred, in a letter to his archbishop Wulfsige (830-837) showed himself concerned to protect his flock from heresy; another is known to have built churches in his diocese. Eardwulf, the bishop who eventually decided that he must abandon Lindisfarne, was praised for the pastoral solicitude he showed for the distant possessions of his see, and his devotion was manifested by the pains he suffered during his seven-year-long struggle to preserve the relics of St. Cuthbert from desecration. In the first half of the century its monks produced their *Liber Vitae,* with its letters in gold and silver. Continental contacts were not entirely lacking; in 852 Lupus of Ferrieres wrote to Abbot Eadsige of York asking to borrow books from the library and Archbishop Wigmund, Wulfsige's successor, issued coins in imitation of those of Louis the Pious. Coins of Wigmund and King Osbert (849-867) found on the site of the abbey prove that Whitby was not abandoned before the middle of the century despite its exposed location, and confirms the impression that the early Danish raids caused great alarm but did little permanent damage.

Such fragmentary notices concerning bishops and monasteries, which are all that remain to us of the formal history of the Northumbrian church, are not the only evidence of the vitality of Christianity in northern England in the years before the Danish invasions. Whether the credit for it should be given to pastorally minded bishops preaching in the farflung villages and hamlets of their dioceses, or to those upland clergy for whom Bede translated the Creed and the Lord's Prayer and for whom on his deathbed he was translating the Gospel of St. John, it is worth remembering that Christianity came to ordinary countryfolk through men who spoke to them in their own tongue. Books were rare and men unlettered, but there is ample evidence throughout the Anglo-Saxon period that poetry was listened to eagerly by all classes of society and that vernacular poetry became a powerful medium of religious instruction.

The first reference to the adaptation of minstrelsy to the purposes of the Church comes in Bede's story of the cowherd Caedmon. Bede tells us that occasionally in the evenings the villagers entertained one another by taking turns in singing to the music of the harp; but Caedmon's inability to versify shamed him, so that when his turn came near he left the gathering and slunk out to the stable. On one such night he had a dream in which a visitor came to him and asked why he had left the entertainment. Caedmon explained that he could not sing, but the visitor answered, ' " Nevertheless you must sing to me." " What ", he said " must I sing? " And the other said, " Sing of the beginning of creation." On receiving this answer he at once began to sing in praise of God the Creator verses which he had never heard.' When it became apparent that this marvellous talent was a permanent endowment Caedmon entered Hild's monastery, where

> he used to compose songs suited to religion and piety; so that whatever he learned by translators from the divine Scriptures, he soon after put into poetic words with the greatest sweetness and humility, and brought it forth in his own language, that is, English. By his songs the minds of many were often fired with contempt of the world and with desire for the heavenly life. And indeed others after him in the English nation attempted to compose religious poems, but no one could equal him.

Only nine lines of Caedmon's poetry certainly survive but there is ample confirmation of Bede's statement that vernacular poetry continued to be written. Most of it is contained in four manuscripts which were compiled in about the year 1000; it is impossible to ascribe definite dates to the poems they contain but it is virtually certain that they were written before the period of Danish invasions and probable that they were composed in Northumbria. Some of the poems, such as *Genesis, Exodus,* and *Daniel* are verse paraphrases of Bible stories of the type that Caedmon is said to have composed. Others are far more than this; they reveal not only a formal knowledge of Christian teaching but an intensity of feeling which demonstrates that Christianity had penetrated deeply into the consciousness of the poet. In the *Dream of the Rood,* composed early in the eighth century, the cross tells the story of the Crucifixion.

> The soldiers on their shoulders bore me,
>   until on a hill-top they set me up;
> many enemies made me fast there.
>   Then I saw, marching toward me,
> mankind's brave King;

He came to climb upon me.
I dared not break or bend aside
against God's will, though the ground itself
shook at my feet. Fast I stood,
who falling could have felled them all.

Almighty God ungirded Him,
    eager to mount the gallows,
unafraid in the sight of many;
    He would set free mankind.
I shook when His arms embraced me
    but I durst not bow to ground,
stoop to Earth's surface.
    Stand fast I must.

I was reared up, a rood.
    I raised the great King,
liege lord of the heavens,
    dared not lean from the true.
They drove me through with dark nails:
    on me are the deep wounds manifest,
wide-mouthed hate-dents.
    I durst not harm any of them.
How they mocked at us both!
    I was all moist with blood
sprung from the Man's side
    after He sent forth His soul.[1]

Such poetry provides the best explanation of the fundamental fact concerning the religious life of the ninth century, both in Northumbria and in those parts of Mercia which were to be occupied by heathen Danes; that Christianity was so deeply rooted in the countryside that within a few years the pagan conquerors had been converted to Christianity through the force of their English neighbours' practice and precept, without benefit of missionary activities from those parts of England which remained unconquered, and despite the fact that the bastions of organized religion in their own areas had been destroyed.

Bishoprics and monasteries were among the first casualties of the Danish attack. Of the Northumbrian bishoprics only York survived, though with difficulty; for a time, between 865 and 872 its archbishop, Wulfhere, lived in hiding in Wharfedale, and for many decades after his return York remained obscure and poverty stricken.

---

[1] The translation is that of M. Alexander, *The Earliest English Poems* (London, 1966), pp. 107-8.

Hexham disappeared, as some time later did Whithorn; in 875 the bishop and community of Lindisfarne abandoned their church. In all this area monasticism became extinct, though a few small and undistinguished communities may have limped along for some time in a quasimonastic guise. Yet the destruction of churches and monasteries and the disappearance of the heads of the ecclesiastical hierarchy did not mean the end of Christianity in Northumbria.

Halfdan's successor at York, Guthfrith, was one of the earliest notable converts; with his permission the community of Lindisfarne at last ended its wanderings and settled in 882 at Chester-le-Street; the slow work of reconstruction could now begin in earnest. The conversion of the Danes to Christianity was the most remarkable memorial of the ninth century Northumbrian church.

In political terms the eighth century saw the eclipse of Northumbria and the ascendancy of Mercia; the emergence of Wessex still lay in the future. By contrast, in the spheres of scholarship and the arts, though the influence of Theodore, Hadrian, and Aldhelm was far from exhausted in southern England and interesting developments were beginning to take shape in Mercia, Northumbria remained for long supreme. In these years some of the triumphs of Anglo-Saxon learning and craftsmanship were produced in Northumbrian monasteries.[1]

In all the English kingdoms churchmen were more influenced by Pope Gregory's *Book of Pastoral Care* than by any other book except the Bible, and readily concurred in its vigorous condemnation of ignorant teachers and in its insistence on the need for an educated clergy. Theodore and Hadrian doubtless brought books with them to Canterbury, but the learning of Northumbria was more broadly based. At Wearmouth-Jarrow Benedict Biscop established a fine library furnished with the books he bought in Mediterranean lands which was supplemented by splendid additions made by Abbot Ceolfrith. Though no identifiable books from Whitby have survived, the work of Abbess Hild suggests that she had assembled a useful library, an assumption confirmed from the compilation there, between 704 and 710, of the earliest biography of Pope Gregory,[2] which drew its information from the *Liber Pontificalis* and many

---

[1] P. Hunter Blair, *The World of Bede* (London, 1970) combines lucidity with learning in his account and discussion of the Northumbrian achievement.

[2] *The Life of Gregory the Great by an anonymous monk of Whitby*, ed. B. Colgrave (Kansas, 1968).

of Gregory's own works. No books survive from Hexham though Wilfrid's pupil Acca is known to have collected there ' a very splendid library consisting of a great many books '. By the middle of the century the greatest of the Northumbrian schools was at York, where successive masters built up a substantial library which Alcuin, a former master and later a leading figure in the Carolingian renaissance of learning, described at length. It still enjoyed a continental reputation nearly a century later.

The purpose of the book collections was utilitarian, to encourage the study of the Bible and the commentaries made on the Bible by the early Fathers of the Church. The prime requisite for such work was the establishment of good editions of the texts and to have them copied. At Jarrow a revised and edited version of the whole Bible based on the best available manuscripts was produced. Three copies of this work were made, one of which, now known as the *Codex Amiatinus*,[1] Abbot Ceolfrith took with him on his last journey to Rome, the finest gift which his monastery could offer to their protector. The work of Ceolfrith in producing a good text of the Bible was the necessary preliminary to Bede's work as commentator.

The affection and respect felt by the monks of Wearmouth and Jarrow for their abbot found early expression in a biography of Ceolfrith, written by one of them before 716. Valuable by reason of its account of religious life in Northumbria, and of Wearmouth in particular, it has an additional interest as being an early historical work from the monastery which produced Bede, the greatest glory of Northumbrian scholarship.

Bede's mind comprehended all that was known to the men of his day, despite the fact that his whole life, since boyhood, was lived within the precincts of his monastery. In terms of sheer physical labour his was a stupendous achievement. The difficulties of writing in that age are vividly described in a letter written in 764 by Abbot Cuthbert of Wearmouth to Archbishop Lull of Mainz; Cuthbert had sent to Lull Bede's writings on St. Cuthbert in prose and verse:

[1] So called because it eventually found its way to the monastery of Monte Amiato in the central Apennines. When the monastery was suppressed, in 1782, the Codex was transferred to the Laurentian Library in Florence, its present home. It is the subject of a fascinating article, ' The Art of the Codex Amiatinus ', by R. L. S. Bruce-Mitford, *Journal of the British Archaeological Association*, XXXII (1969). He emphasizes the material resources required to produce a book like this: its 1,030 folios ' represents the utilization of the skins of 1,550 calves . . . with its protective wrappings and travelling case and original covers it must have weighed a good ninety pounds, practically the same as a fully grown Great Dane '.

And if I could have done more, I would gladly have done so. But the conditions of the past winter oppressed the island of our race very horribly with cold and ice and long and widespread storms of wind and rain, so that the hand of the scribe was hindered from producing a great number of books.

Despite all the obstacles, Bede with the help of the monks of the Jarrow scriptorium wrote a series of commentaries on the books of the Bible, treatises on chronology, the lives of St. Cuthbert referred to by his namesake, translations from Latin into English, and a number of miscellaneous works, as well as the book which to historians, though perhaps not to himself, is his masterpiece, *The Ecclesiastical History of the English People*. Without that work no account of the years between the coming of the Saxons and the early eighth century could profitably be attempted.

Bede did not assemble a miscellaneous collection of materials to be subsequently stitched together like a patchwork quilt. His purpose was clearly defined, to describe the conversion of the English and to give an account of the history of the Church in England; with that object in view he wrote to his contemporaries in the southern kingdoms to discover from them anything they knew relevant to the work in hand. The information so gathered he put into shape; he was no mere chronicler but a historian who saw it as his function to explain the relationship between events, their causes, and their consequences. If it sometimes appears that he was concerned principally to demonstrate that a good king and a godly people were rewarded by prosperity and that wickedness was visited by dire retribution, it must be conceded that he taught that lesson with considerable skill and sophistication, and that he seldom fails to provide an apparatus of solid information which can be put to other uses. It can fairly be said that Bede was less than generous in his appreciation and recognition of the successes of Celtic Christianity, and he sometimes appears unduly concerned to minimize the animosities shown by some of the Roman champions for one another; but these are minor blemishes. A recent discussion of Bede's account of Augustine's mission, while demonstrating that he was not completely successful in his search for the relevant material, only enhances our respect for what, with such limited sources at his disposal, he achieved.[1] Bede's history is so well integrated and so informative within its self-prescribed limits that the reader may come to feel

---

[1] See p. 69, *supra*.

that it provides him with all the knowledge of early Anglo-Saxon England that he needs; yet it tells almost nothing, save incidentally and by implication, about civil institutions and social and economic conditions. Such things were not directly relevant to Bede's purpose and were consequently relegated to the background; the historian of later days may regret that Bede did not see fit to inform us of many matters which he took for granted but of which we are ignorant, but it is precisely the selective quality of Bede's mind which provides the clearest evidence of his genius and gives to his book those qualities which make it both a work of art and the fundamental authority for the history of early Anglo-Saxon England.

His distinction did not go without recognition, even in his own day; almost from the beginning he was a European as well as an English figure. In England he stood alone. Four hundred years later William of Malmesbury could truthfully say that no man since Bede had attempted a historical work on a comparable scale, and William deliberately set himself to do for the history of England since Bede what Bede had so triumphantly accomplished for the earlier period. He took Bede as his model, and reflecting his master's virtues he took considerable trouble to identify the authorities on which his statements depended, and showed a like concern to relate causes and events. Though for these reasons he is to modern historians perhaps the most congenial of twelfth-century scholars, by general consent his work falls well short of that of its exemplar; nor did the later medieval centuries in England produce a historian comparable in quality to Bede.

Bede's death provided the occasion for Cuthbert, Lull's correspondent and a former pupil of Bede, to write a most moving letter to a friend in another monastery. Itself a fine Latin composition, the letter is historically important because it reveals so much about the character of Northumbrian monasticism, and in particular about the importance of academic studies in relation to the other activities of the professed monk. Cuthbert recounted the onset of Bede's illness and described how the community at Jarrow spent the days between Easter and Pentecost. Bede continued to teach regularly and to busy himself with the translation of the Gospel of St. John and the compilation of a selection from Isidore of Seville's book *On the Wonders of Nature*; the rest of the day he spent chanting the Psalter 'as best he could'. Most of each night he prayed, with brief intervals of sleep. Cuthbert continued:

6*

When it came to the Tuesday before Ascension Day, his breathing became very much worse, and a slight swelling had appeared in his feet; but all the same he taught us the whole of that day, and dictated cheerfully, and among other things said several times: 'Learn your lesson quickly now; for I know not how long I may be with you, nor whether after a short time my Maker may not take me from you.' But it seemed to us that he knew very well when his end should be. So he spent all that night in thanksgiving, without sleep; and when day broke, which was the Wednesday, he gave instructions for the writing, which we had begun to be finished without delay. We were at it until nine o'clock; at nine o'clock we went in procession with the relics, as the custom of that day required. One of us stayed with him, and said to him: 'There is still one chapter short of that book you were dictating, but I think it will be hard on you to ask any more questions.' But he replied: 'It is not hard. Take your pen and mend it, and then write fast.' And so he did. At three o'clock he said to me: 'I have a few treasures in my box, some pepper, and napkins, and some incense. Run quickly and fetch the priests of our monastery, and I will share among them such little presents as God has given me.' I did so, in great agitation; and when they came he spoke to them and to each one singly, urging and begging them to offer masses and prayers regularly on his behalf, and they promised with a will. But they were very sad, and they all wept, especially because he had said that he thought they would not see his face much longer in this world. . . .

This he said, and other things, to our great profit, and so spent his last day in gladness until the evening. Then the boy of whom I spoke, whose name was Wilberht, said once again: 'There is still one sentence, dear master, that we have not written down.' And he said 'Write it.' After a little the boy said: 'There! Now it is written.' And he replied: 'Good! It is finished; you have spoken the truth. Hold my head in your hands, for it is a great delight to me to sit over against my holy place in which I used to pray, that as I sit there I may call upon my Father.' And so upon the floor of his cell, singing 'Glory be to the Father and to the Son and to the Holy Spirit' and the rest, he breathed his last.[1]

All Bede's vast learning was put to the service of the Church, which he served with total dedication and selflessness. Different from Aidan and Cuthbert in his intellectual distinction, he shared with them the qualities of devotion, humility, simplicity, and love for their fellow-men, which made them such superbly effective missionaries.

Most of the texts written in the monastic scriptoria were designed for daily use and study, but the Bible was the Word of God and some Bibles were produced with the primary intention of honouring the

[1] The translation is that of B. Colgrave in *Bede's Ecclesiastical History of the English People*, ed. B. Colgrave and R. A. B. Mynors (Oxford, 1969), pp. 583-5.

sacred text. Wilfrid, though himself no great scholar, appreciated a splendid manuscript and he gave to his church at Ripon a copy of the four Gospels written in letters of gold on purple-dyed parchment, with a gold case set with precious gems to contain it—' a marvel of beauty hitherto unheard of in our times ', observed his biographer. Boniface thought that the ignorant men to whom he preached would be impressed by magnificent appearances and asked Abbess Eadburh of Minster-in-Thanet to write for him a copy of the Epistles of St. Peter in letters of gold, ' to secure honour and reverence for the Holy Scriptures when they are preached from before the eyes of the heathen.' Such motives led to the production of marvellously illuminated manuscripts of the Scriptures.

In Northumbria Irish influences, exemplified in the Book of Durrow, came directly into contact with Mediterranean influences introduced in the books brought by Benedict Biscop from Gaul and Italy and were blended to create masterpieces of which the best known is the Lindisfarne Gospels, which was probably written and illuminated by Bishop Eadfrith of Lindisfarne between 698 and 721. In the Lindisfarne Gospels the text is of Mediterranean origin but it is written in an Irish half-uncial hand and the portraits of the evangelists are strongly influenced by Italian models; but the decoration combines Celtic spirals, Irish illuminated capitals and decorated 'carpet' page with Germanic ornaments and interlace. The same combination of Celtic and Mediterranean influences is to be seen in the series of free-standing stone crosses of which the most remarkable are those of Ruthwell and Bewcastle. The figures carved on these crosses are naturalistic and some of the decoration, such as the vine-scroll inhabited by animals and birds, is Mediterranean in style, but many of the decorative patterns resemble those of the Lindisfarne Gospels.

In architecture, too, Northumbria was more advanced than elsewhere, though in this activity indebtedness was exclusively to the Continent. Wilfrid and Benedict Biscop brought stonemasons from Gaul to supervise their buildings. Wilfrid's biographer claimed that no church north of the Alps could compare with his hero's church at Hexham, with its high, long walls, winding passages and spiral staircase. The cathedral at York, rebuilt by Archbishop Aethelberht (786-792), was an imposing building with a great number of upper apartments and thirty altars.

Political decadence was compatible with artistic excellence in eighth-century Northumbria.

7

SOUTHERN ENGLAND IN THE EIGHTH CENTURY: THE MERCIAN SUPREMACY

1. POLITICAL NARRATIVE

ÆTHELBALD of Mercia (716-757) succeeded Ceolred in 716, after a long period of exile; the death of Wihtred of Kent in 725 and the abdication of the West Saxon kingdom by Ine in the following year left him without a rival.[1] No details are known of the stages by which Aethelbald's position was secured, but the range of his power was made explicit by Bede; he gave the names of the bishops who were alive in 731 and the peoples whom they served, and added: 'All these kingdoms and the other southern kingdoms which reach right up to the Humber, together with their various kings, are subject to Aethelbald, king of Mercia.' His statement is confirmed by other evidence. Charters of the early 730s which record Aethelbald's sale of land in northern Somerset to Glastonbury and a grant of land in Berkshire to Canterbury show that by then he exercised control over substantial areas south of the Thames formerly in West Saxon hands. Of the same date are charters to the abbess of Minster-in-Thanet and to Rochester granting them remission of toll on one ship a year at London which illustrate his authority over London and Middlesex; this territory, originally part of the kingdom of the East Saxons, had for long been coveted and sometimes ruled by Aethelbald's predecessors, and was now finally incorporated into Mercia. We have no similar corroborative evidence of his relations with the kings of Kent and of the East Angles, but the councils of the whole southern province of the Church over which Aethelbald presided lend weight to Bede's statement. A charter of 736 styled

---

[1] Though written as long ago as 1918 little has since been written which adds to or subtracts from the account Sir Frank Stenton gave in ' The supremacy of the Mercian kings ', *Preparatory to Anglo-Saxon England* (Oxford, 1970).

him, ' King, not only of the Mercians but of all the provinces which are called by the general name South English '; and its witness list is headed by *Aethelbald rex Brittania,* king of Britain. Aethelbald's ambitions may even have embraced the conquest of Northumbria. On one occasion at least, during the absence of Eadberht from his kingdom whilst campaigning against the Picts, he invaded Northumbria.

The only reverse which Aethelbald is known to have suffered occurred in 752 when he was defeated by Cuthred of Wessex. The battle may have secured West Saxon independence for a year or two, but it did no more. Cynewulf, who succeeded to Wessex in 757, acknowledged his subordination by attending the Mercian court and witnessing one of Aethelred's last charters, issued shortly before the end of his reign.

Aethelbald was murdered by his bodyguard in 757. His death was followed by civil war in Mercia and the collapse of that authority over southern England which he had built up, but by the end of 757 Offa, like Aethelbald a descendant of Penda's brother Eowa, had driven out the rival claimant. Time and favourable circumstances were needed before Mercian supremacy over the other kingdoms was restored. Record of a battle between English and Welsh at Hereford in 760 suggests that the Welsh took advantage of Offa's initial difficulties. Wessex recovered most of the provinces lost to Mercia and even, temporarily, secured lands north of the Thames. Charter evidence reveals, however, that in the south-east Mercian fortunes revived quickly. Offa's authority in Sussex from an early period in his reign is shown by his confirmation of grants made by South Saxon kings in the centre and west of their kingdom; in 771 he conquered the district of Hastings and in 772 a certain Osmund, in 770 a king, attested a charter as *dux* or ealdorman. In 764 Offa confirmed grants made by a Kentish king to the bishop of Rochester and in 774 he made two grants to the archbishop of Canterbury without reference to the local ruler. These initial successes were followed by a serious reverse and the decade 775-785 appears as a crucial period of the reign. Kent rebelled against him and after a battle fought at Otford in 776 Offa's rule there seems to have ended for a period of almost ten years; in 784 a Kentish king Eahlmund granted land to Reculver without reference to him. But in the following year the series of Offa's charters in Kent resumes and thereafter Kent was no more than a province of the Mercian kingdom, though Offa continued to feel the need to guard against a resurgence of local feeling there.

Cynewulf of Wessex held his own against Offa for at least fifteen years. He made his first recorded appearance at Offa's court in 772 but this constitutes no proof of resumed dependence; the critical date here was 779 when Cynewulf was defeated at Bensington, a battle which resulted in the Mercian acquisition of the disputed lands on either side of the river Thames. Cynewulf was present with Offa in 786 at the synod of the southern province attended by the papal legate. In that same year he was killed as the result of an internal feud and thereafter Wessex fell completely under Mercian influence. In the contention for the succession which followed Cynewulf's death Beorhtric, whose ancestry is unknown, confronted Egbert, probably a son of the Kentish king Eahlmund who had led the resistance to Offa. If this was so it would explain why Offa supported Beorhtric, with the result that Egbert was driven into exile. The subordination of Wessex to Offa was assured when Beorhtric married one of Offa's daughters in 793. Little is known about East Anglia during the eighth century but in 794 its king, Aethelberht, was beheaded at Offa's command. Mercian interest north of the Humber is shown by the marriage of one of Offa's daughters in 792 to King Aethelred, the son of Aethelwald Moll, who, after ten years of exile, had returned to Northumbria in 789. In 791 Offa died, at the height of his power.

2. THE CHARACTER OF THE MERCIAN SUPREMACY

Despite Bede's implicit recognition of the dominion of Aethelbald over southern England he omitted his name from his formal enumeration of those kings who had exercised such authority. Yet the power of Aethelbald, still more that of Offa, was greater than that of any previous bretwaldas. It was expressed more directly and more consciously. And because between them the two kings spanned almost a century it acquired an aura of permanence and normality. The necessary corollary to their conception of a kingdom of Britain was the formal subordination of the royal dynasties of the client kingdoms to themselves.[1] Aethelbald's charter of 736 which styled him *rex Brittannia* was attested by Aethelric, *subregulus atque comes,* under-king and ealdorman, though his

---

[1] Offa's treatment of subject peoples is contrasted with Alfred's, *infra*, pp. 225-7.

father Oshere had been styled king. Offa's charters reveal both the continued subordination of the rulers of the Hwicce and a similar reduction in the status of the kings of Sussex and Kent. They attended his court and witnessed his charters; within their own territories their independence was radically curtailed. When Egbert, king of Kent, made a grant of four sulungs to his reeve in Canterbury, Ealdhun, it was subsequently annulled by Offa on the grounds 'that it was wrong that his thegn should have presumed to give land allotted to him by his lord into the power of another without his witness'. Egbert's lands were deemed to have been allotted to him by Offa and the king himself referred to as though he were a mere official (thegn) of the Mercian over-king. In 781, in a council at Brentford, grants made by the rulers of the Hwicce were annulled by a judgment of a similar kind. Not only was the permanent alienation of lands by subject-kings prohibited, save by permission, but it appears to have been wise to obtain Offa's confirmation even if royal interests were not directly involved; a grant made by Oslac, ealdorman in Sussex, in 780, at Selsey was corroborated by Offa at Irthlingborough in Mercia several years later. Conversely, Offa himself granted lands and privileges in dependent kingdoms at will; Ealdhun's confiscated lands in Kent were distributed by Offa to his thegns.

The ecclesiastical history of the eighth century reveals with equal clarity the enhanced character of the Mercian supremacy. The Northumbrian bretwaldas had exercised some degree of authority over the Church in England.[1] Oswald had been associated with Cynegils of Wessex in establishing a bishop's see at Dorchester-on-Thames. Whether the attendance of prominent ecclesiastics from outside Northumbria at Whitby made that meeting an assembly of the English Church under Oswiu's tutelage is debatable, but on the death of Deusdedit, archbishop of Canterbury, soon afterwards, Oswiu and the Kentish king took counsel together on the choice of his successor Wighard, and when Wighard died before his consecration it was to Oswiu that Pope Vitalian wrote promising to find a replacement. But such interventions were occasional rather than normal, and after Oswiu's death political conditions in England made it impossible for a single ruler to preside over the whole Church. Provincial councils were presided over by Theodore and Berhtwald, but the synod of Hatfield in 680 was said to have assembled at the command of Ecgfrith of Northumbria, Aethelred

[1] See especially, John *op. cit.* pp. 14-19.

of Mercia, Aldwulf of the East Angles, and Hlothere of Kent. During these years both provincial councils and councils of the clergy of the separate kingdoms assembled.

The establishment of a separate northern province of the English Church in 735 left the province of Canterbury territorially coterminous with the secular dominion of the Mercian king. Within a few years Aethelbald's ascendancy in southern England assumed institutional form in assemblies presided over jointly by the archbishop of Canterbury and the king of Mercia, attended by all the prominent churchmen of the kingdoms of southern England and by the chief councillors of the Mercian king. At the synod of Clovesho in 742, attended by bishops from all southern England, Aethelbald confirmed the privileges of the Kentish Church. Five years later, in response to letters of reproach addressed by Boniface to King Aethelbald and Archbishop Cuthbert a reforming synod met, again at Clovesho; it was presided over by the archbishop and attended by bishops from all southern England in the presence of King Aethelbald and his counsellors. Similar councils were held throughout Offa's reign. The course of the visit of the papal legates George, bishop of Ostia, and Theophylact, bishop of Todi, in 786, provides a further illustration of Offa's supremacy in southern England. On their arrival they first visited Archbishop Jaenberht at Canterbury and then proceeded to Offa's court where they were well received. A council was subsequently held at which in addition to Offa only Cynewulf of Wessex, of the southern kings, was present. The legates afterwards separated; the bishop of Ostia went to Northumbria, where King Aelfwald arranged for a council to be held ' at which assembled all the chief men of the region, both ecclesiastical and secular '; meanwhile the bishop of Todi visited Mercia and Wales. On their return together to Offa's court they introduced the reforming decrees agreed in the Northumbrian council ' to the council of the Mercians, where the glorious King Offa had come together with the senators of the land, along with Jaenberht, archbishop of the holy church of Canterbury and the other bishops of those parts '. The decrees were ratified in this assembly by Jaenberht, Offa, twelve bishops drawn from the kingdoms of Mercia, Wessex, East Anglia, Kent, and Essex, and four Mercian ealdormen.

A clear demonstration of Offa's conception of the proper relationship between ecclesiastical and royal authority, and the most remarkable indication of the control he exercised over the English Church is revealed by the progress of a project which was broached during the legatine visitation. Prominent among Offa's reasons for welcoming the legates so graciously was a political motive. The resistance of Kent to his dominion had been particularly prolonged and bitter and its king, Egbert, had found a supporter in Archbishop Jaenberht, who was probably Kentish by birth. The potentially dangerous situation created when the head of the southern province of the English Church was identified with the aspirations of a subject kingdom to independence explains Offa's determination to establish an archbishopric within his own hereditary kingdom. This matter must have been discussed with the legates and justified on the grounds that the province of Canterbury was too large for effective supervision. In the following year he overrode the opposition of English churchmen, expressed in a contentious synod at Chelsea, and secured its approval for the establishment of a new archbishopric at Lichfield.

Unlike any of his predecessors King Offa was a European figure, the reality of whose power was appreciated by foreign rulers.[1] In a letter to Charlemagne Pope Hadrian professed his disbelief in a rumour, which had reached him through the Frankish king with a disclaimer, that Offa had suggested to Charlemagne that they should depose him and appoint a Frankish pope; it is a measure of the respect in which Offa was held that so bizarre a rumour could engage even the momentary attention of the greatest ecclesiastic and the greatest layman of his day. It may be significant that it was only shortly afterwards that Hadrian, though with misgivings, acquiesced in Offa's plans for the archbishopric of Lichfield and sent a pallium for Bishop Hygeberht. In 789 Charlemagne, incomparably the dominant lay figure in the West, showed his respect for Offa by asking for one of his daughters as a wife for his son Charles; perhaps reluctant to deliver up a hostage to the court of so great a ruler without a measure of insurance, Offa countered with the suggestion that Charlemagne should give one of his daughters in marriage to his son Ecgfrith. When Charlemagne refused to consider the exchange a period of coolness followed during which time both kings imposed an embargo on traders from the other's country. The quarrel was ended through the mediation of Alcuin, who by this time had left

[1] Offa's relations with Charlemagne have been admirably discussed by J. M. Wallace-Hadrill, ' Charlemagne and England ', *Karl der Grosse: Lebenswerk und Nachleben,* ed. W. Braunsjels (Düsseldorf, 1965-68).

York and now lived at Charlemagne's court, and Gervold, abbot of St. Wandrille, who, according to the chronicle of that house, was a friend and intimate of Offa by virtue of the many diplomatic missions he had undertaken to the Mercian court on Charlemagne's instructions. It seems that Offa mistrusted Charlemagne's interest in English affairs, which extended beyond Mercia and comprehended both secular and ecclesiastical politics. Even before his Imperial coronation in 800 Charlemagne regarded himself as the champion of Christendom in the West; he corresponded with the Northumbrian court and gave hospitality to political exiles; more serious, in Offa's eyes, was that between 789 and 792 he provided a refuge for Egbert of Wessex after he had been driven out by Offa's protégé, Beorhtric. In a letter to the archbishop of Canterbury Alcuin attempted to disarm Offa's suspicions that Charlemagne was following a deliberate policy of harbouring his enemies by declaring that his master's only motive in receiving them was to effect a reconciliation between them and their king. Ecclesiastically, Frankish interest in English affairs had been shown when the papal legates were accompanied to England by the Frankish abbot, Wigbod, and when Charlemagne sent to England the canons of the counil of Nicea (787) which had been favourable to the cult of images. Despite the occasional frictions of the earlier years friendly relations with Charlemagne were maintained in the last period of Offa's reign and Offa received gifts from the loot taken by Charlemagne when he captured the Avar treasure hoard in 795.

Offa was conscious of his great position, and his court officials occasionally attempted to find formulae which expressed the character of their master's authority. In most of his charters Offa is described simply as king of the Mercians, but occasionally his scribes borrowed a usage which is first known to have been used in the last year of Aethelbald; they styled him, ' king not only of the Mercians but also of the nations around '. Sometimes they went further than this. Aethelbald's formula had confined his superiority to the nations of the southern English, but the description of Offa as *rex Anglorum,* and on one occasion as *rex totius Anglorum patriae,* went further; it asserted Offa's supremacy over all the English people in Britain, including Northumbria.

Despite the range and degree of his power Offa was aware of the fragility of the foundations upon which it rested. His predecessor, despite his triumphs, had in the end been murdered by men of his own retinue; in the following year Oswulf of Northumbria had been killed in similar circumstances; in 786 Cynewulf, King of Wessex, was killed in the course of a vendetta; Aelfwald and Aethelred, kings of Northumbria, were murdered in 788 and 796 respectively. Across the Channel the kingship of the Franks had recently been trans- ferred from the Merovingians to the noble but non-royal Carolings. In order to strengthen the basis of his authority Offa exploited to the full those sanctions which, in addition to the material force that all kings needed, could justify the exercise of royal rule. He emphasized simultaneously the authority conferred on a ruler by virtue of his legitimacy and the sanctification conferred upon that authority by God's grace. An early charter described him as ' king of the Mercians, sprung from the royal stock of the Mercians and made king by appointment of Almighty God '. He took pride in declaring his descent from that Offa, king of the continental Angles, whose name he bore; but he tried also, following Carolingian example, to invest his rule with the aura of divine approval. In 781 Charlemagne's sons Pippin and Louis journeyed to Rome to receive papal unction; in 787 Offa had his son Ecgfrith anointed king, either by his new archbishop or by the papal legates. This was the first time that a son had been consecrated king in England in his father's lifetime; Ecgfrith was associated with his father in ruling the kingdom and the future of the dynasty made more secure.

Considerations of this nature suggest that Offa's court was not only more formal in aspect but more sophisticated in its thinking than the courts of earlier kings. Offa was more than a warrior; he won fame as a lawgiver whose code was used by Alfred a century later—it may have been to these laws that Alcuin referred when he wrote of ' the good, moderate and chaste customs which Offa of blessed memory established '. Alcuin knew that Offa possessed a copy of Bede, for in one of his letters to the king he referred to a letter of Pope Gregory which was included in the *Ecclesiastical History* and advised the king to look it up. The skill of Mercian court scribes was not confined to devising novel formulae to describe their master's dignity; the greatest authority on Anglo-Saxon charters has drawn attention to the crude provincial script of a South Saxon charter, contrasting it with the practiced hand of its endorsement, written at the Mercian court.[1] Political strength and renewed contacts with

[1] F. M. Stenton, *The Latin Charters of the Anglo-Saxon Period* (Oxford, 1955), p. 37.

the Continent probably contributed to an efflorescence of Mercian culture which manifested itself in a variety of ways. Many historians are disposed to accept the suggestion that the *Beowulf* poem originated at Offa's court and that the St. Chad Gospels, now at Lichfield, were written in the late eighth century not very far away.

Amidst much that is vague and uncertain the most impressive testimony of Offa's power is still visible. In the last years of his reign a great earthwork was built from the river Dee to the Bristol Channel to define the border between Mercians and Welsh.[1] It reveals a high degree of engineering skill and the control of material resources far beyond those of any earlier king. The line adopted for the Dyke left considerable tracts of English settled land on the Welsh side of the new frontier; it could only have been chosen by a ruler confident of his ability to impose unpopular decisions on his own people in the interests of peace.

3. The Effects of Mercian Supremacy on the Church

How far the control which Aethelbald and Offa exercised over the Church was detrimental to its interests is a question which cannot be answered with confidence, since materials for the history of the southern province are meagre and even the archbishops of Canterbury are little more than names. But the situation in the middle of the eighth century is indicated by the canons of the reforming synod of Clovesho (747). How these are interpreted depends on whether they are compared with an ideal picture of a healthy Church or whether they are juxtaposed with, for example, the canons of the synod of Hertford and Theodore's *Penitential,* with the object of assessing the change which had taken place during the intervening eighty years. The synod was presided over by Archbishop Cuthbert and attended by all the bishops of the southern provinces except Eanfrith of Elmham and its decrees covered every aspect of Church life. By comparison with the earlier canons those of 747 are chiefly remarkable for the positive role enjoined on the bishops. Their first concern is to be for the pastoral care of the districts committed to them; they must conduct a visitation of their dioceses each year to preach, admonish, and prohibit sins of all kinds. Clerics aspiring to the priesthood are first to be examined and approved by their

[1] For a full account of all matters concerning the Dyke, C. Fox, *Offa's Dyke* (London, 1955).

bishops and after ordination priests must live in accordance with their vocations, setting a good example of life to their people and being diligent in baptizing and preaching to them; they must know the words of the mass, the service of baptism, the creed, and the Lord's Prayer in English. There is much detailed instruction concerning the practice of religion both for priests and laity in chapters dealing with the fasts of the Church, almsgiving and the like. There were obviously pseudomonasteries in southern as in northern England which, nonetheless, the bishops must visit and help; abbots and abbesses are to be encouraged to live according to rule. Here again the bishop can be seen taking a positive role for, whereas the synod of Hertford was concerned to preserve the freedom of monastic communities from episcopal interference, this duty was now specifically imposed upon them. Bishops in 747 were made responsible for making known the reforming canons throughout their dioceses and requiring them to be observed; if they failed to secure observance they were instructed to report the offenders to the archbishop in synod. The chapters of the synod show that the practice of the English Church left much to be desired, but also that it compared favourably with the Church of Theodore or with the church life of Gaul at this time; order was maintained through a territorial episcopate and its collective action at Clovesho shows both that it knew what needed amendment and that it intended reform.

Such evidence of continuing zeal for reform and the fact that provincial synods continued to meet during the eighth century is generally discounted because of the evil reputations of Aethelbald and Offa who successively dominated southern England. At the source of such judgment is a letter sent from Francia in 746 by Archbishop Boniface and seven other missionary bishops to King Aethelbald and the controversies generated by Offa's encroachment on the primacy of Canterbury by his creation of a third archbishopric in England. Boniface's letter begins with praise for the king, who had acquired a reputation for generous almsgiving, for suppressing crime, and maintaining good order within his kingdom; it continued with reproach. Boniface has heard that Aethelbald has no wife but many women and compounded his sins by committing them in monasteries with nuns consecrated to God. Since the king's example will be followed by his subjects the English people will become degenerate, unable to defend themselves in battle and, deserted by God for their crimes, will be destroyed by Him. The letter continued, ' it has been told us that you have violated many privileges of churches and monasteries and have stolen from them certain revenues . . . he who seizes the money of his neighbour commits iniquity; but he who takes away the money of the church commits sacrilege ', and concludes with the warning that royal debauchery and attacks on ecclesiastical privilege were unknown until the times of Ceolred, king of the Mercians, and Osred, king of the Deirans and Bernicians, both of whom were punished by the Almighty for their wickedness.[1]

The charges against Aethelbald's personal morality rest on hearsay, whereas the knowledge that as a young man and an exile he was an intimate friend of the hermit Guthlac of Croyland rests on unimpeachable authority. If true, it should be remembered that Alcuin's hero Charlemagne would hardly have satisfied the ethical standards demanded by Boniface. Similarly, the complaint that Aethelbald violated ecclesiastical privileges and appropriated ecclesiastical revenues may also be true, but nevertheless defensible in the eyes of any but the most prejudiced ecclesiastics. In southern as well as in northern England the mutiliplication of pseudomonasteries ruled by laymen and bearing less than their fair share of secular obligations may have threatened to produce the same disastrous consequences as Bede lamented had already occurred in Northumbria. Aethelbald may have had good reason for imposing heavier burdens on ecclesiastical land—like Eadberht of Northumbria's suppression of pseudomonasteries and Charles Martel's use of Church lands for the endowment of his military followers, it was an answer to the problem of compelling a wealthy but powerful Church to accept a share in the defence of the kingdom. Any solution generated ecclesiastical protest. It is possible that the accusations of immorality brought against Aethelbald were no more than the inevitable corollary of a policy which limited ecclesiastical privilege.

That Offa's actions in establishing a third archbishopric were inspired by political motives is as certain as that they ensured the

[1] The nature of the Mercian kings' violation of ecclesiastical privilege is debatable. Stenton, *Anglo-Saxon England*, p. 204 followed W. H. Stevenson in *E.H.R.*, XXIX (1914) in thinking that ecclesiastical lands were from the beginning subject to military service and inclined to the view that the exactions complained of were financial. E. John has argued, *Land Tenure in Early England* (Leicester, 1960), pp. 64-79, that Church lands were originally exempt from military service and that Aethelbald imposed on them the burdens of bridgework and fortress work, to which Offa added the obligation to fyrd-service. An important contribution to the discussion has been made by Brooks, ' Development of military obligations in eighth and ninth century England ', in *England Before the Conquest*, pp. 69-84.

hostility towards him of all subsequent ecclesiastical historians; but they are evidence neither of his hostility to the Church nor of indifference to to its interests. How far Hadrian was reluctantly persuaded to fall in with the king's wishes we do not know, but the excuse for the division, that the province of Canterbury was too large, was reasonable. Alcuin, who was not backward in commenting adversely on ecclesiastical developments in England, shows no sense of outrage in his letters, though he was pleased when the rights of Canterbury were restored; even then he pleaded that Hygeberht of Lichfield should retain his pallium so long as he lived. Alcuin's letters to Offa are markedly friendly in tone, and that this was not mere flattery is shown in a letter he wrote to the Mercian ealdorman, Osbert, soon after the king's death: 'Admonish all the race of the Mercians diligently to observe the good, moderate and chaste customs, which Offa of blessed memory established for them.'

The other important ecclesiastical event in Offa's reign, the legatine visitation of 786, shortly preceded the negotiations for the creation of the Lichfield archbishopric, and shows the king in a more favourable light. The legates were received with honour by the king and a southern council promised to reform all the matters which, in the pope's view, needed amendment. On the return of George of Ostia from Northumbria a Mercian council undertook to observe the additional decrees which the legate had there formulated. The atmosphere in which the legation was accomplished appears to have been friendly throughout and in his report to Pope Hadrian, George emphasized the respect for the papacy which he encountered at Offa's court. There is little in the legatine decrees to substantiate the notion of a Church in need of reform.

Whatever the personal deficiencies of the Mercian kings may have been they do not appear to have affected the Church adversely and their shortcomings were more than counterbalanced by the internal peace which their power imposed. It is even arguable, from the viewpoint of Latin Christianity, that the exploits of English missionaries on the Continent give the eighth century a better claim than the age of Theodore of Tarsus to be regarded as the golden age of the Anglo-Saxon Church. The concern with which their enterprises were followed and the support which they received from all parts of England from both men and women, argues that religious enthusiasm was maintained at a high level.

8

ENGLAND AND EUROPE

1. BEFORE THE EIGHTH CENTURY

WHILE Britain remained part of the Roman Empire contacts with the Roman world of western and southern Europe, with the lands north of Hadrian's Wall, and with Ireland were varied and close. Even forty years after the legions had withdrawn it seemed natural to some Britons in time of adversity to appeal to the Roman governor of Gaul, and Gallic churchmen continued to feel a measure of responsibility for their co-religionists. But after the middle of the fifth century Britain contained two mutually hostile cultures and contacts between the lowland zone of Britain and the old Roman world became increasingly tenuous as Germanic attacks on the lands on both sides of the English Channel became more intense. Britain did not, in consequence, become isolated from Europe. Instead of administrators and traders from Rome, Gaul, and the Rhineland, shiploads of foreigners from the lands adjacent to the North Sea and the Baltic came to eastern England to conquer and settle. Meanwhile western England remained for long in British hands and in the last half of the fifth century and for long after, the Irish Sea was the centre of a Celtic province in which Britain and Ireland were closely linked. Between this area and southern Gaul and the Mediterranean the traditional connections were maintained by traders and churchmen; Mediterranean pottery of sixth-century date has been discovered on Cornish, Welsh, Scottish, and Irish sites, and it has been shown that the Latin inscriptions of Celtic Britain borrowed their styles not from Roman Britain but from Gaul, the epigraphy of Wales in particular being modelled on that of the Lyon-Vienne district. Even eastern

England, although cut off from southern Gaul and Italy, did not entirely lose its cross-Channel contacts with northern Gaul. There were Saxon settlements on the southern coast of the Channel as well as in Britain and certain place names near Boulogne have been explained as originating in a settlement from early Saxon Britain; there is also a considerable body of evidence from Kent pointing to substantial contacts with the Franks.[1] In the fifth and sixth centuries the geographical range of British overseas relations was wider than ever before.

In the first confused years after settlement migration was determined largely by the fluctuating fortunes of war, nor was it confined to the movement of victorious Germanic peoples westward. In the second half of the fifth century and again in the second half of the sixth century substantial migrations of Britons transformed Armorica into Brittany. At about the middle of the century Procopius, the Byzantine historian, retailing information supplied to him by Franks at Constantinople reported that each of the three races which inhabited Britain, Angles, Frisians, and Britons was so prolific that it sent large numbers of people every year to the Frankish lands, where they were settled in sparsely populated areas of the kingdom. This statement accords both with our knowledge of the British migration to Armorica and with the general situation which obtained in the years after Mount Badon when the Saxon advance had been halted and no new lands for settlement were available to them. No literary evidence exists which would enable any reliable estimate to be made as to how far relations were maintained between the conquerors and their native lands but they may safely be inferred from our knowledge of contacts yet further afield. Scandinavian archaeologists are satisfied that a close connection existed in the fifth and sixth centuries between southern Norway and the coastal districts of England and France. More recently the study of the objects found in the Sutton Hoo burial has convinced many historians that intercourse between Sweden and Suffolk began in the first half of the sixth century and was to some extent maintained until the beginning of the next: Swedish objects were found in the Suffolk grave while Suffolk-made sword pommels have been found in Sweden.

By the middle of the sixth century evidence begins to accumulate which suggests that more settled political conditions were assisting

[1] *Supra* pp. 26-7.

a tentative resumption of traditional contacts with western Europe. Though the *History* of Gregory of Tours contains only two references to England, both relating to the marriage of Chariberht I's daughter to King Aethelberht of Kent, and his narrative totally ignores the activities of Irishmen in Gaul, it is clear that the dynastic marriage was a culmination rather than a starting point of contacts between the Frankish kingdom and the Kentings. That slaves were an early export to the Continent is proved by the fact that Pope Gregory I saw English boys in the slave market at Rome between 574 and 578 and some years later he ordered that English boys should be bought in Gaul and educated in monasteries. With the despatch of Augustine direct relations between Rome and England were established and in consequence political and cultural relations with Gaul, the country through which all travellers passed, were intensified. More remarkable was the intensified impact of Ireland on the area of the Roman world. Conversion came late, but Christianity rapidly took root and, after a period in which British ecclesiastics from Wales gave much assistance to the new Church, Irishmen, some years before Augustine's mission, began not only to evangelize their transmarine and still pagan neighbours in Pictland but to travel and work on the Continent, while still maintaining friendly relations with western Britain. Before 565 Columba was established on Iona; Columbanus left the schools of Bangor and before his death in 615 had founded monasteries at Annegray, Luxeuil, and Bobbio.

Contacts with western Europe multiplied in the course of the seventh century. A Frankish charter provides evidence of the presence of English traders at the fair of St. Denis and references in saints' *Lives* suggest that merchant ships from Britain sailed regularly to ports on the north coast of France. An English slave, Balthild, became queen of Clovis II, king of the Franks (639-657). But numismatic evidence points to the danger of over-emphasizing the contribution made by commerce to overseas relations at this period[1] It appears probable that during the reign of Aethelberht a few gold coins were struck copying Merovingian models, but judging from their rarity the demand for them was so small that the practice of minting them was abandoned. The absence of any English coins from

[1] P. Grierson, ' La function sociale de la monnaie en Angleterre aux VIIe-VIIIe siecles ', *Moneti e scambi nell alto medioevi* (Settimane di studio del Centro italiano di studi sull alto medioevi VII) (Spoleto, 1961), and, more generally, the same author's ' Commerce in the Dark Ages: a critique of the evidence '. *T.R.H.S.* fifth series, IX (1959).

those found at Sutton Hoo, together with the absence of coins from Kentish finds of the first half of the seventh century, suggests that in the middle of the seventh century there was still little use to be found for a gold coinage. By contrast, the Crondall hoard of about 670 contained seventy-two English coins and twenty Merovingian and Frisian coins, the English coins derived from Merovingian models but minted in a number of places all in south-east England. The evidence suggests a growing need for coinage, created by the trade in luxury goods and by its utility for the payment of wergilds and fines, but also that the uses of coined money were restricted to these purposes and to an area narrowly confined to south-eastern England. The stimuli to European exchanges at this time were still primarily political and, still more, ecclesiastical.

Gaul was one of the refuges to which English political exiles fled; in 627 Sigeberht, king of the East Saxons went there, was converted and on his return established schools in imitation of those he had seen in France. After Edwin's death in battle in 633 his sons were despatched for protection to the Frankish king Dagobert. At this time too, a number of English princesses became nuns in Frankish monasteries.[1] Gaulish bishops were to be found in England: Felix in East Anglia was a Burgundian; Agilbert, though educated in Ireland, was a Frank by birth; Wine, though a Saxon, received his orders in Gaul; Hlothere was Agilbert's nephew. Conversely, Bishop Wilfrid was as much at home on the far side of the Channel as in England for he had spent five years of study in Gaul and Italy. During the course of his first visit to Rome in 654 he spent some months at Lyons, and returning, lived there for three years as the protégé of the bishop. He was involved in Frankish politics and only saved from the death penalty by virtue of his foreign birth. After the synod of Whitby he went to Gaul for consecration. In 676 he was instrumental in arranging for the return of Dagobert II from his exile in Ireland to Austrasia, thereby incurring the enmity of Ebroin, mayor of the palace of Neustria. Ten years before, English interest in Frankish affairs had seemed so real and potentially dangerous that Ebroin had detained Archbishop Theodore and Abbot Hadrian in Gaul, because he suspected them of having undertaken some mission from the emperor (Constans II) to the king of Northumbria which might be directed against the kingdom which he controlled. Wilfrid's friend Benedict Biscop lived at Lérins for two years and on several

[1] *Supra* p. 96.

occasions during his six visits to Rome broke the journey for a time in Frankish cities like Vienne where he had friends who bought for him the books he wanted for the library he was building up at Wearmouth; it was in Gaul that he recruited masons and glassmakers.

Often Gaul was crossed simply because it was on the route to Rome. English churchmen were fully conscious of the papal primacy over the English Church, nor was their veneration for Rome confined to ecclesiastics. Alchfrith, Oswiu's son, had hoped to visit Rome in the company of Benedict Biscop though the project never materialized. But Caedwalla, king of the West Saxons, relinquishing his kingdom in 689, went to Rome and died there; his successor Ine after a reign of thirty-seven years did the same. In 709 Cenred of Mercia and Offa, king of the East Saxons, went to Rome, were tonsured and died there. These kings founded just outside Rome a hostel or hostels for English pilgrims where they lived as a separate community, the *schola Saxonum*. Women as well as men undertook the pilgrimage and Boniface later complained that the towns of northern Italy were overrun with English prostitutes, reduced to desperate straits because they set out without adequate provision for the journey. Bede's comment on the Roman pilgrimage, ' the which practice in these days many Englishmen, both noble and common, spiritual and temporal, men and women were to do ' had ample substance.

A remarkable characteristic of the seventh century was the extent to which Irishmen continued to contribute to the religious and cultural life of the western world, including Britain. Following the paths pioneered by Columba and Columbanus they travelled in significant numbers to Britain, Gaul, and Italy. North Britain was converted by Aidan and his helpers. An Irish scholar, Maelduibh, founded a community distinguished for its learning at Malmesbury, and Dicuil evangelized in Sussex from a base as Bosham. To East Anglia came Fursa who having founded a monastery at *Cnobheresburg* (Burgh Castle) left it in charge of his brother to settle at Lagny-sur-Marne; he founded a new monastery at Péronne which became head of a confederation of churches and a lively centre of Irish activities. His successors at Péronne were his brothers Ultan and Foillean, who founded a monastery at Fosse near Namur, then Cellan, a correspondent of Aldhelm. Nivelles, one of the dependencies of Péronne, had an Irish abbot some time before 684. An Irish bishop, Ronan, is found in charge of a monastery at Mazerolles in the diocese of

Poitiers. Bobbio, in northern Italy, was another monastic centre where Irishmen left their distinctive mark; they worked in the scriptorium revealing their presence by their use of Irish abbreviations, modes of decoration and script.

Ireland not only despatched pilgrims and scholars to the West but was itself receptive to influences from the outside world, while the renown of its scholarship and asceticism attracted pilgrims from other lands. The works of Isidore of Seville (c. 570-636) reached Ireland with remarkable rapidity. Many Englishmen migrated there both before and after the synod of Whitby and Bede testifies that they were treated generously by their hosts, given food, and taught without charge. Chad, later bishop of Lindisfarne and Lichfield, and Aethelwine, bishop of Lindsey, had both studied in Ireland. Ecgfrith's expedition to northern Ireland in 684, which did great damage, was lamented by Bede because ' the Irish had ever been great friends of the English nation '. On at least one occasion, as we have seen, Ireland was the refuge of a continental political exile; when Grimoald, mayor of the palace in Austrasia, attempted to secure the royal title for his son, the Merovingian king Dagobert II was tonsured and sent there. The total incorporation of Ireland into the western world was symbolized by the delegation which went to Rome in 630 to obtain further information about the Easter question and on its return confirmed the southern Irish in their decision to adopt Roman ways. By the end of the seventh century England and Ireland were more closely linked with the Christian world of the West than at any time since the collapse of the Empire.

Among educated men there was a great interest in the outside world, especially those parts of it which formed the scene of the Bible narrative. Adomnan wrote about the Holy Places, though he had travelled no further east than Northumbria; his principal informant was a Gaulish bishop, Arculf, who had visited the Holy Land, Egypt, and Constantinople and on his return been ship-wrecked off the coast of Britain; but Adomnan took pains to supplement Arculf's story with details culled from the books in his library. King Aldfrith of Northumbria ordered the book to be copied for use in Northumbria and further revealed his geographical interests by giving an estate to Wearmouth in exchange for a book on cosmography which Benedict Biscop had bought on one of his visits to Rome.

If, by contrast with the scattered though ample evidence for the unity of the Roman and Christian world provided by ecclesiastical writers, little can be gleaned from the literary sources concerning its contacts with the still pagan peoples of north and north-west Europe, other evidence is not lacking. Direct communication with Norway and the Baltic countries probably petered out, but only because northern trade became increasingly dominated by Frisians, whose activities in England are well attested. Bede tells of a Northumbrian thegn who, taken prisoner by a Mercian nobleman, was sold in London to a Frisian; and the reception afforded to Wilfrid by the Frisian king Aldgisl does not suggest that Englishmen were unknown there. But the most convincing evidence of trading connections between England and Frisia is numismatic. The minting of a gold coinage in England had begun late and was of brief duration; by the last quarter of the seventh century it was replaced by a silver currency. Silver coins were struck on both sides of the Channel by English and by Frisian mints and whatever their origin they were of similar weight and type. They reached a peak circulation in the second quarter of the eighth century and have been found widely distributed from southern France to Scandinavia; they indicate close and important trading links between England and Frisia from before the end of the seventh century.

Despite their commercial vitality the Frisians remained obstinately pagan. Their heathenism was reinforced by their hostility to the Christian Franks, always threatening their independence, and was unchallenged because of the inertia of the Frankish Church. Within a very few years of the synod of Whitby Englishmen had made it their concern to remedy this situation and the missionary zeal of the Northumbrian Church had extended the field of its activities to include the lands inhabited by their continental kinsfolk.

2. ENGLISH MISSIONS TO THE CONTINENT: ALCUIN

The first mission, to the Frisians, came about almost by accident. Wilfrid, driven from Northumbria in 678, appealed to Rome.[1] His

---

[1] W. Levison, *England and the Continent in the Eighth Century* (Oxford, 1946) is fundamental; it should now be supplemented by J. W. Wallace-Hadrill, 'A background to St. Boniface's Mission', *England Before the Conquest*, pp. 35-48. The same author's reviews of T. Schieffer, *Winfrid-Bonifatius und die christliche Grundlegung Europas* (Freiburg, 1954) in *E.H.R.*, LXIX (1954); and of *Sankt Bonifatius, Gedenkgabe zum zwölfhunderdsten Todestag* (Fulda, 1954) in *E.H.R.*, LXXI (1956), make available in English the results of much recent German scholarship.

recent involvement in Frankish politics having incurred for him the enmity of Ebroin, mayor of the palace of Neustria, it was impolitic for him to travel through Gaul by the most direct route via Quentovic. Instead, he landed in Frisia where he stayed for some months in the winter of 678-9, hospitably entertained by King Aldgisl. He engaged in missionary work, and temporarily he achieved spectacular success. But, undertaken without preparation, his efforts lacked support from England, and Aldgisl's successor Radbod was less accommodating. Though it was later believed in Northumbria that Wilfrid's pioneer work laid the foundations for that of Willibrord, his successor found there little to encourage him. The initiative for the second mission came from an Englishman vowed to permanent exile from his native land and living in Ireland; his story is told in some detail by Bede. This man, Egbert, was eager to engage in the work of converting the heathen kinsmen of the English overseas, but it was revealed to one of his monks in a dream that he must remain in Ireland. In his place he sent Wictberht, another monk, to the Frisians. After two years Wictberht returned home having achieved no success. Undismayed, Egbert despatched Willibrord and eleven companions to make another attempt.

Born in 658 in Northumbria Willibrord while still a boy had been given to Wilfrid's Ripon; from the beginning he was taught to venerate the authority of Rome. In the same year as Wilfrid was driven from his bishopric Willibrord migrated to Ireland where he remained for twelve years. His new master, Egbert, shared both Wilfrid's devotion to Rome (it was he who persuaded the community at Iona to adopt the Roman Easter) and his missionary zeal. In 690 Willibrord and his companions landed in Frisia at a time when the political situation was propitious. Pippin, mayor of the palace of Austrasia, had defeated the Neustrians at Tertry in 687 and thereby reunited the Frankish kingdom, ruled nominally by a Merovingian, in reality by himself. The first task he set himself was the restoration of Frankish frontiers and his first campaign to this end was directed against Radbod in Frisia. Under Pippin's protection Willibrord began his work in the newly conquered territories between the sea and the Zuyder Zee. Shortly afterwards he visited Rome in order to secure papal blessing and support for his mission. During his absence his associates elected one of their number, Suidberht, bishop, and sent him to England where he was consecrated by Wilfrid during the vacancy at Canterbury which followed the death of Archbishop

Theodore; but Suidberht soon left Frisia to work in Westphalia and Willibrord's leadership in Frisia was unaffected.

In 695, on Pippin's initiative, he went to Rome for the second time. The purpose of this visit was to secure his consecration as archbishop of the Frisians, an office which would give him authority over a new province of the Church. Consecrated by Pope Sergius and given the Roman name Clement, on returning to Frisia he established his archiepiscopal see at Utrecht. Pippin's death in 714 was followed by five years of civil discord which encouraged Radbod to revolt against Frankish domination and impeded the progress of the mission, but the accession to power of Charles Martel permitted its resumption. For twenty years more, until his death in 739, Willibrord continued to work in western Frisia, the area under Frankish control.

Willibrord's mission was not only the first of the large-scale overseas ventures but in several important respects was typical of the whole Anglo-Saxon missionary effort of the eighth century. Willibrord took with him to Frisia the English veneration for the papacy. As soon as he had secured Pippin's backing he turned to Pope Sergius for approval and support, and brought back from Rome relics for his new churches. All Willibrord's successors showed a similar concern to enter into a direct relationship with Rome. That concern was shown not only by visits to Rome but in the organization adopted by their churches in the newly converted lands and in those areas of older Christianity which Boniface subsequently supervised. Among the Franks the authority of the metropolitans, the governors of the Roman ecclesiastical provinces, had become almost extinct; but the English Church had from the beginning been organized on a provincial basis and it had become the normal practice for an elected metropolitan to receive from the pope a pallium, a band of white wool, which was both symbol and authority for the exercise of his function as head of the province. It became customary for the bearer of a pallium to be styled 'archbishop' and during the seventh century the terms metropolitan and archbishop became interchangeable. Only the pope could confer a pallium, which gave to its recipient a share in papal authority, and before receiving it the archbishop-elect made a written profession of faith to the pope. When Willibrord visited Rome for the second time it was with the object of creating a new province of the Church, ruled by an archbishop whose authority, derived from Rome, was symbolized by his possession of a

pallium. Willibrord was a monk and in this respect, too, he anticipated future developments; all the eighth-century missionaries were
monks and one of their first concerns was to establish monasteries
in the newly won territories. In this there was nothing incompatible
with the desire to establish a regular diocesan episcopate; the role
of the monastery within the diocese was first as the spearhead of
missionary endeavour; then, as Christianity became firmly established, the monastery became a permanent centre in which the
monastic ideal might be fully translated into reality and a centre
of religious instruction within the diocese. Willibrord's mission was
typical also of those which followed in the interest it aroused among
Englishmen at home. He had been given eleven companions, they
were joined by others, and their achievements were known to, and
followed with concern by, the inmates of monasteries all over England. On his last journey to Rome, in 703, Wilfrid deliberately went
out of his way to visit Willibrord on the scene of his first missionary
enterprise. Most important of all, Willibrord's mission enjoyed
throughout the support of Charles Martel, who is credited with the
initiative which led to the creation of the achbishopric of Utrecht.
More than to anyone else it was a vital interest of Frankish rulers
to establish stability in the lands beyond the Rhine. Charles Martel's
encouragement of missionary work in Frisia and still more in Germany—for the Carolingians were great territorial lords in the Rhineland—was rooted in a shrewd appreciation of political realities.

Willibrord's success, though striking, was limited. The separate
Frisian province did not survive him but was incorporated into the
German archbishopric of Boniface and eventually Utrecht became
a diocesan see in the province of Köln. The Frisian lands to the
east of the Zuyder Zee as far as the Weser were still heathen and
attempts to extend Christianity beyond the area of Frankish political
control were unsuccessful. Suidberht had been compelled to withdraw from Westphalia and two more Englishmen, brothers named
Hewald, had been martyred while attempting to preach to the
pagan Saxons. Willibrord himself journeyed to Denmark, bringing
back Danish boys whom he hoped might be trained as missionaries
there, but this initiative similarly met with total failure. During
Willibrord's own lifetime the fame of the West Saxon Wynfrith had
eclipsed that of his one-time leader.

Wynfrith was born in western Wessex about 675. In childhood he
entered the monastery at Exeter and later moved to Nursling near

7

Southampton. On one occasion he was chosen by King Ine and a West Saxon synod to act as their envoy to the archbishop of Canterbury; and in 717 the Nursling community chose him as their abbot. He was clearly destined for a distinguished ecclesiastical career. But already by 716 he had declared his determination to evangelize abroad; in that year he went to Frisia, but missionary work being impracticable at that time because the Frisians were in rebellion against the Franks, he returned to Nursling. In 718 he again left England, never to return. Following the precedent set by Willibrord his first move was to seek support from the pope, and in 719 he received a papal commission to preach to the heathen; like Willibrord he received a new name, Boniface, by which thereafter he has almost universally been known. His first preaching was in Thuringia, but on receiving the news of Radbod's death and the resumption of the Frisian mission he joined Willibrord. Willibrord wished to keep him, but in 722, having been invited to Rome by Pope Gregory II, Boniface offered a profession of faith as was usual for bishops of the metropolitan district of the pope, was consecrated bishop, and made a sworn promise of obedience and fidelity to St. Peter, to the pope and his successors. No more direct relationship with the papacy was conceivable, and it was maintained throughout his life. During the next years Boniface sent reports to Rome on the progress of his mission and referred there for answers to the problems that arose. When a pope died Boniface renewed his subjection and promise of service to the Holy See and asked that the new pope should continue to show friendship towards him.

Commended by Gregory II to Charles Martel's protection, Boniface returned to work, first in Hesse then in Thuringia. In this area Christianity was not unknown but it lacked both discipline and organization. Assisted by a ' great multitude ' of English helpers, monks, clerics, and nuns, Boniface founded churches and monasteries. The heads of Boniface's new communities were at first predominantly English—Wigbert, abbot of Fritzlar; Leoba, abbess of Tauberbischofsheim; Thecla, abbess of Kitzingen—but they were soon to be assisted by Germans. The success of the mission was formally recognized when in 732 Pope Gregory III sent a pallium to Boniface and made him archbishop, head of the German province of the Church, though as yet without a metropolitan seat. A further phase of expansion appeared to have been prepared by Charles Martel's defeat of the Westphalian Saxons in 738 but that victory did not reduce the Saxons permanently to submission; it did, however, lead to Boniface's third visit to Rome and to the reorganization of the German Church. On his return Duke Odilo invited him to reform the Bavarian Church which was divided by him into four territorial dioceses. In 741 Hesse, Thuringia, and southern and northern Franconia received bishops, three of them Anglo-Saxons. Archbishop Boniface now possessed eight suffragans, though he still lacked a diocese of his own.

On the death of Charles Martel in 741 the government of the Frankish kingdom was shared by his two sons; Pippin ruled Neustria while Carloman governed Austrasia, the eastern part of the kingdom, which included the territories east of the Rhine over which Boniface was spiritual head. Both kings were eager for Boniface to assist them in the reformation of the Frankish Church. One of Carloman's first acts was to summon an Austrasian synod in 742, the first to have been held for forty years. The purpose of the assembly was to promote reform by bringing the practice of the Franks into line with that of Frisia and Germany. Another Austrasian synod met in the following year and in 744 Pippin convened a Neustrian synod at Soissons. In 745 and 747 synods of the whole Frankish Church assembled which, under Boniface's direction, promulgated reforming decrees relating to clerical celibacy, the observance of marriage laws and other matters. A beginning was made towards re-establishing the provincial organization of the Frankish Church when, after the synod of Soissons, the pope was asked to send pallia to the bishops of Rheims, Soissons, and Rouen, though only Rouen achieved archiepiscopal status immediately. In 745 a proposal for erecting Köln into an archiepiscopal see for Boniface had been defeated by the opposition of the Austrasian nobility, but soon afterwards he received the see of Mainz. Newly reorganized under Boniface's direction the Frankish Church was now brought into a direct relationship with Rome. A list of twenty-seven questions of canon law was sent to Pope Zacharias for answer; the synod of 747 sent a formal profession of obedience to Rome; even Boniface's opponents appealed to papal authority.

At the time of the synod of 747 Boniface was more than seventy years old and increasingly desirous of exchanging the arduous administrative and supervisory burdens of his office and the uncongenial contacts which life at court imposed upon him for the more straightforward hazards of the missionary. Having arranged for his

English disciple Lull to succeed him at Mainz and for his own eventual burial at his monastery at Fulda in Hesse he returned to Friesland in 753 to preach to the heathen in the lands north-east of the Zuyder Zee. In the following year, with Eoba, the Anglo-Saxon bishop of Utrecht and more than fifty companions, he was killed by pagans at Dokkum in Friesland.

While recognizing the importance of Boniface's achievement it remains possible to doubt whether he was the prime agent through whose work the Frankish Church accepted the teaching that the pope was the supreme head of the Church; or that he was the architect of the crucially important alliance between the papacy and the Carolingians. Of the closeness of the Anglo-Saxon Church to Rome and the lively awareness of Anglo-Saxon churchmen of all they owed to the papal emissaries Augustine, Theodore, and Hadrian there is no doubt. But there is little evidence for the commonly held views, either that the Anglo-Saxon Church was regarded by popes as enjoying a uniquely close relationship to Rome or that the Frankish Church lacked contacts with Rome and was unconscious of the Roman primacy. At Whitby the official leader of the Roman party had been the Frankish Agilbert, later to become bishop of Paris; Roman influences are identifiable in Frankish liturgical practice and the cult of St. Peter was strong in the Frankish lands. Letters passing between popes and Frankish kings and bishops took for granted their friendship and the dependence of the Frankish Church on the Roman. It is true that the collapse of royal authority in the late Merovingian period had permitted the local landed aristocracy, and the higher clergy with whom they were linked, to assume a substantial measure of independence of central control, and in some regions this state of affairs had led to a relaxation of ecclesiastical discipline. But it was by no means general and it implied no loss of regard for Rome. Once given an effective lead many Frankish ecclesiastics proved eager to press on with reforms and needed no urging to establish close contacts with the papacy. Many of the abuses which Boniface legislated against in the Frankish Church were also to be found in the English Church—the canons of the English Council of Clovesho were to a large extent modelled on the decrees of the reforming Frankish Councils—yet they existed in England despite the veneration felt for Rome. If Boniface directed the reform and reorganization of the Frankish Church it remains true that the initiative came from Carloman and Pippin and that Boniface could be assured of a substantial degree of support from within the Frankish Church. The lay rulers, most of all, were conscious that the regeneration of secular and ecclesiastical authority went forward together. They encouraged reform, but they also controlled it. Charles Martel had alienated ecclesiastical possessions to provide endowments for his military followers: when the reformers attempted to secure their resumption they were defeated because the security of Carolingian rule depended on them. In a real sense Boniface was a willing instrument of Carolingian policy, which achieved its ultimate, though not necessarily long-anticipated, triumph when Boniface crowned Pippin king of the Franks.

The Anglo-Saxon missions on the Continent, irrespective of the role ascribed to Boniface, exercised an important if unconscious influence in England. The Frisian mission was a predominantly Northumbrian enterprise, but that of the West Saxon Boniface drew helpers from all the English kingdoms. His fortunes were closely followed, with pride and sometimes with anxiety, by the men and women of all races with whom Boniface corresponded, in Northumbria, Mercia, Kent, and Wessex; they wrote letters of encouragement to him and sent gifts which were gratefully received. The continental mission must have exercised a definite though imponderable influence on the process of eroding the consciousness of tribal differences among the English peoples, for this was a common enterprise whose agents were Englishmen irrespective of their local origins. The anniversary of Boniface and his companions was celebrated as a feast day by the whole English Church.

Boniface's decision to resume his missionary work in 753 shows his conviction that the work of reorganizing and reforming the Frankish Church could safely be left in Frankish hands. Under the direction first of Pippin and then of Charlemagne the provincial organization of that Church was completed and synods continued to be held fairly regularly which concerned themselves with emphasizing the authority of the bishops in their dioceses and improving the condition of the clergy. Such success had attended the reformers' efforts to establish direct communication between the Frankish Church and Rome that there was no longer need for Englishmen to act as intermediaries. Before the end of the century there were even indications that the earlier current was in reverse and that reformed Frankish practices were beginning to exert influence on England.

The ideal of a common life for cathedral and collegiate clergy which had been popularized by Chrodegang, bishop of Metz, was emphasized by the papal legates to England in 786 and was for a time accepted at Canterbury. In about 800 the office of archdeacon was introduced into Kent, though it failed to take root.

But not all parallel developments on the Continent and in England at this time should be explained in terms of conscious borrowing. When contacts between two areas are close it is natural to assume that when innovations appear in both at about the same time the practice of one area has been borrowed from the other; but parallel developments may be the consequence of the independent operation of the same influences in both areas. It is, for example, doubtful whether the practice of anointing kings was borrowed by the English from the Franks. The first evidence for the ceremony among the Franks was at the coronation of Pippin in 752. In England the practice was referred to generally for the first time in the canons of the legislative council of 786, and the first specific recorded anointing was that of Offa's son Ecgfrith in 787. The close juxtaposition of the dates could be misleading. Kings of Dalriada and of Ireland may have been anointed, as those of Visigothic Spain certainly were, in the seventh century, all of them basing the practice on the Old Testament record of Samuel's consecration of David. It is possible that the special mention of unction in 787 is explicable on the grounds that it occurred in the course of a ceremony which invited special comment on other grounds; it was the first occasion on which a son was made king during his father's lifetime; it may not have been the first royal anointing in England.

The manner of Boniface's death proved that much remained to be done in the missionary field and in this work Englishmen continued to be prominent. The conversion of Frisia was completed after Boniface's death from the mission centre at Utrecht, in which Englishmen were prominent. Between 754 and about 775 it was committed to the care of a Frankish abbot, Gregory, assisted by an English collaborator, Aluberht, who in 767 was consecrated bishop at York. Anglo-Saxons are known to have attended Gregory's school and Frisians came to York for study. The Englishman Lebuin was sent by Gregory to Deventer in the eastern Netherlands, where he worked and died. In about 770 the Northumbrian Willehad was sent to Friesland by the Northumbrian king (Alhred 765-774) and his synod; after working for a time in eastern Frisia Charlemagne sent him into the Saxon lands between the Weser and the Elbe, recently conquered by the Franks. A Saxon rebellion in 782 compelled Willehad to abandon this territory temporarily, but when Widukind, the Saxon leader, submitted and accepted Christianity Willehad returned. In 787 he became the first bishop of Bremen, where two years later he died; this was probably the first see established in Saxon territory. At Mainz Boniface was succeeded by his English pupil Lull, who not only preserved many of his master's letters but in his own correspondence demonstrated that the contacts between the exiles and their homeland continued in the same ways as before.

Soon after Boniface's death Archbishop Cuthbert of Canterbury wrote to Lull proposing a renewal of the community of prayer established by Boniface with the church of Canterbury; in 773 King Alhred of Northumbria and his queen Osgifu similarly asked for Lull's prayers for themselves, their friends and relations in return for the prayers offered for Lull and his associates in all the monasteries of Northumbria. Presents continued to be exchanged, the missionaries being particularly concerned to secure books of all kinds which would be of practical use to them in their labours. Lull asked the abbot of Wearmouth and Archbishop Aethelbert of York for works of Bede and books of cosmography, sending the abbot, in his turn, the gift of a silk robe for Bede's relics and a multicoloured coverlet to protect him from the cold. The abbot on another occasion had sent Lull twenty knives and a robe made of otter skins by the hand of a priest on pilgrimage to Rome, but never learned whether they had arrived safely because the priest died at Benevento. Benedict Biscop, a century earlier, had sought glass-makers in Gaul to work on his new church, but they did not instruct the natives in their craft; the abbot asks Lull that if there is anyone skilled in making glass vessels he may be sent to Wearmouth ' because we are ignorant and destitute of that art '; the same letter tells Lull that it would delight the abbot if he sent a harpist as well. Like Boniface, Lull, also a West Saxon, wrote to all regions of England.

The incessant demands made by them for books reflects the recognition by the English missionaries that the education of a native German clergy was an essential task if the work of preaching was to bear permanent fruit. It was a role that they were ideally fitted to perform, for since the time of Theodore, Hadrian, and Maelduibh

Latin scholarship in England had been at a high level, and in many English centres books were collected, read and written. The first concern of education was to produce a clergy able to understand the Latin used in church, able to read and understand the Scriptures and the Fathers, and to interpret them to the laity. But the missionaries were too typical of the tradition in which they had themselves been trained to be satisfied with elementary education. Boniface had been a scholar before he left Nursling; he wrote complicated verse and was regarded as something of an authority on such matters. English schools did not confine their interests within the field of narrowly ecclesiastical learning; from Theodore's time onwards secular learning had been encouraged on the grounds that it assisted in the understanding of the scriptures, and in the middle of the eighth century the Canterbury tradition was still maintained at York, by then the most famous of English schools. The manuscripts which found their way to monastic libraries in Germany and France were both ecclesiastical and secular in content; the missionaries established schools in their newly founded monasteries and in them books were both studied and copied. In this way Willibrord, Boniface, and their assistants contributed significantly to the success of the Carolingian renaissance.

The educational effort which they began culminated in the work of Alcuin, the last of the great Englishmen to leave their mark on the history of western Europe in the eighth century. But whereas Willibrord and Boniface had themselves taken the initiative in their missionary work, the impulse which attracted Alcuin to the Continent was Charlemagne's. Alcuin was the third and greatest of the distinguished scholars produced by the school of York in the eighth century, following Archbishops Egbert and Aethelberht as its master when Aethelberht was promoted to the archbishopric. He was both a scholar and a man of affairs. He accompanied Aethelberht to Rome before 767 and was sent by him on a mission to Charlemagne. Again in 780 Alcuin went to Rome to receive the pallium for Aethelberht's successor Eanbald, and meeting Charlemagne on his return journey in the following year he was invited to join the distinguished group of scholars who had been assembled at the Frankish king's court. Between 782 and 793 Alcuin divided his time between Northumbria and Francia, but from 793 until three years before his death in 804, when sickness necessitated his residence at his abbey of St. Martin of Tours, he lived mostly in the royal court. During these years Alcuin was Charlemagne's principal assistant in his efforts, centred in the palace school, to promote education among both clergy and laity. Though not a powerful nor an original thinker Alcuin was a born teacher who transmitted to the Continent the spiritual and intellectual heritage of the school of York, which in Charlemagne's court was cross-fertilized by the contributions of the other great scholars of the age, Paul the Deacon, Paulinus of Aquileia, and Theodulf of Orleans. Their work transformed the intellectual condition of Gaul. Since it had been Alcuin's personal fame as a scholar which had attracted Charlemagne's attention he, unlike his missionary predecessors, was not attended and followed by a large group of personal disciples. Yet Alcuin never lost contact with England and continued to correspond regularly with his compatriots in both ecclesiastical provinces, and a few Englishmen were appointed to important positions in the Frankish Church. His successor as abbot of Ferrières was the Anglo-Saxon Sigulf who had been his pupil at York, his cousin Beornred became archbishop of Sens, and an Englishman, Fridegis, succeeded him at Tours.

3. DIPLOMATIC AND ECONOMIC CONTACTS

Although the cause of ecclesiastical reform in the Frankish lands now under Charlemagne's rule no longer needed external assistance, in other respects contacts between England and the Continent were fully maintained. Diplomatic relations between the Frankish court and the kings of Mercia and Northumbria became closer than ever before and they occasionally provide evidence of strongly maintained economic links.

In view of the Northumbrian mission effort it was natural that Northumbrians and Franks should be interested in events in each other's kingdoms. Kings of Northumbria and archbishops of York exchanged letters with Charlemagne, and the early Northumbrian annals incorporated into Symeon of Durham's *History* include notices of Charles's campaigns. Conversely the murder of King Ethelred in 796 so outraged Charlemagne that he withheld gifts intended for Northumbrian churches. When Ethelred's successor Eardwulf was expelled from Northumbria in 808 he first took refuge at the Frankish court and next year returned home accompanied by envoys from the pope and the emperor. With Offa of Mercia Charlemagne's contacts were, as we have seen, frequent and variable.[1]

---

[1] *Supra* pp. 167-8.

An interesting byproduct of the negotiations for a marriage alliance between the two royal families was a period of coolness during which Charlemagne prohibited the entry of English merchants to Gaul, to which Offa replied with an embargo on Frankish merchants wishing to come to England. Some years later, a letter from Charlemagne to Offa gives some indication that both parties regarded the trade as worth fostering and suggests that it was economically important. Charlemagne alleged that English merchants had been masquerading as pilgrims with the object of evading their customs dues; if discovered they would be required to pay the normal tolls on their goods. He agreed that English merchants in his dominions and his subjects in England should be under the protection of the kings of their respective countries and if they were oppressed might appeal to royal officers for justice. In reply to Offa's request for certain ' black-stones ' Charlemagne suggested that if Offa would send a representative who knew exactly what was wanted he would ensure that they were provided and asked in return that Offa should ensure that the cloaks exported by the English merchants conformed in size to those sent in former times.

This exchange of letters poses the question how far English trade had been affected by changes which may have occurred in the economy of western Europe in the late seventh and eighth centuries. By some historians it is argued that since European trade had been predominantly a commerce in luxury goods from the eastern Mediterranean, the closing of that sea to Christian traders during the late seventh century, which was a consequence of Islamic expansion, must have affected the economy of western Europe adversely. Whereas Merovingian Gaul was wealthy and still able to operate a money economy based on gold, Carolingian Gaul was poor, with an economy based on great landed estates each striving for self-sufficiency as a consequence of the breakdown of commercial exchanges; the disappearance of gold currencies in both Francia and England was a symptom of the decline.

The tendency of more recent research has been to reject the notions of a healthy Merovingian economy and of Carolingian recession. Merovingian Gaul was in a sorry plight before the effects of Islamic conquest had made themselves felt; the check to Mediterranean trade was of brief duration and quickly resumed, though now through Islamic Spain and Venice instead of the traditional entrepot of Marseilles; the importance of the northern and eastern trade routes handled by the Frisians is more fully recognized than in the past and it was unaffected by political changes in southern Europe. The replacement of a gold by a silver coinage, while partly explicable as the consequence of a physical shortage of gold, far from being a symptom of regression reflected an economy in which the needs of local markets serving the needs of broad sections of society were satisfied; it was healthier and more vigorous than the narrowly based commerce in luxury goods carried over great distances for which gold had been the most suitable means of exchange. If, then, the effects of Islamic expansion in the Mediterranean are discounted as a serious impediment to continental commercial activity, a favourable circumstance for its expansion was that in the eighth century both in Gaul and in England internal peace was better maintained than in previous centuries. By comparison with the endemic civil wars of Merovingian Gaul Carolingian wars were directed towards territorial expansion, while in England, though resentment of Mercian domination provoked strong opposition in Kent, the power of Aethelbald and Offa was sufficient to check the constant warfare between the lesser kingdoms which characterized the period of the Heptarchy.

It seems reasonable to conclude that both western European and English trade expanded during the eighth century. For England, evidence of the kind which has been presented for the earlier period continues to be available. Bede described London as ' a market frequented by the merchants of many nations '; the life of a Frisian saint mentions a Frisian colony at York; an Englishman named Botto was settled in Marseilles. Already the most important English export was wool and woollen cloths, while wine from the Rhineland, glassware, rare pottery, and precious goods from the east continued to be imported. The principal English ports were London, York, and Southampton (Hamwih) and on the Continent, Dorestad on the Rhine and Quentovic on the Canche. But now, for the first time, it can be seen that kings have become aware of the revenue-producing potential of foreign trade. Aethelbald remitted royal tolls on ships for the benefit of the churches at Rochester and Worcester, and for the abbess of Minster in Thanet.

More remarkable testimony to the importance of commercial exchanges are developments in the coinage of both Gaul and England. Up to this time both in England and in Merovingian Gaul the coinage, irrespective of its intrinsic quality, had been the product of individual moneyers, not regarded by the ruler as a royal prerogative. Doubtless the moneyers paid for their privileges and kings exercised a measure of control over the weight and standard of the coins produced; but in England coins never bore the name of a king, and seldom the name of either moneyer or mint while in Gaul they occasionally bore the king's name, albeit only as a compliment to the ruler, but nearly always the name of the moneyer and the mint. But in 755 the Merovingian denier was made official and from about 780, at the latest, Charlemagne established the relation of 240 denarii to the pound; these coins bore the name of the king on the obverse side, and of the mint but not the moneyer on the reverse side. In England the introduction of an official coinage began in Kent, the kingdom with the closest links with the Continent, at the Canterbury mint between *c.* 775 and *c.* 780 and it was modelled on the standards and format of the Frankish denarius, except that the moneyers name rather than the mint is found on the reverse side. In the middle of of the 780s the Kentish kingdom became a dependency of Offa and the Canterbury mint substituted the name of Offa for that of the Kentish Egbert, but it continued for a time to produce pennies of the same type as before. The subsequent development of Offa's coinage in design owed nothing to its continental counterparts, but the continuing conformity of the English and Frankish relation of 240 pence (denarii) to the pound provides strong support for the view that Anglo-Frankish trade had assumed substantial proportions.[1]

Travel for all purposes, which had increased as a consequence of comparative political security in both England and western Europe, became more difficult with the turn of the century. After Offa the Mercian dominance of southern England was not maintained by his successors and the rivalry between Mercia and Wessex was resumed. After Charlemagne's death his empire gradually disintegrated and fell victim to civil wars. Before either of these developments had progressed far the sack of Lindisfarne in 793 and of Iona in 795 by

---

[1] For Offa's coinage, C. E. Blunt, in *A(nglo)-S(axon) Coins: (Historical Studies Presented to Sir Frank Stenton)*, ed. R. M. H. Dolley (London, 1961). As to the volume of coinage in Carolingian Gaul and in Offa's England and its significance as an index of both internal and foreign trade, numismatists hold strong but divergent views. The debate may be followed in Grierson, ' Money and coinage under Charlemagne ', in *Karl der Grosse* and ' The volume of Anglo-Saxon coinage ', *Economic History Review*, second series XX (1967), whose views are controverted by D. M. Metcalf, ' The prosperity of Europe in the eighth and ninth centuries ', in the next issue of that journal.

Viking pirates provided early warning that intensifying assault would drive every kingdom in the west back on its own resources in a struggle for survival.

In the face of so many hazards it might appear surprising that English pilgrims continued to visit Rome, yet the latter part of the journey had always been difficult and additional obstacles gave added merit to the enterprise. The *schola Saxonum*, burned down during the pontificate of Paschal, was rebuilt with papal assistance. Kings, archbishops, and bishops continued to be prominent among the pilgrims. King Aethelwulf of Wessex visited Rome himself ' with great state and remained there a twelvemonth ' having previously despatched his son Alfred there. After his expulsion from Mercia King Burgred settled in Rome and was eventually buried in the church of St. Mary in the English quarter. During the pontificate of Nicholas I ' certain Englishmen came to Rome and placed a *tabula* of silver in the chapel of S. Gregory '. A letter of Pope John VIII provides evidence of the continued existence of the English colony; he wrote to the English archbishops, informing them that all the leading Englishmen then living in Rome, having been assembled, agreed to give up the native form of dress and to clothe themselves in tunics reaching to the knee in Roman fashion.

A group of letters written in the middle of the ninth century by Lupus, abbot of Ferrières, to correspondents in England sheds a vivid light on the difficulties of maintaining communications with Gaul and the eagerness with which they were resumed at the earliest opportunity. Ferrières had close connections with England. It was one of the monasteries given to Alcuin by Charlemagne and he had been succeeded there as abbot by an English pupil. Lupus had received his early teaching at Ferrières and before returning as abbot had studied at Boniface's monastery of Fulda under one of Alcuin's most distinguished pupils, Hrabanus Maurus. In 852 in a letter to Wigmund, archbishop of York, he deplored the long break which war had caused and expressed the hope that now that peace was restored mutually advantageous contacts would be resumed. His other letters give an indication of the benefits he hoped for; from abbot Eadsige of York he asked for the loan of works of Jerome, Quintilian, and Bede, which he wished to have copied at St. Judoc, a cell of Ferrières, by a certain Lantram who was known to Eadsige—this letter has a particular interest because it suggests that the library at York had still at this time a considerable reputation and it is also the last evidence of learned intercourse between Northumbria and the Continent before the Danish settlement. A letter from Lupus to King Aethelwulf of Wessex, asking for lead for the re-roofing of his church, provides evidence of contact between Frankish ecclesiastics and the West Saxon court and incidentally reveals that Aethelwulf employed a Frankish secretary, Felix, who was instructed by Lupus to see that the lead was sent to Quentovic.

Commercial exchanges which had been expanding in the late eighth century were particularly hard hit by Viking activity, for the ports of the North Sea and Channel coasts were attractive and vulnerable targets for piracy. Dorestad, the most important European market was looted in 834 and thereafter the coasts of Flanders, Francia, and England were subjected to regular visitations. Yet trade did not cease entirely. Between 837 and 854 Archbishop Wigmund of York issued coins in imitation of those of Louis the Pious. Dorestad effected a measure of recovery despite further attacks until its destruction in 863, and in 864 the continued economic vitality of Quentovic is vouched for by Charles the Bald's edict of that year which nominated it as one of the nine official minting-places of the West Frankish kingdom—it was soon afterwards destroyed. There are two references to British traders in the *Life* of Charlemagne written by Nottker of St. Gall.

Viking piracy made international exchanges difficult but it did not inhibit them entirely and as soon as more peaceful conditions returned, in the last decades of the century, they were speedily resumed. A series of papal letters shows that popes, though ignorant of English affairs, were eager to exercise an oversight over the English Church, while the *Chronicle* records payments of Peter's Pence to Rome taken by royal embassies from England. Alfred turned to Archbishop Fulk of Rheims for assistance in recruiting continental churchmen to assist him in the work of ecclesiastical reform. Foreign merchants like the Norwegian Ohthere were welcomed at Alfred's court. Contacts could be made from even further afield; both Alfred and Charles the Fat, king of the Franks, received letters and gifts from Elias, patriarch of Jerusalem; that to Alfred has not survived, but the letter to Charles asked for money for the rebuilding of churches and if Alfred's letter was similar it may have stimulated him to think of sending alms to India. Even in the worst times diplomatic exchanges had not entirely ceased. In 856 at Compiègnes, on his return from Rome, Aethelwulf of Wessex married Judith, daughter of Charles the Bald. She subsequently married Aethelwulf's son and successor Aethelbald and after his death she married Baldwin I, count of Flanders; her son Baldwin II married Alfred's youngest daughter, Aelfthryth.

With the restoration of peace England would participate more fully than ever before in the economic and diplomatic life of western Europe; though relations with Rome would become more tenuous the explanation would lie in the politics of Italy rather than in the indifference of Englishmen to religion.

9

POLITICAL AND ECCLESIASTICAL
DEVELOPMENTS IN SOUTHERN ENGLAND

B Y comparison with the modest wealth of materials which makes it possible to write the history of the two centuries between the arrival of Augustine and the death of Offa with some degree of confidence the first half of the ninth century is a period for which the literary sources are both meagre and enigmatic. Politically these years lack any obviously significant development. Wessex emerged from the dependence into which it had been thrust by King Offa and became the strongest of the English kingdoms, but save for a brief period its kings seem not to have aspired to extend their authority outside their own realm. Mercia, still powerful for twenty years after Offa's death, suffered a series of disasters in the third decade of the century but apparently recovered subsequently. The East Anglian kingdom, suddenly, very temporarily and inexplicably, emerged from obscurity, inflicting military defeats on Mercia. Northumbria continued to be, as for long she had been, a cipher in political affairs. In the middle of the ninth century there seemed to be no convincing reason why any of the kingdoms of the Heptarchy should establish a lasting authority over the others. Periodically, after 830, England was subjected to Viking attacks, but though destructive and damaging they appeared to contemporaries to have no political significance.

Concerning the state of the Church, and of society in general, we know even less than of the political happenings, and what we know suggests more problems than it resolves.

The political uncertainties were terminated by the abrupt and violent intrusion of a new factor from outside England, the great Danish army which landed in East Anglia in the autumn of 865.

Soon there could no longer be contention for hegemony between the English kingdoms for only Wessex remained, and for a time it would seem doubtful whether even Wessex would survive.

1. Mercia and Wessex

The wide-ranging authority which Offa had established rapidly disintegrated on his death. His son Ecgfrith survived him for less than five months and his kingdom then passed to a distant relative, Cenwulf (797-821). Kent rebelled again in 796; the murder of Aethelred of Northumbria and the death of Beorhtric of Wessex summarily ended Mercian influence in those kingdoms. Only in Kent was Mercian control re-established after a brutal two-year campaign; Cenwulf then established his brother Cuthred as king and on his death in 807, Bealdred, whose origins are unknown, was appointed king.

It is likely that Cenwulf's interests differed from those of Offa. Although on the day that Egbert, Beorhtric's successor, was enthroned as king of Wessex a Mercian force attacking into Wessex was defeated by the men of Wiltshire, this was an isolated act of hostility. Cenwulf was more concerned with his Welsh frontier than with the territory south of the Thames. It is not clear whether his actions were punitive, taken in response to Welsh raids into Mercia, or whether he deliberately reversed Offa's policy of containment behind the Dyke in order to extend the Mercian border westwards. It is possible that his Welsh campaigns were an unwelcome diversion, but it seems more probable that they represent a deliberate change of policy. In 796 a battle was fought at Rhuddlan and in 798 Caradog, king of Gwynedd, was killed by the English; Snowdonia was harried in 816 and the small Welsh kingdom of Rhufuniog, between the rivers Clwyd and Elwy, was annexed to Mercia; Dyfed was ravaged in 818. Cenwulf's death at Basingwerk in Flintshire suggests his intention of mounting yet another expedition. The offensive was maintained by his cousin and successor Ceolwulf (821-823), who destroyed the Welsh fortress at Deganwy and overran the kingdom of Powys. Despite these preoccupations, and though they could not and did not lay claim to the authority exercised by Offa, Cenwulf and Ceolwulf were the strongest kings in England of their time. Mercian control over both the kingdom of Kent and the archbishopric of Canterbury remained unimpaired and both kings continued to preside over ecclesiastical synods attended by all the bishops of southern England.

During Cenwulf's lifetime Egbert (802-839) had been content to consolidate his position in Wessex; the only recorded event in the early years of his reign is a ravaging of Cornwall in 815. If he began to take advantage of the more favourable circumstances now presenting themselves, with the consequence that the forward policy in Wales favoured by Cenwulf and Ceolwulf met with opposition in Mercia, it might explain why Ceolwulf was deposed in 823. Of the origins of Ceolwulf's successor, Beornwulf, nothing is known; it was now the turn of Mercia to suffer the fate of kingdoms ruled by non-royal stocks.

For Beornwulf Wessex was more important than Wales and in 825 he led an army into Wessex. It was defeated at Ellendun (Wroughton) in Wiltshire and Egbert followed up his victory by offering his leadership to the other kingdoms of the southern English which had suffered Mercian domination for a century. A detachment of his army under his son Aethelwulf and Bishop Eahlstan of Sherborne entered Kent and drove out the Mercian puppet Bealdred; the people of Kent, Surrey, Sussex and Essex submitted to Egbert immediately and the king of the East Angles appealed to him for peace and protection. Beornwulf responded by attacking the East Angles, by whom he was defeated and killed. He was succeeded by Ludeca, previously an ealdorman. In 827 he, too, led a Mercian army against East Anglia; it met the same fate as that of his predecessor, the Mercians were defeated and Ludeca was killed. How the East Angles with their slender resources were able twice to defeat the Mercians in battle in three years has never been satisfactorily explained; not even the names of their kings are known.

In 829 Egbert, taking advantage of Mercian disasters, assumed the offensive. He expelled their new king, Wiglaf, from his kingdom and conquered Mercia and everything south of the Humber. His campaigning took him as far as Dore in North Derbyshire and culminated in the submission of the Northumbrians to his lordship. A campaign waged in the following year against the north Welsh reduced them to humble submission. The *Chronicle* described Egbert as the ' eighth king who was bretwalda ', but even disregarding the chronicler's refusal to recognize the nature of the dominion exercised by Mercian kings, this was more encomium than sober truth. His superiority over the Mercians was shortlived. Wiglaf recovered his kingdom in

830 and though he did not succeed in regaining the south-eastern territories lost by Beornwulf he successfully maintained the integrity of Mercia, including London and Middlesex, and by 836 his position was so far restored that he presided over an assembly attended by the archbishop of Canterbury and eleven bishops of the southern province. Though gravely weakened, and threatened henceforth by the emergence of a strong Welsh kingdom in Gwynedd, Mercia was never again in danger of subjection to Wessex. The recovery of Mercian independence must have terminated West Saxon superiority over Northumbria.

Both Egbert and Wiglaf died in 839. In Wessex Egbert's son, Aethelwulf, became king; to Mercia succeeded Beorhtwulf, another king of whose origins nothing is known. These changes made little difference to the balance of power between the two kingdoms, though it is surprising to learn from a charter of 844 that Beorhtwulf at that time held land on the Berkshire side of the river Thames. But once again, and this time of necessity rather than of choice, Mercian interests began to be directed westwards as Rhoddri the Great, who succeeded to the throne of Gwynedd in 844, rapidly extended his rule over the whole of north Wales and much of the south. Yet Aethelwulf showed no disposition to embarrass either Beorhtwulf or his successor Burgred, who became king at some time between 851 and 853. In 853 Burgred asked for, and obtained, West Saxon assistance in a campaign against the Welsh; two years later Burgred married Aethelwulf's daughter.

2. The Church from the Death of Offa to the Danish Conquest

Offa's death made possible the reversal of his unpopular ecclesiastical policy. Cenwulf still desired to diminish the authority of the archbishop of Canterbury but to do so in a manner which might be less obnoxious to ecclesiastical sentiment than Offa's device of creating a third archbishopric. He proposed to Pope Leo III that the unity of the southern province should be restored by the relegation of Lichfield from its archiepiscopal status and the establishment of the archbishopric of the province in London. This ingenious proposal possessed for the Mercian king all the advantages of a metropolitan see in Mercian territory; and having the virtue of appearing to conform to Pope Gregory the Great's original plan for the organization of the English Church it might be expected to secure a measure of ecclesiastical support in England. But by this time reverence for and loyalty to the church of Canterbury had become so much a tradition of the English Church that its leaders showed no more enthusiasm for London than for Lichfield. The pope, made aware of English hostility to Cenwulf's plan, was reluctant to acquiesce, alleging the undesirability of reversing decisions so recently taken in favour of yet another novelty. More important than these hostile reactions, Cenwulf's success in reasserting Mercian authority in Kent made insistence on the diminution of the authority of the archbishop of Canterbury less pressing. Cenwulf withdrew his proposal and in 802 Pope Leo III conferred on Aethelheard of Canterbury a privilege confirming the ancient rights of the see of Canterbury over all the churches of southern England and wrote to King Cenwulf informing him of the contents of the privilege. At the synod of Clovesho in 803 it was decreed that no power whatsoever should diminish the rights and honours of the see of Canterbury and that the metropolitan dignity given to Lichfield be abolished.

The resistance of the Kentings to Mercian domination, which was the context of the involved transactions of these years, had temporarily disrupted the ecclesiastical order of the southern province when Aethelheard, archbishop of Canterbury between 793 and 805, whose Mercian sympathies were obnoxious to his flock, had allowed himself to be persuaded by the community of Christ Church to flee from his see. Alcuin censured Aethelheard for his flight and exhorted him speedily to repair the damage done; he must ' especially bring into the house of God the zeal for reading. . . . And also let your preaching be done in all places, and before all bishops in the general synod . . . and be zealous to do away with the most vain style of dress and the immoderate habit of feasting ' which was prevalent among all degrees of the clergy. He had previously reproved the clergy and people of Kent for driving out their archbishop and warned them of the damage inflicted and the dangers incurred by rebellion. But whatever harm the Church had suffered was quickly repaired. Hygeberht of Lichfield was very different in temperament from Wilfrid of York and acquiesced passively in his demotion. In the long term the primacy of Canterbury in the southern province appears to have been strengthened by the attack made on it, for in these years comes the first evidence of a custom which subsequently became generalized. Henceforth newly elected bishops made a written profession of faith and a promise of obedience to their archbishop.

The principal interest of the lengthy pontificate of Wulfred, archbishop of Canterbury from 805 until 832, from the narrowly ecclesiastical point of view, is the evidence it provides of the influence of a continental reforming movement on the English Church. To counter the laxity of his familia Bishop Chrodegang of Metz (742-766) had drawn up a Rule for his cathedral clergy: they were required to use a common dormitory and refectory and though they were not compelled to give up all their property they received equal allowances of food and drink from the bishop. This Rule was widely followed in Francia and its influence extended to England. A decree of the English synod of 786 required that 'the bishops take diligent heed that all canons shall live canonically and all monks and nuns according to their rule'. Wulfred's reforms were modelled on those of Chrodegang; he allowed his clergy to retain their property but insisted that they should regularly attend services of the church, make use of the common refectory and dormitory, and observe regular discipline. How far Wulfred's efforts were effective lack of evidence makes it impossible to determine; they may well have been stultified by his protracted disputes, first with Cenwulf of Mercia then with Egbert of Wessex.

Disturbed political conditions and the dislocation and destruction caused by Danish raids were obstacles to the maintenance of a high level of religious observance in the middle years of the ninth century but evidence that they disrupted the work of the Church is hard to find. The West Saxon dynasty of Egbert was outstandingly pious. When, in 839 King Aethelwulf wrote to the emperor asking permission to pass through the Frankish kingdom on his way to Rome he incidentally warned him that careful attention should be given to the safety of the souls subject to him, for unless Christians behaved better God would allow them to be punished! In 853 he sent his son Alfred to Rome with a large retinue, and two years later went himself, taking Alfred with him. Throughout his reign Aethelwulf was a notable benefactor of the religious communities of his kingdom. Nor was Alfred the only one of his sons to inherit his devotion; Asser reported that King Aethelred refused to join battle with the Danes at Ashdown in 871 until the mass which he was attending was completed. Of the West Saxon bishops during these years little is known; Eahlstan, bishop of Sherborne, appears several times in the *Chronicle*, always engaged in fighting, and his successor Heahmund was killed in battle; but there were good precedents for warrior bishops in the history of the Church and it is probable that a pastor who defended his flock with arms against the heathen was more admired than criticized for his conduct. Swithun, bishop of Winchester, left a reputation for sanctity and was canonized in the reign of Edgar. Of religious life in Mercia in the early ninth century tantalizingly little is known. Cynewulf, the best vernacular poet of the eighth century and a competent Latinist, was a Mercian; there is some evidence that book production still flourished in some centres and the capability of western Mercia to provide teachers for Alfred suggests that learning was well maintained there. The piety of King Burgred is attested by his choice of Rome as a new home after he had been driven from his kingdom.

The most direct evidence on the state of the Church in the later ninth century is a group of letters written to English ecclesiastics by popes during King Alfred's reign, when as a result of the Danish war conditions might have been expected to be at their worst. Between 873 and 875 Pope John VIII wrote to archbishops Aethelred of Canterbury and Wulfred of York telling them that the English clerics living in Rome had agreed to give up their voluminous but short native style garments and to clothe themselves in robes reaching to the ankle after the Roman fashion; he hoped that the English clergy in England would follow their good example. The real interest of this letter lies in its evidence of the pope's attempt to maintain contact with the see of York, for its suggestion of insularity in the dress of the clergy is scarcely criticism of their behaviour. Later letters condemn the English clergy for their failure to impress on their flocks the teaching of the Church on marriage. This charge could have been made against Englishmen in all previous Christian centuries and was certainly not new in the ninth century. The most serious accusations occur in a letter written by Pope Formosus (891-896) to all the bishops of England in which he declared that though paganism has reasserted itself in England the bishops have kept silence. He had, however, heard from Archbishop Plegmund that the bishops were now more active in their missionary efforts and commanded them to continue the work; they were to take particular care to ensure that when bishops' sees fell vacant they should be speedily filled, so that evangelization would not be checked. If enthusiasm was lacking, these papal letters display no awareness of scandalous shortcomings.

Nevertheless, by this time it is clear that two important changes had taken place within the Church during the ninth century; learning had decayed and the monastic ideal was in eclipse. Alcuin's correspondence with friends in both English provinces at the beginning of the century had already revealed concern for the condition of scholarship. He lamented the lack of teachers in England where once they had been plentiful and pressed on Archbishop Aethelheard the need to encourage study among the community at Christ Church; but the tone of his letters betrays anxiety rather than alarm. The corrupt Latin of ninth-century charters shows that Alcuin's fears had been realized. Still more explicit is the statement made by King Alfred towards the end of the century in the letter written by him to Bishop Waerferth of Worcester when he sent the bishop his translation of the *Pastoral Care*; ' So general was its decay [of learning] in England that there were very few on this side of the Humber who could understand their service-books in English, or translate a letter from Latin into English; and I believe that there were not many beyond the Humber. There were so few of them that I cannot remember a single one south of the Thames.' Alfred did not believe that the Danes were entirely responsible; ' I also remembered how, before everything was ravaged and burned the churches throughout all England stood filled with treasures and books, and likewise there was a great multitude of the servants of God. And they had very little benefit from these books for they could not understand anything in them, because they were not written in their own language.' Even where there was no shortage of priests many of them had been illiterate. Yet it is worth remembering that in southern as in northern England the decline in Latin culture had been partly compensated for by the development of vernacular English poetry, which was used both to teach the Christian virtues and to express religious sentiment.[1] For some purposes English had superseded Latin—Alfred's translators recognized the fact—and when the attempt is made to assess the spiritual climate of the age the existence of this religious poetry must be taken into account. The decay of Latin learning did not necessarily involve a comparable decline in the strength of religious feeling, though the lack of an educated clergy would have made the maintenance of high standards of observance difficult to sustain over a long period.

Asser, in his biography of King Alfred, prefaced his account of the

[1] *Supra* pp. 153-5.

king's attempt to revive monasticism with the comment that ' for very many years past the desire for the monastic life had been utterly lacking in all that people . . . although there still remain many monasteries founded in that land, but none properly observing the rule of this way of life '. This marks a dramatic change from the conditions of a hundred years earlier. Admitting that many so-called *monasteria* in pre-Alfredian England were never more than communities of clerics and that many others were not even that—designated in their own time as pseudomonasteries—yet there had been many religious communities which professed to follow a rule; and though there may have been almost as many rules as monasteries the influence of St. Benedict was strong in many of them, and some had been outstanding for the quality of the life they fostered. Jarrow, York, Ripon, Ely, Peterborough, Malmesbury, and Glastonbury had been, in the strict sense, monasteries. In Asser's view nothing of this remained. Although it is possible that by the time he wrote only communities which followed the Benedictine Rule as interpreted by Benedict of Aniane at Aachen in 817 would have qualified as monasteries ' properly observing the rule ' even by the more elastic criteria of the earlier epoch his assertion would stand. In so far as his generalization can be tested by reference to the histories of individual monasteries only St. Augustine's Canterbury might be excepted.[1] Even the greatest monasteries of Mercia and Wessex had either declined into churches served by communities of clerics, often married, who made no profession of obedience to a rule, or had fallen into the hands of laymen.

It is obvious that in areas overrun by the Danes the destruction of buildings, libraries, and ecclesiastical furniture of all kinds, and the appropriation of landed endowments by pagan settlers, would have made impossible the continuance of genuine monastic life. Yet, just as Alfred did not attribute the decay of learning to the Danes, nor could they be blamed for the contemporary indifference to the monastic ideal in Wessex even though many West Saxon monasteries had suffered heavy material damage; and Asser knew this. He professed not to understand what had happened but was more inclined to blame the nation's ' too great abundance of riches of every kind ' than ' the onslaughts of foreigners '. A later analyst of monastic

---

[1] D. Knowles, *The Monastic Order in England* (Cambridge, 1940), p. 695. This work is indispensable for the history of monasticism between Alfred's reign and the Norman Conquest.

fortunes, Aethelwold, bishop of Winchester, attributed decline to
' secular domination '. By this he implied several things. The prevalence of the notion that a religious house belonged to its founder
and that rule over it might properly be confined to the founder's
kindred was likely to produce unsuitable abbots and even monasteries directly ruled by laymen. Such men sometimes treated the
lands of their communities as private possessions which might be
granted away to kinsfolk. In times when the protective authority
of the king was weak, local lords used their power to appropriate ecclesiastical endowments and at such times too, abbots might
well make grants to influential laymen in their localities in return for protection. In these ways secular domination might
damage the monasteries and it seems that they had all been present
in the ninth century. The monastic reforms of Wulfred's contemporary, Benedict of Aniane, appear to have had no influence in
England.

Monasticism was dead but it did not necessarily follow that the
clerical community often found occupying an old monastic site was
totally despicable; they might well maintain a decent level of religious observance if they did not aspire to the heights.

In general the evidence suggests that during the ninth century the
Church experienced a continuous and delicately balanced struggle
between reforming churchmen and the natural tendency for ecclesiastical communities to accept relaxations in discipline or to fall under
lay control, and that neither tendency predominated.

3. The Early Phases of Danish Attack

An important reason for the development of friendly relations
between the kings of Wessex and Mercia after more than two hundred years of continuous hostility[1] was the appearance of a danger
equally threatening to both kingdoms.

The looting, in 834, of Dorestad, the biggest trading centre in
northern Europe, by Vikings was followed in the next year by the
devastation of the Isle of Sheppey. This event signalized the beginning of a period of endemic raiding on England.

Few phenomena of the early middle ages have engaged the attention of historians more than the assault of the Vikings on western

[1] *Supra* p. 201.

Europe in the ninth century.[1] Sporadic attacks had occurred in the last decades of the eighth century, the more terrifying because totally unexpected. On hearing of the sack of Lindisfarne in 793 Alcuin wrote, ' It is some three hundred and fifty years that we and our forefathers have inhabited this lovely land, and never before in Britain has such terror appeared as this we have now suffered at the hands of the heathen. Nor was it thought possible that such an inroad from the sea could be made.'

The early ninth century saw a respite from Viking attacks until the 830s; thereafter they were resumed, to be continued with greater frequency and increasingly large forces as time passed. The raid of 793 had been a disaster which Alcuin found inexplicable in terms of his knowledge of the world and he therefore attributed it to a visitation of the Divine wrath on the sinful Northumbrians. Later historians reject Alcuin's interpretation of events but are not agreed on an alternative explanation. It is likely that no single cause can do more than secure acceptance as a contributory factor in explaining a phenomenon which embraced three peoples and more than three centuries; in which sea-power, uniquely important for two of the peoples concerned, was largely irrelevant for the third.

It has been argued that the Scandinavian races were notoriously fast-breeding whereas the area of easily cultivated land was restricted by the harsh climate and the vast areas of mountain, forest, and marsh; the search for new lands to farm was consequently the response to population pressure. This is certainly true of the coastal area of western Norway whose inhabitants were early compelled to supplement their harvests by resort to trade, piracy, fishing, and hunting. The first record of the Northmen in England tells of Norwegians from Hordaland who were thought by the king's reeve of Porchester to have come to trade; their first settlements abroad, in the Shetlands and Orkneys, were made by Norsemen concerned not to loot but to settle and farm in their traditional ways. King Alfred's guest, Ohthere the Halogalander, was among the foremost men in his land; even so ' he had not more than twenty head of cattle and twenty sheep and twenty pigs, and the little that he ploughed he ploughed with horses '. His principal wealth was derived partly

[1] Good general books on the Vikings are T. D. Kendrick, *A history of the Vikings* (London, 1930); J. Brønsted, *The Vikings* (London, 1965), Gwyn James, *A History of the Vikings* (London, 1968); and P. H. Sawyer, *The Age of the Vikings* (London, 2nd edn, 1971): this last, throughout sceptical of received opinions, is particularly valuable for its use of numismatic evidence.

from fishing walrus and whale but chiefly from tribute in skins and furs levied from the Lapps who lived further north, and it was in order to dispose of these valuable goods that he travelled to Kampang, Hedeby, and even to England. Othere's description of Norway provides ample explanation of Norwegian enterprise abroad. ' The land of the Norwegians ', he said, ' was very long and very narrow. All of it that can be grazed or ploughed lies alongside the sea, and that, moreover, is in some part very rocky. And wild mountains lie to the east, above and parallel to the cultivated land.' Jutland, too, was infertile. By contrast, the Vik area of Norway, the Danish islands, and much of southern Sweden, were flat and productive and the seas adjacent to them were famous for their wealth of fish. These areas were well able to maintain a substantial population and even in the fourteenth century, when in many parts of Europe populations were greater than the available land could sustain. Sweden was a country with land to spare.

Other authorities emphasize the importance of political changes within Scandinavia which resulted in the emergence of fewer and stronger kings. Assisted by the natural physical barriers which separated their different regions, rule over all these Scandinavian countries in the centuries after the age of migration had been highly fragmented. But by the beginning of the ninth century the kings of Uppland had created a Swedish kingdom by asserting their superiority over the mainland Geats and the islanders of Gotland. In Denmark Godfred (*c.* 800-810) and his son Horik established some measure of unitary authority over Jutland, the islands and Scania; it collapsed after Horik's death in 853/4 but was re-established by Gorm the Old well before the middle of the tenth century. Norway had been divided between three major regions, Vestfold, Trondelag, and the south-western coastal area, each of them controlled by numerous kings and jarls; during the long reign of Harald Fairhair, a king of Vestfold (*c.* 870-945), all of them were loosely drawn together in a single kingdom. Political consolidation sometimes resulted in the expulsion of rivals who had to seek a settlement elsewhere; some preferred to leave their native land rather than endure a superiority which they found insupportable; others left their homes in the hope that successful piracy would provide the resources and the reputation with which to return and sustain their claims. As early as 826 Harald Klak, one of Horik's unsuccessful rivals for the Danish throne, was established in Frisia by Louis the Pious, and his kinsmen continued to live there throughout the century; the most substantial Norwegian emigration to the Shetlands, Orkneys, the Hebrides, and Iceland is traditionally associated with the departure of a freedom-loving people unable to tolerate the tyranny of Harald Fairhair.

But neither population pressure nor the concentration of political authority will explain the fact that the period of greatest Danish activity against Francia and England occurred in the second half of the ninth century when Danish political unity was temporarily lost. A strong king was often reluctant to see the dissipation of the military resources of his country in expeditions which he did not control and from which he did not profit, though sometimes he might be glad if some of his more turbulent subjects removed themselves from the domestic scene. The establishment of strong kingship in the north contributed to the flow of emigrant warriors but did not initiate it; and when Viking enterprise was harnessed by royal authority its character changed. Although in degree there was a difference between the strong kings and the kinglets they superseded, and though they imposed a measure of internal order upon their subjects, they realized that their authority, like that of their predecessors, depended on their successes in war and their ability to reward those who served them loyally. They too were sea-kings and Vikings, but they operated on a larger scale than had been customary and they used their power for political rather than narrowly economic ends. The objectives of Swegn and Cnut were very different from those of the sons of Ragnar Lodbrok.

It has also been argued that Charlemagne's conquest of the Saxons which advanced the Imperial frontier to the Eider, and his alliance with the Slavonic Abodrites, whom he encouraged to move into east Holstein, stimulated the mutual awareness of Danes and Westerners in several ways. By the extension of their power and influence in the north the Franks threatened Danish control over the two important trading routes on which their prosperity depended; the east–west route leading across the base of the Jutland peninsula and the north–south route up the peninsula. This threat may well have facilitated the task of Sigfred, who died in about 800, and his successor Godfred in strengthening their authority over Denmark; and it certainly drew their attention to the areas immediately to the south. Sigfred had given shelter to the Saxon chief Widukind and in 804 Godfred staged a demonstration on the frontier with a strong fleet and army to warn Charlemagne of the consequence of further advances. On this occasion a peace was negotiated, but a few years later Godfred ravaged the territory of the Abodrites, captured their king, and destroyed their commercial centre, the town of Reric. Shortly afterwards Godfred ordered the construction of a rampart to protect the base of the Jutland peninsula and to provide a safe, all-Danish route for east–west traffic. Charlemagne, preoccupied with other problems, reacted feebly to the defeat of his allies and in 810 King Godfred with a powerful fleet raided in Frisia without encountering more than local opposition. Godfred's murder in that year was followed by a period of confusion in Denmark while contenders for the succession to his kingship fought one another. Louis the Pious resorted both to direct military operations and to intervention on behalf of one of the rivals but by 827 Horik, son of Godfred, had secured the kingdom which he retained until his death. But if Carolingian expansion engendered a Danish response it is also true that Charlemagne's reputation and the coastal defences he caused to be made preserved his country from harm until the aggressive Godfred was dead and that further Danish attacks were thereby postponed for two decades.

Whatever elements of truth these varied explanations contain it is probable that our understanding of Viking activity has been obscured by the feeling that it can only be made intelligible if it is possible to identify changes in Scandinavian society at about this time which compelled the inhabitants of a hitherto remote and backward area to undertake novel and hazardous martial ventures overseas. Yet as more is learned about Scandinavia in the pre-Viking period it becomes clear that the activities characteristic of the Viking age were in themselves no novelties: they reflect a traditional way of life extended from the Baltic into a far wider geographical context. The facts of Scandinavian geography are from the earliest times reflected in the importance of communication by water, whether in the Norwegian fiords, among the enclosed waters and sounds of the Baltic, or by the rivers and lakes of Sweden. Traditionally, the abundance of fish in Baltic waters encouraged every farmer to be as well a fisherman. By virtue of their position in the north of Europe the Scandinavian peoples possessed commodities greatly in demand in the south and west and had needs, particularly of silver, which they could not satisfy from their own resources. They were farmers, fishermen, and traders according to the season of the year; and long before they troubled the West they had preyed on one another as opportunity offered. From the beginning the Swedes were predominantly traders and their enterprises only secondarily maritime in nature; their penetration of Latvia and Estonia and towards the southern shores of Lake Ladoga began earlier than the raids of the Norwegians and Danes and their trading centre at Birka was well-established by 800. The critical fact which transformed the Norwegians and Danes into the Vikings of history was the development of a seaworthy and manoeuvrable sailing ship which could carry a crew of thirty or more men and accommodate them, if necessary, for weeks at a time. This happened only on the eve of the Viking period, and it made commonplace voyages which would have been inconceivable earlier, to remote Greenland and to the Mediterranean. The new ships first extended the range of traditional activities and then made possible the satisfaction of a long felt need for cultivable land, first realized when the Norwegians sailed to the Shetlands and beyond. The Danes were only temporarily inhibited by domestic problems and the defensive dispositions of Charlemagne and Louis the Pious. Both peoples, Norwegians and Danes, whatever their conscious intentions may have been—to trade, to steal, or simply to see what lay beyond their familiar world—quickly discovered that in Ireland, the Frankish Empire, and in England there were riches that could often be taken without the formalities of trade. It took them little longer to realize that in these countries there were fertile lands which could be appropriated without much effective opposition from their nominal rulers. The Norwegian route westwards took them to the Faroes, Shetland, Man, and then Ireland, where they found a country shared by mutually warring kings, an easy prey to conquest; the Danes operated mainly on the North Sea coastlands where they found conditions substantially similar.

After the attack on Sheppey in 834 our next information is that in 836 a Viking fleet joined forces with the Britons of Cornwall, but the allies were defeated by Egbert and the West Saxon army at Hingston Down. Thereafter Danish raids increased in intensity and duration; in 840 the ealdorman of Hampshire destroyed a Viking force at Southampton, but the ealdorman of Dorset was killed at Portland and his army defeated. Raids are recorded in 841, 842, 843 and 845.

A more serious phase of Viking operations began in 851 when the raiders took to wintering on island bases in the river mouths, conveniently situated for a quick resumption of campaigning as spring approached. After wintering on the isle of Thanet an army of 350 ships' crews stormed Canterbury and London; it routed the army of Beorhtwulf of Mercia but was then defeated by the West Saxons under Aethelwulf and his son Aethelbald. Although all the advantages in this kind of warfare lay with the attackers, Aethelwulf, his sons, and his local commanders were a good deal more successful than their Frankish counterparts, and the *Chronicle* records some notable victories.

Only one reference to attacks on English kingdoms other than Wessex appears in the *Chronicle* (s.a. 841), but it would be mistaken to infer that they were immune. Northumbrian tradition testifies to the killing of a King Raedwulf and one of his ealdormen by a heathen army in 844, and a Mercian charter of 855 refers to pagans in the area of the Wrekin. There can be little doubt that the whole of eastern England suffered from raiding, but it does not appear that the English fully realized the significance of the mounting pressure. To Burgred of Mercia, as we have seen, the Welsh were for long more important than the Vikings. There appeared to be support for this view in the comparative tranquillity of the decade after 855, during which only one raid was reported, but in fact the respite was due to a concentration of Viking attacks on Francia rather than to a loss of interest in England.

This fortuitous immunity from attack was fortunate for Wessex for these years were not lacking in domestic incident. In 855 Aethelwulf went on pilgrimage to Rome, absenting himself from Wessex for about a year and a half, leaving his eldest son Aethelbald in charge. On his return with a young bride, the daughter of Charles the Bald, king of the Franks, he found Aethelbald unprepared to deliver back the kingdom. It was probably felt that despite the diplomatic and military advantages implicit in a Frankish alliance Aethelwulf would have been more profitably occupied in England than in visiting the shrines of the saints in Rome. The threat of civil war in the kingdom was avoided when Aethelwulf agreed to accept the subordinate kingship over the south-eastern shires which Aethelbald had previously held; nor was there any protest when on Aethelwulf's death Aethelbald married his father's widow. Two years later, in 860, Aethelbald died and was succeeded by his brother Aethelberht (860-865); since Aethelwulf's death Aethelberht had ruled the south-eastern province, which was now reunited with the kingdom of Wessex.

The *Chronicle* states that his was a reign of good peace and tranquillity marred only by the storming of Winchester by a great pirate host, which was in turn put to flight by ealdormen Osric and Aethelwulf and their men of Berkshire and Hampshire. Of Mercia between 855 and 865 we know nothing. During these years events on the Continent were determining the course of events in England. In 862 Charles the Bald, king of the Franks, defeated the Vikings of the Seine, and though they again plundered the Paris area in 865-866 in the latter year the Franks paid 4,000 pounds of silver for a ten-year truce. In Ireland, its high king, Aedh, had recently won victories. In both regions a stiffening resistance developed at a time when the easiest pickings had been taken. Much remained, but in the circumstances England, immensely wealthy and with only its coastal districts so far ravaged, became an increasingly attractive target for attack.

The peaceful reign of Aethelberht was the calm which heralded the storm to come. Within a few years the course of English history had been changed.

10

KING ALFRED 'THE GREAT'

1. The Great Army of 865

A NEW phase of operations began in 865. A Danish army came
to Thanet and induced the Kentishmen, for the first time, to
buy peace; but under cover of the peace and the promise of
money the host went secretly inland by night and devastated all the
eastern part of Kent. Far more important, in the autumn of that
year a great heathen army came to England and took up winter
quarters in East Anglia. Under the leadership of two great Viking
chiefs Halfdan and Ivar the Boneless, the sons of that Ragnar
Lodbrok who had led the force which sacked Paris in 845, it was a
larger and more unified force than had ever previously come to
England; and it was prepared to quarter itself in England until it
had exhausted all the possibilities of plunder which a rich country
offered.

The East Angles submitted and provided the invaders with horses
with which they moved into Northumbria, capturing York in the
autumn of 866. At this time two rivals, Osbert and Aelle, were
contending for the Northumbrian throne; belatedly they joined
forces and attacked the Danes in York in March 867, but they were
crushingly defeated and both killed.[1] The Danes now appointed an
Englishman, Egbert, as puppet king of Northumbria, to hold office
at their pleasure. That winter they moved into Mercia and took up
winter quarters at Nottingham; King Burgred appealed for help to
his brother-in-law the king of the West Saxons, and Aethelred (who
had succeeded Aethelberht in 866) and his brother Alfred led an
army to assist in the siege of Nottingham; but no battle ensued and
the Mercians made peace with the enemy who retired to York where

---

[1] *Supra* p. 148.

they remained for a year. From York the army moved, in autumn 869, across Mercia into East Anglia taking up winter quarters at Thetford. In the following spring they destroyed the army which King Edmund of East Anglia led against them and killed the king. Within four years Northumbria, north-eastern Mercia, and East Anglia were under Danish control.

At about this time Ivar the Boneless disappears from sight, but in December 870 Halfdan struck at Wessex, establishing a fortified camp at Reading. King Aethelred and Alfred took the initiative and defeated the Danes at Ashdown, twenty-five miles to the west, with considerable loss, but in another battle at Basing two weeks later the Danes were victorious and in March the West Saxons again suffered defeat near Marlborough. At Easter, 871, King Aethelred died. Though he left children his brother Alfred was immediately proclaimed king. Alfred's accession made no immediate difference to the situation; the first recorded event of his reign is a battle he fought against the whole Danish army at Wilton which resulted in another defeat. The *Chronicle* entry for 871 reads, 'during that year nine general engagements were fought against the Danish army in the kingdom south of the Thames, besides the expeditions which the king's brother Alfred and [individual] ealdormen and king's thegns often rode on, which were not counted. And that year nine [Danish] earls were killed and one king.' Yet this was a year of moral, if not of military victory. Wessex alone of English, indeed of west European, kingdoms, under the leadership of its royal family, had offered stern resistance to the Danes, inflicting heavy losses on them and causing them to realize that plunder and land could be more easily acquired elsewhere. The Danes made peace with Alfred and withdrew to London.

For the kingdoms north of the Thames the West Saxon resistance had dire consequences. After moving from London into Northumbria in 873 the Danish army took up winter quarters at Torksey in Lindsey, and in the following year it moved to Repton. King Burgred of Mercia was driven into exile and the Danes established a puppet king, Ceolwulf, in his place, 'who swore oaths to them and gave hostages that it [Mercia] should be ready for them on whatever day they wished to have it, and he would be ready himself and all who would follow him, at the enemy's service'. This is the first unambiguous evidence that the Danes had determined to make their homes in England, but it was soon to be confirmed elsewhere. Shortly afterwards the great army split up. Halfdan took part of it into Northumbria where, after ravaging Bernicia and the territory of the Picts and Strathclyde Britons, in 876 he settled his followers in the area corresponding to the modern county of Yorkshire. Three other kings, of whom Guthrum was the most important, went to Cambridge where they remained for a year. In 876 Guthrum resumed the assault on Wessex. His force evaded the West Saxon army and occupied Wareham, but after hard fighting they accepted Alfred's peace terms, offering important hostages and swearing oaths that they would leave Wessex immediately. They broke their oaths, stole away from Wareham by night and hurried to Exeter, with Alfred in hot but unavailing pursuit. But the Danish fleet which supported the land operations met with disaster off Swanage, losing many ships, and once again Guthrum gave hostages and promised peace. His army moved into Mercia which in 877 was partitioned; the Danes took the area north of the river Welland, the remainder was left to Ceolwulf.

Guthrum's headquarters at Gloucester were not far from the frontier of Wessex, and he effected complete surprise when he drove south into Wiltshire in the middle of next winter. At about the same time another army commanded by a brother of Ivar the Boneless and Halfdan which had been wintering in south Wales raided the Devonshire coast. This force was defeated by Odda, the ealdorman of Devon, but by Easter 878 Alfred had been driven back into the marshes of Athelney. They were admirably suited for defence and in the heartland of the West Saxon kingdom, but the king had no army now, save for the members of the household. These weeks marked the nadir of his fortunes. But the attachment of the West Saxons to their ruling dynasty was signally demonstrated when in answer to Alfred's summons the levies of Somerset, Wiltshire, and west Hampshire concentrated in the seventh week after Easter at a point east of Selwood, and two days later fought a battle with Guthrum's army at Edington, twelve miles south of Chippenham. It was a great and decisive victory which drove the Danes back into their camp and caused them to surrender unconditionally a fortnight later.[1] They gave hostages and promised to leave Wessex, and Guthrum undertook to accept baptism. Three weeks later Guthrum, with thirty of his leading men were baptized in the river Aller near Athelney,

---

[1] R. H. C. Davis, 'Alfred the Great: propaganda and truth ', *History*, LVI, no. 187 (1971), takes a less enthusiastic view of the victory.

Alfred acting as sponsor to the Danish king. This time the Danes honoured their oaths and moved to Cirencester and thence in the following year to East Anglia, where they settled. Alfred's success was reflected in the fact that when in 879 a Viking fleet encamped at Fulham it preferred to sail away again and wage war in the Frankish kingdom rather than to fight in England.

2. THE SURVIVAL OF WESSEX

Between 865 and 873 the kingdoms of Northumbria, East Anglia and Mercia had been destroyed in battle. In 876 the best part of Northumbria, in 877 north-eastern Mercia, and in 878 East Anglia, had been settled by the rank and file of Danish armies. That Wessex alone retained its ruling dynasty and its territorial integrity was not due to mere chance.

During the middle years of the ninth century the English kingdoms north of the Thames were in a weaker position to resist attack than at any time since their establishment. East Anglia had long been overshadowed by Mercia and though recently it had enjoyed a moment of glory and was now independent it was a small kingdom. The line of Mercian kings descended from Penda had ended in 823 with Ceolwulf, since when the throne had passed to a number of kings of uncertain origins whose hold on the loyalty of their subjects was accordingly diminished; in 865 the Mercian king was Burgred who, judging from his failure to engage the Danes in battle at Nottingham in 868 despite West Saxon support, was no warrior. Northumbria, politically disturbed since the death of Aldfrith, was in a state of civil war. In Wessex alone was the dynastic fabric of the kingdom unfrayed by internal frictions, which, though potentially present, had been happily resolved through the forbearance of Aethelwulf's sons and the cooperation of the great men of the kingdom.

In the course of their early raiding the Danes must have been made aware of the fragility of the northern kingdoms, whereas the resistance offered in Wessex had made it a relatively unattractive theatre of operations. When they turned seriously to England their attack was first directed to those regions where least resistance was to be anticipated. They rapidly overran the kingdoms north of the Thames, but deferred taking over their conquests until Wessex, too, was subdued. That was the purpose of the campaign of 871. The resistance they encountered was a tribute not only to Alfred, who became king only after Easter in that year, but to all King Egbert's descendants who by their efforts had maintained a military organization and a level of morale sufficiently high in the face of frequent defeat to enable Alfred to engage in nine major battles in a single year. The result of the campaign was to persuade the Danes that it was better for them to consolidate their earlier gains than to prolong their attacks on Wessex. In the sequel no more favourable opportunity ever recurred. The great army was dissipated by the settlement of Hastein's men in Yorkshire and of other Danes in Mercia; henceforth 'they were engaged in ploughing and making a living for themselves'. Guthrum's army in 878 was a less powerful force than that which had attacked Wessex in 871 and its principal military asset was that his assault, mounted in midwinter, took Alfred by surprise.

The *Chronicle* annal for 878 is instructive. It describes how

> the enemy army came stealthily to Chippenham, and occupied the land of the West-Saxons and settled there, and drove a great part of the people across the sea, and conquered most of the others; and the people submitted to them, except king Alfred. He journeyed in difficulties through the woods and fen-fastnesses with a small force. . . , And afterwards at Easter, king Alfred with a small force made a stronghold at Athelney, and he and the section of the people of Somerset which was nearest to it proceeded to fight from that stronghold against the enemy. Then in the seventh week after Easter he rode to Egbert's stone east of Selwood, and there came to meet him all the people of Somerset and of Wiltshire and of that part of Hampshire which was on this side of the sea, and they rejoiced to see him.

Here is revealed the unique strength of the West Saxon dynasty. With their king apparently reduced to desperate straits and calling on his people to rally to him in support of what must have seemed a forlorn venture, 'they rejoiced to see him'. Soon afterwards he won a resounding triumph. Alfred owed much to his predecessors; yet having admitted so much, the fact remains that the first great military victory over the Danes was achieved through his own leadership, courage, pertinacity, and military skill.

3. The Reorganization of Defence: Alfred's Last Wars

For some years after 878 Wessex enjoyed a respite from attack; military operations never ceased entirely but they were no longer the king's sole concern. The opportunity was taken to reorganize the defences of the kingdom to ensure that its recently gained security would not be lost and that West Saxon military capacity would be increasingly augmented. The Danes had been especially formidable because their seaborne forces could land at any point along a coast far too long to be effectively protected. King Aethelwulf had occasionally fought against them on the sea but no English king before Alfred so clearly realized the importance of a fleet both for offence and defence. In 875 and 882 he used naval forces and in 885 took the initiative by sending a ship army to East Anglia. In 897 the *Chronicle* records that 'king Alfred had long ships built to oppose the Danish warships. They were almost twice as long as the others. Some had sixty oars, some more. They were both swifter and steadier and also higher than the others. They were built neither on the Frisian nor the Danish pattern but as it seemed to him himself that they could be most useful.' The size of the new ships made them difficult to handle but the advantages in having a substantial fleet were demonstrated both now and later. Edward the Elder assembled a fleet in 910 and Athelstan's Scottish campaign of 934 was waged by combined land and sea forces.

Effectively to secure the English coast from Danish seaborne forces would have required far greater resources than Alfred could hope to command. But by building strong points in strategic positions on the coast and on his frontier with Mercia it was possible to discourage attack from Danish occupied territories, to protect the inhabitants of the adjacent countryside and to provide bases from which armed forces could operate offensively against the invader as opportunity offered. The military utility of fortified strongholds had been demonstrated by the Franks both as defence against the Northmen and as a means of holding down newly conquered lands in Saxony. The Danes themselves understood the value of fortifications; they fortified their shore bases, their first move on mounting their attack on Wessex had been to establish an entrenched camp near Reading, and later in the 'seventies they availed themselves of the defences of Wareham, Exeter and Gloucester; when they settled it was as armies around fortified centres. King Alfred recognized the value of such strongpoints and ordered their construction, but such orders were unpopular because of the labour involved and were not always carried out—when the Danes came to the mouth of the Lympne in 893 they successfully stormed one of these forts which was occupied by a few peasants and only half built. Alfred's appreciation was correct but its execution on a large scale was the work of his successor King Edward.

In another respect Alfred prepared for the future. One perpetual problem facing any medieval military commander was that of maintaining an army in the field for a long period; men did not care or dare to spend months away from their homes to the neglect of their holdings. Alfred's attempt to solve this difficulty is recounted in the *Chronicle annal* for 892, which explains that besides maintaining permanent garrisons in the fortresses he divided his levies into two sections which alternated between service in the field and work at home. Initially this arrangement revealed weaknesses. In the next year the English field army defeated and then besieged the Danes on Thorney Island; but when they had completed their tour of duty and had come to an end of their food they dispersed homewards before the second division of the field army could arrive to relieve them, thus allowing the Danes to escape. These defects must have been eliminated by his successor, for Edward the Elder could keep an army in the field for more than a year when he wished to sustain protracted offensive operations. King Alfred's military reorganization was soon to prove its worth.

The English Chronicler, shrewdly aware that the easing of Danish pressure after 878 was partly due to the greater vulnerability of the Frankish kingdom at this time, carefully recorded the movements of Danish armies on the Continent during these years. A large Danish force established itself in Amiens in 884 and when, in the following year, it divided, one part moved to Louvain while the other besieged Rochester. Its garrison held out until Alfred arrived with a relieving army and drove the enemy back to their ships. Some of the invaders returned to the Continent but others, after agreeing peace terms, twice raided the country south of the Thames and established a camp at Benfleet on the north side of the Thames estuary. This band received support from that part of Guthrum's Danes now settled in East Anglia; a punitive fleet sent by Alfred against the East Anglians won a victory at the mouth of the Stour but on its homeward voyage was badly mauled by a superior Danish force. More important than these skirmishes was Alfred's recovery of London and its surrounding territories in 886; it is likely that London had been in Danish hands since Halfdan had used it for his winter base in

871-872, and though it may not have been a permanent military headquarters its strategic importance was considerable. For long it had been an important port and minting-place so that as well as having symbolic significance as the first territorial gain made by the West Saxons it was a valuable material acquisition. The sequel to the recovery of London was that all the English people that were not under subjection to the Danes submitted to him. Alfred had become the recognized leader not only of the West Saxons but of all the English, and could now count on the support of the inhabitants of that part of Mercia not under Danish domination.

For four years after the recovery of London no further engagements in England are recorded, though the Danes continued to ravage the Frankish lands until in 891 they were heavily defeated near Louvain by Arnulf, king of the East Franks. In the following year the defeated army moved westwards to Boulogne and having collected a great number of ships it crossed to Kent and established its base at Appledore, at the head of the estuary of the river Lympne. It met little opposition. Shortly afterwards another Danish fleet under the command of a famous leader named Hastein, who had been fighting on the Continent for the past fifteen years, sailed up the Thames Estuary and made its base at Milton near Sittingbourne. The arrival of these forces stimulated the Danes of Northumbria and East Anglia into renewed activity which Alfred tried unavailingly to check by securing promises that they would not assist the newcomers and taking hostages in the attempt to ensure that the oaths would be honoured. Throughout the campaigning which followed, Alfred's strategy was complicated by the assistance which the seaborne forces from the Danish occupied areas of England gave to their compatriots and by the covered route for withdrawal to their ships provided by the Danish controlled territories of northern and midland England.

Alfred prevented Hastein's band at Milton combining with the force at Appledore by positioning his army between them and soon afterwards that threat was temporarily removed when Hastein left Milton and established himself at Benfleet on the north side of the Thames Estuary. For some time operations between English and Danes were confined to local skirmishes in the Weald. After Easter in 893 the Appledore Danes broke out of their encampment, despatched their ships to Benfleet and ravaged Hampshire and Berkshire; but when they attempted to cross the Thames with the intention of joining Hastein and their own ships at Benfleet they were intercepted by Prince Edward, Alfred's eldest son, at Farnham and put to flight. The retreating Danes were besieged on Thorney Island for some weeks, but Edward's army had used up its provisions and completed its term of service before King Alfred arrived with the army under his command; although ealdorman Aethelred brought help from London Edward was compelled to negotiate with the Danes, accepting hostages from them as a pledge that they would leave Wessex.[1] This force made its way to Benfleet where it was attacked by an English army. Hastein's band was out on a raid and the English stormed the fortress and took everything within, both goods and people, including Hastein's wife and two sons. They were taken to King Alfred but because one son was his godson and the other a godson of ealdorman Aethelred both were restored to Hastein together with generous gifts of money. The combined Danish armies then established a new base, further down the river at Shoebury, and prepared for a raid into the Midlands.

The Danes had escaped disaster at Thorney because King Alfred's relieving force had been compelled to countermarch westwards to deal with an attack on Exeter by a seaborne army of Danes from Northumbria and East Anglia. The king's arrival raised the siege but operations in the south-west continued to occupy his attention while the Danes from Shoebury, reinforced by their Northumbrian and East Anglian allies, struck into the heart of England. They followed the Thames and then the Severn. A large English force gathered from every borough, West Saxon and Mercian, which could spare men for the operation, led by ealdorman Aethelred of Mercia and the ealdormen of Wiltshire and Somerset, and supported by a contingent of Welshmen, pursued them. At Buttington, near Welshpool the Danish force was overtaken and besieged for many weeks until famine forced them to break out from their camp. The English were victorious but could not prevent elements of the defeated force making their way safely to their base in Essex. Pausing only to put their women, ships and property in greater safety in East Anglia the Danes once again combined with a large army of their compatriots from Northumbria and East Anglia and moving by day and night they established themselves in the fortress of Chester, frustrating by their speed an English attempt to intercept them on the way.

The march to Chester was a remarkable tactical exploit but achieved no wider success. An English force ravaged the Wirral and

[1] *Supra* p. 221.

the Danes, driven by hunger, moved into Wales, which they devastated and plundered as far as the Bristol Channel. The expedition made its way back into East Anglia in the summer of 894, choosing a route through Northumbria which obviated the possibility of contact with English forces. A new camp on Mersea Island was occupied for only a short period and before the year ended the Danes had built a fortress on the river Lea, twenty miles above London. Here they remained until the following autumn. Nor had the Danish army in the south-west fared better; in 894 it turned homewards and while plundering near Chichester was badly mauled by the garrison of the borough. The initiative had now passed to the English. An attack on the Danish encampment on the Lea in the summer of 895 was repulsed, but in the autumn King Alfred personally conducted large-scale operations. The course of the river was diverted so that the Danes could not get their ships downstream, and forts were built on either side of the river. The Danes abandoned their camp and having placed their women in safety in East Anglia once again struck across the Midlands and encamped at Bridgnorth where they stayed the winter. 'And afterwards in the summer of this year [896] the Danish army divided, one force going into East Anglia and one into Northumbria and those that were moneyless got themselves ships and went south across the sea to the Seine.' Seaborne armies of Northumbrian and East Anglian Danes continued to harry the south coast of Wessex throughout the year and did considerable damage but they were successfully contained by the new warships which King Alfred had designed. The last three years of Alfred's reign were peaceful.

The *Chronicle* commented on Alfred's last war that: ' By the grace of God, the army had not on the whole affected the English people very greatly; but they were much more seriously affected in those three years by the mortality of cattle and men, and most of all in that many of the best king's thegns that were in the land died in those three years.' After the Danes left their camps in Kent only the coastal districts of southern England had been affected by seaborne armies, while on land they had been confined to raids which though spectacular in the distance covered had each time been countered by a sharp reaction from English forces. They were damaging rather than dangerous. The Danish assault had lost impetus; the last raiders had received support, recruits, and a refuge when things went badly from their compatriots already settled in England, but the crises of 871 and 878 had never threatened to recur.

When Alfred died in 899 the military situation was stable. Wessex and western Mercia, defended by a line of border fortresses, a re-vitalized fyrd, and the mutual understanding and military abilities of the West Saxon king and the Mercian ealdorman, were unlikely now to lose their independence. The offensive capacity of the Danes was almost exhausted and they were unlikely to receive significant warrior reinforcements either from Francia or from their homeland; but in much of England they were solidly entrenched. Alfred's unique achievement was to ensure the survival of his kingdom, but even at the end of his reign the prospect of conquering the Danish con-trolled areas of England appeared remote.

4. ALFRED'S CONCEPTION OF KINGSHIP: THE FOUNDATION OF ENGLAND

Had Wessex been conquered the range of Alfred's remarkable qualities could never have been revealed. Yet it was not military prowess alone which made him a great king; there had been great war-leaders before his day and his own son, Edward, was to show himself at least as competent a general as his father. What distin-guishes King Alfred from any other Anglo-Saxon king was the com-bination in him of outstanding military ability with an originality of mind and breadth of outlook which gave a new dimension to English kingship. His conception of royal authority, adopted and developed by his successors in easier political circumstances, made acceptable to all their subjects the expansion of the ' tribal ' kingdom of Wessex into the territorial kingdom of England. In this lies Alfred's title to greatness.

Alfred was the first king in England who identified himself with the ' English ', irrespective of their local affiliations. His predecessors, whether kings of Northumbria, Mercia, or Wessex, had been rulers who waged war on neighbouring kingdoms with the intention of reducing them to subjection and imposing tribute upon them.[1] The men of Kent or of Lindsey might be unable to reject the demands of a king like Offa, but they could hardly be expected to show him spon-taneous loyalty, and they rebelled against his authority as soon as they dared. That tribal kingship could be the focus of powerful

[1] Hart, ' The Tribal Hidage ', *op cit.* has argued that the very high assess-ment of 100,000 hides attributed to the West-Saxons in that document reflected the wish of Mercian kings to burden their only potential rivals as heavily as possible.

loyalty within the people was strikingly demonstrated in Wessex in the 870s but in its traditional guise it could have no wider appeal. The attitude of king to subject peoples would have to change if the West Saxon rulers were to take advantage of the Danes' destruction of the other English kingdoms.

Signs that such a changed attitude might be realized had already appeared in the ninth century; the contrast in the policies of Offa of Mercia and Egbert of Wessex to the Kentings is revealing. Offa subdued the Kentings by force and repressed their rebellions ferociously; he sought to undermine the authority of their archbishop over the English Church by establishing a rival to him within the confines of his own kingdom. But in 823 the people of Kent, Surrey, Sussex, and Essex, submitted to Egbert of Wessex; what arrangements he made for them are unknown, but his son Aethelwulf treated them not as conquered lands to be exploited but as an apanage for his son Aethelbald. Supported by his ealdorman Eahlhere, Aethelbald led the Kentings to victory over the Danes at Sandwich in 851. In 860 Aethelberht succeeded to both kingdoms, which were never subsequently separated. From Egbert's time successive West Saxon kings were careful to maintain good relations with the archbishops of Canterbury who, in the tenth century, became the most prominent props of the English throne. Such a policy, given time, could yield results on a larger scale.

In the face of a common danger the traditional animosity of Mercians and West Saxons had given way to occasional cooperation even before 865 and increased thereafter. Burgred of Mercia married a daughter of Aethelwulf of Wessex and West Saxons assisted the Mercians against both Welsh and Danes. This policy was taken further by King Alfred, who married the daughter of a Mercian ealdorman and arranged the marriage of his daughter Aethelflaed to the Mercian ealdorman Aethelred, who had assumed the military leadership of English Mercia by 883 after the Danish puppet Ceolwulf disappears from sight. Alfred's decision to entrust London to ealdorman Aethelred after its capture was an act of high statesmanship. Formerly the capital of the East Saxons, London had been annexed to Mercia by King Aethelbald; briefly taken from Mercia by King Egbert of Wessex, but recovered by Wiglaf and held by the Mercians until its conquest by the Danes, London was by now recognized as a Mercian town. By acknowledging this fact Alfred's action showed a diplomatic regard for Mercian sentiment at a time when

a simple annexation to Wessex appeared the obvious sequel to victory. Hostility and suspicion were gradually replaced by cooperation,
which in turn was to be transformed into a relationship of Mercian
dependence on Wessex achieved not by force but by diplomacy and
the recognition of common interests. Under Aethelred Mercia preserved a measure of autonomy; the ealdorman issued charters for
English Mercia in assemblies of Mercian lay and ecclesiastical councillors and he led the military forces of the kingdom, but at the same
time he recognized Alfred's superiority. For his part Alfred willingly
looked to Mercia to find churchmen better qualified to assist in
ecclesiastical and educational reform than any he could find in
Wessex, elevating one of them to the archbishopric of Canterbury.

Even in his dealings with the Danes Alfred established a pattern
which his successors could successfully follow. King Guthrum of East
Anglia had accepted Christianity in 878 and Alfred had acted as his
sponsor at baptism; Hastein's sons were godsons, one of Alfred, the
other of Aethelred of Mercia. With the Danish leaders Alfred tried to
establish relations of trust which if persevered with would generate
mutual tolerance. After the capture of London he concluded a treaty
with Guthrum which, while concerned to secure for Englishmen
living under Danish rule the best terms possible, yet fully recognized
Guthrum's authority east of Watling Street and was designed to
reduce occasions for friction between the two races.

Alfred's enlightened attitude to Mercians and Danes reflected his
adoption of a conception of the kingly office which though previously
given verbal currency had hitherto lacked practical content. Before
the end of the seventh century a Mercian king had claimed to be
king by God's grace, but Aethelred of Mercia showed no awareness of
what this implied, nor did his successors allow their political objectives to become obscured by the obligations of doing justice and
showing mercy. God's favour provided a support for authority, not
an indication of how authority should be exercised. The private
lives of the Mercian kings presented to their subjects little that
evoked the approval of their bishops, and Offa's predecessor was
rebuked by St. Boniface because his evil life set a bad example to his
people.

By contrast, the West Saxon ruling house from Aethelwulf onwards
was almost morbid in its religiosity. Whenever military exigencies
permitted, Alfred's thought was concentrated on the effort to live as

a Christian and to rule as a Christian king. The quality of his mind is well indicated by the character of the Latin works he selected for translation into English—the *Dialogues* and *Pastoral Care* of Pope Gregory; Bede's *History*; the *Books against the Pagans* of Orosius; Boethius's *Consolation of Philosophy*; the *Soliloquies* of Augustine; and, most of all, in the personal commentary which he freely interpolated into the texts of the later translations.

Augustine wrote at the beginning of the *Soliloquies*: ' Thou art one God, one eternal and true Substance; in whom is no discrepancy, no confusion, no change, no lack, no death; with Whom is fullness of harmony, of certainty, of content, of life. Thou art He Whom all things obey.' Alfred accepted this view of the universe and its corollary, that the end of living was the knowledge and understanding of God. ' Therefore it is needful that thou look straight with the eyes of thy spirit to God, as straight as a cable stretches taut from a ship to her anchor . . . And with those anchors wisdom, humility, prudence, moderation, justice, mercy, reason, maturity of mind, goodwill, cleanness and abstinence—with these thou shalt fasten firmly to God the cable that shall keep safe the ship of thy soul.' In his Preface to that work Alfred insisted that life on earth is a preparation for the life to come. ' It is for every man to live and work on earth in such a way that he may pass on with sure and certain hope to the eternal dwelling, to the work which has no end, the infinite increasing of knowledge in the nearer Presence of God.' The king's thought was epitomized in the last sentence of the Preface to the *Soliloquies*; ' He who created both [Heaven and Earth], may He grant that I fail not in either, but give it to me to fulfil my service here and, above all, to reach that house beyond.'

The role of a king in a world so conceived was burdened with obligations and unremitting service to the people entrusted to his care. He was responsible for his subjects' welfare; he must educate them in the truth and create the material conditions in which it could more readily be apprehended; the power which God had placed in his hands was a trust for which he would have to answer to God. Since no one man could supervise all his subjects it was particularly necessary that his efforts should be seconded by those of his subordinates, both ecclesiastical and secular, and for this to be effective they must understand and approve his purposes, and have sufficient skill and knowledge to implement them.

It was with this object in view that the king embarked on a programme designed to produce educated leaders for the service of the
kingdom and the Church. Since knowledge of Latin was almost dead
the first step to be taken was to

> turn into the language which we can all understand some books, which
> may be most necessary for all men to know; and bring it to pass . . .
> that all the youth now in England, born of free men who have the means
> that they can apply to it, may be devoted to learning as long as they
> cannot be of use in any other employment, until such time as they can
> read well what is written in English. One may then teach further in the
> Latin language those who one wishes to teach further and to bring to
> holy orders.

Since it was impossible to find West Saxons sufficiently learned to
perform the tasks of translation Alfred turned to Mercian scholars
for assistance. Plegmund, appointed archbishop of Canterbury in
890, came from the north-western area of Mercia; Waerferth was
bishop of Worcester; two other Mercian priests are known to us by
name. Our informant in these matters is the Welshman Asser, bishop
of St. David's who was also recruited by the king and wrote an
account of his life. The choice of Pope Gregory's *Pastoral Care* as one
of the first books for translation reflects the king's practical concern.
It lays down the duties of a bishop, emphasizing his responsibility for
educating the laity; a copy of the translation was sent to every see in
the kingdom. The translation of parts of Bede's *Ecclesiastical History*
made Englishmen aware of their past and especially of the traditional cooperation of kings and churchmen. Alfred's efforts were
concentrated on his court circle, for he knew that if the greatest men
in his kingdom could be fired with his own enthusiasm they in turn
would influence their dependants. If his bishops taught assiduously
the next generation of clergy would be better equipped for their
work. It was a programme which, however successful, would not
show results for a long time.

From Bede Alfred would have learned of the great part played by
monasticism in the religious life of England in more prosperous days.
With Latin learning, according to Asser, it had totally decayed
during the ninth century. Alfred decided to found two monasteries,
one for men at Athelney, and one for women at Shaftesbury. Asser
tells us that since no noble or freeman of English birth would now,
of his own accord, enter the monastic life, inmates for the new community had to be brought from overseas, principally from Gaul.

John, the Old Saxon, who probably came from the revived Benedictine monastery at Corbie, was appointed abbot of Athelney. Very soon dissensions broke out and the abbot narrowly escaped murder by one of his monks. Little is known of the later history of the monastery which may even have ceased to exist before the great revival of Edgar's reign. Alfred contemplated the foundation of a second monastery at Winchester; his intention was accomplished by his son, but though its head was Grimbald of St. Bertin's, described as priest and monk, it is unlikely that the New Minster was, even at its beginning, a monastic community. The nunnery at Shaftesbury, whose abbess was Alfred's daughter, Aethelgifu, may have been more successful, but it never achieved distinction and neither of the daughters of Edward the Elder who entered nunneries chose to go there. Alfred's attempt to revive monasteries was premature; for two more generations the greater churches would continue to be served by communities of secular priests.

In this sphere, too, it was only possible for Alfred to do what time and circumstances permitted. The letters from popes to which reference has already been made and the frequent references in the *Chronicle* to embassies carrying alms to Rome show that contact with the papacy was fully maintained.[1] Letters from Archbishop Fulk of Rheims to King Alfred and to Archbishop Plegmund show that contacts with Francia were not limited to the physical contacts made by travellers on their way to Rome. Yet even at Winchester no more than the years of the bishops' consecrations are known between 862 and 909.

For most of his reign preoccupied with survival and with the military measures that survival demanded of him it was only in his later years, and then only in limited fashion, that King Alfred could translate his ideas into practice. Even the code of laws which was promulgated towards the end of his reign is more concerned to preserve the best of the past than to introduce novel principles of action. The introduction to the *Laws* places them firmly in a Christian context; it begins with the Ten Commandments and is followed by the Mosaic law of Exodus, so that the English code could be seen as a local version of the law of Christendom. English was not synonymous with West Saxon, for Alfred claimed to have taken the most just laws that he could find in earlier collections, whether West

[1] *Supra* p. 204.

Saxon, Mercian, or Kentish. But though consciously Christian and English, the most striking feature of Alfred's code is its conservatism, expressed both in the description of the way in which it was formulated and in the content of its clauses. ' Then I, King Alfred, collected these [laws] together and ordered to be written many of them which our forefathers observed, those which I liked; and many of them which I did not like, I rejected with the advice of my councillors, and ordered them to be differently observed. For I dared not presume to set in writing much of my own, because it was unknown to me what would please those who should come after us.' In the code there is a new emphasis on the importance of abiding by the pledged word and on lordship; but it is still only as a last resort that the king will intervene directly to ensure conformity to the judgments of the courts, when a plaintiff has been denied justice by his adversary or by royal reeves, or when overmighty subjects deny right to their neighbours. The last half of the code, more than thirty clauses, consists of a table of compensations for private wrongs and personal injuries of the kind to be found in Aethelberht's earliest Kentish laws.

The importance of the Alfredian laws lies in the fact that it was the first legislation in England since the reign of Offa, that it applied to all lands under English rule, and that it projected aspirations which could be translated into practical forms by his successors. The king had accepted his responsibility to God for the welfare of his people. In order to fulfil the Divine mandate it might be necessary for him to extend his intervention into areas which earlier kings had ignored because in them they had no personal interest or profit; in so doing his authority would be vastly augmented. The West Saxon kings of the tenth century were to accept Alfred's conception of royal duty; in so doing they made possible the creation of England.

Alfred's abilities as warrior, military administrator and diplomat emerge very clearly from the narrative of his wars against the Danes. A novel and remarkable feature is that such a narrative can be composed with a certainty and wealth of detail unparalleled for earlier, and much of later, Anglo-Saxon history. That this is possible is no mere accident, but the consequence of measures taken by a king who realized that military victories could continue to be won only if the internal fabric of his kingdom was strong enough to sustain the incessant strains imposed on it by continuous warfare. Alfred's greatness lay in the combination of widely diverse qualities in one man whose whole life was dedicated to the purpose of defending his kingdom and mobilizing all its latent strength. Winning battles was only part of his function; he must also provide for the good government of his kingdom, a task which necessitated the cooperation of his subjects. Of his thoughts on these matters and its practical application to the business of government something has already been said, but his success in large part depended on making full use of the affection felt for his dynasty and the prestige it had acquired during the wars. It was probably with this practical purpose in mind that the history of the house of Cerdic was written, perhaps under Alfred's direction, at least with his encouragement.[1]

The compiler of the *Chronicle* had at his disposal Bede's *Ecclesiastical History*, a few sets of earlier West Saxon annals, and miscellaneous materials such as a few northern annals, some royal genealogies and king lists, and lists of bishops. In its early sections it reflected the limitations of its sources, comparatively full for some decades and almost barren for others; it deals fragmentarily with all the English kingdoms, but the link which gives the work its unity is its account of the West Saxon royal dynasty. Its real purpose becomes apparent as it reaches the middle years of the ninth century when it begins to relate the story of how the sons and grandsons of Egbert fought valiantly against the Danes and under Alfred finally repulsed them. Now that the other kingdoms were destroyed it is clearly, in the words of one of its great editors, ' a national Chronicle as opposed to merely local annals ',[2] and from 865 until 891 the history of the wars and of Alfred's successful leadership is related in considerable detail. This was court history written for propaganda purposes, to magnify the achievement of King Alfred and to mobilize support for him. Versions of the *Chronicle* in this form, down to 891, were probably circulated to the greatest churches in the kingdom, just as the translations of Pope Gregory's *Pastoral Care* was distributed to every bishopric in the kingdom. All seven extant manuscripts of the *Chronicle* are broadly identical as far as 891. Thereafter the manuscripts diverge in their content; there is no longer one *Anglo-Saxon Chronicle* but as many chronicles as there are extant manuscripts,

---

[1] But see Stenton, *Anglo-Saxon England,* who argues (p. 692) that ' the Chronicle has definitely the character of a private work '. The whole section pp. 688-94, is an invaluable review of the manifold problems presented by the Chronicles.

[2] C. Plummer in *Two of the Saxon Chronicles Parallel* (repr., Oxford, 1952 with an appendix by D. Whitelock), vol. II, p. civ.

and there must have been many other versions which have been lost.[1] After 891 some local versions of the *Chronicle* were kept up to date by adding to the parent manuscripts further materials supplied from the court or by adding such materials as fell into the hands of the local compiler; sometimes the manuscript was totally neglected for long periods. At Winchester the *Chronicle* was continued faithfully until 920 and so provides a full account both of Alfred's last years and most of the reign of Edward the Elder. In another version was incorporated an invaluable group of annals which provide details concerning events in Mercia up to 924, and materials drawn from northern sources were incorporated into two other manuscripts in their record of events between 925 and 957. But the impulse to historical writing was not long sustained, perhaps because it became less necessary. After 920 the *Chronicles* provide an inadequate framework on which to base a narrative of English history, until the miserable events of the reign of Aethelred stimulated a monk at Abingdon to take up once again the challenge of historical narrative; thereafter ensued another period of neglect until the reign of Edward the Confessor. But that it is possible to write a detailed account of the reigns of Alfred and his son is not the least important of the benefits conferred on posterity by Alfred's many-sided genius.

It is an equally remarkable and fortunate circumstance, but in this case a fortuitous consequence of Alfred's practical concern to secure the best available teachers for his kingdom, that he was the subject of the only secular biography written in England until that of Edward the Confessor a century and a half later.[2] For this reason Alfred's personality, character and objectives are more familiar to us than of any other pre-Conquest king, and of almost any post-Conquest king until Henry VIII. Indirectly, through Bishop Asser's ' Life ' every English child is familiar with Alfred's love of scholarship, illustrated by the story of how, as a small boy, the youngest of several brothers, he acquired from his mother a book of Saxon poetry which she had promised to give to whichever of her sons could soonest understand and repeat it to her. But there is more to Asser's

---

[1] One such was used by ealdorman Aethelweard, whose Latin version of the Chronicle has been edited by A. Campbell, *The Chronicle of Aethelweard* (London, 1962).

[2] This work, originally edited by W. H. Stevenson, was reprinted, with an additional introduction by D. Whitelock, *Asser's Life of Alfred* (Oxford, 1959). Its authenticity has often been challenged, recently by V. H. Galbraith. ' Who wrote Asser's Life of Alfred ', in *An Introduction to the Study of History* (London, 1964); but see D. Whitelock, *The Genuine Asser* (Reading, 1968).

biography than a collection of anecdotes. The bishop knew Alfred well and was in a position to know the facts which he relates, and he could appreciate the stature of a king who drove himself to ceaseless activity despite the handicap of crippling illness. Asser's ' Life ' is an essential companion to the *Anglo-Saxon Chronicle* for anyone concerned to understand the history of King Alfred's reign, for much of that history was the product of the king's genius.

That so much depended on the king's energy and determination is perhaps indicated by the fact that for many years after his death, the *Chronicle*, the translations and the biography had no adequate sequels.

Ripon•

•York

Tortsey• Lincoln (918)•

•Chester
•Farndon
Derby (917)• Nottingham (918)•
Repton•
Tettenhall•
✗ 910
Bridgnorth• Leicester (918)• •Stamford

Huntingdon (917)•
Northampton• Cambridge (917)•
Bedford (914)• •Tempsford
Buckingham• Witham (912)•
Gloucester•
Benfleet•
Chippenham• London• Sandwich•
Ashdown
Edington ✗ 878 ✗ 871 Canterbury•
Athelney• •Glastonbury •Winchester
Exeter• Wareham•

OFFA'S DYKE

The Danish wars 865-954

I I

THE MAKING OF ENGLAND

THE area of England over which the Danes had imposed their rule is conveniently known to historians as the Danelaw. Its territorial limits were largely determined in a treaty concluded *c*. 890 between Alfred and Guthrum, king of the East Anglian Danes. The frontier between the Danes and English Mercia followed the Thames Estuary as far as the mouth of the river Lea, leaving London in the English zone; it followed the Lea to its source and then went in a straight line to Bedford; from Bedford it followed the Ouse as far as Watling Street. All England north and east of this line as far as the Tees was the Danelaw. It was not a homogeneous area, nor was all of it heavily settled by Danes; it was simply the area in which as a result of the settlement of a Danish aristocracy on the land Danish law prevailed. In 899 it covered about half of England. Not since Alfred's capture of London thirteen years before had the native English made any inroads on Danish occupied territory.

If this situation appeared unpromising in reality the events of the last twenty years of Alfred's reign had significantly altered the balance of forces between Danes and English in favour of the English. The unity of the Danish army of 865 was an uncharacteristic and temporary feature of Viking activity created by the great reputation of its leaders, who had attracted under their command diverse bands of Danish warriors which normally operated as independent units under their own kings and jarls. After their departure from the scene and the piecemeal settlement of Danes on English soil all unity was lost. Their settlement pattern reproduced the character of their military organization, a congeries of independent districts which combined only in the face of imminent danger. Nor were Danish farmers working their holdings on the land as eager to engage in prolonged and hazardous military adventures as their Viking for-bears; they might engage in profitable forays against their English neighbours but they had no stomach for serious military operations. Finally, the prospect that English-based Danes might be stimulated into further activity by the arrival of large new seaborne armies from the Continent was a threat which receded further with each year that passed. The English by contrast, both West Saxons and Mercians, were united in their support of King Alfred's son, Edward, who was quickly to prove himself a military commander of genius, fully able to put his father's military reforms to the new uses which a changed political and military balance of power made possible. Edward demonstrated that fortified ' burhs ' and the reorganized fyrd could be as effective in offensive operations as in the past they had been in the defence of Wessex.

The reconquest of the Danelaw begun by Edward the Elder was not concluded until thirty years after his death; concurrently with conquest West Saxon institutions were modified and applied to the newly won territories, so that they might be permanently incorpor-ated into the new kingdom which was in process of creation.

1. The Reconquest of the Danelaw

The early years of Edward's reign (899-924) held little promise of the triumphs which were to follow. For the first time since the friction between King Aethelwulf and his son Aethelbald the internal harmony of the West Saxon ruling house was disturbed when Edward's cousin Aethelwold, son of Alfred's elder brother and pre-decessor Aethelred, rebelled against him. He received little support in Wessex, but having taken refuge among the Northumbrian Danes he was accepted by them as their king. In 901 a fleet under Aethel-wold's command secured the submission of Essex and in the follow-ing year he induced the East Anglians to break the peace and raid into Mercia and northern Wessex as far as Braydon in Somerset. Edward retaliated by penetrating East Anglia as far as the fens but suffered a tactical reverse when part of his army failed to obey his orders to withdraw; its Kentish contingent was overtaken by the Danish army and suffered heavy losses. Though the Danes remained in possession of the battlefield their dead included Aethelwold and Eohric, the East Anglian king, and the challenge to Edward's posi-tion, never serious, disappeared.

Some sort of peace between Edward and the Danes of East Anglia and Northumbria was made in 906, but in 909 it was Edward's turn to take the offensive and he launched a combined West Saxon and Mercian army on a five week raid into Northumbria. In the following year while the king was in Kent awaiting the mustering of his fleet the Northumbrian Danes retaliated by raiding into Mercia as far as the Bristol Avon. Edward reacted rapidly by mobilizing a West Saxon and Mercian army which intercepted the retreating Danes at Tettenhall in Staffordsire and there won a decisive victory which contributed to put an end to their aggressions for the remainder of the reign. Perhaps a more important factor explaining the passivity of the Northumbrians after 910, but a factor which also complicated the military problem confronting Edward and Aethelred of Mercia, was that these years witnessed a considerable immigration of Norse Vikings from Ireland into north-eastern England between the Mersey and Solway Firth. The first intimation of the new danger is the entry in the *Chronicle* that the fortifications of Chester were restored in 907, a measure clearly designed to protect Mercia from the new settlers in the Wirral. But English concern with the newcomers was no greater than the apprehension of the Danes of Northumbria; fears of the Irish Norsemen distracted them from participation against Edward during his campaigns of reconquest in the east and north Midlands.

In 911 Aethelred, ealdorman of Mercia, died and henceforth the cooperation between Wessex and the Mercians, now ruled by the lady Aethelflaed, Edward's sister, was closer than ever before, even though Edward took this opportunity of detaching London and Oxford and their adjacent territories from Mercia and subjecting them directly to himself. In 912 he was ready to take the initiative. His operations rested strategically on the assurance of Mercian cooperation and tactically on the building of fortifications which both secured his frontiers and provided firm bases from which offensive action could be mounted. Each year the frontiers were pushed forward and previous advances consolidated. In 912 Aethelflaed built forts at Scergeat (unidentified) and Bridgnorth, while Edward having built two forts at Hertford on either side of the river Lea to protect his northern flank, moved eastwards against the Danes of Essex; the building of a fort at Witham secured London from attack and effected a substantial territorial advance. In the next year Aethelflaed built Tamworth and Stafford, while Edward consolidated. In 914 offensive operations were delayed by a need to meet a Viking force from Brittany, which sailed up the Severn estuary and ravaged the coastal districts of Wales. The high standard of military efficiency of the English forces in both offensive and defensive operations was displayed in this campaign. The Mercian garrisons of Hereford, Gloucester, and the neighbouring boroughs concentrated and defeated the raiders, killing two of their leaders and extracting hostages as guarantee that they would leave the country. Meanwhile, West Saxon forces were deployed along the northern coasts of Somerset, Devon, and Cornwall, and though the enemy fleet twice attempted to make landings they were both times driven back to their ships and forced to take refuge on an island in the Bristol Channel until, driven from it by lack of food, they sailed to Pembrokeshire and thence to Ireland. This diversion served only to postpone the next stage of Edward's grand design which was resumed in the autumn of the same year. Aethelflaed built forts at Eddisbury and Warwick while Edward after building fortresses on both sides of the river Ouse at Buckingham received the submission of Thurketel, the leader of the Danes of Bedford and many of his leading men; their action was quickly followed by some of the Danes of Northampton. The fighting of the next two years followed the same pattern, of small gains firmly secured.

The campaign which opened in April 917 was different in character and consequences from those of previous years. For fifteen months successive contingents of the Mercian and West Saxon forces were continuously in the field, conducting a series of operations which extended along the whole length of the Danish frontier. The Danes, exponents of the raid but ill-equipped to deal with the steady and unrelenting pressure now applied by Edward, at no stage in the fighting operated under a unified command. Edward was able to deal with the Midland, East Anglian, and the Essex Danes in detail. At a critical moment of the war Aethelflaed struck in the rear of the armies facing King Edward and successfully assaulted Derby. By the end of 917 the armies of Northampton, Huntingdon, and Cambridge, together with the East Anglian Danes had made their submission to Edward, to be followed soon after by the army of Leicester which submitted to Aethelflaed. Within the next twelve months Nottingham and Lincoln surrendered without fighting, and all England south of the Humber was in English hands. The Danes, disunited, receiving no support from abroad, and looking over their shoulders at the Irish Norsemen had little heart for fighting an English army better led and better organized for war than their own. Early in 918 the leading men of York offered their allegiance to Aethelflaed, though nothing came of it because she died in June that year; but their act testifies to the readiness of the Danes to accept English rule. When the Irish Viking, Raegnald, established himself as king in York in 919 the reason for their action became apparent.

This event faced Edward with a new challenge; the new ruler of York could count on a constant stream of reinforcements from Ireland and in 920 an army from Dublin under Raegnald's cousin, Sihtric, raided into Mercia. Edward built new forts to protect his borders and prepared for an invasion of Northumbria, but before the expedition materialized the kings of York, Scotland, and Strathclyde, and Ealdred of Bamburgh submitted to him at Bakewell and acknowledged his overlordship. The agreement at Bakewell reflected both recent events in the north of England and Edward's recognition that as much territory had been recovered as could, for the time being, be assimilated into the new kingdom he was creating. The wisdom of this course of action was confirmed by the events of the last year of his reign. On the death of Aethelflaed Edward had assumed direct rule over Mercia, but as danger from the Danes receded so did the disposition of the Mercians to acquiesce in West Saxon rule; while the Welsh princes, who had sought Edward as their lord in 918, had no wish to see a much stronger ruler implementing traditional Mercian policy at their expense. In the summer of 924 the Mercian inhabitants of Chester with Welsh support rebelled against Edward; the rising was suppressed but shortly afterwards Edward died. His military genius has always been recognized but his wisdom in adjusting the pace of territorial advance to the resources at his disposal and the political realities of his day is generally ignored.

Edward the Elder's successsor Athelstan (924-939) was endowed by nature with high qualities and his Mercian upbringing made him more acceptable than was his father. Initially he was prepared to accept the situation established at Bakewell and in January 926 he gave a sister in marriage to Sihtric, who had succeeded his cousin Raegnald as king of York in 921. But Sihtric died in 927 and was succeeded by a son by a previous marriage, Olaf, who was supported by his uncle Guthfrith, king of the Dublin Norsemen. Aethelstan responded with an invasion of Northumbria. He captured York, drove Olaf and Guthfrith out of their kingdom, and brought southern Northumbria directly under his rule. At Eamont, near Penrith, the kings of Scotland and Strathclyde, and the ruler of Bamburgh reiterated their promises made at Bakewell to King Edward. The strength of Athelstan's position was remarkably demonstrated when in 934 he led a combined land and sea force against the king of Scotland. His army, containing English, Danes, and Welsh, penetrated on land as far as Fordun in Kincardineshire, while the fleet ravaged the coast as far north as Caithness. This demonstration of power was sufficient to convince all the neighbouring rulers that the West Saxon king was a threat to their independance. A coalition which was formed under the leadership of the king of Scotland and whose other members were the king of Strathclyde and Olaf, son of Guthfrith, since 934 king of the Dublin Norsemen, invaded England in 937. It is known that their army penetrated deep into England before being brought to battle, but the site of the engagement is still unidentified, despite the fact that it is named *Brunanburh* in a vernacular poem which describes the battle, and that it was a great victory for the combined West Saxon and Mercian forces under the king's generalship. A son of the king of Scots and five kings and seven earls from Ireland were killed; English losses were also heavy. The coalition was shattered, though the sequel suggests that the battle settled little in the longer term. Athelstan had successfully defended his acquisitions but no significant change in the balance of forces in northern England resulted.

Athelstan's death in 939 was followed immediately by a new invasion led by Olaf Guthfrithson, king of Dublin, who, before the end of the year had re-established himself in York. In the following year, after a vigorous campaign, he compelled King Edmund, Aethelstan's successor (940-946), to cede to him the whole district of the north-east Midlands known as the Five Boroughs. In 941 he turned northwards and his armies penetrated into Bernicia as far as Dunbar. In two years Olaf exposed the fragility of Athelstan's military achievement, though his death in 941 prevented a further deterioration in the situation. He was succeeded as king in York by his cousin, that Olaf Sihtricson who had been expelled from York in 927 and who again demonstrated his lack of martial quality. In 942 Edmund recovered the Five Boroughs and in the following year the Northumbrians expelled Olaf Sihtricson and chose Raegnald, brother of Olaf Guthfrithson, to be their king. Taking advantage of the rivalry of Olaf and Raegnald, Edmund invaded Northumbria in 944, expelled both of them and recovered York. The losses of the first year of the reign were now fully recovered, but Edmund's consciousness of weakness caused him to cede Cumbria to Malcolm, king of Scots, on condition that Malcolm ' became his helper by land and sea '.

When Edmund died in 946, to be succeeded by his brother Eadred (946-955), the Northumbrians swore fealty to him and promised their obedience, but their hostility to English rule quickly manifested itself again when, on the arrival of Eric ' Bloodaxe ', they immediately accepted him as their king. Eric was the son and successor of Harald Fairhair, king of Norway: some years previously he had been driven out of his kingdom and had then acquired a great reputation as a Viking leader. Eadred responded to the defection of the Northumbrians by leading an army into the north and though it was defeated in battle he was able to compel the Northumbrians to desert Eric and accept his rule. Two years later, however, the Northumbrians received Olaf Sihtricson once again as their king and he maintained himself in York until in 952 Eric Bloodaxe returned, drove him out and ruled as king for two years. Eric was killed in an ambush in 954 in circumstances not clearly understood, whereupon Eadred's control over Northumbria was re-established. The history of the years between the death of King Athelstan and 954 shows the continued hostility of the inhabitants of northern England to West Saxon rule, which imposed a serious check on what had hitherto been a gradual but uniformly successful process of reconquest and peaceful assimilation. But by 954 the subjection of all England to the West Saxon dynasty had been successfully accomplished.

For a hundred years West Saxon kings were preoccupied first with defending their own kingdom and then with extending its boundaries by incorporating into Wessex the territories of the English kingdoms which had been overthrown by the Danes. How considerable an achievement was this? In the early phases of war victory over the Danes was hard won, but already, before the end of the ninth century, the Danish assault had lost its momentum. King Alfred had demonstrated that they were not invincible and had taken measures to provide effectively for both defence and attack against them. Yet more than fifty years passed before Northumbria finally accepted King Eadred.

A great deal of debate has centred on the size of the Danish armies.[1] It has justly been remarked that both contemporaries and later historians grossly exaggerated the numbers of fighting men involved. Medieval writers did not conceive of numbers in exact terms; their concern was to indicate whether they were describing the exploits of a few ships, a raiding expedition, or a large fleet. The attribution to a Danish force of a fleet of several hundred ships means nothing more than that it was a large-scale expedition. A contemporary chronicler asserted that 700 ships and 40,000 men were involved in the siege of Paris in 885; such figures are incredible, and even smaller fleets when counted in hundreds of ships arouse misgivings as to how their crews fed themselves for long periods and organized themselves effectively during a campaign. Nor do the camps which they established, when identifiable, seem large enough to accommodate thousands of even temporary inhabitants. Sometimes too, the fighting men were accompanied by their women and children, which further reduced the effective size of the armies. The Danish armies were almost certainly considerably smaller than used to be thought, though it is difficult to accept the argument they seldom numbered more than a few hundred men.

A more important problem, and hardly related to the size of the armies, is the question of the density of Danish settlement on the land. The warriors were joined by later settlers who took advantage of the victories of the armies; that this phenomenon is virtually undocumented should cause little surprise—so too, is the settlement of a substantial Norse population in north-west England at this time which is well attested by place names. But the density of this settlement, which could have taken place over a prolonged period is highly debatable. It is a matter of fact that, in large areas of northern and eastern England the shires were divided into wapentakes not hundreds, land was measured in carucates not hides, and the unit of money was the ora not the penny; the peasant population was in general substantially freer than in the south and west, and so on; these peculiarities have generally been interpreted as evidence of heavy Danish settlement. The validity of this premise has been attacked on the grounds that such peculiarities could equally well stem from the dominance of a numerically small Danish aristocracy

[1] P. H. Sawyer in ' The Density of Danish Settlement in England ', *University of Birmingham Historical Journal*, VI (1957) and, *The Age of the Vikings*, argues that the size of Danish armies and the density of Danish settlement have been exaggerated.

able to impose its familiar customs on a subject native peasantry, and in themselves provide no evidence for a heavy settlement of Danish peasantry on the land.

There is, however, a general agreement that it is the linguistic rather than the legal or agrarian evidence which is crucial; this too, has been subject to considerable reinterpretation of late. It was traditionally argued that the linguistic evidence pointed conclusively to a fundamental distinction between the land lying between the Welland and Tees and the rest of England. In Normandy, which the Danes also conquered, the Scandinavian language quickly disappeared because the Danish element in the population was small, and being unable to communicate with the predominantly Frankish peasantry, was compelled to adopt the language of the conquered; conversely, the preservation and survival of elements of the Scandinavian language in northern England was held to be evidence of heavy Danish settlement. To this it is answered that the apparent persistence of the Scandinavian language in the north of England is equally well explained by the general similarity between the English and the Scandinavian languages in the late ninth century, which facilitated a degree of mutual assimilation. Many apparently Danish place names in the north and east are simply old English names combined with a Scandinavian personal name, though evidence that the lordship of such villages had passed into Danish hands reveals nothing as to the racial composition of their inhabitants; and when the first occurrence of Scandinavian place name forms is in Domesday Book they similarly provide no evidence of early Danish settlement. Nor can it be safely argued that all the persons with Scandinavian names who are encountered in tenth century records are of Scandinavian descent; it has been shown that by the end of the twelfth century between half and three-quarters of the inhabitants of East Anglia bore Norman names—but they were clearly not Norman in origin; personal names are very much a matter of fashion. The conclusion drawn from the evidence as to the size of armies and their subsequent settlement on the land is that the Danish settlers were too few in number to overwhelm the English and that they settled where they could, often on land which the English had not yet occupied.

There is some cogency in all these contentions, but in evaluating them it is essential to remember the long entered caveat of the traditionalists—that the term ' Danelaw ' is one that must be taken literally—it was the area in which the law administered in the local courts was Danish; it implies a Danish aristocracy but nothing as to the density of the Danish population within it. East Anglia was part of the Danelaw but the evidence argues strongly that there the Danish immigrants formed only a small minority of the population;[1] and this is equally true of the south-east Mercian shires. The problem at issue is accordingly confined geographically to the area of southern Northumbria, Lincolnshire, and the north Midlands, and the balance of the evidence so far adduced strongly suggests that here the Danes settled thickly. Since by the end of the twelfth century East Anglia was largely populated by men with Norman names it is the more remarkable that in northern England and the north Midlands more than half the total number of personal names recorded in the second half of the twelfth century are Scandinavian; this conservatism is hard to explain in terms other than of a substantial Danish population. Still more difficult to explain, on the assumption of close similarity of speech between the Scandinavian invaders and the Anglian inhabitants of Northumbria and Mercia, is the linguistic frontier which by the eleventh century had cut the old Mercian kingdom in half, leaving Oxfordshire clearly ' English ' and Leicestershire ' Scandinavian ' in their personal and place nomenclature. Much more will be written on this important problem[2] but it seems probable that the Danish settlement was sufficiently dense to render the conquest of the northern Danelaw a considerable military task.

2. THE INTEGRATION OF WESSEX, MERCIA, AND THE SOUTHERN DANELAW

The previous history of Anglo-Saxon England offered ample proof that conquest and the subsequent imposition of a forced subjection on the conquered was no permanent basis on which to build a state. Alfred's successors pursuing the policies adumbrated by him, did their best to reconcile both the Mercians, with their long tradition of hostility to Wessex, and the inhabitants of the recently conquered territories to rule by a West Saxon king, and at the same time they worked vigorously to provide for them the institutional machinery which would make that rule effective. The problems presented by

[1] R. H. C. Davis, ' East Anglia and the Danelaw ', *T.R.H.S.*, V (1955).
[2] A recent important contribution is J. M. Kaye. ' The Sacrabar ', *E.H.R.*, LXXXIII (1968).

English Mercia, the southern Danelaw and Northumbria were similar in kind, but different in degree.

King Alfred had established close ties with Mercia and its ealdorman Aethelred, which amounted to a formal acceptance of his lordship. While Aethelred lived the relationship established by Alfred was maintained by Edward the Elder who sent his son Athelstan to be nurtured at the Mercian court. A further step towards integration was taken when, on Aethelred's death, Edward detached the regions dependent on London and Oxford from Mercia and incorporated them into Wessex. The close cooperation of Edward and his sister in the campaigns of the following years shows that Aethelflaed did not resent her brother's action. On Aethelflaed's death in 918 Edward occupied Tamworth, the capital of Mercia, and all Aethelflaed's subjects accepted him as lord, though for some months her daughter Aelfwynn was allowed to exercise a nominal authority. Even this was shortlived, and when in the following autumn she was removed to Wessex the fiction of Mercian independence was brutally exposed. In the last year of his life Edward was faced with a Mercian revolt. But it is interesting to note that just as the ecclesiastical position of Kentish Canterbury had been accepted by the West Saxons, so did Edward's assumption of direct rule in Mercia signalize West Saxon identification with traditional Mercian policy towards the Welsh.

Since the death of Rhoddri the Great of Gwynedd in 878 at the hands of the English his sons had continued his policies, extending their influence in south Wales while retaining their independence of both Mercians and Danes. It was to secure protection from both Gwynedd and the Mercians that after Alfred's victory over the Danes in 878 the minor kings of the south placed themselves under Alfred's patronage. Meanwhile Aethelred of Mercia continued to follow the established Mercian policy of aggression in north Wales, but was heavily defeated in 881 by Rhoddri's eldest son Anarawd. Anarawd's response to Alfred's increasing strength was first to seek alliance with the Danish king of York, but when he proved an unsatisfactory ally Anarawd decided that his best security lay in accepting Alfred's overlordship in return for protection. During the campaigns of the 'nineties West Saxons, Mercians, and Welsh fought as allies. King Edward initially continued his father's protective role towards the south Welsh princes in return for their recognition of his overlordship; when a Viking host from Brittany raided up the Severn and

captured the bishop of Llandaff Edward paid the ransom for his recovery. But the new Norse settlement in the Wirral peninsula appears
to have stimulated the Mercians into more vigorous independent
action on their north-western border. Aethelflaed's fortresses were
built primarily to protect Mercia from Norse attack but those on
her western frontier threatened the Welsh. In 916 she led a punitive
expedition into Brycheiniog and it is possible that before her death
she had brought many of the Welsh princes nominally under her
control. Edward continued his sister's policy towards the Welsh and
his power was so great that the Welsh princes were reluctantly compelled to accept him as their lord, though the rebellion of 924 when
Mercians and Welsh combined against him reveals that neither were
reconciled to their new status.

Edward's successor Athelstan enjoyed an advantage denied to his
father, for having been educated at Aethelred's court he was not
regarded as an alien by the Mercian aristocracy. They elected him
king at Tamworth independently and prior to his election as king by
the West Saxons and throughout his reign there was no manifestation
of particularist disaffection. The great victory at Brunanburh in 937
was as much a Mercian as a West Saxon triumph. Athelstan pursued a
characteristically Mercian policy towards the Welsh, transforming
their formal submission into real subordination when in 926 or 927
he summoned the Welsh princes to Hereford and imposed a tribute
on them, fixing the Wye as the boundary between the two races in
that part of the country. At this time the dominant figure in Wales
was Hywel the Good, a prince of south Wales and a grandson of
Rhoddri the Great; he recognized the need to maintain close relations
with the English king, and other Welsh princes followed his example.
Welsh princes were frequent witnesses to Athelstan's charters, often
attending his court, and they abstained in 937 from joining the great
coalition against him. Athelstan fully implemented Mercian aspirations with regard to their Welsh neighbours.

Once again, in 957, Mercian self-consciousness manifested itself
when the Mercians rejected the rule of King Eadwig, but it was a
repudiation of the man not of the dynasty for they chose his brother
Edgar as their king. The division of the kingdom was shortlived, for
on Eadwig's death two years later the West Saxons accepted Edgar.
It is possible that the alignment of the supporters of Edgar's two
sons, rival claimants to the throne in 978, was affected by local
preferences, but of this there is no unambiguous evidence. By the

middle of the tenth century Wessex and Mercia were genuinely integrated; there were still local differences, and a twelfth-century writer could still distinguish the region of England in which Mercian law prevailed, but by then political aspirations to independence had long been dead. Even so, despite the presence of several favourable circumstances, unification had taken a long time.

Contrary to what might have been expected the southern Danelaw was absorbed into England more easily than was western Mercia. The Danish invasion had completely destroyed the old framework of society and administration and except in the north Midlands a Danish minority was settled among the English population. The Danes enjoyed no vestige of political unity, the English lacked any native focus of their loyalty. Accordingly, as Edward the Elder steadily advanced into East Anglia and the east Midlands the newly conquered areas were brought under West Saxon control without great difficulty. In this he was greatly aided by the rapidity with which Christianity had been accepted by the Danes. By 900 a cult of St. Edmund, the East Anglian king killed in battle against the Danes thirty years earlier, was firmly established. It was not long before men of Danish descent had risen to the highest positions in the Church; Oda, whose father was said to have fought in the army of Ivar the Boneless, was appointed bishop of Ramsbury in 926, and was later promoted to the archbishopric of Canterbury. Edward was a diplomat as well as a warrior, and did not scorn peaceful methods of strengthening his position. Even before mounting his great offensive, charters relating to land in districts as far apart as Bedfordshire and Derbyshire show him encouraging Englishmen to buy land from their Danish owners, and in 919 he assisted the migration to Francia of Thurketel, one of the Danish jarls of the east Midlands whom he had recently defeated. In the north Midlands, in the district of the Five Boroughs, Leicester, Lincoln, Nottingham, Stamford and Derby, where the Danes were settled intensively, the determinant factor was the establishment of Norwegians in York. As early as 918 the Danes of York had made overtures to Aethelflaed; the rule of King Raegnald there confirmed the Danes of the north Midlands in their belief that they had more in common with the English than with the Irish Norsemen. In 939 the king of York annexed the area of the Five Boroughs; the reaction of their inhabitants to King Edward in 942 when he recovered the territory was to receive him as a deliverer from oppression.

The further integration of England by the incorporation into it of the land and peoples north of the Humber was to present greater difficulties.[1] Northumbria was inhabited by a mixed population of English, Danes, and, after the beginning of the tenth century, Irish Norsemen, none of whom had reason to welcome the rule of a West Saxon king. The native English, who inherited a tradition of hostility to those of the south, were as prominent as the other peoples in opposing Athelstan and his successors. A late tradition recorded that it was the Northumbrians who persuaded Guthfrith to rebel against Athelstan in 927, on the grounds that they had always been independent of the kings of the southern English. Athelstan was a conspicuous benefactor of northern churches, particularly Ripon, Beverley, St. Cuthbert's and York, but even the leaders of the Church were not won over, and after his death one of the most powerful protagonists of Northumbrian independence was Wulfstan, the English archbishop of York. If the antipathy of the Danes for the Norsemen was exhibited first in 918 and again in 942, the equally strong antipathy of Northumbrians for Southumbrians is demonstrated by the career of Archbishop Wulfstan. Wulfstan accompanied King Olaf in his campaign of conquest of the Five Boroughs in 939, but accepted the consequence of King Edmund's later victories and in 946 promised obedience to Eadred; within a short time he had broken his promise and was eventually imprisoned by Eadred and deprived of his archbishopric. The circumstance most favourable to Wessex was that though no element in the population welcomed her kings or felt any positive loyalty towards them the different races of Northumbria felt an even greater dislike for one another. To make Northumbrians of all races feel themselves Englishmen was the most important problem which Eadred's successors faced, and for its accomplishment there was to be little time.

Even so, by comprehending the aspirations and traditions of the old tribal kingdoms into the policies of the new territorial kingdom, by waging war with armies drawn from all Southumbria, and by treating the Danes not as a conquered people but as subjects whose interests were as much to be considered as those of the native English, the West Saxon kings did much to promote a sense of common loyalty and common interest in England which transcended particularist traditions.

---

[1] D. Whitelock, ' The dealings of the kings of England with the Northumbrians ', *The Anglo-Saxons*, ed. P. Clemoes (London, 1959) is an excellent survey.

3. GOVERNMENTAL INSTITUTIONS OF THE ENLARGED KINGDOM

The motivation for such enlightened policies stemmed from the royally held determination that they would be kings of all men who lived in England, not merely kings of the West Saxons. Their success stemmed from the wholehearted conviction with which they embraced the image of kingship which King Alfred had put before them, and by the vitality of two notions concerning kingship which they did their best to foster; that the king was supreme lord of all men in his kingdom; and that he was God's vicar on earth, exercising a delegated authority from on high. Both notions vested the king with a wide authority; neither notion conceived of that authority as irresponsible.

The principle of lordship was deeply rooted in Anglo-Saxon society and Alfred's code of law had insisted that the tie of lordship was the strongest bond that could exist between men, stronger even than the tie of blood. From the reign of Edward the Elder it became customary for the great men of the kingdom to affirm the obligations which bound them to the king by swearing oaths of fealty to him, and to undertake ' to love all that the king loves and to shun all that he shuns '. As the West Saxon conquest proceeded the leading men of the conquered territories accepted the king as lord. At Colyton King Edmund's counsellors swore to be faithful to him ' even as it behoves a man to be faithful to his lord '. Loyalty to the king was the subject's first duty and they commanded that ' no one conceal a breach of it in a brother or a relative of his, any more than in a stranger '. But the concept of lordship was not onesided; as well as the lord's authority it comprehended the lord's obligation to protect and serve the interests of his men. The universal lordship of the king implied his protection of the rights of all his subjects.

But the king was not merely the most dignified of temporal lords; he was king by God's grace. Churchmen taught, and would continue to teach this doctrine with increasing fervour as the century progressed, until near its close one of them would write that a consecrated king ' has dominion over all the people, and they cannot shake his yoke from their necks '. On earth the king's power was absolute, nor was he answerable to his subjects. Yet his authority, delegated from on high, was held by him for the purpose of advancing the Christian welfare of his subjects, and ultimately he would have to answer to God for the manner in which he had performed his divinely appointed function.

These ideas concerning the nature of royal power impelled kings, in fulfilment of the obligations of their office, increasingly to extend the range and intensity of their activities in government; and induced subjects willingly to accept the increased degree of royal authority which flowed from such activities. To ensure that justice was done to all men they exerted their authority in supporting the proper functioning of the local courts; anyone failing to attend a court when summoned was fined, and anyone who refused to take part in measures against a man who refused to pay the fine was himself fined; where Alfred had exhorted his reeves to do justice, under his successors the denial of justice by a royal official or a lord incurred a heavy fine and loss of office. Since one of the king's first concerns was the maintenance of internal peace those offences most productive of disorder were made subject to the particularly heavy penalties traditionally imposed on offenders against the king's peace. Athelstan's second code laid down that ' it is to be announced in the meeting that everyone is to be at peace with everything with which the king will be at peace, and to refrain from theft on pain of losing his life and all that he owns ', the king and his counsellors thus agreed that the king might determine what constituted a breach of the peace and laid down the extreme penalty for its breach. King Edmund imposed limitations on the responsibility of a guilty man's kindred for his crime, a practice which could give rise to vendettas lasting for generations; Edmund isolated the criminal by declaring that if his kindred chose to disclaim responsibility for him they should be exempt from the feud, and if thereafter any of the murdered man's kindred took vengeance on anyone other than the actual slayer he would forfeit all his possessions. A procedure was laid down by which the leading men of the district were assigned responsibility for settling feuds peacefully. The same code declared concerning *mundbryce* (violation of the king's protection) and *hamsocne* (forcible entry of a house or injury to the persons inside), ' that anyone who commits it after this is to forfeit all that he owns, and it is to be for the king to decide whether he may preserve his life '. In this way the most serious offences against the peace came to be regarded as offences against the king. Later kings, while sometimes mitigating the penalties for such offences, extended their range and concerned themselves to improve the machinery for enforcing the decisions of the courts.

Good intentions were made practically effective by the development of institutional machinery to enforce them. North and east of Watling Street the governmental arrangements of the old kingdoms had been destroyed; in Wessex and English Mercia it is probable that the exigencies of war had necessitated a temporary reorganization of the kingdom on a military basis. One of the great achievements of the tenth century monarchy was its successful adaptation of the institutions of Wessex to meet the needs of the enlarged kingdom. By the time of King Edgar the English had become familiar with a royal court frequented by great men from all parts of the kingdom; with subdivisions of the kingdom known as shires, each of which possessed a court which met at regular intervals; and with subdivisions of the shires known as hundreds (in the Danelaw, wapentakes) which also had courts which met regularly.

Despite Danish invasions the governmental structures of Wessex and western Mercia continued to function and surviving evidence sheds a clear light on the activities of both West Saxon and Mercian assemblies. The highly complicated business relating to the succession to the West Saxon throne after Aethelwulf's death was determined in a series of councils and with the approval of the counsellors. To ensure their effectiveness land grants by kings to subjects and the testamentary dispositions of kings and their great men were made in conditions of greatest publicity in such assemblies. The participation of the counsellors was emphasized by King Alfred in the introduction to his code of laws. The composition and functions of the Mercian council in 896 are catalogued in the preface to a document of that year:

> Earl Aethelred summoned together at Gloucester all the Mercian council, the bishop and the earls and all his nobility; and this he did with the cognizance and leave of king Alfred. And then they deliberated there how they could most justly govern their people, both in spiritual and in temporal matters, and also do justice to many men, both clerical and lay, with regard to lands and other things in which they had been wronged.

After the death of ealdorman Aethelred no more is heard of the Mercian council and as Edward the Elder and his successors integrated Mercia and the Danelaw into their kingdom the court and council of the king of Wessex became the court and council of the king of England. Its nucleus continued to be the royal family and a small group of household officials and intimates who discharged the routine business of government, but often it was enlarged by the attendance of great men from all parts of the king's dominion. Of the detailed organization of routine work very little is known except that King Alfred tried to reduce the burden on his officers by arranging that their tour of duty should be limited to one month in three. In contemporary accounts of the Carolingian successor kingdoms signs of departmentalism in the household can be readily identified; hall, chamber, and chapel had each its own staff. It is reasonable to suppose that a comparable development occurred in England but there is no evidence for it. King Eadred's will mentions seneschals, chamberlains, butlers stewards, chaplains, and 'other priests', but there is no indication of specialization of function; the highly idiosyncratic formulae of Aethelstan's charters does suggest, however, that during his reign there existed a writing office staffed by trained clerks.

The counsellors with whom the king chose to discuss the affairs of his kingdom, irrespective of their number, were his 'witan'; they might be few or many. An example of a large session of the court is the assembly which met at Nottingham in 934 in which King Athelstan granted Amounderness to the church of York; it included the archbishops of Canterbury and of York, three Welsh princes, sixteen bishops whose dioceses ranged from Cornwall to Chester-le-Street, seven ealdormen, and six earls from the Danelaw. Meetings as well attended as this were infrequent, nor did they usually meet beyond the confines of old Wessex, but the assembly of 934 was not unique in either respect. They transmitted the old tradition of consultation which recognized that royal policies which failed to secure the cooperation of the great men of the realm would be inefficiently carried out. But it would be mistaken to think that in Anglo-Saxon England there was an institution styled 'the Witenagemot' whose members represented in any formal way the people of England, met at regular intervals, and possessed defined powers in government: the most important men in Kent and of the towns of Exeter and Totnes were similarly styled 'wita'. Attendance at the king's court was determined by the king's will; his chosen counsellors dealt with such business as he chose to put before them and at such times as he felt the desirability of consultation; there was no way of compelling a king to enlarge his court or to accept the advice of his counsellors. Nevertheless, such was the practical utility of bringing together the magnates of the kingdom that tenth-century kings were glad to provide frequent occasions for their meeting, and this practice must have contributed something towards the development of a unitary realm.

There were few matters on which the king might not seek the advice of his council. Kings continued to emphasize the elements of consultation and consent in the preambles to their legislation and to secure the assent of their counsellors before making grants of privileged land and, since they naturally wished to impress the representatives of foreign rulers with visible evidence of their dignity, foreign embassies were often received on occasions when the king was surrounded by the great men of his kingdom. An embassy from Hugh, duke of the Franks, was received by King Athelstan in a large assembly at Abingdon in 924, and a further embassy from Hugh twelve years later came to him at York. The comprehensiveness both of the membership and the business of the king's council is illustrated by an assembly held at Grately in Hampshire, attended by Archbishop Wulfhelm and ' all the nobles and counsellors whom the king could gather together '. The laws published on this occasion while primarily concerned with the maintenance of order affected all manner of people and many aspects of their daily lives. They dealt in turn with the measures to be taken against thieves, the lord who supported a guilty man, treachery to a lord, breaking into churches, and witchcraft, as well as edicts relating to the repair of boroughs, coinage, minting and a variety of other topics.

The wide-ranging character of the legislation and the importance of ecclesiastics in the king's council are a direct reflection of the way in which political authority was regarded. The preamble to Edmund's second code begins: ' I, King Edmund, inform all people high and low, who are under my authority, that I have been considering with the advice of my councillors both ecclesiastical and lay, first of all how I could best promote Christianity.' Such a definition of purpose might leave no activity immune from royal intervention and demanded that a prominent place among the counsellors should be reserved for the highest officials of the Church, whose advice and guidance would be particularly valuable.

While a king lived all initiative lay in his hands; but occasionally it might pass briefly to the great men of the kingdom who normally constituted the inner circle of his councillors. Generally there was no doubt about the succession; in 871 Alfred, in 899 Edward, in 924 Athelstan, in 939 Edmund, and in 946 Eadred were all so obviously fitted for kingship that their election was no more than a formality. Nevertheless this was no triumph for the principal of primogeniture; in 871 Alfred, and in 946 Eadred, were crowned, although their predecessors had left sons. In theory the whole royal family continued to be regarded as throneworthy and from its members he who appeared fittest to rule was chosen as king. Circumstances kept alive the principle of election. In 924, when there was no certainty that the union of Wessex and Mercia would be maintained, Athelstan became king of the Mercians but was not accepted by the West Saxons until the next year. In 955 Eadwig the eldest son of King Edmund was crowned king of England, but two years later the Mercians rejected him in favour of Edgar. On Edgar's death the reality of election was underlined by the need to choose between his two sons by different marriages. On this occasion the strength of the principle of ' blood-worthiness ' as an indispensable attribute of a king was demonstrated with equal force by the absence of any rival candidate for election, despite the fact that neither of Edgar's sons was old enough to exercise effective rule. Such occasions were rare, and a king, once crowned, was free of any constitutional limitations on his power.

The king's will was made known to his subjects and royal oversight of the workings of local government was maintained through the activities of local institutions, the courts of shires and hundreds.

By the middle of the ninth century Wessex had long been familiar with subdivisions of the kingdom styled shires, governed by officials entitled ealdormen. In Mercia royal officials bearing the same title frequently witnessed the charters of Mercian kings but they seem to have been numerous and there is no evidence which associates them with fixed territorial districts. Of local government in the rest of England before the Danish wars nothing is known for certain. In the tenth century the West Saxon shire system of local government was extended to cover all England south of the Mersey and the Tees. This achievement testifies to both the administrative ability of the West Saxon kings and their material strength.

In the ninth-century annals of the *Chronicle* the West Saxon shire appears primarily as a military district, and its ealdorman as the leader of the shire levies; in 837 ' ealdorman Aethelhelm fought against a Danish army at Portland with the men of Devon '; in 847 ' ealdorman Eanulf with the men of Somerset and bishop Eahlstan and ealdorman Osric with the men of Dorset fought at the mouth of the Parret '. Alfred's *Laws* reveal the ealdorman presiding over a moot, so it is probable that the shire was also a judicial unit. How well the system operated during the wars is uncertain, but it seems likely that military considerations encouraged the concentration of power and for some part of the time there may have been only two ealdormen in Wessex, while in some frontier districts the fortified boroughs became the administrative as well as the military centres for their adjacent countrysides. Crisis conditions did not last long enough for these arrangements to establish themselves. The few extant charters of Edward the Elder that survive show that early in his reign every shire in Wessex had its own ealdorman and the diocesan reorganization of 909 appears to assume that every shire ought to have its own bishop.

As lands north of the Thames were brought under West Saxon control they were assimilated into the West Saxon system, with the difference that whereas the southern shires were the culmination of many years of political development those further north were either artificially created by the royal will or represented the governmental arrangements of their Danish settlers now accepted by their English rulers; in either case the new shires were, from the first, based on fortified boroughs. The shires of English Mercia were probably created by King Edward in the last years of his reign. His concern was to establish efficient units of local government which would not encourage or revive traditional loyalties. The shires of Gloucester, Worcester, and Warwick were carved out of the old kingdom of the Hwicce; Shropshire comprised lands which formerly belonged in part to the Magonsaetan and in part of the Wreocensaetan. In the reorganization the Mercian ' capital ', Tamworth, was ignored. In the areas of Danish settlement the newcomers had introduced the methods of government which they knew. When the independent Danish armies settled on the land their leaders established themselves in the fortified boroughs of Bedford, Cambridge, Huntingdon, Northampton, Leicester, Derby, Nottingham, Stamford, and Lincoln, around which the rank and file grouped themselves. The borough was the administrative centre of the men of the army in time of peace and their rallying point in time of war. These areas were the natural products of Danish settlement. They bore no relation to pre-existing territorial divisions and were in no way the product of external authority. The boundaries of their territories were fixed by mutual arrangement. When the Danelaw was reconquered no attempt was made to change the territorial divisions which the Danes had created.

The shiring of the Danish Midlands did not occur all at once:

its timing depended on the date at which they were brought under West Saxon control. Nor until some time after 945 could the land between the Humber and the Tees, which had been occupied by Halfdan's army, become Yorkshire, while the lands north of the Tees and the Mersey remained unshired until after the Norman Conquest. It is probable, too, that even in the Midlands shire boundaries did not achieve stability for many years. When King Eadred made his will he left money in trust for the relief of the inhabitants of the southern shires should need arise; each was mentioned by name. For Mercia only general provision was made; ' Bishop Oscytel is to receive four hundred pounds and keep it at the see of Dorchester, for the Mercians.' A charter of 958 still refers to ' a certain estate in the province of the Magonsaete '. The large size of Domesday Gloucestershire is probably due to its absorption of the former shire of Winchcombe early in the eleventh century: the lands of the army of Stamford became part of Lincolnshire.

By the middle of the tenth century the shires were subdivided into districts styled hundreds, or, in those areas where Scandinavian influence was strongest, wapentakes. Since the shires of midland and northern England were the creations of West Saxon kings and took no account of earlier territorial arrangements it is clear that their subdivisions, whether styled hundreds or wapentakes, were also the products of the governmental initiative of West Saxon kings. The West Saxon shires, whose existence as we have seen is attested at a time well before the Danish invasions, had come into existence either through the grouping of early provinces into new administrative units or by their creation by West Saxon kings out of lands newly conquered from the British.[1] Whatever its origin it is obvious that a territorial unit as large as the shire would be too unwieldy for many purposes of government and that there was always a need for a convenient local unit for tax collection, the raising of armies and the determination of disputes. Though one tradition maintained that the West Saxon hundreds were created by King Alfred it is far more probable that many of them originated much earlier, in the subdivision of early provinces which had themselves been merged into shires. The extreme irregularity of assessment of the West Saxon hundreds in the tenth century, which contrasts sharply with the remarkable symmetry of the midland hundreds all neatly assessed at round hundreds of hides, argues for their antiquity.

[1] *Supra* pp. 139-40.

Surprisingly, the first mention of the hundred by name occurs no earlier than the reign of King Edmund, but within two decades it merited special legislation. These considerations suggest that Edmund and his successors put an old institution to new, or, at any rate, more important uses than those for which it had hitherto been employed. By them the hundred was made an essential part of the machinery for the enforcement of internal order. In the early years of Edgar's reign the hundred appears primarily as the instrument for the prevention of the most prevalent of all occasions leading to disorder, theft, particularly of cattle, and for ensuring that if thefts were committed the offenders would be apprehended and punished. A man wishing to buy cattle was required to give notice of his intention to his neighbours; if he made a purchase unexpectedly he had to inform his village immediately on his return —if this was not done the villagers had to inform the head of the hundred. In every hundred twelve permanent witnesses were chosen, two or three of whom were required to witness every purchase within the hundred so that in the event of a dispute they could vouch for the legitimacy of the transaction. If a theft occurred the men of the hundred were required to go in pursuit of the thief and failure to participate in the chase was punished by fine to the hundred and to the guilty man's lord; for a second offence a double fine was imposed and the penalty for a third offence was outlawry. If a fugitive escaped into another hundred the chief man of that hundred was responsible for taking up the pursuit and if this was not done a fine was payable to the king.

Though its police function was the aspect of hundredal activity stressed in legislation it had other uses. For the administration it continued to be the basic sub-unit for tax collection while for the individual it was a court in which private pleas were determined according to the customary law. Distraint of property was forbidden until justice had been sought three times in the hundred court. Non-attendance at the hundred court incurred the penalty of a fine. The court met every four weeks under the presidency of the king's reeve.

The effectiveness of this elaborate hierarchy of courts was maintained by a matching hierarchy of royal officials. Directly subordinate to the king were his ealdormen. In ninth-century Wessex every shire had its own ealdorman, Kent had two, and there were a considerable number in Mercia. During the reign of Edward the Elder their number was greatly reduced and for most of the tenth century there were generally only eight ealdormen south of the Trent, five in the midlands and East Anglia and either two or three in Wessex; in the Five Boroughs and Northumbria were a number of men of Danish race who styled themselves 'eorls' but who exercised no official functions. As a result of the expansion of the English kingdom the territorial area of the ealdorman's activities was similarly enlarged and he became more like a provincial governor entrusted with the general oversight of a group of shires than a local administrator and military leader. The ealdorman's principal functions were presiding over the shire court, the publicizing and carrying out of royal commands within his ealdormanry and the execution of the law against those who had set it at defiance. For his labours he was rewarded by monetary privileges of various kinds, an elevated status, and by estates permanently and officially connected with the office.

Despite the enhanced status of the ealdorman he remained a royal official, nor was his office hereditary, despite occasional appearances to the contrary. Although sons frequently succeeded fathers, as Athelstan of East Anglia was followed by his son Aethelwine and in Mercia Aelfric succeeded his father Aelfhere, yet a brother of Aelfhere had obtained an ealdormanry in Wessex to which he could have possessed no hereditary claim. The succession of son to father, when it occurred, reflected the monopolization of political power in England at the highest levels by a group of great families few in number and closely connected both with the royal family and with each other. It was no longer possible for kings to marry the daughters of other English kings nor did they seek brides overseas and it may have been deliberate policy on their part to establish marriage ties with the greatest figures in the countryside calculated to assist in binding the kingdom together more closely. King Alfred, who himself married the daughter of a Mercian ealdorman, gave a daughter to ealdorman Aethelred of Mercia and at least two of his son Edward's three wives are known to have been the daughters of ealdormen. King Edmund's second wife, Aethelflaed of Damerham, was the daughter of an East Anglian who had been an ealdorman in Wessex —her sister married ealdorman Byrhnoth. King Edgar's first wife was the daughter of ealdorman Ordmaer; his second wife, previously the wife of Aethelwold, ealdorman of East Anglia, was the daughter of ealdorman Ordgar. The brothers Aelfheah and Aelfhere, ealdormen in Wessex and Mercia respectively in the reigns of Eadwig and

Edgar, were described as the king's kinsmen. From among the members of this narrow group of kinsfolk the king's choice as ealdormen fell on men who had been for some years in attendance on him and had proved their loyalty and capacity in his service. Promotion did not detach the ealdormen from the royal court. The charters of tenth-century kings were generally witnessed by some of their ealdormen who in their persons formed links between the court and the provinces. At times, as during the disturbances which followed the death of King Edgar, the power latent in the office became apparent as political factions aligned themselves behind Aelfhere, ealdorman of Mercia, and his opponents, Aethelwine of East Anglia and Byrhtnoth of Essex.

Associated by Asser with the ealdormen in the task of administering justice in the localities were reeves and thegns. Their concerns extended to all matters in which the king interested himself. Edward's law commanded that the local assembly which preceded the hundred court should meet every four weeks under the presidency of the district reeve, who was commanded to see that every accusation and complaint of injustice brought to his notice was heard and determined. Suits concerning folkland were decided before him in this court, and to help maintain public order traders travelling upcountry were required to produce publicly in court the men they intended to take with them, their number being limited to such as they could guarantee to bring to justice in the event of their wrongdoing. In Aethelstan's reign the reeve was one of the local dignitaries whose witness validated any exchange of cattle and he was made responsible for pursuing the trail of cattle reported stolen. It is difficult to be precise about the king's reeves' functions because the legislation which describes it reveals that lords other than the king made use of reeves and that the king might well employ several reeves within a shire not all of whom were necessarily employed for the same purposes. Whether the reeves who supervised the royal estates within the shire and were responsible for ensuring that royal tithes were fully paid were sometimes or always or never the same men who presided over the local courts is not clear; but that one group of reeves performed special functions in the boroughs is well attested, as is also a class of high reeves whose authority presumably extended over a wider territorial area and perhaps embraced a more extended range of business than was committed to the ordinary reeve. All reeves were immediately subject to the king's will; if they failed to enforce the law they were subject to fining, expulsion from office and loss of status.

The most important reeves were likely to be king's thegns, local landowners owing direct allegiance to the king. In the reign of King Alfred their military role in the kingdom was most prominent, but as the century progressed the effective operation of local government can be seen to have depended largely on their activities and they assumed a key role in the public assemblies of shires and hundreds. They were the most dignified members of a much larger class of men who, in the tenth century, were styled ' thegns '.[1] The term ' thegn ' had originally meant ' servant ' but by this time its use was restricted to describe the highest échelon of the servants of great lords and it thereby acquired the significance of ' nobleman ' whose holder enjoyed the nobleman's wergild of 1,200 shillings. Thegnage was an hereditary rank but not a closed caste. An early eleventh-century document declared that ' if a ceorl prospered, that he possessed fully five hides of his own, a church and a kitchen, a bell-house and a castle gate, a seat and a special office in the king's hall, then he was henceforth entitled to the rights of a thegn '. A merchant could attain thegn-right by three times crossing the sea at his own expense. The rank could be acquired either through personal service to the king or a great lord or through the acquisition of a sufficient estate in land, but not until the qualifying criteria had been satisfied by three generations did the possessor of thegn-right become permanently ennobled. Rank could be forfeited for cowardice in battle or the betrayal of a lord, for pronouncing false judgments or promoting injustice. Five hides of land was the notional norm associated with thegnly rank but because the rank was hereditary and territorial holdings were partible the range of thegnly estates varied widely; some were minute, no more than a peasant might possess, but others comprised lands in several shires. The thegnage, in consequence, embraced men of widely differing degrees of importance. Not only were there Danish thegns and English thegns, but also king's thegns and king's thegns ' who stand nearest to him ', all of whom paid heriots or death duty of varying amounts; as well there were the thegns of bishops and

[1] Although the most specific documentary evidence relating to thegnage comes from the first half of the eleventh century there is little reason to suppose that its content is novel. See H. R. Loyn ' Gesiths and Thegns in Anglo-Saxon England from the seventh to the tenth century ', *E.H.R.*, LXX (1955) the same author's ' The King and the structure of society in late Anglo-Saxon England ', *History*, XLII (1957), and *Anglo-Saxon England and the Norman Conquest*. ch. 5.

lay noblemen, who might themselves have dependants who styled themselves thegns.

The thegnly class provided valuable contacts between the king and the local communities and in innumerable ways the effective operation of local government depended on their activities. The greatest among them might be found at times in personal attendance on the king, sometimes leaving him to engage on some piece of royal business. Some of them were so dignified that they were served in the king's hall by their own thegnly retainers and so immersed in royal business that their thegnly inferiors might be authorized to represent them in actions before the local courts. The importance of the king's thegns to him was such that jurisdiction over them was reserved to the king. Far more numerous were the ordinary thegns whose activities were concentrated in the public assemblies of shires and hundreds. A man accused of certain offences had to find at least one thegn among his oath-helpers if he sought to rebut the charge. In the Danelaw a jury of twelve leading thegns in each wapentake was required to denounce men suspected of serious crime and to assist in their arrest by the reeve. Everywhere they formed the main body of the suitors of the shire court. Increasingly, too, the thegns assumed importance for the jurisdictional powers they came to enjoy over their estates and their dependants; by the eleventh century many thegns held courts which adjudicated in land disputes between free tenants on their estates, punished breaches of agrarian routine and heard accusations against men accused of having stolen goods in their possession. In this lay profit for the landowner, but it also served the king's purpose of maintaining the vitality of the machinery of justice, and if Edgar's enactment that thegns giving unjust judgments were liable to lose their rank was enforceable it left a powerful sanction in the king's hands.

Recognition of the governmental achievements of the tenth century and of royal concern for the maintenance of internal peace must not obscure the facts that they were made possible and necessary by successful war and that to Anglo-Saxon kings military pre-occupations continued to be paramount. Until 954 they were constantly required to fight first Danes then Norsemen, and some years, like 937, the year of the Brunanburh campaign, were militarily critical. Edgar's peace partly depended on the respect which his army and navy inspired in his neighbours and after his death the resumption of

Danish attacks underlined the importance of adequate defences. The late Old English kingdom was made by, and continued to be organized for, war and even where kings granted privileged estates to favoured churches or laymen the obligation to the military burdens of fyrd-service, bridge-building and the construction of fortresses was reserved to the king. Despite the importance of military institutions, and though it is clear that after their reform by King Alfred English armies proved adequate to the demands made on them for both defensive and offensive operations, there is little agreement among historians concerning their composition and recruitment, nor is there agreement as to the extent to which, if at all, after Alfred's day older institutions continued to be modified to meet the needs of the enlarged kingdom in an age of rapid social change.

The conquests had been accomplished by war bands; after their establishment on the land the circumstances of the settlers often resembled those of the early immigrants in North America, who, living always in danger of Indian attack, at any moment might be compelled to lay down their farming implements and take up their weapons. The fighting role of the peasant is attested by the weapons found in graves of the pagan period, too numerous to be explained as the possessions of kings and their retinues; by the clause in Ine's *Laws* which laid down a penalty for the ceorl who failed to perform his military service when summoned; and by the vitality of the principle, which survived the Norman Conquest, that all freemen were required to possess arms. But increasingly, after the settlement was secure the peasant's efforts had to be concentrated on extracting a living from the reluctant soil with the primitive tools available to him. By the time that the tribal kingdoms were established it appears that fighting had become predominantly the business of kings and lords together with their retainers, an aristocratic exercise in which the role of the peasant was limited to that of a carrier of provisions for the fighting troops and general labourer. The peasant element in the armies led by Aethelfrith to Chester, by Penda to the Winwaed, or by Egbert into Derbyshire was probably very small. It seems reasonable to suppose that while the free peasant continued to be liable for service at his king's command practical considerations confined his use to defensive operations in the vicinity of his home. A charter of Cenwulf of Mercia (797-823) may reveal an attempt by the king to improve the quality of service rendered by the peasant element by substituting selective service for the principal of universal conscription; it records the grant of an estate of thirty hides on terms which demanded the service of only five men when the fyrd was called out.

By the eleventh century selective service had become customary in certain areas of England but what progress, if any, it had made by the age of Alfred we do not know. The threat posed by the Danes was new and urgent, and whatever arrangements for military service had been adequate in a previous age were now insufficient. Alfred himself divided his people into those who prayed, those who fought, and those who worked, and allocated one-third of the revenue he reserved for secular uses to pay his fighting men and the thegns who served him at court. But such distinctions were unreal in emergency conditions; prominent among West Saxon military commanders were a number of bishops, and peasants would fight in defence of their homesteads. The armies which fought the Danes appear to have been differently composed according to the nature of the operations on which they were engaged. The ninth-century annals of the *Chronicle* are replete with entries recording how ealdormen led the forces of their shires against bands of marauding Danes; on such defensive operations of brief duration and limited geographical range local landowners and peasants might be expected to fight without regard to precise social status and legal obligations. In 878 the small company of household retainers which Alfred led into Athelney was subsequently reinforced by ' all the people ' of Somerset, Wiltshire and part of Hampshire. But in 893 the English army which pursued the Danes to the Upper Severn under the command of three ealdormen was composed of king's thegns ' from every borough east of the Parrot, and both east and west of Selwood and also north of the Thames and west of the Severn, and also some part of the Welsh people '; in the battle which ensued ' the king's thegn Ordleah and many other king's thegns were killed '. In his summing up of the effects of the last campaigns of Alfred's reign the chronicler reflected that one of the most serious injuries that the kingdom had suffered was ' that many of the best king's thegns that were in the land died in those years '. The prominence of the king's thegns in the warfare of both Alfred and Edward the Elder leaves no doubt that they bore the brunt of the fighting; but both in local engagements under their ealdormen, and in battles fought by royally commanded armies, the lesser landowners and free peasantry had an important part to play. Asser tells us that the noble thegns who served the king were divided into three companies, each serving for one month at court and then returning home for two months; Alfred's division of the fyrd into two sections with alternating periods of active service may have extended the principle to the landowners and free peasantry of the shires. Even after the English had moved to the offensive the methods of warfare favoured by Edward the Elder depended on the availability of second-line troops who could be used to drain rivers and to build fortifications. In later campaigns the forces employed by kings were probably smaller numerically and more specialized in their training, but the events of Aethelred's reign would show that in an emergency larger armies could still be mobilized and kept in the field for long periods. The size and the composition of armies long continued to be determined by the judgment of the king and his councillors as to what was necessary for the operation in hand. How Alfred, Athelstan and Edgar recruited their naval forces is unknown.

Some measure of the success which attended the efforts of the kings between Alfred and Eadwig in their objective of creating a unified kingdom is indicated by at least three quite different kinds of evidence.

The poem on the battle of Brunanburh in the *Anglo-Saxon Chronicle* reveals the solidarity of West Saxons and Mercians in 937:

. . . The whole day long the West Saxons with mounted companies kept in pursuit of the hostile peoples, grievously they cut down the fugitives from behind with their whetted swords. The Mercians refused not hard conflict to any man who with Olaf had sought this land in the bosom of a ship over the tumult of waters, coming doomed to the fight.

And the poem annal recording the recovery of the Five Boroughs in 942 speaks of King Edmund, ' the lord of the English, protector of men, the beloved performer of mighty deeds ' and relates that, ' the Danes were previously subjected by force under the Norsemen, for a long time in bonds of captivity to the heathens, until the defender of warriors, the son of Edward, king Edmund, redeemed them, to his glory '.

In these passages the spontaneity of Mercian and Danish acquiescence in West Saxon rule finds expression.

In a tangible and visible way the reality of the king's power was manifested to his subjects almost every day in their lives. King Athelstan decreed that ' there is to be one coinage throughout the king's realm and no man shall mint except in a town ', and this enactment went on to regulate the number of moneyers in each town. Every coin bore on its face the imprint of the king's head. Central control was assured since all dies were cut at a central workshop from which they were distributed to or collected by the local moneyers. Infringements of coinage regulations were savagely punished; the hand of a moneyer found guilty of issuing base or light coins was cut off and fastened to the mint. This close royal supervision of the coinage was never to be relaxed throughout the Anglo-Saxon period, even though the number of mints and of moneyers steadily increased. Control of the coinage was a profitable perquisite of the crown and the proliferation of minting places in the tenth century suggests that peace provided a considerable stimulus to internal trade which through its need for coined money made a handsome contribution to royal revenues, already increased by the extension of the king's profits from the operations of the courts.

Finally, the unity, and consequently the strength, of the kingdom was attested by its prominent role in the political affairs of western Europe.

3. The Resumption of Diplomatic Relations with Continental Rulers

The kingdom created by the military prowess of King Alfred's descendants was a more considerable power than even the England which Offa had ruled. Though the cessation of Viking raids would in any event have favoured the resumption of contacts of all kinds with Europe, yet the assiduity with which continental rulers courted the alliance of English kings is striking testimony of the respect in which England was held abroad during the first half of the tenth century. A combination of English military strength, the confused political situation in western Europe during these years, and the availability of English princesses generated diplomatic relationships with foreign courts on an unprecedented scale. The renewal of friendly relations with Flanders had already been symbolized when King Alfred gave his daughter Aelfthryth in marriage to Count Baldwin; when Edward the Elder married a daughter, Eadgifu, to Charles the Simple, king of the west Franks, England was brought into the mainstream of western European politics.

In Francia during the latter part of Edward's reign the authority of Charles the Simple was being challenged, internally by his great vassals, of whom Robert, count of Paris, was the most prominent, and externally by Henry I, king of Germany, who coveted Lotharingia. Both of them sought to secure English support or, at least, English neutrality. In 922 Charles the Simple lost effective power over his kingdom and after his death in 929 his son Louis, King Athelstan's nephew, was brought by his mother to the English court where he lived under Athelstan's protection until 936. Before this, in 926, an embassy had come to Athelstan from Hugh, count of Paris and son and successor of Robert, who, though he had himself refused to accept the French crown none the less wished to establish ties with England on his own account; before the year's end he had married Athelstan's sister, Eadhild.

The domestic troubles of the Frankish kingdom had given Henry I of Germany the opportunity to seize Lotharingia; his concern was to prevent the English king providing support for Charles's exiled son Louis. He, too, sent an embassy to England seeking an alliance; in 928 Edith, another of Athelstan's sisters, married Henry's son Otto, the future king of Germany and emperor. It is said that Henry was given the choice of two sisters and that the less favoured one subsequently became the bride of the king of Burgundy. In 936 the opportunity arose for the restoration of Louis to his father's kingdom. The initiative was taken by Hugh of Paris, who for a second time had refused to accept the Frankish crown for himself; he again sent an embassy to Athelstan to negotiate terms. Satisfied that Louis would be well received if he returned, Athelstan provided the escort which conveyed Louis back to his kingdom. Three years later the Lotharingian magnates sought to emancipate themselves from German control and revert to their Carolingian allegiance, confronting Athelstan with the choice between the conflicting claims of two sisters. An English fleet was despatched to assist Louis. Though the military intervention proved ineffective the diplomatic exchanges of these years indicate the importance attached by the greatest continental rulers to maintaining good relations with the king of England.

Louis was not the only political refugee to seek protection at Athelstan's court. Alan Forkbeard, a Breton magnate, came to England in 931 after taking part in a disastrous rising against the Vikings, who occupied much of Brittany. He was well received and with Athelstan's support returned in 936 to Brittany, where he established himself in the counties of Vannes and Nantes.

Athelstan's importance was recognized even further afield, in Scandinavia, where the establishment of Harald Fairhair, king of Westfold, as ruler of a united Norway gave to the rulers of Norway and England a common interest in controlling the piratical operations of independent Viking fleets. Harald sent an embassy to Athelstan to establish friendly relations, which brought with it as a gift a magnificent warship. A further token of Harald's respect was the despatch of his younger son Hakon to be brought up at Athelstan's court. This alliance subsequently bore fruit when Hakon, having succeeded to his father's kingdom, sent for a bishop and priests from England to assist in the establishment of Christianity in Norway.

Though a remote Irish monastic chronicler recording Athelstan's death styled him ' the pillar of the western world ' the circumstances which made England appear as the arbiter of western Europe were of brief duration. For some years after Athelstan's death his successors were preoccupied with Norse aggression in the Five Boroughs. A more permanently important reason for the diminution of English influence was that in Europe, the preponderance of German power and the disintegration of Francia destroyed the balance of forces which had made English support or neutrality a factor which had to be taken into account by their rulers.

One last continental intervention was attempted by Edmund, in the last years of his life. King Louis had been captured by the Vikings of Rouen and though freed through the efforts of Hugh of Paris the count showed no disposition to re-establish him on his throne. Edmund sent an embassy to France to attempt to persuade Hugh to assist Louis, but before anything could materialize Edmund had been killed.

12

THE APOGEE OF THE ANGLO-SAXON KINGDOM

1. The Reign of Eadwig

Despite the remarkable growth of royal authority the king was still far from being absolute. The developing uniformity of governmental institutions and of the hierarchy of officials which supervised their operation never ensured automatic and immediate obedience to the king's will throughout the country; and beneath the apparent tranquillity at the centre fragments of evidence hint that the court could be the scene of intrigue between magnates attempting to secure influence over the king.

Asser had complained that King Alfred's plans were often dislocated ' by those unwilling to submit to any, or but little, service for the common necessity of the kingdom ' and of Danish successes made possible because fortresses which the king had ordered to be built were not begun, or, begun too late, were still unfinished at the time of attack. Alfred began by exhorting his officials to govern well, but if exhortation proved inadequate he threatened to punish the disobedient. The reiteration of measures against violence and theft in tenth-century legislation argues that there was a serious gap between intentions and execution; the Prologue to Athelstan's fifth code says, ' our peace is worse kept than I should like and that it was pronounced at Grately; and my councillors say that I have borne it too long '; his successor Edmund was murdered by a thief. The *Laws* of Alfred's successors included measures to deal with overmighty lords who unjustly supported their men in the public courts.[1] The enlargement of the king's authority went hand in hand with the increasing power of his greater subordinates in government, and only a strong and energetic king could keep them in subordination to the royal

[1] *Supra*, p. 231.

will. The power of landed magnates, even in southern England and in the face of the interests of a member of the royal family, is revealed in the account of a lawsuit in the reign of Edward the Elder. Eadgifu, the king's third wife, claimed an estate in Kent occupied by a certain Goda; but even after judgment had been pronounced in court in the queen's favour ' she could not get possession of the estate until her friends induced King Edward to declare that Goda must restore the estate if he wished to hold any land at all '. Already in Athelstan's reign a West Saxon landowner and namesake of the king, promoted into the East Anglian ealdormanry, was known as Athelstan Half-King, by reason of his wealth and power; King Edgar was subsequently to marry his son's widow.

It is unlikely that Anglo-Saxon kings were spared the dangers of court intrigue. Though they matured early they also died young and frequently left as successors boys in their 'teens; occasionally there was uncertainty as to the succession to the throne. It would have been remarkable if aristocratic factions had not competed with one another to secure influence over young kings in order to manipulate the royal authority to their own advantage or to secure the election of preferred candidates. Often the natural interest of the great magnates in the crown at such times was enhanced by the practice whereby tenth-century kings married the daughters of ealdormen. Edward the Elder was challenged by his relative Aethelwold. Even Athelstan was threatened by disaffection; William of Malmesbury asserted that his accession was opposed by a certain Alfred, of whom nothing more is known, and that Athelstan's brother Edwin was involved in the plot. This story finds some confirmation in contemporary sources both English and continental. A Northumbrian annalist categorically asserted that in 933 ' King Athelstan ordered his brother Edwin to be drowned at sea ', while the *Annals of St. Bertin* state more moderately that Edwin was driven from the kingdom as a consequence of some disturbance. The unpopularity at court of the highly born Dunstan, later to become archbishop of Canterbury, in the reign of Athelstan, his disgrace in the reign of King Edmund, and again in the reign of Eadwig occurred long before monastic reform became a political issue, and it is hard to believe that royal actions reflected no more than the antipathy felt for a pious courtier by others more dissolute. Problems of this kind recurred, but generally they were resolved by the early maturation of the members of the West Saxon dynasty; Eadwig's reign exemplified them and revealed how much still depended on the personal ability of the ruler.

Eadwig became king of the West Saxons, Mercians, and Northumbrians on the death of his uncle Eadred in 955. Two years later the Mercians and Northumbrians withdrew their allegiance and chose his younger brother Edgar as their king. Legend quickly explained these events as the consequence of Eadwig's licentiousness and hostility to religion. It was said that on the day of his anointing he insulted the assembled notables of the realm by prematurely leaving the coronation feast. Dunstan and his kinsman, the bishop of Lichfield, despatched by archbishop Oda to bring him back, found Eadwig happy in the compromising company of a young woman and her mother, both intent on seduction. The king was compelled to return from the feast and in revenge drove Dunstan into exile. There is little credibility in this rigmarole. The young woman accused of diverting Eadwig during the coronation feast was a noblewoman who subsequently became his wife, probably the sister of ealdorman Aethelweard the chronicler; in her will she made considerable bequests to monastic foundations and was honoured by the New Minster as a benefactress. Nor is there substance in the charge that Eadwig was indifferent, still less hostile, to the interests of the Church. Charters reveal that he made substantial grants to churches, and even after the defection of the Midlands and the north prominent reforming churchmen continued to attend his court.

In 955 Eadwig was thirteen years old; whatever happened in the early months of his reign can hardly be attributed to his initiative and in all probability his uncle's counsellors continued to rule in his name. In 956 three men destined to be prominent in politics and government during the reign of the exemplary Edgar, his supplanter, were promoted into ealdormanries: Byrhtnoth of Essex, Aethelwold of East Anglia, and Aelfhere of Mercia. The very large number of grants made in his name in 956 suggest that far from pursuing any positive policy an attempt was being made to satisfy all interests.

It is likely that the young king soon began to assert himself. The woman he chose to marry, though perfectly respectable, was probably too nearly related to him for the marriage to be acceptable to ecclesiastics, and perhaps was linked by family ties to a group of West Saxon magnates whose predominant influence at court was unacceptable to the magnates established beyond the Thames. Rewards to new friends may sometimes have involved others in loss; Eadgifu, the third wife of Edward the Elder, was despoiled of all her property. The choice of Eadwig's brother Edgar as king by Mercians and Northumbrians proves that the movement against Eadwig was not separatist in origin, a fact confirmed by the subsequent acceptance of Edgar by the West Saxons. Their defection from Eadwig was caused not by his moral lapses nor by an imaginary dislike of churchmen but by his lack of statesmanlike qualities. Only by hindsight was the killing of Eric Bloodaxe in 954 clearly to be seen as making an end to the age of Viking adventures in England. To contemporaries this was not apparent and much of King Eadred's will consisted of provision for the relief of his people in the event of their being obliged to pay tribute to the Danes again. With the situation in the north unresolved and the domestic business of the kingdom demanding continual application from men of exceptional ability a king like Eadwig was intolerable if a suitable alternative lay at hand.

2. The Reign of Edgar: Secular Politics

The vulnerability of the new monarchy was concealed for a time by the brevity of Eadwig's reign and by the tale of uninterrupted triumphs which ensued. Edgar's reign (959-975) contrasts sharply with the confusion which came before and the disasters which followed. Coinciding largely with the thirty years of peace which prevailed between the end of one series of Viking attacks and the beginning of a new wave, Edgar's reign is generally regarded as the period during which the developments in monarchical power and towards the unification of the kingdom inaugurated by Alfred came to climax and completion.

Near contemporary writers were unanimous in regarding him as a king fully worthy to stand beside the best of his predecessors. The author of one version of the *Chronicle* inserted a verse eulogy of Edgar into the annal recording his accession to the throne.

> In his day things improved greatly, and God granted him that he lived in peace as long as he lived; and, as this was necessary for him, he laboured zealously for this; he exalted God's praise far and wide, and loved God's law; and he improved the peace of the people more than the kings who were before him in the memory of man. And God also supported him so that kings and earls willingly submitted to him and were subjected to whatever he wished. And without battle he brought under his sway all that he wished. He came to be honoured throughout

the countries, because he zealously honoured God's name, and time and again meditated on God's law, and exalted God's praise far and wide, and continually and frequently directed all his people wisely in matters of Church and State.

Only one fault is recognized:

He loved evil and foreign customs and brought too firmly heathen manners within this land, and attracted hither foreigners and enticed harmful people to this country.

Abbot Aelfric placed Edgar in the same category as Alfred and Athelstan, describing him as, ' the strongest of all kings over the English nation '. Already in Aethelred's reign Edgar had the reputation of a lawgiver. ' Let us take as our example what former rulers wisely decreed, Athelstan and Edmund, and Edgar who came last ', and it was recognized that things were better then than now, ' since the days of Edgar Christ's laws have waned and the king's laws dwindled '. His good reputation survived the Norman Conquest. William of Malmesbury held ' that no king, either of his own or former times in England, could be justly and fairly compared to Edgar ' while to Henry of Huntingdon he was ' that second Solomon '. By contrast the reign of his son Aethelred, who succeeded him after a short interval, has always appeared as a time of unrelieved and ignominious failure. The monk who wrote the *Chronicle* at this time castigated the folly and ineptitude of the king and his chosen advisers, whose inadequacies were highlighted by the terms of the invitation to return from his exile in Normandy in 1014, ' if he would govern them more justly than before '. William of Malmesbury commented that ' his life is said to have been cruel in the beginning, wretched in the middle, and disgraceful at the end '.

The monopoly of writing by churchmen, especially by monks, is adequate explanation for the universal praise of King Edgar; little that he did could be wrong. His only admitted fault, the propensity to favour foreigners, was not elaborated by contemporaries. William of Malmesbury explained that they were attracted to the court by Edgar's fame; unfortunately ' from the Saxons they [the English] learned an untameable ferocity of mind; from the Flemings an unmanly delicacy of body; and from the Danes drunkenness '. It is likely that the peaceful conditions which obtained in England in his time encouraged traders and others to come to England but William's explanation is no more enlightening than the silence of contemporaries. William admits that in his time stories illustrating

Edgar's cruelty and sexual licentiousness were current; he related them in detail but confined comment to observing that his abundant virtues more than compensated for his vices.

Modern writers have been more critical in their estimate of Edgar. To them the association of the king with the movement of monastic reform has appeared less admirable than to the monk-historians and hagiographers. But it is possible that because so little has been recorded of the reign other than the story of reform a false impression of his preoccupations may have been inferred. The *Chronicle* credited Edgar with three achievements; support for the Church; the maintenance of a better peace than any king before him; and the imposition of his authority on the rulers of neighbouring lands. Of his concern with internal order and his ' foreign policy ' far less is known than of his ecclesiastical policy but their recognition by the chronicler provides a warning that they should not be neglected.

As a lawgiver Edgar followed in the steps of his predecessors, perfecting the working of the machinery which they had devised. The code of law, usually known as I Edgar though it may have been promulgated by Edmund, provides us with our first detailed knowledge of the hundred and its court. By this time, too, the shire and its court were sufficiently established to be the subject of legislation. The court met twice a year in the presence of the bishop and the ealdorman, and was attended by the principal landowners of the shire. The bulk of its business consisted of the determination of disputed claims to land in accordance with the verdict of local men. As well it was a centre of financial administration and later it became a court in which some offences against the king were heard. Even more valuable to the king was its usefulness as the place where royal commands were sent and given publicity and where the enactments of his council were made widely known to the inhabitants of the countryside. Edgar's fourth code of law, though concerned mainly with the Danelaw, states; 'And many documents are to be written concerning this, and sent both to ealdorman Aelfhere [of Mercia] and ealdorman Aethelwine [of East Anglia] and they are to send them in all directions, that this measure may be known to both the poor and the rich.'

This fourth code has a particular interest in its indications of the manner in which he hoped to reconcile the Northumbrians to acceptance of his lordship.[1] This was the most important problem facing

[1] Whitelock, *op. cit.* pp. 73-79.

an English king in 960 and an estimate of the quality of Edgar's statesmanship depends on the view taken of its effectiveness. It was a conservative policy designed to win confidence gradually. He recognized and respected the different local custom of the Danelaw: ' It is my will that secular rights be in force among the Danes according to as good laws as they can best decide on. Among the English, however, that is to be in force which I and my councillors have added to the decrees of my ancestors, for the benefit of all the nation.' Yet even in the Danelaw royal measures deemed crucial for the maintenance of order must be obeyed—' this measure is to be common to all the nation whether Englishmen, Danes or Britons in every province of my dominions '—though conformity is qualified by allowing the Danes to determine the punishments appropriate to the offences specified. Because he owed protection to the inhabitants of the Danelaw he was prepared to ravage Thanet in 969 to punish men who had maltreated a party of merchants from York. More positively, evidence that many Englishmen were established north of the Humber by the end of the tenth century suggests the possibility that during Edgar's reign English thegns were encouraged to settle there, just as earlier Edward the Elder had encouraged English infiltration into the Danish midlands. Consciousness of the limitations of royal authority combined with the lack of royal lands in Northumbria probably explains the failure of monastic reform to extend into Yorkshire. But the ecclesiastical isolation of the north, broken down when Osketel bishop of Dorchester was appointed to the archbishopric of York, was not allowed to recur. Oscytel may have occupied both sees until his death, thus establishing the practice whereby York was often held in plurality with a southern bishopric, a practice which combined the economic advantage of compensating for the poverty of the see of York with the political virtue that an archbishop, much of whose income was derived from a southern see, would be unlikely to support separatist movements in the north. Beginning with Osketel the men chosen for the see combined loyalty to the king with Danish affinities which made them acceptable to their subjects; Osketel, Oswald, and Eadwulf, successively archbishops, had close connections with the eastern Danelaw.

In the administration of the recently acquired Northumbrian lands Edgar took advantage of opportunities which occurred but took no initiatives. Eric Bloodaxe had been betrayed to his murderer by Oswulf, the English lord of Bamburgh, who had then received from

King Eadred the whole Northumbrian earldom. Oswulf's death in 966 enabled Edgar to divide Northumbria; Oswulf's son Eadwulf kept an earldom between the Tees and the Forth but the area between the Humber and the Tees was given to Oslac, a Dane with East Anglian connections. Edgar was alive to the danger that a quasi-hereditary earldom might become established and took measures to prevent it

In the light of subsequent events the doubt remains whether Edgar did as much as was possible in the time available to him. All West Saxon rulers were handicapped in their dealings with the Danelaw because they lacked an adequate landed endowment in the Danish settled areas. A medieval king, like any other lord with a large household to provide for, was compelled to arrange his travels so that the bulk of his time was spent on his own estates; if he did otherwise he imposed a heavy burden on the inhabitants of the countryside which had to support him and his court. Had the conquest of the Danelaw been followed by wholesale confiscations the West Saxon kings could have acquired lands in northern England—as did King William after 1066—but such a policy would have defeated the royal attempt to secure voluntary acceptance of their rule, and since their landed endowment in southern England was always adequate for their needs it did not seem desirable on other grounds. Accordingly, lacking lands in the Danelaw, kings seldom penetrated far into the north save when campaigns made their presence there necessary, and they continued to hold their courts in Wessex and the south Midlands. The great magnates of the Danelaw, both lay and ecclesiastical, attended the king, but the lack of direct links between the king and the lesser landowners inhibited the generation of that spontaneous affection and loyalty which had been achieved in the south and was maintained by personal contacts with the ruler; for such men the king was always a remote figure. In this way the conciliatory attitude of Edward the Elder and his successors created problems for the future. Edgar could not hope that his northern subjects would feel genuine affection for him but he attempted to transform antipathy into acceptance by relying on the material advantages which firm rule brought in its train. His policy was simple, unspectacular, and as far as time allowed, effective.

Perhaps the most remarkable demonstration of Edgar's authority found no mention in contemporary historical sources, although it was recorded by the thirteenth-century chronicler, Roger of Wendover.[1] He stated that in 975, because the old money had become so corrupt from clipping that the penny had become worth little more than a halfpenny, King Edgar ordered a new coinage to be struck. The date given by Wendover may not be acceptable, nor is the reason, for the earlier pence of Edgar's reign were not significantly lighter in weight than those of the last issue; but numismatic research has confirmed that late in his reign Edgar effected a great recoinage, which may from its inception have envisaged further changes of type at regular intervals. Not only was the old coinage called in and replaced but the number of mints, already more than forty, was increased to about seventy by the end of the century. An increased number of mints was partly the natural response to an increasing volume of internal trade, but it may also have been made desirable by the adoption of the policy of regular recoinage, which required men to travel to the nearest mint to hand in their old coins. What is remarkable is the success with which government policy was enforced. Of the thirty three coin hoards discovered within territory under the effective control of Anglo-Saxon kings which contained coins struck between 975 and 1066 no fewer than fifteen were composed substantially of coins of a single issue and a further seven were composed of coins from no more than two successive issues. Between *c.* 975 and 1066 twenty-four successive coin types were issued; at first each type was current for six years, though later in the period recoinages occurred more frequently. On the debit side of the balance-sheet and indicative of the limitations on Edgar's authority it must be recorded that, after Edgar's reign as before, the most northerly of English mints were at Chester and York.

It would have been understandable if the Celtic kings and princes of the west and north had reacted strongly against the increasing authority of the king of England. In 920, feeling themselves threatened by the establishment of Raegnald's kingdom at York, the kings of the Scots and the Strathclyde Britons and the ealdorman of Bamburgh had sought support and leadership from Edward the Elder. The West Saxon chronicler declared that the northern rulers ' chose him [Edward] for father and for lord ', although in sober fact he was recording nothing more than the establishment of an anti-Norse coalition. But not long afterwards the power of King Athelstan

[1] R. M. H. Dolley and D. M. Metcalfe, ' The reform of the English coinage under Eadgar ', in *A.S.Coins* but note, too, the cautionary words of P. Grierson in ' Numismatics and the Historian ', *Numismatic Chronicle,* seventh series, II (1962).

had replaced the threat from Raegnald as the chief danger to the independence of the northern rulers and the English claim to lordship had acquired genuine significance. In 927 the northern princes made submission to Athelstan and in the same year the Welsh princes paid him tribute. The scribes of Athelstan's charters showed their consciousness of the nature of their king's claims to superiority when they styled him not merely *rex Anglorum* but as *rex et primicerius totius Albionis,* and sometimes *basileus,* and as 'elevated by the right hand of the Almighty to the throne of the whole kingdom of Britain'. Athelstan claimed hegemony over all Britain, including its Celtic parts. It was not surprising that the rulers of these Celtic regions combined once more, this time against the English king, but their crushing defeat at Brunanburh made Athelstan's lordship more real than ever before. After Athelstan's death West Saxon authority in the north suffered a severe setback, but the final elimination of the kingdom of York after the death of Eric Bloodaxe made Edgar a more formidable neighbour than Athelstan had ever been. Yet whatever disposition they may have felt to challenge him was held in check by their fear of his military and naval forces. In his relations with Scotland and Wales Edgar maintained peace by constantly demonstrating his readiness for war. Every year, after Easter, his fleet, organized in three squadrons, patrolled the coastal waters. His strength was such that in 973, 'the king took his whole naval force to Chester, and six kings came to meet him, and all gave him pledges that they would be his allies on sea and on land'. They undertook not to attack England and promised assistance if England was attacked. The kings involved were those of the Scots, the Cumbrians, and of the Islands, together with the most important Welsh princes. But there was no element of aggression in his policy and he was more concerned to define the limits of his territorial frontiers than to extend them. Soon afterwards Edgar proved his pacific intentions by granting Lothian, the district between the rivers Tweed and Forth, to Kenneth II of Scotland, in the hope of confirming their friendship.

It has been shown that half a century earlier, when the strength of King Athelstan made England an attractive ally, contacts with continental courts were frequent and wideranging.[1] It would be natural to expect that a similar situation would recur under Edgar, especially since the king was criticized for his fondness for foreigners,

[1] *Supra,* pp. 266-8.

but of such relations there is practically no evidence. The *Life* of
St. Oswald mentions an embassy sent by Edgar to the Emperor Otto I
bearing magnificent gifts, and its return with even more remarkable
presents, and in general terms it states that neighbouring kings
praised his generosity and feared his ferocity, but this is all. Yet it
would be rash to infer from the paucity of the evidence that Anglo-
continental relations were more attenuated in this reign than before.
Quite apart from the close links known to have been maintained
by English churchmen with Rome, Fleury and the monasteries of
Flanders and Lorraine, and the favourable conditions for foreign
trade which obtained, there are indications that the interest of
Englishmen in Germany was fully maintained. Early in the next
reign ealdorman Aethelweard corresponded with Matilda, abbess
of Essen, the granddaughter of Otto I and Edward the Elder's daughter Edith; he wrote to tell the latter ' what is known of our common
family ' (Aethelweard was himself descended from Alfred's brother
Aethelred) and about ' the migration of our nation ', and he wrote
a *Chronicle* of English history for her instruction. He was well aware
of the Germanic origins of the English for he referred to ' the arrival
of our ancestors in Britain from Germany '. The *Anglo-Saxon
Chronicle* annal for 982 similarly reveals the interest taken in the
fortunes of the ruling house of Germany; recording the death of Otto
of Swabia in 982 it mentions that ' he was the son of Liudolf the
atheling, who was the son of Otto the Elder and of king Edward's
daughter'. It is worth remembering in this context that our knowledge of Athelstan's wideranging foreign alliances is due largely
to the notices concerning the marriages of English princesses with
foreign rulers; it may well be that our comparative ignorance of King
Edgar's diplomatic activities stems from no deeper cause than a lack
of royal ladies whose exotic marriages had naturally evoked comment
from contemporary writers in the earlier reign.

This tenuous account of Edgar's secular activities complements the
more frequently cited evidence of his religious fervour. He was,
without doubt, a vigorous and active ruler with a capacity for occasional acts of violence. His reputation as a peace-loving king who
brought peace to his kingdom was achieved because men were as
well aware of his firmness as of his piety. It was reported of him that
on his return from the summer cruise with the fleet he was accustomed to travel throughout England, making enquiry into the
decisions of local officials and chastening the negligent.

10

Apart from the submission of the Celtic kings to him at Chester the best known event of Edgar's reign was the great ceremony staged at Bath in 973. It has often been stated that this was Edgar's coronation, deliberately postponed by the king until the year in which he reached the age of thirty, the age below which no one could be ordained to the priesthood, and that the purpose of the delay was to emphasize the sacerdotal quality of kingship. An account of the service at Bath is given in the nearly contemporary *Life* of St. Oswald; it is lacking in lucidity and coherence but it generates considerable doubt as to whether the ceremony it describes was the first anointing and coronation of the king.[1] What took place at Bath was certainly unusual, because tenth-century West Saxon kings were generally crowned at Kingston-on-Thames and at the earliest opportunity. It is also true that no specific evidence exists recording a coronation of Edgar at Kingston in 959, but it would be rash to conclude that a coronation did not take place early in the reign for it is often only by chance that such evidence survives and normality provides no ground for comment. That Edgar's coronation was deferred until 973, for any reason, seems improbable, for an unconsecrated king lacked the strongest of the sanctions for his rule. An alternative explanation of the ceremony, which occurred just before Edgar's journey to Chester to meet the Celtic kings, is that at Bath in 973 he was anointed and crowned for a second time, thereby solemnly and publicly rededicating himself to the task of ruling his enlarged dominion. Whatever its exact nature, and whether or not the writer who described it had access to the coronation order used then or on a later occasion, the central fact remains that henceforth the coronation of an English king was to be primarily a religious ceremony which emphasized the priestly character of the king and in which the central role was played by churchmen. The identity of objectives of kings and churchmen in the late Anglo-Saxon kingdom was made explicit in the undertakings which kings gave to their people on the day of their coronation.

> In the name of the Holy Trinity! I promise three things to the Christian people who are under my authority.
> Firstly, that true peace shall be assured to the church of God and to all Christian people in my dominions.
> Secondly, I forbid robbery and all unrighteous deeds by all classes of society.

[1] Richardson and Sayles, *Governance of Medieval England* (Edinburgh, 1963), pp. 397-412.

Thirdly, I promise and enjoin justice and mercy in the decision of all cases, in order that God, who liveth and reigneth, may in his peace and mercy be brought thereby to grant us all his eternal compassion.

In this formal statement of the purposes for which God invested kings with authority can be seen the reasons both for the uninhibited cooperation of kings and religious leaders and also for the voluntary acceptance of the augmentation of royal authority by their subjects which, in combination, gave to tenth-century English kingship its unique quality.

3. ECCLESIASTICAL REFORM

In his conduct of secular affairs Edgar continued the policies of his forbears, but in his support of the monastic order, which transformed the Church in his kingdom, he was an innovator.

Alfred's attempt to revive monasticism in England had failed miserably. The reason may well have been that to contemporaries it appeared to take little account of the most pressing problems which beset the Church in their day. Over much of England the Danish wars and the settlement of a heathen population on the land had destroyed ecclesiastical organization; everywhere buildings had been destroyed and territorial endowments had fallen into secular hands. The strength of Christian religion among the native population and the lukewarmness of the Danes' attachment to their paganism had enabled Christianity to survive and to begin to effect the conversion of the heathen, yet its hold on the inhabitants of the Danelaw, whether native or alien, would have been precarious had not reconquest been quickly begun and followed by measures to restore the supply of trained clergy to the territories recovered. In such circumstances the maintenance of a decent level of ecclesiastical order in Wessex and English Mercia and the restoration of the Church in the Danelaw must have seemed more urgent needs than the revivification of an institution which appeared both moribund and ill-suited to the tasks in hand. Although in the seventh century the English had been converted largely through the efforts of the inmates of ' monasteries ' that term had since become so much more rigorously defined that the monastery of the tenth century was ill-adapted to be a centre of evangelistic endeavour.

Alfred's successors abandoned his premature pursuit of a monastic revival, but were almost equally zealous in their care of the Church.

Their effort was attended by gradual and unspectacular advances, but it seldom receives recognition. The contemporary sources for the history of the Church in the first half of the tenth century are once again scanty; there is a lack of colourful figures and dramatic events. And when the history of the monastic revival was recorded its chroniclers were monks whose zeal to demonstrate the greatness of their heroes led them to display the premonastic Church in its worst guise and to conceal the magnitude of the debt which the monks owed to their secular predecessors.

The piety of Alfred's descendants found expression in grants to religious communities both in England and abroad. Edward the Elder completed his father's plans for the New Minster at Winchester. William of Malmesbury wrote of Athelstan that there was scarcely a minster in England which he did not enrich with buildings, ornaments, books, or estates. He was a benefactor to established communities and himself founded Milton Abbas and Muchelney. His generosity was almost as conspicuously displayed to Chester-le-Street and other churches in northern England as to Bath and to Malmesbury, where he was buried. By the favour of King Edmund, Dunstan was given Glastonbury to restore and King Eadred himself paced out the dimensions of the first buildings of Aethelwold's Abingdon. Their munificence was not confined to England. Edward sent help to the clergy of St. Samson at Dol in Brittany and in return was enrolled in the confraternity book of that house; his generosity was continued by Athelstan who also sent gifts to a number of German monasteries and was similarly enrolled in their confraternity books. Athelstan was a benefactor of St. Bertin's in Flanders where his brother Edwin was buried. Three of Edward's daughters renounced the world, and the daughter who married King Henry I's son Otto was remembered for her goodness.

As opportunity offered they reconstructed the diocesan organization of the Church, increasing the number of bishoprics and appointing worthy bishops mindful of the importance of instructing and overseeing their clergy. Occasionally in the past bishops had been helped by assistants, bearing the title of bishop but without established sees, but there had been too few of them. The deaths of Denewulf of Winchester and Asser of Sherborne in 909 facilitated a radical reorganization of the Church in Wessex. On his return from a visit to Rome Archbishop Plegmund consecrated bishops for Berkshire and Wiltshire, for Somerset, and for Devonshire, whose sees were established at Ramsbury, Wells and Crediton respectively; he also re-established the bishopric of Selsey. In the same year he initiated the restoration of diocesan supervision in the area of the old sees of Lindsey and Leicester by consecrating a bishop for Dorchester-on-Thames. The new dioceses were small enough for effective supervision although it became apparent in time that their endowments were inadequate. Diocesan reconstruction in southern England was completed when, after a campaign in Cornwall in 926, Athelstan created a new bishopric at St. Germans over which he placed a bishop with a Celtic name, Conan. As the Danelaw was absorbed its needs were met in the south by Dorchester, and by the extension of the authority of the archbishop of York into the north Midlands and Lindsey. For East Anglia, which had recently been under the supervision of the bishop of London, the see of North Elmham was revived in 956. It is probable that attempts were made to re-establish other bishoprics, for a bishop of Lindsey reappears for a brief period in the middle of the century, but that they came to nothing for lack of endowments. Less progress was made in Northumbria. It proved impossible to re-establish the bishoprics of Hexham and Whithorn and for the whole of the tenth century the archbishopric of York, itself impoverished, had only one subordinate bishopric, Chester-le-Street, which was moved to Durham in 990.

Among the royal appointments to bishoprics were a number who were men of distinction. Beornstan and Aelfheah the Bald, who encouraged the future monastic reformers Dunstan and Aethelwold, were bishops of Winchester of enviable reputation; Theodred of London was styled ' the Good '. Oda, appointed successively bishop of Ramsbury and archbishop of Canterbury, in his concern for the wellbeing of the Church in the localities and his sympathy for reforming movements of continental origin, may well be numbered among the great English archbishops of the middle ages. The influence of bishops in the king's councils is revealed not only in the wording of the preambles to their legislation but in its content. Not only were kings generally concerned with ' how best to promote Christianity ' but they legislated specifically against heathen cults and for the maintenance of ecclesiastical discipline and ecclesiastical revenues. Athelstan's first code of laws exhorted his officers to take the greatest care rendering in full the tithe due from royal lands and to ensure that other ecclesiastical dues were paid promptly by all men.

English churchmen fully shared in the increasing contacts with the Continent which, never ceasing entirely even in time of war, reached a climax in the reign of Athelstan. Not only did they bear gifts from their royal masters to foreign churches but ecclesiastics figured prominently in the diplomatic embassies which frequently crossed the Channel. The visit of Bishop Cenwald of Worcester to several German monasteries in 929 was probably connected with negotiations for the marriage of Athelstan's sister Edith to Otto of Germany. Bishop Oda visited Francia in 936 on a mission to the court of Hugh the Great. England provided a refuge for foreigners against the Northmen early in the century and for opponents of monastic reform later. Refugees from St. Judoc were given shelter in the New Minster and in Edmund's reign clerics from St. Bertin's who refused to accept the new discipline of St. Gerard of Brogne were settled at Bath by the king. Other continental churchmen were to be found in England though the circumstances which brought them here are unknown.

Throughout this period of reorganization and conversion the kings of England were at war, and the task of both political and religious leaders had been made more difficult by the arrival of the new wave of pagan Irish Norsemen in the north-west and at York. In war the Church suffered from both sides, as was shown when Eadred's army burned down the minster at Ripon during the campaign of 947. Despite these circumstances and primarily through the continued support of his successors King Alfred's hopes for the English Church were gradually fulfilled. The King's own works continued to be copied, as were the Latin writers of earlier times; intellectual life may have been undistinguished but learning was far from extinct in the households of Oda and Aelfheah of Winchester, and Dunstan at Glastonbury found no obstacles to study. Concern for pastoral care is shown in the *Constitutions* of Archbishop Oda which instructed bishops to visit their dioceses annually, to enforce canonical life on the clergy and insist on the observance of marriage laws by the laity; they emphasized the duties of almsgiving, fasting, and the payment of tithes.

At first sight it is strange that England remained for all this time apparently unaffected by the remarkable revival of monasticism in western Europe which stemmed from the foundation of Cluny in 910 and from the efforts of Gerard of Brogne in Lorraine. Inaction is explicable by neither ignorance nor indifference. As early as 925

Aelfheah of Winchester witnessed a charter as ' priest and monk ' and when Oda became archbishop he sent to Fleury-sur-Loire, recently reformed from Cluny, requesting the monastic habit. Dunstan and Aethelwold were both members of the household of Bishop Aelfheah, who encouraged Dunstan to take monastic vows. Oda sent his nephew Oswald to Fleury for instruction in the best monastic discipline and other Englishmen followed him there. That monastic reform progressed so slowly in England despite an awareness of the continental reforms and the sympathy felt for them by leading churchmen requires explanation.

Some men may have felt it undesirable to concentrate spiritual energy in monasteries until pastoral provision in the dioceses was more adequate; in the next century reforming archbishops of York took this view. Partly it may be that the efforts of bishops like Oda had been too successful; the Church they fostered worked well enough to secure the loyalty and affection of a great many Christian people. It continued to attract the munificence of the wealthy. By the standards of the age the communities of clerics, sometimes married and enjoying prebends and private property, maintained a respectable standard of worship and were not scandalous. King Alfred's successors certainly showed no eagerness to resume his policy of monastic reformation. The royal foundation of New Minster at Winchester continued to be a house of clerics; King Athelstan gave Abingdon to a German priest Godescalc; the Flemish clerics to whom King Edmund gave Bath were fleeing from the introduction of the monastic rule. There were as well formidable material difficulties in the way of monastic reform.

Before monasticism could re-establish itself in England two things were necessary; men willing to submit themselves to the monastic discipline, and land on which to build monasteries and provide for the material needs of monastic communities. King Alfred could not find free-born Englishmen who would accept the monastic way of life: further witness to the success of the post-Alfredian bishops is that by the middle of the tenth century the problem of recruiting monks had been resolved and the reformed monasteries of Edgar's reign were never short of men. But the provision of endowments continued to be a more serious problem. A genuinely monastic community on the model of the best Benedictine houses of tenth-century Europe required substantial wealth for its maintenance. Lands owned by monastic churches in earlier times had often been dispersed and acquired by kings and local landowners; the remaining large religious foundations were now served by communities of clerics who jealously guarded their possessions. The refoundation of monasteries depended on the substantial generosity of kings and the readiness of great laymen to restore the annexations of their predecessors and supplement them with additional grants; as well it might involve the dispossession of clerics to make way for their replacement by monks. Enthusiasm for monasticism might be communicated to the laity, but in time of war the military needs of kings and their great men probably compelled them to use such lands as they could afford to grant away for the endowment of fighting men. This problem was eased by the ending of the Danish threat. The expropriation of clerical communities was difficult, for the clerics attached to the wealthier churches were often well-born, the kinsfolk of local magnates, both ready and able to concert opposition to such changes. Only the king had sufficient resources of land and power to endow new monasteries and enforce changes on the old foundations. For these reasons, despite its influential sympathizers, the reforming movement in England made a late start and slow progress.

It was not until about 943 that the first genuinely monastic community was established, and apparently almost by accident. Among King Edmund's courtiers was a young man, Dunstan by name, born of noble stock in the vicinity of Glastonbury in about 909. After an education at Glastonbury, which at that time was served by a small clerical community, though it still possessed a large library, he had been introduced to Athelstan's court by his uncle, Athelm, archbishop of Canterbury. There, according to his first biographer, who knew Dunstan and wrote within twenty years of his death, his purity of life aroused the enmity of his dissolute associates who achieved his expulsion from the royal court. He took refuge in the household of another uncle, the reforming Aelfheah, bishop of Winchester (934-951), and was by him, together with another of the leaders of the later reforming movement Aethelwold, ordained to the priesthood. With Aelfheah's encouragement he subsequently took monastic vows. On Athelstan's death Dunstan was restored to favour for a time and returned to court, but once again he became a victim of intrigue and King Edmund resolved to exile him. Dunstan had already made arrangements to leave England in the company of a foreign embassy which was visiting Edmund's court at Cheddar when the king miraculously escaped death while hunting in the vicinity of Glastonbury; his hounds pursued a stag over the edge of Cheddar Gorge and his own horse pulled up on the brink of the precipice. Made aware at the moment of imminent death of his injustice to Dunstan, the king, in thanksgiving for his safety and in amends for the wrong he had committed, resolved to re-establish Glastonbury as a regular monastery and to appoint Dunstan as its abbot.

By Dunstan the derelict buildings were restored and the community he assembled there lived a truly monastic life based on the Rule of St. Benedict probably supplemented by the *Ordo Qualiter* of the late eighth century, ' the order how brethren in a monastery should live and serve God '; it was less complicated than the practice which Benedict of Aniane had attempted to make uniform in the Empire and more emphasis was laid on instruction than on physical austerities. When King Eadred succeeded Edmund, Dunstan was fully restored to royal favour and numbered among the king's principal counsellors; Glastonbury was used by the king as a repository for treasures and archives.

Dunstan had attracted disciples but it seems that the regimen he laid down was not strict enough to satisfy the more ardent of them. Aethelwold, his contemporary in the household of Bishop Aelfheah, received the monastic habit from Dunstan but wanted to go overseas ' to perfect himself in learning and monastic discipline '. At about this time Oswald, a nephew of Archbishop Oda, who ruled a community at Winchester which his uncle had bought for him at a stiff price, was sent by Oda not to Glastonbury but to Fleury. Other Englishmen followed him there, among them Germanus, also from Winchester. In order to keep Aethelwold in England the queen mother Eadgifu persuaded King Eadred to give him the site of the old monastery at Abingdon, at that time derelict and neglected, consisting only of mean buildings, possessing only forty hides of land and served only by clerks or not at all. The land, in this as in many other places, had reverted to the king. Taking with him a small group of followers from Glastonbury, Aethelwold, with the king's personal support, began to re-establish a second genuinely monastic community in England. The abbot was largely responsible for the education of the king's nephew, Edgar. Yet despite the support of King Edmund, Queen Eadgifu, and King Eadred, and Dunstan's own work at Glastonbury, when Eadred died in 955 only Glastonbury and Abingdon had been reformed.

Though the new ruler, Eadwig, had no ecclesiastical policy the sequel to internal discord was that Dunstan again fell into disfavour. He was exiled in 956 and found refuge at the reformed abbey of St. Peter's in Ghent; the contacts established between Dunstan and Flanders were important for the future but bore no immediate fruit. At this time, too, Aethelwold sent one of his monks, Osgar, to join Oswald at Fleury and another to Corbie to learn church music, but this did nothing to redress the damage done to the cause of monastic reform in England by the exile of Dunstan.

The accession of Edgar in Mercia in 957 was a momentous event. Dunstan was immediately recalled and on the death of Bishop Cenwald he was appointed to the see of Worcester, to which later was added the bishopric of London. On the death of Eadwig in 959 and Edgar's assumption of the whole kingdom, Dunstan was promoted to Canterbury, where a vacancy had been artificially created by the arbitrary return of Archbishop Byrhthelm to the see of Wells, whence he had come. By Dunstan's influence Oswald, now returned from Fleury, succeeded him at Worcester and began to establish a small community of monks at Westbury-on-Trym under the rule of Germanus, hastily recalled from Fleury. In 963 Aethelwold became bishop of Winchester. Within a few years of the accession of a new king his appointment of three monks to the greatest sees in the kingdom had radically transformed the situation. In the following year the second phase of monastic reform was initiated with the dramatic expulsion of the clerks of the Old Minster at Winchester under the eye of the king's minister, Wulfstan of Dalham; they were replaced by monks from Abingdon.

From Glastonbury, Abingdon, and Westbury colonies of monks were sent to restore strict observance of the Benedictine Rule in old foundations and to make new plantations. Dunstan reformed Bath, Malmesbury, and Westminster and founded several monasteries in the west country. Aethelwold's reform of the Old Minster was followed in the next year by the expulsion of the clerics from the New Minster. But his most remarkable achievement was the extension of monasticism to the Danelaw by the restoration of the Fenland monasteries of Peterborough, Ely, and Thorney. The *Liber Eliensis* retails vividly the local tradition concerning the destruction of a once great monastery and its restoration after years of degradation. After constant Danish attack

> In the end everything was devoured by fire and the sword nor was anything left which the impious hands of the barbarian did not destroy

. . . almost all the clergy were killed and any who survived were taken into captivity. Thus miserably the place remained, in every respect empty of divine service . . . none who would carry on the service remained. Of the clerks who had been dispersed after some years eight returned, some of whom remained there, in decrepit old age until the reign of King Eadred. These carried out their duties as well as they could, but to them succeeded clerks, who lived not canonically but most irreligiously; on account of their insolence God drove them out.

In 970 Ely was a place without cult and reverence which lay open to all who might pass by; its lands were in the king's hands. King Edgar gave Ely to Bishop Aethelwold and provided it with an adequate endowment. Brihtnoth, formerly a monk of Abingdon, was appointed abbot, and within a few years it had become one of the most celebrated of English monasteries. Bishop Oswald of Worcester was equally zealous. Uneasy about the security of his community at Westbury because the property belonged to the bishopric and he could not be certain that his successors would be sympathetic to monks, he asked the king for a place for them to be settled; but eventually he accepted from Aethelwine, ealdorman of East Anglia, the fenland site of Ramsey. Ramsey flourished and from Ramsey the abbey of Winchcombe was colonized.

Such rapid advance created problems. Though united in their general aims the traditions represented by Dunstan, Aethelwold, and Oswald were, in detail, different. Dunstan had restored Glastonbury on traditional lines and had spent his exile in a reformed Flemish abbey at Ghent; Glastonbury had not satisfied the more ascetic ideal favoured by Aethelwold who, though himself remaining in England, sent his disciples to Fleury and Corbie; Oswald's knowledge of the monastic life had been wholly learned at Fleury. Nor could the leaders exercise close personal supervision over all the new foundations. Competing with one another in a striving for perfection their enthusiasm threatened to degenerate into extravagance and divergence from the Rule of St. Benedict. To combat these dangers, at the king's command, a synod assembled at Winchester, attended by all the bishops, abbots, and abbesses in the kingdom, and by monks from Fleury and Ghent. Its object was to establish a uniform code of observance which all the reformed houses would undertake to follow. The result of the synod's deliberations, written down by Aethelwold, was the *Regularis Concordia,* ' The Monastic Agreement of the Monks and Nuns of the English Nation '.[1] The

[1] T. Symons, *The Regularis Concordia* (London, 1963).

greater part of this customary consists of detailed instructions for the observance of the liturgical functions of the day and year, which, if followed, would bring the monastic life of England into line with the best continental practice. The Preface to the *Concordia* is of more general interest. It gives a brief account of the origins of the revival, explains why King Edgar summoned the Winchester assembly, records some further instructions which Archbishop Dunstan added to the previously agreed conclusions, and lays down some general rules which, if obeyed, would maintain the health of the monastic order.

The *Concordia* serves to focus two of the most discussed aspects of the reform movement; the respective parts played by its leaders and the degree to which the English reform was influenced by continental movements and models. The period of nearly fifteen years which intervened between the refoundation of Glastonbury and of Abingdon contrasts sharply with the fifteen years which followed the expulsion of the clerics from the Old Minster, during which nearly forty monasteries and houses of women were founded or restored; the ninety years between the death of Edgar and the Norman Conquest saw the addition of only another twenty houses. It is clear from these statistics, from the prominence which contemporaries gave to the king's role on particular occasions—such as the events at the Old Minster, his summoning of the Winchester synod which produced the *Concordia*—and from his generosity in providing sites and endowments, that King Edgar backed the reformers to the hilt and that their conspicuous success depended in large measure on his support. How far he set the pace of reform is a more difficult question.[1] In 957 when Edgar became king in Mercia he was only thirteen years old, hardly of an age to hold independent views on important political or ecclesiastical issues; the elevation of Dunstan to the episcopate must have been the work of magnates who supported Edgar rather than a manifestation of the royal will. The first dramatic event in the story of reform is the expulsion of the clerks from the Old Minster in 964, after which a hectic pace was maintained until the king's death. The king certainly came to power under the aegis of a political party which included zealous reformers; either he continued to be dominated by them until his death or, alternatively,

---

[1] E. John has included some of his important papers on the tenth-century reform movement in *Orbis Britanniae op. cit.*; they include, ' The king and the monks in the tenth century reformation ', pp. 154-80.

having made Aethelwold's ideals his own, their rapid realization was the product of the king's driving will, operating without hindrance because for the first time the country was relieved of distracting warlike commitments. In the light of Edgar's reputation and what is known of his activities in secular affairs the second alternative is to be preferred. Tenth-century kings matured early; by 964 Edgar was no longer in tutelage, and in character he was energetic, even wilful, rather than docile. The appointment of his teacher Aethelwold to the bishopric of Winchester—the last of the great triumvirate of reformers to be promoted to the episcopate—may have been one of the first expressions of the king's initiative in affairs, to be quickly followed by a vigorous monasticizing policy which in its disregard for vested interests could only have been carried through with the king's active cooperation.

The nearly contemporary lives of Dunstan, Aethelwold and Oswald throw little light on their relative roles in the reforming movement or on their relationships with one another. The *Life* of Dunstan, written by a priest, has surprisingly little to relate of Dunstan as a monastic reformer. Dunstan's passivity at Glastonbury for fifteen years after his appointment as abbot and the dissatisfaction felt by Aethelwold at the regimen that obtained there, the ecclesiastical legislation of the early years of Edgar's reign characterized by concern for the maintenance of secular churches, his acquiescence as archbishop in the 'unreformed' state of his own community at Christ Church, which did not become fully monastic until the archiepiscopate of Aelfric; all suggest that though genuine in his zeal for reform he was content to effect changes gradually. That he established monasteries we know, but his performance in that field was outstripped by both Oswald and Aethelwold.

Perhaps the most significant fact to emerge from Dunstan's biography is that by virtue of his family connections he was destined to be from his early manhood a prominent figure at court and in the affairs of the kingdom. As we have seen, his relations included an archbishop of Canterbury and a bishop of Worcester, and another uncle was Cynesige, bishop of Lichfield; his kinsmen were also to be found among the secular aristocracy, and we know one of them by name, Aethelflaed, who lived near Glastonbury and was a niece of King Athelstan. It was for his participation in court politics that Dunstan fell under suspicion of three kings and it is far more likely that his activities related to secular than to religious politics. His party achieved power and Dunstan himself secured ecclesiastical promotion with the accession of Edgar. But in an age when bishops were so closely identified with politics and government at all levels,—in the king's council, as co-presidents of their shire courts, and as local lords,—bishops were as much involved in the business of the court and kingdom as in those matters which today would be deemed fitting for a bishop's attention. It may well be that Dunstan's concern for monastic reform was only one facet of the manifold activities appropriate to an archbishop of Canterbury, and that its importance to him has been exaggerated because so much of the history of the times in which he lived was written by monks, themselves reforming zealots. If this is true perhaps Dunstan was more like Archbishop Oda in outlook and temperament than like either Aethelwold or Oswald. In the circumstances of Edgar's reign a politically sophisticated prelate, aware of the animosities which the precipitate changes taking place after 964 were arousing and fearful of the dangers that might ensue, might well have felt that he would best serve the monastic cause by moderating the enthusiasm of his associates. In 975 his influence was to be successfully exerted in a political crisis when his support secured the succession to the throne of Edward, the elder of King Edgar's son.

If Archbishop Dunstan's role has been correctly diagnosed it would appear that the leader among the monastic reformers was Aethelwold. He it was who gave a lead to the forcible expulsion of clerics from their communities and whose concern to secure adequate endowments for his new houses of monks took little account of other men's rights. Whether Oswald more resembled Dunstan or Aethelwold is debatable. Like Aethelwold he transformed his see into a monastic community; whether, as used to be thought, it was effected gradually or by a sudden coup, is uncertain.[1] Attempts to portray the differing characters of the monastic leaders based on the evidence presented by their biographers is an unprofitable exercise; to Aelfric of Eynsham and Wulfstan, the precentor of Winchester who wrote of Aethelwold, and to the Ramsey monk who wrote of Oswald, their heroes were immaculate. Perhaps unconsciously, historians have often cast Aethelwold and Oswald in the roles of St. Peter and St. John, the vital energy of Aethelwold being contrasted with the dove-

[1] The case for gradualness was made by J. Armitage Robinson, *St. Oswald and the Church of Worcester* (London, 1919); it has been rejected by John, *Orbis Britanniae*, pp. 230-49.

like sweetness of Oswald; for this dramatization there is little warrant in the sources. And it should be remembered that to the mute sufferers from their enthusiasm both must have appeared equally bigoted and ruthless. In any event their common purpose was far more significant than any temperamental difference between them. That purpose was realized in only a very limited way until the accession of Edgar, an event which marked the turning point in monastic affairs.

The importance of continental influences on the English movement is apparent at every stage in its development, from the time when Oda sent to Fleury for the habit to the presence of foreign monks at the Winchester synod. The procedure of the synod was modelled closely on that at Aachen in 817 and of the *Concordia* it has been remarked that ' it was the normal use of western Europe, inherited in part from the traditions of Glastonbury and other English churches but chiefly through information and training received from Fleury and Ghent '.[1] Like the continental houses the reformed English monasteries followed a life which devoted the greater part of each day to liturgical prayer and praise in common. But in a number of important respects the English revival differed from continental reforming movements. The most obvious contrast between Cluny and Lorraine was in their attitude to the lay powers which had made reform possible; Cluny desired independence of secular control while the houses reformed by Gerard retained close contacts with their lay patrons. Again, whereas Cluny sought exemption, from diocesan authority the Lotharingian reformers cooperated with their bishops. The attitude of the English reformers to both secular power and episcopal authority reflected the origins and subsequent history of the reform movement within England.

The English reformers owed everything to royal support and were fully aware of their vulnerability to the greed of lay magnates. Unlike Cluny, and with greater conviction than Lorraine, they deliberately sought to bind themselves to the lay power, or rather, to the monarchy; they put themselves under royal protection; even, convinced of the righteousness of their patron, under royal control. The *Concordia* is unique in the number of special prayers for the king and queen which it prescribes for daily recital by the monks. It laid down that though the election of abbots and abbesses must be made according to the Rule ' they must also be conducted with the advice and

---

[1] Knowles, *op. cit.* p. 44.

consent of the king '. While forbidding monasteries ' to acknowledge the overlordship of secular persons, a thing which might lead to utter loss and ruin as it did in past times,' it commanded ' that the sovereign power of the king and queen—and that only—should ever be sought with confident petition '.

The success of the monastic reform movement had been made possible by the work of the previous generation of bishops; it was an extension of their achievement, not a reaction from it. Oda's admiration for the continental monastic reformers complemented his zeal to reform the secular clergy. Whereas Cluny demanded emancipation from diocesan control, and the Lotharingian bishops though supporting monastic reform had not become closely involved with it, in England in Edgar's reign monks captured the episcopate. Uniquely, in England important cathedral churches were transformed into monasteries; the *Concordia* ensured that they would remain monasteries by laying down that their bishops should be elected by their communities of monks—subject to the royal prerogative—and should, after election, conform in all respects to the monastic rule. At the time of the Winchester synod only Winchester and Worcester were affected by this ruling, but before long Christ Church and Sherborne became monastic. Even in the secular cathedrals monk-bishops predominated; out of eighty-seven appointments to bishoprics made between 960 and 1042 no fewer than fifty-six were certainly monks. But though they brought to their cathedrals an awareness of the spiritual aspirations of the monks they cannot be accused of indifference to the world outside. Sometimes one suspects that their biographers have unwittingly, in their enthusiasm for monastic reform, done their principals less than justice by causing them to appear narrower in their interests than in fact they were. The reformers' determination to extirpate abuses and impose the highest standards of monastic life in the greatest churches in the land never caused them to lose sight of the need to raise the standards of Christian observance in the far greater number of houses of secular clergy, and among the isolated priests of the upland parishes.

This truth is revealed in one of the earliest enactments of Edgar's reign, issued at a time when it might have been thought that the minds of the king and his advisers were preoccupied with their plans for the monasteries. Their concern was to ensure that all types of churches were adequately provided for. For the first time the payment of tithe was enforced under threat of heavy penalties for disobedience.

If, however, anyone refuses to render tithes in accordance with what we have decreed, the king's reeve and the bishop's reeve and the priest of the church shall go to him, and without his consent shall take the tenth part for the church to which it is due, and the next tenth shall be allotted to him [the king]; and the remaining eight parts are to be divided into two, and the lord of the estate is to succeed to half and the bishop to half.

The detailed provision made for the application of this law provides a salutary reminder that the tenth century witnessed not only the spectacular achievements of Dunstan and his colleagues but, concurrently, the undramatic proliferation of parish churches to serve the spiritual needs of the laity. Edgar's law, which distinguished between minsters and various categories of private church, was concerned with the allocation of ecclesiastical revenues. Within the large areas served by the minsters, which were generally royal or episcopal foundations served by communities of priests, lesser churches had subsequently been built, generally by laymen. The process of fragmentation of the territories of the minsters had begun as early as the seventh century, though how far it had proceeded and how it had been affected by the dislocation which accompanied the Danish invasions is unknown. But by the middle of the tenth century it had become normal for substantial thegns to build themselves churches in villages on their estates, and to appoint the priests who officiated in them. Edgar's legislation permitted the thegn who owned a church which possessed its own graveyard to pay one-third of his tithe to the priest of his own church, the remaining two-thirds being paid to the minster of the district from which the lesser church had been severed. The parish church was already well established in Edgar's day and his legislation may well have encouraged the foundation of more of them. Dunstan's predecessors, his associates, and his successors all concerned themselves to ensure that the services of these churches were decently maintained and that their incumbents were properly instructed in their duties.

High-ranking churchmen had always been prominent in royal councils and this tradition was fully maintained by the monk-bishops and abbots of the new dispensation. Separate ecclesiastical assemblies met only rarely because the interests of religion were well represented in the witan. In one respect the late Anglo-Saxon Church became more involved with the laity than ever before. In his desire to enrich his new foundations and to secure them from the depredations of local magnates King Edgar began to grant them jurisdictional powers over their territories, which involved abbots in regularly holding courts in which they dispensed justice to their tenants and which rendered them immune from the normal operations of courts of shire and hundred.

The conclusion must be that though the forms and organization of English monastic life had been strongly influenced by continental, and especially Lotharingian models, the spirit which informed it was characteristically English. In its involvement with and concern for the whole Christian congregation of England it was coloured more by Bede's *Ecclesiastical History* and Dunstan's statesmanlike practicality than by continental practice.

Discussion of the relationship between monasticism and the society of which it was part threatens to obscure the fundamental fact that the life of the individual monk centred on the performance of the common liturgical services of his community, through which he hoped to achieve his salvation. To this object all else was secondary. But for the seemly performance of claustral duties noble buildings and furniture were necessary. The services of the conventual church demanded a knowledge of music, particularly as the liturgy became more elaborate. These requirements, in themselves narrowly ' religious ', provided stimuli to the monastic craftsman and musician. Dunstan worked in metals, designed a stole for a noble kinswoman to embroider, played the harp, and composed chants. Athelwold was a great builder and his biographer describes his design for the church at Abingdon—it had a round chancel, the nave was twice the size of the chancel and also round, and it had a round tower. He made an organ with his own hands and a golden wheel studded on its circumference with precious stones and many bells. Oswald was apparently less interested than his colleagues in these activities but there are frequent references to his presence with the monks during the building of Ramsey, and his patron Aethelwine ordered a reredos covered with sheet silver and studded with gems for the church there. Much of the monks' time was spent in the copying of books, mostly service books for daily use of the community in chapel and books for the monastic school and library, but in circumstances comparable to those in eighth-century Northumbria the old English art of illumination was revived. At first influenced by continental manuscripts it quickly developed its own style. The two Winchester communities associated with Aethelwold were its most famous exponents, but the art was widespread in England.[1] Monastic revival once again brought in its train an artistic revival.

[1] F. Wormald, ' Decorated initials in English MSS. from 900 to 1100 '. *Archaeologia*, XLI (1945).

13

THE NADIR OF ANGLO-SAXON KINGSHIP

1. Civil War and Anti-monastic Reaction

KING Edgar died two years after his visit to Chester, at the early age of thirty-two. His surviving sons were both youths, the elder, Edward, about sixteen years of age, the younger, Aethelred, not more than eleven. If either succeeded their father it was probable that for some years effective power would fall into the hands of that group of magnates which succeeded in gaining the confidence, or controlling the person, of the young king. The claim of Edward, Edgar's son by his first wife, Aethelflaed, was supported by Archbishop Dunstan, his fellow bishops, and probably by ealdorman Aethelwine of East Anglia. Aethelred's cause was championed by his mother, Edgar's second wife, Aelfthryth, and ealdorman Aelfhere of Mercia.

The issues involved in the succession dispute were and remain obscure, because they were complicated by the opportunity which Edgar's death afforded to the opponents of monastic reform to express their hostility to the ecclesiastical developments of recent years. The rapid proliferation of monasteries had in many cases involved the expropriation of influential persons and, if the history of Ely is at all typical, foundation had been followed by purchases and exchanges sometimes made under duress; certainly after Edgar's death the monks were involved in a vast number of land pleas. Edgar's policy of granting to monasteries wide jurisdictional privileges also aroused opposition. Peterborough exercised judicial control over the eight hundreds centred on Oundle; Ely was similarly privileged in the two hundreds of the Isle and the five and a half hundreds of Wicklaw in south-east Suffolk; Worcester was the centre of a huge judicial immunity. Such a policy was objectionable not only on the selfish grounds that it encroached on a profitable sphere of activity more properly performed by laymen but also because it might diminish the effectiveness of local government. Moreover, if monasteries should continue to be founded and endowed at the rate attained in the preceding fifteen years they would soon own half the country. Edgar's enthusiasm had deprived the crown of revenue which it needed if the royal resources were to continue to meet the demands made upon them. After his death lands which he had given to Abingdon were withdrawn ' by the decree and order of all the leading men ' of the kingdom, on the grounds that they were properties appropriated to the support of the king's sons. Even when lands granted away were undeniably the king's to give, those who lived on them could suffer hardships. When King Edgar restored to Winchester those parts of the great Taunton estate which had fallen into his hands he ' commanded every one of his thegns who had any land on the estate that they should hold it in conformity with the bishop's wish, or else give it up '. For one of them, even though Queen Aelfthryth interceded for him, this meant nothing more than the recognition of his and his wife's life interest in this land ' and after their death the land should go to Taunton, with produce and with men '; this ungenerous settlement was concluded with great difficulty. It was possible for men to oppose such manifestations of monastic influence in high places without being necessarily hostile to monasticism.

The bitterness generated by a disputed succession and a sharp division of opinion and sentiment on the issue of monastic reform was not dissipated by the choice of Edward as king, probably through the influence of Dunstan. The party which supported Aethelred was unwilling to accept the verdict, and a civil war ensued which fully vindicated the appreciation of the monastic leaders that their well-being depended on the support of a powerful king. The Mercian monasteries were particularly vulnerable and they suffered severely for their close association with Aelfhere's political opponents. Germanus was driven from Winchcombe and took refuge at Fleury, Pershore was dispersed, and Deerhurst ceased to be an abbey. At Evesham the monks were driven out and replaced by a few canons; some of its lands were appropriated by Aelfhere and others were distributed among his relations and supporters. Animosity against the reformers found expression outside Mercia; in south-east England they were opposed by ealdorman Edwin, and at about this time the see of York suffered serious losses, which Archbishop Oswald made the subject of a memorandum. Everywhere popular sentiment was hostile to the monks though they found powerful supporters in Aethelwine, ealdorman of East Anglia, and Byrhtnoth, ealdorman of Essex.

The sequence of events in Edward's reign (975-978) is irrecoverable, but it appears that a nominal peace was restored fairly quickly although Aethelred's supporters did not accept the political settlement. In March 978 Edward was treacherously murdered by Aethelred's supporters at Corfe, a residence owned by Queen Aelfthryth. With Edward dead Aethelred had no rival; even so, his coronation was effected by Archbishop Dunstan at Kingston, 'very quickly' within the year.

2. THE RESUMPTION OF DANISH RAIDING AND ITS EFFECTS

Aethelred succeeded to a difficult inheritance. Though accepted by all, the consequences of the civil war continued to be felt and the dubious circumstances surrounding Edward's death were long remembered. In the year after the murder the body of Edward, which had been buried at Wareham without royal honours, was disinterred and taken to Shaftesbury 'with great honour' by ealdorman Aelfhere. The event symbolized the formal reconciliation of the contestants, and afterwards official attempts were made to obliterate the memory of the disputed succession. In a charter to Abingdon, which can only be dated within the broad limits 990-1016, it was said, with a flagrant disregard of the facts, that all the magnates both lay and ecclesiastical unanimously had chosen Edward as king. But the truth of the matter could not be glossed over and, though Edward's unsuitability for kingship had been reasonably urged against him in 975, he rapidly acquired the reputation of a martyr. Miracles were declared to occur at his tomb and the strength of popular sentiment was such that in 1008 Aethelred and his councillors decreed that St. Edward's festival should be celebrated all over England on 18 March every year.

The domestic difficulties confronting Aethelred and his advisers were compounded by the resumption of Danish attacks upon England. In 980 districts as far apart as Southampton, Thanet, and Cheshire were ravaged; in 981 it was the turn of Devon and Cornwall; in 983 of Dorset. Since the death of Hywel Dda in 952 the resumption of internecine warfare between the Welsh princes had encouraged the renewal of raids on the Welsh coast from the Norse settlements in Dublin, Limerick, and Man; in the 980s the raids were intensified and often came from further afield; St. David's was sacked four times between 982 and 989. The renewal of the Scandinavian assault was caused by political changes in the Scandinavian world and by its material need for silver after it was cut off from its traditional sources of supply; but that the attacks were concentrated on Britain reflected the political weakness of England and Wales at a time when the Frankish lands and Ireland were less vulnerable to assault. Normandy, in particular, now under the rule of a Norse dynasty, far from being a target for attack was used as a convenient base and refuge for fleets operating against England. Aethelred cannot fairly be blamed for the resumption of Danish raids but the ineptitude of his government in dealing with them naturally encouraged the raiders to continue their expeditions.

The great men who had surrounded Edgar and been prominent in the government of his kingdom gradually disappeared from the stage in the early years of the new reign. Of churchmen, Aethelwold of Winchester died in 984, Archbishop Dunstan in 988 and Archbishop Oswald in 992; of the ealdormen, Aelfhere of Mercia died in 983, Byhrtnoth of Essex was killed in battle against the Danes in 991, Aethelwine of East Anglia died in 992. With Danish raiding continuing with unabated ferocity during the next twenty years the king's power of making appointments was more than ever crucial. Aethelred proved to be a poor judge of men, and though he sometimes showed the ability to make a just appreciation of political and military problems he lacked the steadfastness necessary to bring sound plans to a successful conclusion. Not only did he fail to select able and trustworthy subordinates but he was himself both arbitrary and inconstant.

In some respects, particularly in his attitude to Northumbria, he was fully alive to the intensification of the difficulties created by the new wave of invasion. The long-standing and intractable problem of translating antipathy into acquiescence in English rule was compounded by the arrival of more Danes, and throughout Aethelred's reign the northern borders of Northumbria were threatened by the ambitions of the king of Scots. The north needed strong government, but it must be in the hands of a man whose loyalty to the king could be guaranteed yet whose presence there did not irk the king's nominal subjects. Unlike Edgar, Aethelred could not regard time as his ally; he had to take positive measures to strengthen his position. After Earl Oslac had been banished, early in the reign of King Edward, he had been succeeded in the southern Northumbrian

ealdormanry by a certain Thored; a later tradition recorded Aethelred's attempt to secure his loyalty by marrying one of Thored's
daughters. When the ineffectiveness of Thored's military leadership
was demonstrated in the campaign against the Danes in 992 he lost
his earldom and was replaced by Aelfhelm, a Mercian with large
estates in both English and Danish-occupied territories south of the
Humber, whose brother Wulfric Spot, the founder of the monastery
of Burton-on-Trent, was also a great landowner with widely diffused
territorial interests. Aelfhelm's appointment was an intelligent con-
tinuation of Edgar's policy of sending officials, both ecclesiastical and
lay, from the eastern Danelaw to govern the lands north of the
Humber. Its failure, for Aelfhelm and his two sons were murdered
in 1006, apparently on the king's orders, is more a comment on
Aethelred's incompetence in selecting subordinates, or on his inability to trust his chosen instruments, than on the unsoundness of
the policy it represented. The murder of Aelfhelm was followed by the
reunification of the Northumbrian earldom under Uhtred of Bamburgh; once again Aethelred attempted to secure loyalty by means
of a marriage alliance and gave Uhtred one of his daughters as his
third wife. Other members of the royal family made friends in the
Danelaw. In his will Aethelred's eldest son Athelstan made bequests
to Sigeferth and Morcar, the greatest thegns in the north Midlands.
More remarkably, after their assassination in 1015 and King Aethelred's confiscation of their lands, Edmund Ironside, the king's eldest
surviving son, married Sigeferth's widow. Edmund was accepted as
lord by the Five Boroughs and an army from the Danelaw rallied
to his support. The policy of attempting to bind great magnates to
the crown by means of marriage alliances was pursued not only in
Northumbria but in East Anglia as well when a daughter of Aethelred's married its ealdorman, Ulfketel; and in Mercia when another
daughter married Eadric Streona, who became ealdorman there in
1006. The conception was statesmanlike but in its application it did
not succeed because as a rule the individuals in whom Aethelred
reposed his trust were ill-chosen.

Even in the conduct of war Aethelred's failure lay in execution
rather than planning. Recognizing the advantage which a friendly
base in Normandy gave to the Danish fleets he took advantage of
Pope John XV's mediation to make a treaty with Duke Richard I
by which both rulers undertook not to shelter the other's enemies.
In 1002 he again showed his awareness of the value of Norman friend-

ship by taking as his second wife Emma, sister of Duke Richard II. On numerous occasions careful preparations were made for the campaign which had inevitably to be fought in the following spring; sometimes impressive sea and land forces were equipped and assembled. Between 1007 and 1009 Aethelred took advantage of a respite in Danish attacks to restore his fleet; every three hundreds of his kingdom had to furnish a ship of sixty oars and provision was made for arming their crews. Always the land and sea forces were destroyed, by the treachery of some or by the incompetence of others of their commanders.

Aethelred's intelligent awareness of what needed to be done was more than cancelled by his lack of those personal qualities even more essential to a king in a time of crisis. His arbitrariness generated first mistrust and ultimately disloyalty. On the death of Aelfhere of Mercia his son Aelfric succeeded to the ealdormanry; two years later he was driven into exile. In 993 Aethelred had Aelfgar, son of earldorman Aelfric of Hampshire, blinded; this was probably done in revenge for his father's treachery in the previous year, yet the guilty father continued to hold office. In 1002 Aethelred ordered that all the Danes in England should be massacred on St. Brice's Day, ' because he had been told that they intended to kill him and all his counsellors; and afterwards to possess his kingdom '. Impracticable of execution in those areas of England where Danes had settled heavily, where the command was obeyed its consequences were disastrous. Among the Danes massacred at Oxford was Gunnhild, sister of King Swein of Denmark, whose previous disposition to attack England was hardened into a determination to obtain revenge. The slaughter of St. Brice's Day was an act of folly inviting savage reprisals. In 1006 Aelfhelm, ealdorman of southern Northumbria, was killed at the king's orders and his two sons blinded. Well before this Aethelred had forfeited his subjects' support and from Essex had come evidence of the seriousness of unrest and pro-Danish sympathies in a plot to receive Swein of Denmark.

Much of the blame for the progressive undermining of morale must be attributed to the king's disastrous appointments to high offices. The city of Exeter was sacked in 1002 through either the negligence or the treachery of the Norman whom Queen Emma had appointed as her reeve there. Byrhtnoth's successor as ealdorman of Essex, Leofsige, negotiated with a Danish fleet and killed the king's high-reeve Aefic. Sometimes incompetence and worse were overlooked.

In 992 ealdorman Aelfric warned the enemy of an impeding English attack and then deserted from the army; eleven years later ' a great English army was gathered from Wiltshire and from Hampshire, and they were going very resolutely towards the enemy. Then ealdorman Aelfric was to lead the army but he was up to his old tricks. As soon as they were so close that each army looked on the other, he feigned him sick, and began retching to vomit and said that he was taken ill, and thus betrayed the people he should have led.' The classic example of royal folly was the appointment of Eadric Streona to the ealdormanry of Mercia. When, in 1009, the Danes were cornered and eager to retreat to their ships and the English eager to attack, ' it was hindered by ealdorman Eadric, then as it always was '. In 1015 Eadric was blamed for the murder of Sigeferth and Morcar, and he subsequently joined Cnut against the king and Edmund Ironside; in alliance with Cnut he was said to have advised the killing of Uhtred of Northumbria. On Aethelred's death Eadric was readmitted into King Edmund Ironside's confidence—' no greater folly was ever agreed to than that was ', commented the Chronicler—but when battle was joined at Ashingdon, ' then ealdorman Eadric did as he had often done before; he was the first to start the flight with the Magonsaete, and thus betrayed his liege lord and all the people of England '.

The measure of the king's culpability for the appointment of incompetents and traitors to military command is underlined by the evidence which shows that when properly led the English levies could still give a good account of themselves. In 988 the men of Devon strongly resisted the raiders; in 1004 though ' the flower of the East Anglian people, under the command of ealdorman Ulfketel was destroyed, the battle might have been won had his army been at full strength, and the Danes said ' that they never met worse fighting in England than Ulfketel dealt to them '. Even in 1010 when an immense Danish army under command of two famous chiefs Thorkell the Tall and his brother Hemming invaded East Anglia, though the East Anglians incontinently fled, ' the men of Cambridgeshire stood firm against them ' and suffered heavy casualties. The invulnerability of the city of London was several times demonstrated. Olaf Tryggvason and Swein, son of Harald, king of Denmark, attacked the city in 994 but were driven off, and ' there they suffered worse harm and injury than they ever thought any citizens would do to them '; in 1010, though several times attacked, the city held out;

Oxford and Winchester submitted to Swein without a fight in 1013, but the Londoners ' would not yield, but resisted with full battle '; successful resistance was offered again in 1016. Most striking evidence of English resilience after years of military defeat was their rally to Edmund Ironside in the summer of 1016 when Edmund led his army in five separate battles against Cnut.

But heroic local defence could not compensate for the feebleness of central direction. The exasperated compiler of the Abingdon version of the *Chronicle* recorded the story of gradual demoralization, indicating both its causes and its progress.

993. . . . Then a very large English army was collected, and when they should have joined battle, the leaders, namely Fraena, Godwine and Frythegyst first started the flight . . .

999. . . . And then they [the Danes] seized horses and rode wherever they pleased, and destroyed and ravaged almost all west Kent. Then the king with his councillors determined that they should be opposed by a naval force and also by a land force. But when the ships were ready, one delayed from day to day, and oppressed the wretched people who were on the ships. And ever, as things should have been moving, they were the more delayed from one hour to the next, and ever they let their enemies force increase, and ever the English retreated inland and the Danes continually followed; and then in the end it effected nothing —the naval expedition or the land expedition—except the oppression of the people and the encouragement of their enemies.

1006. . . . Then after midsummer the great fleet came to Sandwich, and did just as they were accustomed, ravaged, burnt and slew as they went. Then the king ordered the whole nation from Wessex and Mercia to be called out, and they were out on military service against the Danish army the whole autumn, yet it availed no whit more than it had often done before; for in spite of it all, the Danish army went about as it pleased, and the English levy caused the people of the country every sort of harm, so that they profited neither from the native army nor from the foreign army . . .

1010. . . . And when they were in the east, the English army was kept in the west, and when they were in the south, our army was in the north. Then all the councillors were summoned to the king, and it was then to be decided how this country should be defended. But even if anything was then decided, it did not last even a month. Finally there was no leader who would collect an army, but each fled as best he could, and in the end no shire would even help the next.

Almost every year, for more than thirty years, some part of England was harried. In such circumstances it may appear remarkable that resistance was so long maintained. But the raids of the period 980 to 1013 in many ways resembled the assaults of the ninth-century

Vikings prior to the landing of the army of 865. The attackers were concerned with plunder not conquest, so despite the miseries they inflicted on the native population they made no challenge to the established government. Even the army of 1009, which remained in England until the early spring of 1012, did not at first look very different from its predecessors except that it was larger, its commanders were the most celebrated soldiers in northern Europe and it included a strong professional element. The campaign of 1009-12, during which fifteen counties were ravaged, demonstrated that England was now almost defenceless; but it was the sequel to that campaign which determined Swein of Denmark to lead an expedition of conquest.

During this period of uncoordinated raiding the strength of the administrative machine built up by Aethelred's predecessors was strikingly demonstrated. The price of military failure was the levying of huge sums of money to buy peace, yet the increasing demands of the invaders were satisfactorily met. In 991 there was a payment of 10,000 pounds; in 944 of 16,000 pounds; in 1002 of 24,000 pounds; in 1007 of 36,000 pounds; in 1012 of 48,000 pounds; the burden grew heavier as the countryside became increasingly impoverished by tribute and destruction. Archbishop Sigeric had to sell an estate in Buckinghamshire to Bishop Aescwig of Dorchester in order to secure ready cash to pay his share of the tribute demanded in 994; lesser men with fewer resources must have been driven to harsher expedients. The huge sums raised testify not only to the wealth of England but also to the efficiency of the tax-collecting machinery of the Anglo-Saxon kingdom. In view of the difficulties encountered by later kings in the exercise of their right of purveyance it is remarkable that not only money but provisions could be supplied to Danish armies wintering in England, at a time when crops suffered constant damage, and famine, never far away, was in 1005 ' more severe than any that could be remembered '.

Surprisingly, fiscal strains appear to have affected neither the quality of Aethelred's coinage nor the concern of his government to control it. Occasionally, under strain of war, a minting place vulnerable to attack might be abandoned—as were Bruton, Crewkerne, and Ilchester, which were temporarily replaced by a mint at the old hill fort of Cadbury—but the volume of coins issued was greater than ever before. Though the weight of silver pennies minted in different issues fluctuated, the variations in weight show no evidence of a progressive reduction in their silver content. New dies were issued at six-year intervals throughout the reign. Aethelred's legislation shows no relaxation in control over minting places and the number of moneyers who might work in them, but rather an intensification in the determination to protect the quality of the coins produced. Athelstan laid down that the hand of a false coiner should be struck off and set up over his workshop; on certain particularly heinous offenders, ' moneyers who carry on their business in woods or worked in other such places ', that is, men who operated outside the official mints, Aethelred imposed the death penalty.

Throughout these years the king frequently held courts attended by magnates from all over England. From such assemblies emanated no fewer than eight codes of law, mainly repeating and strengthening earlier legislation, but some of it indicating a firmer attitude towards the Danish lands than had been shown by Edgar. It has also been recently suggested that Aethelred's fourth code of laws is in fact a composite document of which the first two articles are not legislation but record the replies to an inquest into the customs of London made about the year 1000.[1] If this were true it would be tribute to the administrative ingenuity of Aethelred's advisers, for it would reveal them directing an enquiry very similar to those made half a century later by the Domesday commissioners of King William.

Dangers more pressing than had been known for more than a century may have stimulated new devices in the area of military organization. In 1008 the territorial divisions of the kingdom were used for military purposes when every three hundred hides were required to combine to provide a ship and its equipment; instances of the groupings of hundreds for this purpose are found in Buckinghamshire, Worcestershire and Warwickshire, thus proving that the levy was made on inland as well as coastal shires. Whether reforms were effected in the methods of mobilizing and recruiting land armies is uncertain, but accounts of the fighting suggest that they continued to be highly flexible. As ever, able-bodied men irrespective of social status and legal obligation would be likely to take up whatever weapons they could lay hands on to repel raiders intent on destroying their homes and looting their possessions. In more deliberately organized operations, as in those of 1003 when Aelfric led a force from Wiltshire and Hampshire, or of 1004 when Ulfketel led the

---

[1] Richardson and Sayles, *Law and Legislation*, p. 28.

East Anglians, an ealdorman commanded the levies of a shire or group of shires against the enemy; sometimes the king ordered a more general mobilization, as in 1006 when the whole of the people of Wessex and Mercia were called to service.

The nucleus of such provincial and natural armies consisted of the great magnates of kingdoms and their retainers, often, though not always, of thegnly rank; the poem *The Battle of Maldon* tells how, after reviewing his troops, ealdorman Byrhtnoth alighted from his horse ' among the people where it pleased him best, where he knew his body-guard to be most loyal ', and the account of the fighting centres on the exploits of this group of warriors who after their leader's death ' desired one of two things, to lose their lives or to avenge the one they loved '. How these élite household troops were now supplemented is a much debated question.[1] The military crisis served to place emphasis once again, as in Alfred's day, on the fighting role of the thegn. It used generally to be thought that all thegns owed personal military service by virtue of their social rank and that in addition to the thegns, the principle of selective service having by now become established, every five hides or six carucates of land contributed one peasant soldier to the fyrd. This view has recently been challenged; both the military liability of all thegns and the importance of the free-peasant element in the armies of the late Anglo-Saxon state are denied. It is urged that there is no unambiguous evidence to support the contention that all thegns owed military service—that a thegn liable to service was liable to the confiscation of his estates if he defaulted and that many thegns were so liable is undoubted, but since the thegnly class comprehended men of widely differing resources there is no compelling reason to suppose that their social status involved them all in the same liability. The eleventh-century document *Rectitudines Singularum Personarum* associates the military service of a thegn with his holding in land, not with his rank; ' the law of the thegn is . . . that he shall contribute three things in respect of his land, armed service and the repairing of fortresses and work on bridges '. The size of the estate is not mentioned, but the frequency with which thegnly holdings of five hides are encountered in the south and Midlands and a Northum-

---

[1] For differing views as to the nature and composition of the fyrd at this period see Stenton, *Anglo-Saxon England*, pp. 583-4; C. W. Hollister, *Anglo-Saxon Military Institutions on the Eve of the Norman Conquest* (Oxford, 1962); Richardson and Sayles, *Governance of Medieval England*. ch. 3; and John *Orbis Britanniae*, pp. 128-53.

brian document which associates the rights of thegnhood with possession of five hides of land, suggest that despite numerous anomalies,
both greater and less, the typical thegn of this period might be
expected to hold that amount of land. The conclusion to be drawn
from the coexistence of a five-hide territorial unit of military service
and the notion that thegnly holdings should be of five hides is that
the typical territorial representative of the units into which England
was by now divided for military purposes was not a peasant but a
thegn. The thegn who held five hides acquitted his estate through his
personal service; but a five-hide unit would often be represented by
a thegn holding less than five hides; and it might, if no thegn were
available, be represented by a member of the ceorl class, among whom
were some who remained or became prosperous.

If these conclusions are justified the army led, for example, by
ealdorman Byrhtnoth at Maldon consisted of the earl and his household retainers supplemented by the territorial levy many, but not all
of whom, would have been landed thegns. Such a development would
seem to accord with the general tendencies of social change in the
century and a half before the Conquest. Certainly warfare was
becoming increasingly professional. To withstand Swein's Jomsvikings[1] with any hope of success it was essential to confront them
with troops equally well trained and dedicated to the skills of war.
This was achieved by the introduction of a mercenary element into
the king's forces. In 1012 Aethelred took Thorkell the Tall with his
forty-five ships and their crews into his pay, and mercenary troops
returned to England with him in 1014. Henceforth stipendiary
soldiers were always an element in the royal army.

It seems possible to believe that armies composed predominantly
of household troops and thegns were normal, yet to doubt whether
the king ever relinquished his claim on the military service of all
the freemen in his kingdom, though he implemented it only in times
of emergency. In 1016 ' an order was issued to the home-force that
every able-bodied man, on pain of the full fine, should come out
for service '. It can be argued that this command applied only to the

---

[1] The Jomsvikings were a community of well-tried soldiers who lived under
strict discipline in Jomsborg, a fortress at the mouth of the river Oder. It has
not been identified, but four other fortresses, datable within the limits 950-1050,
have been excavated in Denmark, all constructed to accommodate large military
forces and all built on royal estates. Trelleborg, the first of them to be found,
consisted of sixteen barrack blocks surrounded by a strong circular rampart with
fifteen further barrack blocks outside the rampart. These bases testify to the
strength of the military resources at Swein's disposal.

five-hide representatives who owed service in the fyrd and that its singularity consisted in its call to all the shires of England rather than to one or several of them, but it would be more natural to interpret it as a summons to all freemen. But in whatever way armies were constituted it remains a tribute to the competence of Aethelred's administration that year after year they continued to be put in the field, and remained there until their leaders deserted them.

Throughout the years of Aethelred's reign large numbers of charters continued to be issued; they give no indication of royal weakness or of any awareness that royal commands might be ignored. Whether military pressures stimulated the interest of the king in the institutions of local government cannot be determined, but it certainly did not inhibit their continuing development.

The increasing importance of the ealdorman as he became the king's viceroy over a large province, together with the need for his frequent attendance at court and his military commitments, created the need for an official who could relieve the ealdorman of some of his duties within the individual shires. In every shire there had been a number of reeves entrusted with the supervision of royal interests within the shire; among the royal reeves one of their number came to be burdened with heavier and wider ranging duties than his fellows, who took over from the ealdorman the routine parts of his administrative functions and acted as his deputy if he were absent. The shire reeve was to have a great future in the history of English local government and he emerged in the reign of Aethelred. For a long time his functions were overshadowed by those of the ealdorman, but as the latter's political importance increased so did the work which the sheriff was required to do.

Contact between the king and the provinces continued to be maintained, through his thegns and through the medium of written instruments conveying the king's command to his subjects. In form the writ was a letter in the vernacular tongue bearing a lord's greetings and conveying his orders to his men, authenticated by the seal of the sender.[1] Of the origins of the sealed writ little is certainly known; an allusion to writ and seal by King Alfred in his translation of Augustine's *Soliloquies* has been taken to indicate that it was a commonplace device even in his day, but the earliest extant examples are no earlier than Aethelred's reign. It is true that since many writs were

[1] The extant writs were edited with an invaluable introduction by F. E. Harmer, *Anglo-Saxon Writs* (Manchester, 1952).

administrative orders they were unlikely to be preserved after the instructions they conveyed had been obeyed, but the number which have survived from the end of the tenth century to the Norman Conquest casts doubt on the suggestion that their ephemeral utility adequately explains their total absence earlier. It is possible that in Alfred's reign the king's letter, and the seal which accompanied it, were separate objects; if so the seal would have provided inadequate evidence of authenticity. Certainty was only secured when the seal was physically attached to the writing. When this practice began is unknown; the frequency of allusions to writ and seal in Aethelred's reign suggests that it was totally innovatory, though it may not then have had a long history behind it. But that the writ was a commonplace instrument of the royal will in Aethelred's reign cannot be doubted; despatched to the leading men of the shire it was the perfect device for publicizing his instructions.

How effective this oversight was in the event of the king's interest differing from that of the local magnate is more dubious. A document of 996 retails an unsavoury story of unpunished crime. On the death of his father a certain Wulfbald seized his stepmother's land and chattels. When ordered by the king to restore the land Wulfbald ignored the command, and his wergild was assigned to the king; this happened twice more. Then Wulfbald seized the land of his kinsman, Brihtmaer of Bourne; the king's order to restore that estate was similarly ignored, and for the fourth time his wergild was assigned to the king. 'Then took place the great assembly at London...then all the councillors that were there . . . assigned to the king all Wulfbald's property, and also placed him at the king's mercy, whether to live or to die. And he retained all this until he died. Afterwards, when he was dead, on top of all this, his widow went, with her child, and killed the king's thegn Eadmaer . . . and fifteen of his companions.' It seems that reality was very different from appearances, even before the Danish attacks had reached their crescendo.

Equally remarkable was the continued vitality of the second generation of monastic reformers. After their tribulations in Edward's reign their activities were resumed, though at a reduced tempo. The monastic hold on the episcopate was unshaken by the deaths of their first champions; in the year 1000 of the eighteen bishoprics in England only one, Elmham, was certainly held by a secular clerk. Christ Church became monastic under Archbishop Aelfric (995-1005) and a few years later Sherborne followed suit. Although King Aethelred himself, when young, was guilty of taking estates from Abingdon he subsequently repented; he never showed enthusiasm for the monks but during his reign the example set by ealdorman Aethelwine under Edgar found several emulators and the flow of benefactions from noble laymen was maintained. Ealdorman Aethelweard founded Cerne and his son Aethelmaer founded Eynsham; ealdorman Ordwulf founded Tavistock; in the north Midlands a wealthy thegn, Wulfric Spot, established Burton-on-Trent.

In the last decade of the century the writings of Aelfric, a former pupil of Aethelwold, reveal more fully than ever before the concern of the monastic leaders that pastoral work in the towns and villages should be adequately carried out. First at Cerne and later at Eynsham where he was abbot, he was commissioned by Bishop Wulfsige of Sherborne and by Archbishop Wulfstan of York to write pastoral letters which impressed on parish priests the high standards of behaviour their vocation imposed on them and instructed them in their duties. He translated many books of the Bible into Old English, and his *Catholic Homilies* were expositions of Christian morality or of passages from the Bible written to be preached or read to their people by clergy whose education fell short of what was necessary for them to provide instruction of their own devising. Judged by intellectual standards these works appear homespun, and their author second-rate by comparison with the scholars of the twelfth century, but Aelfric's writings fulfilled admirably the purpose which their author had in mind.

Exhortation and instruction was reinforced by legislation. Canons, if their endowments permitted, were to have a common refectory and dormitory, but in any event to maintain celibacy and to observe regular lives on pain of forfeiting their prebends. Parish priests must remain celibate and avoid drunkenness and brawling; they must be assiduous in the performance of the services of their churches and in their duties of baptizing and educating children and confessing sinners; the furnishings of their churches and their own vestments must be maintained decently; they must possesss the books needful for church services—a mass book, a copy of the Gospels, the epistles and the psalms; on Sundays they must explain the Gospel to their congregations and ensure that their flocks understood the meaning of the Lord's Prayer. There is evidence too that missionary enterprises were sustained in these years. When Olaf Tryggvason went to

Norway in 995 English clergy accompanied him, and about this time English churchmen participated in the conversion of Sweden.

Aethelred's wars were less disruptive to the Church than the Danish wars of the ninth century. Occasionally communities near the coast suffered; Padstow was sacked in 981, Tavistock was burned in 997 but recovered. Yet there was never any threat to diocesan organization or to the monastic order. The problem which now faced Church leaders was more insidious; the social strains which attended the protracted but generally unsuccessful and humiliating fighting threatened to undermine Christian standards of behaviour among the native English. This challenge could not be defeated from the cloister, but Church leaders attempted to meet it by intensifying their efforts to maintain discipline among both the secular clergy and the laity.

No prelate was more prominent in these efforts than Wulfstan, a monk by training and successively bishop of London, archbishop of York and bishop of Worcester from 1002 to 1016, and archbishop of York until his death in 1023.[1] He was highly influential in national affairs and the last six codes of law promulgated in Aethelred's reign were his work; they combined exhortation with prohibition and threats of punishment against those who denied justice to God or man. ' Men of every order are each to submit to that duty which befits them in religious and secular concerns '; monks and canons must keep their rule; all men must zealously perform their Christian duties, which implied the fulfilment of obligations not only to the Church but also to the kingdom, since ' a Christian king is Christ's deputy in a Christian people '. A considerable scholar, Wulfstan, while still at Worcester, made its scriptorium a centre of learning, especially in canonistic studies, but in his own writings he was severely practical, insisting always on the duties which attended rank. He had also a great reputation as a forceful and eloquent speaker. His most famous, though least characteristic, homily was his *Sermon of the Wolf to the English*; it reveals how little reward had attended his efforts and those of his colleagues and it paints a telling picture of the demoralization of English society during Aethelred's last years :

[1] See, especially D. Whitelock, 'Archbishop Wulfstan, Homilist and Statesman ' *T.R.H.S.*, fourth series, XXIV, 1942, and Wulfstan's most important work. *Institutes of Polity, Civil and Ecclesiastical,* ed. K. Jost (Berne, 1959).

God's dues have dwindled too long in every district within this nation, and the laws of the people have deteriorated all too much, and sanctuaries are violated far and wide, and the houses of God are entirely despoiled of ancient privileges and stripped inside of all that is seemly. And widows are forced into marriage, and too many are reduced to poverty and greatly humiliated. And poor men are sorely deceived and cruelly defrauded and sold far and wide out of this country into the power of foreigners, although quite innocent; and children in the cradle are enslaved for petty theft by cruel injustice widely throughout this people. And the rights of freemen are withdrawn and the rights of slaves are restricted and charitable obligations are curtailed; and in short, God's laws are hated and his precepts despised.

The sermon was a final demonstration of the dependence of ecclesiastical leaders on a ruler who could maintain order within his kingdom. In the conditions which obtained during Aethelred's reign the conversion to Christianity of the new wave of pagan settlers was an easier task than the maintenance of Christian standards among the native population. But if Wulfstan's *Sermon* was a confession of failure it is hard to see what more he and his fellow-bishops could have done, for he did not stand alone. Aelfheah, the monk-bishop of Canterbury, preferred martyrdom to the imposition of further burdens on his flock.

3. THE DANISH CONQUEST

Though the administrative fabric of the kingdom remained intact, by 1013, after years of unrelieved defeat and the experience of almost three years when a Danish army moved through the country at will, the spirit of resistance was at its nadir. In that year Swein, king of Denmark, resolved on conquest. He had raided in England in the company of Olaf Tryggvason in 994 but his desire for easy plunder had been transformed into a personal hostility to King Aethelred by his sister's murder in 1002. He campaigned in England again between 1003 and 1005. In 1012 he suffered a further injury. The mercenary element in the army of 1009 had been drawn from a highly trained corps of warriors which lived under rigid military discipline within fortified bases in Denmark; though not entirely Danish in composition they owed allegiance to King Swein.[1] In the spring of 1012 this army was paid £48,000 to leave England, but not satisfied with that vast amount they demanded a separate ransom for Archbishop Aelfheah. The archbishop forbade that payment should be made for

[1] *Supra*, p. 309 n.

him and in their drunken fury his captors killed him despite appeals for his life made by Thorkell the Tall, one of the Danish commanders. Before the end of the year Thorkell had gone over to King Aethelred and undertaken to assist in the country's defence. This event was decisive. Thorkell's defection was insufferable to Swein, who regarded Aethelred as equally culpable for admitting a traitor into his service.

In August 1013 a large Danish fleet under Swein's command made its landfall at Sandwich, sailed up the east coast into the mouth of the Humber and disembarked at Gainsborough on the river Trent. Immediately Earl Uhtred and the Northumbrians, and then the people of Lindsey, submitted to him; they were followed by the inhabitants of the Five Boroughs and all the Danish settlers north of Watling Street. As insurance against treachery Swein took hostages from every shire. After requiring the natives to provide provisions and horses he marched south, leaving his son Cnut in charge of the base and the hostages. Once across Watling Street the Danes devastated the countryside and with a massive display of force terrified Oxford and Winchester into submission. Repulsed from London by King Aethelred and Thorkell they moved westwards through Wallingford to Bath, where ealdorman Aethelmaer and the leading men of the western shires made their submission. Everywhere hostages were taken. Almost the whole of England was in Swein's hands and shortly afterwards the citizens of London capitulated, fearful that their city would be destroyed. During the campaign Emma and her children had crossed to Normandy to take refuge with the queen's brother, Duke Richard; after Christmas Aethelred joined her there. 'And all the nation regarded him [Swein] as full king.'

Within less than two months on 3 February 1014, Swein died, at Gainsborough. The Danish ships' crews at Gainsborough elected Cnut king, but ' all the councillors of England, ecclesiastical and lay, took counsel and determined that Aethelred should be sent for, declaring that no lord was dearer to them than their natural lord, if only he would govern them more justly than before '. Aethelred's son Edward, sent by his father to England, bore Aethelred's promise ' that he would be a gracious lord to them and reform all the things which they all hated '. On these terms Aethelred returned to England and was joyfully received by his people. Cnut at this time was at Gainsborough preparing, in conjunction with the men of Lindsey, for a raid into Aethelred's territory. Showing unwonted vigour

Aethelred attacked him before his preparations were complete and compelled him to sail away with his fleet, leaving Lindsey and its inhabitants to Aethelred's mercy. Moving south Cnut put ashore all the hostages taken by his father, after mutilating them by cutting off their hands, ears, and noses. He then returned to Denmark.

Though restored to his kingdom Aethelred had learned nothing. During a council held at Oxford in the spring of 1015 Eadric Streona arranged the murder of Sigeferth and Morcar, the two chief thegns of the northern Danelaw. The king involved himself in the crime by seizing their property and ordering Sigeferth's widow to be taken to Malmesbury. Edmund, the king's eldest surviving son, rescued and married her and moving into the Danelaw took over the estates of both thegns. The people of the Five Boroughs accepted him as their lord. Cnut meanwhile, with the support of his brother, the king of Denmark, had mobilized new forces. His principal subordinates were Earl Eric of Hlathir, a famous Viking and the chief prop of Danish influence in Norway, and Thorkell the Tall, who by now had left Aethelred's service—it is said that Thorkell's brother Eilaf had died in England in 1014 in suspicious circumstances which compromised the king. The arrival of Cnut's fleet in southern England led temporarily to a reconciliation between Eadric Streona and the atheling Edmund. The English forces combined, but their mutual distrust was such that no battle was fought. Before the year's end Eadric had joined Cnut and the West Saxons had again submitted to him.

Early in 1016 Cnut and Eadric Streona advanced into western Mercia. Edmund tried to raise an army against them, but since the king was not present to lead the English forces and the Londoners gave no support the army dispersed without achieving anything. A second attempt to raise an army, this time under royal leadership, revealed little enthusiasm for fighting and hints of overt disloyalty. Aethelred returned to London while Edmund made contact with Earl Uhtred of Northumbria. For some time both forces, English and Danish, ravaged the shires of north-west Mercia until Cnut suddenly broke off the campaign and drove northwards into Northumbria. Uhtred hastened back to his earldom and submitted to Cnut, but to no avail. On the advice of Eadric Streona Uhtred was killed and his earldom given to Eric of Hlathir. After the submission of the Northumbrians Cnut returned to Wessex, intending to reduce London, where King Aethelred and Edmund were now established.

Aethelred died on 23rd April 1016. The leading men of the Danish controlled areas immediately elected Cnut as king; meeting him at Southampton they swore loyalty to him and Cnut swore to be a good lord to them. In London all the magnates there and the citizens chose Edmund as king. Cnut assaulted London but was repulsed and while the city remained under siege Edmund counterattacked into Wessex. He was well received by the inhabitants and won victories over the Danes and Eadric Streona at Penselwood and Sherston. Returning to London Edmund relieved the city and continued the reorganization of the West Saxon element in his army. The Danes were driven into Kent and then into Essex. At Aylesford in Kent Edmund allowed himself to be reconciled with Eadric Streona and together they joined battle with the Danes at Ashingdon in Essex; once again Eadric turned traitor and was the first to flee from the battlefield. Cnut won the battle and ' all the nobility of England was there destroyed '. Yet the contestants were still evenly matched and they agreed on a partition of the kingdom which left Wessex in Edmund's hands and Mercia to Cnut. Arrangements were also made for the payment of the Danish army, which took up winter quarters in London. Edmund remained in Wessex. On 30 November he died and was buried at Glastonbury by the side of his grandfather, King Edgar. Without opposition Cnut succeeded to the whole kingdom.

Such is the bare narrative of events. It shows both the demoralization of the English by 1013 and the latent strength of a monarchy which even after continuous reverses could, under a commander of Edmund's calibre, mobilize resources sufficient to defeat Cnut's professional army. The restoration of Aethelred in 1014 despite his frequently demonstrated unfitness for rule reveals the respect still felt for the dynasty of Cerdic and suggests that the Church's teaching on the obligations of a people to the Lord's Anointed had struck deep roots. The readiness of the Five Boroughs to support Edmund argues for the success of Edgar and Aethelred in making the inhabitants of the Danelaw feel ' English '. Further north, the attitude of the Northumbrians indicates that they felt no particular enthusiasm for either of the contenders to the throne. In 1013 they passively accepted Swein who, nonetheless, took hostages from them; in 1014 Cnut left them to their fate, and when he came again he chose to establish himself in Wessex, rather than the Danelaw. Earl Uhtred was able and willing to join forces with Edmund against Cnut and only submitted to him ' out of necessity '. The war between Edmund and Cnut ended with the partition of the kingdom just as the war between

Alfred and Guthrum had ended; but whereas the sequel to 878 was an English reconquest, the sequel to 1016 was that the Danes took all. These conclusions appear clearly from the story told by the English Chronicler. Other things are more obscure and suggest that the picture that we have from him is coloured and distorted by his prejudices. It is difficult to believe that Eadric Streona was responsible for all the crimes attributed to him; harder still to believe that a man with his reputation for treachery would win the confidence of three kings so different as Aethelred, Edmund, and Cnut. But to speculate further on these matters, in default of evidence, is profitless.

14

THE ANGLO-SCANDINAVIAN KINGDOM

1. The Consolidation of Cnut's Authority in England

THE conquest of England by Cnut invites comparison with that by Duke William of Normandy fifty years later. Both conquerors claimed the English crown to be theirs by right and were concerned to take over and continue the governmental machinery, the legal system, and the social structure of the kingdom with the minimum of dislocation. Since their right was disputed they were compelled to fight and they vindicated their claims with the support of small but highly professional armies. After their victories both kings confronted the problems set by the rule of overseas territories in addition to England. Yet detailed comparisons are impossible because whereas the results of 1066 are written in Domesday Book the consequences of Cnut's conquest can only be conjectured. Paucity of evidence, the prominence of Englishmen in the politics of the half-century after 1016, and above all, the subsequent restoration of the Anglo-Saxon dynasty in the person of Edward the Confessor, may have contributed to conceal the importance of the changes which took place during the rule of Cnut and his two sons. It is true that because Cnut after the death of Edmund, unlike William after the death of Harold, was untroubled by native rebellions, his conquest was not followed by a tenurial revolution on the scale of that which followed 1066, which resulted in the extinction of the English aristocracy; but it is possible that the changes effected in the upper ranks of English society after 1016 were more important than has been generally recognized. Though only a comparatively small number of Danes were newly introduced into the ranks of the great landowners and a few huscarls settled in estates in the localities, this, combined with the elimination of the great magnate families of tenth-century England and their replacement by English-born collaborators who owed their positions to the favour of Danish kings, created an aristocracy whose loyalty to Edward the Confessor rested on little more than a calculation of self-interest. When the old dynasty was restored in 1042 it lacked the intangible sources of strength which, in times of difficulty in the past, had sustained it.

The death of Edmund Ironside left Cnut without a rival. Although both Aethelred and Edmund left sons theoretically eligible to rule only Edward, the son of Aethelred and Emma, was of an age to lead a campaign. He showed no disposition to challenge Cnut, nor is it likely that a fifteen-year-old who had so far revealed no ability for military command would have obtained much support. No one wanted further fighting. The issues at stake during the recent fighting had become much less clear cut than in the ninth century when King Alfred and his West Saxons had fought the pagan followers of Halfdan and Hastein. The campaigns of Aethelred and Edmund against Swein and Cnut had developed into a struggle for the English Kingdom between rival contenders, all of whom professed to be Christians and whose leading supporters were not necessarily of the same race as their principals. Aethelred's treachery and incompetence had caused him to forfeit the support of some of his nobles; conversely, as early as 1001 the Danish Pallig, brother-in-law of King Swein, had been in his service. In 1012 Thorkell the Tall took service under Aethelred, and on Aethelred's return from Normandy in 1014 Olaf Haraldsson accompanied him with a force of Norwegians. Edmund fought the Danes with an army raised in the Danelaw. Eadric Streona supported Dane or Englishman indifferently, as self-interest appeared to indicate; English troops, whether willingly or not, fought in Swein's army. Differences of racial origin ceased to be important when intermarriage between English and Danes was commonplace. King Aethelred had taken the great granddaughter of the Viking Rollo as his second wife, Edmund married the widow of a Danish thegn, while Cnut took as wife, ' after the Danish fashion ', Aelfgifu of Northampton, daughter of that ealdorman Aelfhelm who had been killed in 1006 with Aethelred's connivance; though he subsequently married Emma of Normandy Cnut continued to treat Aelfgifu and her sons with consideration. The Northumbrian house which ruled the land between the Tees and the Scottish border was of mixed Danish and English blood; the elder son of Leofwine, ealdorman of Mercia, was named Northman; Thorkell the Tall's wife Edith was perhaps a daughter of King Aethelred; and Earl Godwin of Wessex married Gytha, sister of Earl Ulf, the husband of Cnut's sister Estrith. In the next generation Earl Siward of Northumbria married a granddaughter of Earl Uhtred and named one of his sons after Uhtred's father, Waltheof. Such relationships were established more easily in the eleventh than in the ninth century because the leaders of the second phase of Scandinavian invasion, Olaf Tryggvason, Olaf Haraldsson, Swein, Cnut, and their principal subordinates were nominally Christian. The emphatic prohibition of pagan practices in Cnut's legislation and their denunciation by contemporary homilists testifies to the superficiality of Christianity among the recently settled Scandinavian population, but it suggests also that Danish ways exercised a spontaneous attraction on the native English. One of the rare private letters of this period written by an Englishman confirms this view:

> I will tell thee also, brother Edward, now that thou has asked me, that you do wrong in abandoning the English practices which your fathers followed, and in loving the practices of heathen men who begrudge your life, and in so doing show by such evil habits that you despise your race and your ancestors, since in insult to them you dress in Danish fashion with bared necks and blinded eyes. I will say no more about that shameful mode of dress except what books tell us, that he will be accursed who follows heathen practices in his life and in so doing dishonours his whole race.

In the circumstances it was not surprising that Cnut's succession was achieved without bloodshed. He claimed to be occupying the throne to which he had been chosen at Gainsborough in 1014 and again at Southampton in 1016; according to one account he persuaded the assembled lay and ecclesiastical magnates to agree that Edmund had designated him as protector of his sons and their inheritance until they were old enough to reign.

In his statesmanlike pursuit of political objectives Cnut was in striking contrast to the other great Scandinavian leaders of his time, all of whom were great soldiers in the old Viking tradition. Cnut possessed none of the heroic virtues. His role in England after Swein's death though prudent was inglorious; his military prowess is not emphasized in the accounts of his later campaigns; nor were his military interventions in Scandinavia victorious. Men he mistrusted he ruthlessly destroyed, like Eadric Streona who, having outlived his usefulness, was executed on Christmas Day 1017; men who played him false but whom he failed to defeat in battle were murdered by his orders, like his brother-in-law Ulf, regent of Denmark; men he feared were killed, like Eadwig, the only surviving son of King Aethelred by his first marriage. It was thoroughly characteristic of his statecraft that after an unsuccessful northern expedition in 1026, he prepared for the defeat of Olaf Haraldsson two years later by the lavish distribution of bribes. Yet for Cnut cruelty was an instrument of policy rather than the indulgence of personal vindictiveness. He was determined to rule his kingdom and took such measures as he deemed necessary to that end; they were not incompatible with his wish to govern England as an English king, accepting and maintaining the Christian heritage he had found there.

Having obtained the throne unopposed, Cnut's first concern was to make himself thoroughly secure, by the imposition of military government until all possible rivals and opponents were eliminated.[1] Early in 1017 the kingdom was divided into four parts each under the rule of one man; he kept Wessex in his own hands, gave Mercia to Eadric Streona, East Anglia to Thorkell the Tall, and Northumbria to Eric of Hlathir. In the same year the atheling Eadwig was first exiled and subsequently killed by Cnut's orders; Edward and Edmund, the two young sons of Edmund Ironside, would have suffered the same fate had they not fled to a safe refuge in Hungary. Before the year's end the upper ranks of the Anglo-Saxon nobility, already attenuated by the combination of Aethelred's malevolence and the long wars, were further reduced by the killing of at least four of its leaders, among them Eadric Streona. Finally, in order to neutralize any possibility that Duke Richard of Normandy might support the claims of Aethelred's son by his sister Emma, Cnut married her.

By 1018 Cnut felt strong enough to relax his military rule. Two earldoms were re-established in Wessex and the Mercian ealdormanry was again dismembered by the re-establishment of earldoms in Herefordshire and Worcestershire. The greater part of the force which he had brought with him to England was paid off and sent back to Denmark. The money for this operation was raised by the imposition of a tax of £72,000 with an additional £10,500 from London. Even so, Cnut retained a fleet of forty ships and their crews

---

[1] *Encomium Emmae Reginae*, ed. and trans. A. Campbell, *Camden*, third series, LXXII (London, 1949), is an important but difficult source for the years 1012-42; pp. l-lxix of the Introduction provide a valuable assessment of its historical value.

in England which, together with the force of huscarls which he maintained, necessitated the imposition of a heavy annual tax for their support. At a council held at Oxford in that year ' the councillors determined that above all things they would ever honour one God and steadfastly hold one Christian faith, and would love Cnut with due loyalty and zealously observe Edgar's laws '. Cnut here declared his intention of maintaining continuity with the past. He would defend the kingdom from external attack, protect the Church, promote the Christian way of life and secure to every man, whether Dane or English, justice in accordance with his customary law. In return he expected loyalty and obedience.

In fact the only possible threat to the integrity of Cnut's kingdom came from the ambitions of the long lived Malcolm II, king of Scots. Lothian, ceded to his father Kenneth by King Edgar, was the richest and most fertile part of the Scottish kingdom, and its possession opened up an attractive prospect of further expansion southwards. In 1006 Malcolm had unsuccessfully besieged Durham, but in 1016 in alliance with Owain, king of Strathclyde, he defeated Earl Uhtred of Northumbria at Carham on the river Tweed. Eric of Hlathir, appointed earl after Uhtred's murder, stabilized the military situation, but it was still necessary for Cnut to undertake one expedition into Scotland which secured the submission of King Malcolm and two lesser kings. The danger from Scotland was finally removed by Malcolm's death in 1034. His successor Duncan was fully occupied with internal troubles until in 1040 he was killed by Macbeth and his two sons driven into exile. The elder son, Malcolm, found refuge with Siward, Eric's successor in the Northumbrian earldom, who was probably his uncle by marriage. Whether on his own behalf or as guardian for his ward. Siward extended his authority into Cumbria and successfully maintained the integrity of the northern frontier. Except for the uncertainties in the north Cnut's reign was a period of unbroken internal peace and so firmly was he established that in 1019 he was able to leave England and make the first of his four expeditions to Scandinavia. In the confused and constantly changing politics of that region he exercised a decisive role.

2. England, the Scandinavian Empire and Western Europe

Since the middle decades of the tenth century the kings of Denmark and Sweden had competed in their ambitions to exercise authority in Norway. Their aspirations were temporarily checked when the famous Viking leader Olaf Tryggvason, a descendant of Harald Fairhair, the greatest of Norwegian kings, established himself on the throne in 995; but five years later a coalition of the former rivals with a group of disaffected nobles, of whom the most important was jarl Eric of Hlathir, killed Olaf in battle. From 1000 until his death Swein, king of Denmark, was the predominant power in Norway, and his principal supporter was jarl Eric. On Swein's death his elder son Harald succeeded to Denmark without difficulty, but when Eric left Norway in 1015 to join Cnut's expedition to England Danish influence in Norway was rapidly eclipsed. Almost immediately Eric's brother Swein was defeated in a great sea-battle by Olaf Haraldsson, another prince descended from Harald Fairhair, who quickly secured acceptance of his rule in Norway. Swein's dismembered empire was now shared between Harald in Denmark, Cnut in England and Olaf in Norway.

In either 1018 or 1019 Harald died childless. Cnut, with England quiescent, left Earl Thorkell as regent and sailed to Denmark with a small fleet to claim the Danish throne, thus incidentally ensuring that an interregnum in Denmark would not lead to a resumption of Viking activity against his English kingdom. By Easter 1020 he was back in England having successfully accomplished his intention. Two years later a second visit was necessary in order to deal with Thorkell, who, banished from England in the previous year for reasons not certainly known, had returned to Denmark, where his great reputation as a warrior would always assure him of support in any project he chose to undertake. The sequence of events is as mysterious as their origin, but their outcome was to establish Thorkell briefly as Cnut's regent in Denmark and to promise him the guardianship of Hardecnut, son of Cnut and Queen Emma, while Cnut brought Thorkell's son back with him to England. Shortly afterwards Thorkell disappears from history and at some time between 1023 and 1026 Ulf, husband of Cnut's sister Estrith, became regent of Denmark and Hardecnut's guardian.

Both Olaf Haraldsson and Anund, king of Sweden, felt themselves threatened by Cnut's increasing power and having joined forces they seduced the regent Ulf and his brother Eilaf from their allegiance to Cnut. It was to counter the threat of an invasion of Denmark and the ravaging of the provinces of the English mainland that Cnut took a fleet to Scandinavia, for the third time, in 1026. In a battle fought against the forces of the alliance at the mouth of the Holy river in eastern Scania, Cnut was heavily defeated. But the defeat appears to have involved no disastrous political consequences and in 1027 Cnut's position was sufficiently strong for him to feel free to travel to Rome to attend Conrad's coronation as Roman emperor. The hostile coalition was broken up by the murder of Ulf at his orders and by the undermining of Olaf's position in Norway by bribery and promises made to disaffected Norwegian nobles. Olaf's reputation as a saint was very much the product of forces which operated only after his death; while he lived his personal austerity and the severity with which he pursued measures to stamp out heathenism in his kingdom were deeply resented, so that when Cnut sailed to Norway in 1028 his combined English and Danish fleet met no resistance. Olaf was compelled first to withdraw into southern Norway and then to seek refuge in Sweden. Cnut's mastery of both Denmark and Norway was publicized at a great court held at Nidaros (Trondheim) in which Hardecnut was proclaimed king of Denmark, and Hakon, son of Eric of Hlathir, was appointed regent of Norway. Within months Hakon was drowned at sea and Cnut then sent Aelfgifu of Northampton to Norway to act as regent for her son Swein, who accompanied her. Their reception was delayed because Olaf Haraldsson took advantage of the situation to attempt a restoration, but the small army that he brought with him from Sweden was decisively defeated at Stiklestad near Nidaros. Olaf was killed in the fight and Aelfgifu and Swein were then accepted in Norway.

Cnut had reconstituted his father's empire and his position in England, Denmark, and Norway seemed now to be secure. But his triumph in Norway proved ephemeral and his plans for Swein to succeed him there could not be realized; failure in Norway created problems in Denmark, which in turn affected events in England. The rule of Aelfgifu was detested because it was both alien and harsh, characterized by heavier taxation, heavier public service, and severer penalties for violence than the Norwegians had been accustomed to accept. In retrospect the virtues of Olaf Haraldsson were magnified and within a brief period he came to be regarded as a saint; a year after his death his uncorrupted body was translated to Nidaros and soon miracles were attributed to him. Though the northern area around Nidaros had been the centre of the authority of the pro-Danish Eric of Hlathir and Hakon and the scene of Olaf's death it was also the seat of government, which explains why, by 1033,

Aelfgifu and Swein had been driven from Nidaros into southern Norway. Olaf Haraldsson had left a son, Magnus, who rapidly proved himself a formidable warrior. By the autumn of 1035 he had achieved control over almost the whole of Norway and Aelfgifu and Swein were refugees in Denmark, where Swein died in the following year. When Cnut died in 1035 Magnus, secure in Norway, was threatening to attack Denmark. The situation in the north was completely reversed and the danger to Denmark appeared so pressing that Hardecnut, intended by his father to succeed to both Denmark and England, could not leave Denmark to claim his English inheritance.

Under Cnut England had once again entered the main stream of continental politics. By becoming the ruler of a great northern empire he was inevitably involved in Scandinavian politics, while the uneasy balance of power in the Baltic emphasized the desirability of an alliance with the king of Germany. Long before the end of his reign he was so commanding a figure that any European ruler would be pleased to be on friendly terms with him, while his domination of the North Sea and the English Channel made good relations imperative for some of them. The involvement of England in the politics of northern Europe was a novel though inevitable concomitant of Danish conquest; in western and southern Europe Cnut's reign marked a resumption of traditional contacts.

Friendly contacts between the English and German courts had been maintained intermittently since the time of Athelstan, but between Denmark and Germany there was a frontier dispute of long standing. Cnut's visit to Rome in 1027 had the dual purpose of pilgrimage and of establishing good relations with King Conrad, who was crowned emperor by the pope on Easter Day that year. The encounter was notably successful; valuable gifts were exchanged and mutual concessions granted to travellers and traders. Near the end of his reign a marriage alliance was negotiated whereby Cnut's daughter Gunnhild was betrothed to Conrad's son Henry; as part of the arrangements then made the emperor promised to concede the disputed territories north of the river Eider to Cnut. Of less direct importance, but none the less an indication of the respect in which he was held was the great honour shown to him in the course of this visit by all the princes of the nations from Mount Garganum (in southern Italy) to the North Sea, which Cnut reported with obvious satisfaction to his subjects at home. The king of Burgundy, Rudolf

III, was mentioned specifically among the princes ruling territories traversed by the pilgrim route to Rome who made concessions on this occasion to English travellers. A few years earlier Cnut's presentation of an illustrated Book of Saints to Duke William II of Aquitaine had initiated relations with south-western France which were subsequently maintained by the frequent exchange of embassies and gifts.

With the duchy of Normandy relations were more delicate. Cnut had married Emma, the sister of Duke Richard II, to discourage the duke from supporting the claims of her sons by King Aethelred to the English throne. Yet Richard continued to offer hospitality to the exiles. On the death of Richard in 1026, followed by that of his eldest son in the next year, the duchy passed to Richard's second son, Robert. It took him some time to establish himself firmly but thereafter it is certain that his fear of Cnut's increasing power caused a steady deterioration in Anglo-Norman relations. It is possible, though the evidence is unsatisfactory, that Cnut attempted to maintain friendship by giving his sister Estrith, Ulf's widow, to Robert in marriage, and that her subsequent repudiation by Robert contributed to increase rather than diminish the rulers' mutual animosities. William of Jumièges goes so far as to assert that Robert assembled a fleet for the purpose of establishing Edward and Alfred on the English throne but that the expedition was dispersed by a storm off the coast of Brittany. These stories, though inadequately substantiated, deserve consideration in the light of the certain fact that from 1028 onwards the English athelings became more prominent at Robert's court and witness a number of the duke's charters. The revitalization of the claims of the athelings to the English throne was to have momentous consequences in the future, but while Cnut lived it was Robert who had the greater cause for concern at the way events were shaping.

The restoration of peace, Cnut's unchallenged political position, and his concern for the welfare of the Church greatly stimulated ecclesiastical contacts with the outside world. Early in his reign he despatched Archbishop Lyfing of Canterbury to Rome, whence he returned with messages and letters from the pope. In 1022 Archbishop Aethelnoth travelled to Rome to receive his pallium, accompanied by Abbot Leofwine of Ely; in 1026; Aelfric Puttoc, Wulfstan's successor, was the first archbishop of York known to have visited Rome for the same purpose. Cnut complained to the pope about the excessive sums demanded from archbishops on such occasions and secured a promise that the practice would cease. The king's own pilgrimage to Rome in 1027 was the first undertaken by an English king since the journey of Aethelwulf of Wessex in the mid-ninth century. Less distinguished pilgrims travelled not only to Rome but also to Byzantium and Jerusalem, whether by the overland route through Flanders, northern France, Bavaria, and Hungary or to Italy and thence by sea. During his constant travels Cnut diligently visited famous churches and their shrines and frequently, as at St. Bertin's, demonstrated his piety and munificence. He sent money to assist in the rebuilding of Chartres after a disastrous fire in 1020. He presented to the church of Köln, in return for its prayers, a sacramentary and a psalter which had been given to himself and Emma by Earnwi, the schoolmaster of Peterborough who had written and illuminated them. Foreign churchmen came to England, seeking help of various kinds. Monks from Limoges visited England to study evidence relating to St. Augustine in the hope that it might provide support for them in their campaign to secure the recognition of St. Martial, patron saint of Aquitaine, as an apostle. The bishop of Benevento sought to raise money in England to relieve a famine in his city; Queen Emma bought from him an arm of St. Bartholomew.

English churchmen had been prominent in the conversion of the Scandinavian kingdoms to Christianity and their influence was maintained during the first half of the eleventh century. Under Cnut English churchmen went to Denmark, among them a certain William who acted as the royal secretary and later was appointed bishop of Roskilde. Such promotion was unusual and most Danish bishops were of native or German extraction but since Cnut's control of the Danish episcopate was complete it is not surprising that they were often consecrated by the archbishop of Canterbury despite the protests of the archbishop of Hamburg-Bremen who claimed metropolitan rights over all Scandinavia. Gerbrand, bishop of Zealand, was consecrated by Archbishop Aethelnoth and subsequently captured by Archbishop Unwan of Hamburg-Bremen, after which Cnut undertook not to act in future without reference to the archbishop of Bremen. Hostility to Denmark did not prevent both Olaf Tryggvason and Olaf Haraldsson using the services of bishops and priests from England, and English missionaries from Norway reinforced the efforts of Germans and Danes in Sweden. English practice influenced the national churches of the Scandinavian kingdoms in their church organization, their liturgy, their religious vocabulary, and their architecture. English clerics took with them for the benefit of the kings they served their knowledge of the English writ and seal. Reflecting the value to an English king of men familiar with the continental political scene was the grant of a bishopric to a foreigner —the first since the age of conversion; Duduc, either Lotharingian or Saxon by birth, was appointed to Wells in 1033.

The coincidence of good internal order, Cnut's international prestige, and the beginnings of a revival of economic activity over much of western Europe stimulated trading activity. The range of English foreign trade in the early eleventh century is indicated in a document which details the dues to be paid by alien merchants coming to London; it is generally ascribed to the reign of Aethelred but may well relate to that of Cnut. Dues were paid by merchants coming from Flanders, Lorraine, Ponthieu, Normandy, and the Isle of France, while the subjects of the emperor, chiefly from the Rhineland, were especially privileged. Another text, dateable at latest c. 1024, records the dues which foreign merchants entering Lombardy paid to the royal treasury at Pavia; prominent among them were Anglo-Saxons, who brought horses, slaves, woollen and linen goods, hemp, tin, and swords. They seem to have been an obstreperous company whose resentment at the opening of their baggage by the customs officials had expressed itself in violence. An arrangement was arrived at between the rulers of England and Lombardy, whereby the English merchants made a single payment every third year in lieu of toll. The toll thus paid amounted to fifty pounds of pure silver, two greyhounds with gilded and embossed collars, two shields, two swords and two lances; the official in charge received two pounds of silver; such a payment suggests a trade of considerable value. London was by far the important centre in the kingdom and its mercantile community comprised both Danes and Englishmen; though Winchester had been the principal royal residence of West Saxon kings the economic preponderance of London was at the basis of changes which would soon make it the capital city of England. But London did not stand completely alone. Even before Cnut came to the throne trading links between the Scandinavian population of northern England and their old homelands had been strong. York in the early eleventh century was described by a contemporary as a city of 30,000 inhabitants, filled with the treasures of merchants, chiefly of the Danish race. This estimate of the population was certainly over generous but that trade with Scandinavia flourished is convincingly demonstrated by the vast number of English coins which have been found in Scandinavian hoards. Many of them certainly represent payment of danegeld and of heregeld to warriors who carried them to their homes, but the series of such coins continues long after danegelds and heregelds ceased to be levied and the presence of many of them in hoards, accumulated over a long period and including continental coins suggests that they were the profits of trade; in all three Scandinavian kingdoms English moneyers were employed to strike coins imitated on the pennies of Aethelred's reign.

The last troubled years of Aethelred's reign had not favoured the maintenance of overseas contacts; under Cnut they were closer and more diversified than ever before.

3. CNUT S RULE IN ENGLAND

Cnut's royal position in Denmark and his wide European interests meant that for the first time in history an English king had to divide his time between England and his continental territories. It is noteworthy that just as Duke William of Normandy, after the first five years of his reign in England, encountered more trouble from his Norman followers and from the duchy than from the native English so, too, Cnut's few political problems were set by Danes and by Denmark. There is no hint of English disaffection after 1020; but in 1021 Thorkell of East Anglia was outlawed, in 1026 Ulf and his brother Eilaf rebelled against him, and according to one early tradition the despatch of Earl Hakon, son of Eric of Hlathir, to Norway was a form of banishment. In the early years of his reign Cnut's chosen associates, as revealed in the witness lists of charters, were principally men of Danish extraction who had presumably taken part in his victorious campaign. In his later years his principal subordinates were Godwin, earl of Wessex, probably the son of the English thegn Wulfnoth who had deserted Aethelred in 1008; Leofric, the son of Leofwine, ealdorman of the Hwicce under Aethelred, subsequently promoted to Mercia after the execution of Eadric Streona; and Siward, the Danish earl of Northumbria, whose preoccupations in the north left him little opportunity for further activities. It seems as though Cnut promoted men of whose loyalty he felt confident and who owed everything to his favour without regard to their racial origins.

The composition of Cnut's court reflected the king's determination, as soon as his position was secure, to be king of all men in England whether Dane or English. In 1020 he promised that 'if anyone, ecclesiastic or layman, Dane or Englishman is so presumptuous as to defy God's law and my royal authority or the secular law, and he will not make amends and desist according to the direction of my bishops, I then pray, and also command earl Thorkell, if he can, to cause the evil-doer to do right'. His two letters to the people of England, written in 1020 during his absence in Denmark, and in 1027 after his visit to Rome, were unprecedented. They are remarkable in that their purpose is to tell his subjects of all degrees what he had been doing on their behalf. In 1020 he wrote: 'King Cnut greets in friendship, his archbishop and his diocesan bishops, and earl Thorkell and all his earls and all his people, whether men of a twelve hundred wergild or a two hundred, ecclesiastical and lay, in England': his greeting in 1027 was similarly addressed to the archbishops 'and to all the bishops and leading men, and to the whole race of the English, whether nobles or commoners'. In 1020 he insisted that his object in going to Denmark was to take measures to avert dangers threatening England and reported success: 'I have so settled the great dangers which were approaching us that we need fear no danger to us from there.' In 1027 he explained that his visit to Rome was motivated not only by the admirable desire to visit the threshold of the apostles but also 'for the safety of the kingdoms and of the peoples which are subjected to my rule', and he took advantage of the meeting of so many European rulers to speak with them 'concerning the needs of all the peoples of my whole kingdom, whether English or Danes, that they might be granted more equitable law and greater security on their way to Rome'. As we have seen he complained to the pope at the immensity of the sums exacted from archbishops when they travelled to Rome to receive their pallia.[1] Again he claimed, 'that I have successfully accomplished all that I had desired, just as I had designed'. After recounting the objects of his journeys and the success which had attended them, in both letters the king declared his will that his counsellors left in England should supervise the administration of justice impartially and fearlessly and that his sheriffs and reeves should deal justly with the people under their charge; and he sternly admonished his subjects to pay in full all ecclesiastical dues. In these letters, which achieved the publicity the

---

[1] *Supra*, p. 328.

king wanted for them by being read out in the local courts, Cnut appealed to the loyalty of his subjects by demonstrating the benefits which his rule had brought them and he emphasized the personal contribution he had made: ' I send ahead this letter, in order that all the people of my kingdom may be gladdened at my success, because, as you yourselves know, I have never spared—nor will I spare in the future—to devote myself and my toil for the need and benefit of all my people.'

Symbolic of Cnut's wish to fuse the two races under his rule was his attendance, together with Thorkell, Archbishop Wulfstan, and a great company, at the consecration of a new church at Ashingdon, on the site of the battle. Even more striking was the conspicuous participation of the royal family in the ceremonies associated with the translation of the relics of the martyred saint Aelfheah from London to Canterbury in 1023;

> And the illustrious king, and the archbishop and the diocesan bishops and the earls and very many ecclesiastics and also lay-folk, conveyed his holy body on a ship across the Thames to Southwark, and there entrusted the holy martyr to the archbishop and his companions. And they then bore him with a distinguished company and happy jubilation to Rochester. Then on the third day queen Emma came with her royal child Hardecnut, and they then conveyed the holy archbishop with much glory and joy and songs of praise into Canterbury, and thus brought him with due ceremony into Christ Church on 11 June.[1]

But the most impressive testimony of Cnut's policy in England is, above all, the great code of law he issued between 1020 and 1023, which fulfilled explicitly and in detail his Oxford undertaking to maintain Edgar's law. In form, content, and tone it was thoroughly traditional. Its first chapters related to ecclesiastical matters—rights of sanctuary, peccant clergy, the law of marriage, the payment of ecclesiastical dues of all kinds, feasts and fasts—and they included a good deal of simple moralizing:

> c. 18. We desire and we pray, for the love of God, that every Christian man should readily understand what is for his own good.
> c. 21. And very zealously we enjoin upon all Christian men that ever, from their inmost hearts, they love God and zealously uphold the true Christian faith, and eagerly obey their spiritual teachers, and frequently and often ponder over and enquire into the precepts and laws of God for their own advantage.

[1] The translation is that of D. Whitelock, *English Historical Documents c.500-1042* (London, 1955), p. 230.

The civil section of Cnut's code comprised eighty-four chapters, some of them elaborated by several subordinate clauses; it effected a comprehensive restatement of the secular law. Very little of it was original, though some of its injunctions such as the prohibition of heathen practices and the selling of Christians into slavery may have needed restatement if the new influx of Danes had given new vitality to old bad habits. It insisted that the courts of shire and hundred should operate as in Edgar's day, and there were, as usual, provisions relating to the coinage, buying and selling, thieves and murderers, military organization, heriots, offences against the canon law, and all manner of other topics. An appearance of novelty, as in the clause requiring every free man to be brought within a hundred and a tithing, was probably nothing more than an improvement of detail in the practical implementation of a long-established principle. In this section, too, there is a substantial leavening of moral exhortation. Quite consciously the reign of Edgar was already being looked back on as a golden age and that of Aethelred ignored, even though much of Cnut's code repeated enactments of Aethelred, and its author, Archbishop Wulfstan, was the compiler of Aethelred's later codes. In the Danelaw, however, it is apparent that Cnut was stronger than Edgar or Aethelred. In general, Danish custom continued to prevail there, but Cnut stated his rights in that area with as much certainty as he stated his rights in Wessex and in Mercia. And not only was the king's position as the ultimate executant arm of the law restated in the rule that none should appeal to the king unless he had failed to obtain justice in his hundred, but the royal responsibility for peace and justice now embraced an original jurisdiction. Certain pleas were reserved to the king unless, as a special favour, they were granted to a subject. Jurisdiction over the most serious crimes of all, arson, manifest murder, and treachery to a man's lord—was never granted away; they were so heinous that no payment of money could compensate for them. Such crimes involved outlawry, and the thirteenth chapter of the code laid down that ' if anyone did the deed of an outlaw the king alone shall have power to grant him security '.

Continuity with the past did not lead to ossification. Institutionally, few changes are recorded. The tendency for the ealdormanry to become a provincial governorship was confirmed during Cnut's reign, though his division of the kingdom into the four great earldoms of Wessex, East Anglia, Mercia, and Northumbria in 1017 was not maintained after the military advantages which had determined their creation were seen to be no longer necessary. Cnut's ealdormen, now styled earls after the Danish fashion, continued to exercise the same functions as their predecessors in Aethelred's reign—leadership of the military forces of the earldom, the maintenance of justice and peace, and such executive duties as the king laid upon them. Though the large size of the areas under their supervision gave the earls great political importance they continued to be royal officials. The expectation of an earl's son to succeed his father was sometimes gratified, but royal control was demonstrated by the king's power to alter the territorial composition of the earldoms by appointing officials with the title of earl within the areas of the greater earldoms and by varying the combinations of shires that each earldom contained. Charters of Cnut's reign are few and irregularly dispersed but they show the earls in frequent attendance at the court. Together with the enlarged size of their areas such absences from their provinces may have placed heavier responsibilities on the king's reeves in the shires, but the paucity of evidence makes it impossible to give any detailed demonstration of such a development. No changes were deliberately made in the operation of the local courts, but in his willingness to grant substantial jurisdictional rights to favoured churches Cnut again resembled King Edgar; Bury St. Edmunds received all judicial rights and royal revenues over eight and a half hundreds in west Suffolk and Archbishop Aethelnoth was similarly privileged ' over his own men within borough and without, and over Christ Church, and over as many thegns as I have granted him to have '. It is likely, too, that Cnut made similar grants of hundredal jurisdiction to favoured lay magnates.

In his efforts to maintain continuity and stability Cnut received powerful support from the Church and throughout his reign the long-standing tradition of cooperation between ecclesiastics and the king was strikingly maintained.[1] The absence of change in the upper ranks of the clergy after 1016 contrasts both with the transformation of the lay aristocracy at that time, still more with the wholesale change in ecclesiastical personnel effected by William the Conqueror after 1066. Cnut was a baptized Christian whose piety was abundantly manifested by his benefactions to religious houses and in his concern for ecclesiastical welfare. He quickly showed himself eager to use the

---

[1] For all matters relating to the late Anglo-Saxon church, F. Barlow, *The English Church 1000-1066: A Constitutional History* (London, 1963).
[2] *Rectitudines Singularum Personarum.*

services of his predecessor's bishop. His counsellors' Oxford declaration of 1018 that ' above all things they would ever humour one God and steadfastly hold one Christian faith' was reflected in legislation concerned to assist the Church in its work. In return the archbishops and bishops gave Cnut their unstinted support. Lyfing of Canterbury early in the reign undertook an important mission to Rome for the king; Wulfstan of York drafted Cnut's law codes as he had previously drafted the later codes of King Aethelred. Having inherited bishops with whom he found no fault, Cnut generally maintained the practice of elevating distinguished monks to the episcopate. Lyfing's successor at Canterbury was Aethelnoth 'the good ', formerly abbot of Chertsey and bishop of Wells, while to Wulfstan succeeded Aelfric Puttoc from Winchester, a reformer who began the building of communal buildings at Beverley. The appointments made in the last five years of the reign, whether of monks or of secular clerks were more questionable. Brihtheah, appointed to Worcester in 1033, though a monk and a nephew of Archbishop Wulfstan, left a reputation for nepotism. Other monkish appointments though in themselves not scandalous were inadequate in that the first loyalties of the new bishops remained to their old monasteries, even after their promotion. In 1032 Aelfwine, a king's priest, received the monastic see of Winchester, the first case of elevation to the episcopate in reward for service in the royal household; he proved to be an unworthy bishop. In the following year Duduc's appointment to Wells, though nothing is known to his discredit, was probably due to a knowledge of European affairs which was politically useful to Cnut. By this time the energies of the second wave of ecclesiastical reform were spent, to be followed by a period of mediocrity.

Emphasis on the king's desire to maintain continuity with the past should not be allowed to glamorize the actual condition of affairs; the recent past had been a wretched time for England. Cnut, however willing, could not quickly alter those tendencies in society to which Wulfstan's *Sermon* had drawn attention; in any event his frequent absences abroad made close and continuous oversight of his kingdom impossible. Between 1017 and 1020 Archbishop Lyfing ruefully told Cnut ' that he had charters of freedom in plenty if only they were good for anything '. The *Ramsey Chronicle* relates how Bishop Aethelric of Dorchester impleaded Thorkell of East Anglia and his second wife Edith, who had been accused of murdering her stepson.

Three times the earl ignored the bishop's summons to attend his synod, but a command to attend the king's court was obeyed. Despite his protestation of innocence Thorkell and his wife were ordered to clear themselves by oaths to be taken by themselves and by oath-takers on their behalf. The oath-taking was not satisfactory—Thorkell's beard came away in his hand as he swore—and the court adjudged Thorkell guilty of perjury and his wife guilty of homicide. They were given penances and Thorkell paid compensation to the bishop for flouting his jurisdiction. The judgment and Thorkell's subsequent outlawry show that no man, however great, could defy Cnut's law with impunity; more sinisterly, it shows, too, that lesser authorities could impose little control on a great magnate.

The legislative requirement that local courts should continue to operate as in Edgar's reign could not be enforced since it ran counter to the mainstream of social change. One document from Cnut's reign revealing that the shire court of Herefordshire, at least, was by now confined to important landowners, exemplifies the concentration of authority in a small number of powerful men. The exactions of war and other economic pressures in the reigns of Aethelwold and Cnut must have confirmed the long operative tendency for power and wealth to be concentrated in fewer and fewer lands. In the late tenth and early eleventh centuries not only peasants but even thegns increasingly attached themselves to great magnates. Commendation, the acceptance of lordship in return for protection and support, took many forms; it might involve the payment of services or the acceptance of the lord's jurisdiction; a man might commend himself to one lord or to more than one; or it might involve other obligations; but though the relationship appears to have been revocable, in every form it involved a degree of dependence on the lord. Economic insecurity was compounded by the jurisdictional dependence which resulted from the royal policy, initiated by Edgar and continued by his successors, of granting hundreds and groups of hundreds to favoured subjects both ecclesiastical and lay; whole groups of people were thus effectively removed from the administrative arrangements of the shires in which they lived.

Even the most crucial of all governmental concerns, that of military organization, was in the last days of Anglo-Saxon England increasingly affected by the growth of lordship. Some lords were allowed to accept responsibility to the king for the number of soldiers indicated by the hidage of their estates. When this happened the estate quota served in the fyrd as a discrete military unit under the command of the lord or his deputy; in the reign of Edward the Confessor a certain Eadric, as the bishop of Worcester's deputy, was designated steersman of the bishop's ship and commander of his troops. Provided that the number of troops stipulated by the hidage turned out when summoned, the king had no interest in regulating the manner in which the lord recruited his quota. Lords became free to make whatever arrangements they saw fit; to adhere to the traditional five-hide arrangement, to allocate the whole burden on their estates to particular vills; or even to keep a body of soldiers in their households. Lordly contingents, made up of household retainers and other men holding lands specifically burdened with military service probably formed a large element in the armies of the last pre-Conquest kings.[1]

When thegns were commending themselves to lords and the number of land-owning free peasants was continuously declining the conditions of life of the dependent peasantry was unenviable. For them life had always been harsh, and whether their situation deteriorated with the passage of time and as their numbers increased cannot be determined; but the impression left by the surviving evidence from the late tenth and early eleventh centuries is unambiguously dreary. In Kent and East Anglia, the wealthiest areas of England, and in the northern Danelaw where Danish settlement had been substantial, the peasantry were still able to sustain their legal freedom and economic independence with a substantial measure of success. But in Mercia and Wessex, after allowing that there were many gradations of legal, social and economic circumstances among them, the tenants of the holdings in the village arable were heavily burdened. One treatise on estate management[2] recorded that what was almost certainly the largest group of peasants might be expected to work for their lords for two days in most weeks, and for three days a week during the busiest periods of the farming year, and in addition they would pay money rents and perform further labour services at stipulated times; such services were rendered in return for what came to be regarded in the middle ages as the typical tenant holding, a yardland or virgate of land in the village arable. The holding of another large class of peasants consisted of about five acres in the arable, for which they were required to work for one day a week throughout the year and to perform miscellaneous seasonal services; such men could not have maintained themselves on the produce of

---

[1] Hollister, *op. cit.* 25.
[2] *Rectitudines Singularum Personarum.*

their holdings and must have eked out their livelihood by selling their labour to their lord or to some more prosperous ceorl. This document does not stand alone. A survey of the manor of Tidenham in Gloucestershire after stating the money rent payable from each yardland and detailing the lord's rights over the fishing on the estate prefaces its account of the labour services due from the tenants with the ominous phrase, ' from Tidenham much labour is due '. From Hurstbourne Priors in Hampshire comes the same story of heavy labour services and substantial money rents. Such men enjoyed the freeman's wergild and paid church-scot and hearthpenny as free men should, but legal freedom could be compatible with abject economic dependence. The free peasant owning his own land and knowing no lord but the king was no common figure in the early eleventh century.

Neither lordship nor a dependent peasantry were novelties in Cnut's time, and certainly under Cnut lordly power could not develop into the political threat associated with overmighty subjects, nor did it stimulate regional particularism; but should this aristocracy come to feel no particular loyalty to, or fear of, an increasingly remote king the imposition of mediate lordship on large classes of his subjects might in time threaten the reality of royal authority.

An intelligent alien, Cnut saw the advantages that accrued to him from making no more changes than were necessary. He had acquired a kingdom with an administrative system which, regulated by men dependent on himself, could serve him as well as it had served his Anglo-Saxon predecessors; and a vigorous Church whose leaders were willing to cooperate with him to their mutual advantage. Superficially the Anglo-Danish state appeared to be the Anglo-Saxon state under new direction. Yet in reality much was altered. The close circle of old aristocratic families, interrelated among themselves and with the royal family, had been destroyed and their place taken by Danes and English parvenus; Danish huscarls performed functions linking the king and the localities which had previously been performed by king's thegns; the king's permanent military establishment was maintained by the proceeds of a heavy annual tax; the king himself, often abroad, allowed more latitude than previously to his agents in the earldoms, which had become provinces within which their earls exercised viceregal powers. If the administrative anatomy of the English kingdom remained unchanged the spirit which had animated it had died; acquiescence had replaced that spontaneous loyalty which had buttressed the authority of Anglo-Saxon kings, in southern England at any rate. Despite Cnut's efforts to demonstrate his concern for all his subjects irrespective of their race the ineradicable truth was that he was a conqueror whose authority rested on military force not blood-right. Like any new dynasty, that of Cnut might have established itself on a firm basis, given time and successors of his own high quality; neither was forthcoming.

4. HARALD AND HARDECNUT: RESTORATION OF THE OLD DYNASTY

Cnut's death seems to have been unanticipated, for the circumstances of 1035 were unpropitious for the realization of his intentions for the succession. His designated heir to England and Denmark, Emma's son Hardecnut, was in Denmark and so seriously threatened by the increasing strength of Magnus of Norway that it would have been unwise for him to leave that kingdom. At an assembly at Oxford, which met shortly before Cnut's burial, a party in England headed by Leofric of Mercia and supported by the magnates of the Danelaw and the shipmen of London, chose Aelfgifu's second son, Harald ' Harefoot ', as regent of all England on behalf of himself and Hardecnut. Queen Emma, Earl Godwin, and the magnates of Wessex vainly opposed this arrangement but secured agreement to the proposal that the queen should hold Wessex on behalf of Hardecnut and retain a body of huscarls to defend his interests.

The continued failure or inability of Hardecnut to claim his English inheritance caused support for Harald to gain in strength. Bitterly opposed to Harald, Emma in desperation appealed to the sons of her first marriage. Edward landed in England at Southampton accompanied by a small force, was repulsed, and returned to Normandy. Alfred probably landed at Dover, was captured by Earl Godwin and taken first to Guildford then to Ely, where he was blinded and soon after died of his wounds; most of his companions were either executed, mutilated, or sold into slavery. The degree of Godwin's culpability for this crime is disputable; it is likely that, aware of Harald's increasing strength, he had changed his allegiance since the time of the Oxford council and was eager to demonstrate his change of heart, but whether Alfred was killed by Godwin's men or by Harald's men after he had been handed over to them by Godwin, is unknown. In 1037, while Hardecnut was still preoccupied in Denmark, Harald was recognized as king of all England and Emma was driven into exile. She took refuge at Bruges where she waited hopefully for Hardecnut's arrival which occurred two years later, following a peace arranged with Magnus of Norway. In the spring of the following year, 1040, Harald Harefoot died. Hardecnut was invited to England and a few months later, with Emma, he returned peacefully to England and ascended the throne without opposition.

Hardecnut's reign though brief was not lacking in colourful incident. One of his earliest acts was to order the exhumation of his royal half-brother's body and have it thrown into the Thames. Earl Godwin, having been cleared of guilt for Alfred's death, gained the new king's favour by giving him a splendid war-galley fully equipped with tackle, weapons, and crew. In order to pay for the ships and their crews which had transported him from Denmark to Bruges and thence to England Hardecnut imposed a heregeld of £21,000 and then an additional tax of £11,000. The money was collected throughout England by the king's huscarls. Opposition was offered in Worcestershire and two of the collectors were killed in Worcester by the recalcitrant taxpayers. As punishment Hardecnut ordered the earls of Mercia, Wessex, Northumbria, Middle Anglia and Herefordshire to plunder and burn the city and to lay waste the whole province. For five days their forces ravaged the shire, though most of its inhabitants found safety in flight while others defended themselves on a small island in the middle of the river Severn. Not long after this episode Hardecnut invited to his court Edward, the son of Aethelred and Emma, recognizing him as his heir. Whether this action was motivated by Hardecnut's desire to return to Denmark or designed to disarm the potential leader of the opposition to his harsh government is uncertain, but the latter explanation is the more probable. The *Chronicle* for 1041 added to its notices of the treatment of Worcester and the return of Edward the statement that Hardecnut also in this year betrayed to death Eadwulf, earl of Northumbria, while under his safe conduct; the chronicler's verdict was that ' all who wanted him [Hardecnut] before then were ill-disposed towards him '. In the following year Hardecnut collapsed and died while standing at his drink during the wedding feast of Gytha, daughter of Osgod Clapa, a prominent Dane, to Tofi the Proud.

The interlude of Danish rule was ended. ' Even before he was buried all the people chose Edward as king.' In the person of Edward,

y to explain the slowness of the English conquest. Yet the
groups had much in common. The 'English' language,
comprehending variations of dialect corresponding to the
groupings, became totally dominant wherever they settled.
red the same gods and all save one of the ruling dynasties
kingdoms of the Heptarchy traced their descent from Woden.
political institutions and social organization appear to have
in so far as they are known, substantially similar. Though
nal and tribal differences are identifiable their material culture
basically common to all. The large number of small kingdoms
the settlement period was reduced by internecine warfare to
oduce the kingdoms of the Heptarchy, of which Northumbria,
ercia, and Wessex were the greatest. Contemporaneously, the
omano-Britons were confined to the Highland zone of western
Britain, though Britain was never conquered in its entirety. The Picts
beyond the Forth and the Clyde and the Welsh beyond Offa's Dyke
maintained their independence and in the more westerly parts of
England the Celtic element in the population must have been considerable. Celtic tongues continued to be spoken in the west, assuming divergent forms after the territorial integrity of their lands had
been disrupted by conquest. The Cornish dialect continued to be
spoken into the eighteenth century; Welsh remains a vigorous language; in Strathclyde Celtic disappeared probably in the eleventh
century under the pressure first of Norwegian colonization and then
of Norman conquerors. Before the conquest had achieved its limits
the English peoples had been converted to Christiantity by the
missions from Rome and from Iona. Conversion created another
bond of unity: the Church showed little concern for tribal frontiers.
Archbishop Theodore presided over a council of the whole English
Church and Bede wrote his *Ecclesiastical History of the English
People* which, though recognizing in its arrangement the political
realities of his day, also, by its title, underlined the heritage which
they all shared. Even before England was fully Christianized or
colonized missionaries from the English kingdoms undertook the
evangelization of their continental kinsmen, and their efforts were
followed with interest and concern by their fellow-countrymen irrespective of their tribal affiliations. The eighth century saw a splendid
efflorescence of scholarship and the arts.

From earliest times the ruler of whichever of the English kingdoms
was temporarily dominant aspired to a hegemony over the other

son of Aethelred, the old dynasty was restored; whether the Old
English state was to be restored as well was an open question.

It was improbable that his rule would be unchallenged. In 1038-39
Hardecnut, anxious to make good his rights to England, had made a
treaty with Magnus of Norway by which if either died childless
the other was to inherit his dominions. On Hardecnut's death Magnus
occupied most of Denmark despite the strong resistance offered by
Swein, son of Cnut's sister Estrith, and intended subsequently to
vindicate his claim to England. Swein Estrithson, regarding himself
as heir to his uncle, aspired to succeed him in both Denmark and
England. Until Magnus's death in 1047 Swein maintained his claim
to Denmark with little success but with sufficient determination to
distract Magnus from implementing his plans for invading England.
Magnus bequeathed Norway to his uncle Harald Hardrada, Denmark
to Swein; both kings had designs on England. Edward, the surviving
son of Aethelred and Emma, became king because as a descendant of
both Cerdic and of Rollo he was acceptable to both Englishmen and
Danes, and because, being already in England and having been
adopted by Hardecnut as his heir, he was the only claimant actually
available at the time of Hardecnut's death.

Edward succeeded to a difficult inheritance. Brought up in Normandy since his youth he was now a middle-aged man unfamiliar
with England and lacking close ties either with the greatest men in
his kingdom or with its lesser landed nobility. His power in southern
England, which had been the mainstay of the strength of his dynasty
in the tenth century, was weakened by the authority wielded by
Godwin in the great earldom of Wessex. The other earls were men
appointed by his predecessor, either Danes or Englishmen, more
concerned to secure their vested interests than actively to support
him. Edward's mother, Emma, was thought to prefer the claims of
Magnus to those of her own son. If there was initially no hostility to
Edward there was equally little enthusiasm for him. His one great
stroke of fortune was that Scandinavian entanglements prevented
the threatened invasion of Magnus from materializing. In 1042
Edward's position was unpromising but by no means impossible.

EPILOGUE

In the course of six hundred years the Roman provinces of Britain became the Kingdom of England. The most remarkable achievement of the Anglo-Saxons was their success in conquering their physical environment. In Roman times, despite the activities of the road-builders, the pattern of settlement on the land had been determined by the forces of nature and there were in southern Britain vast tracts of forest, wasteland and marsh. By the time that Domesday Book was compiled England could be described as ' an old country which had passed beyond the colonial stage ' and was more or less fully settled in an economic sense.[1] Though by modern standards there were still large areas of uninhabited land over much of England, few men lived more than fifteen miles from a town important enough to possess a mint, and few men lived more than half a day's walk from their nearest neighbour. The area of land under the plough was as large in the eleventh century as in the early years of the twentieth. England had become vastly wealthy: how wealthy is demonstrated by the huge and escalating sums of money demanded by and paid to Viking raiders at the turn of the tenth and eleventh centuries, and of the capacity of the country to sustain a heavy burden of regular taxation. One may feel scepticism about the precise figures of danegelds supplied by the *Anglo-Saxon Chronicle* but the presence of well over 50,000 silver pennies minted in England between 950 and 1050 in Scandinavian hoards testifies to the substantial truth of the proposition the figures are meant to convey. It is confirmed by other witnesses.[2] Shortly after 1066 William of Poitiers, the biographer

[1] R. L. Lennard, *Rural England 1086-1135* (Oxford, 1959) ch. 1.
[2] P. H. Sawyer, ' The wealth of England in the eleventh century ', *T.R.H.S.*, fifth series, XV (1965).

of William the Conqueror, expresse
England. He said that England wa
mensely fertile, and abundantly pro
Describing the treasures which William
and gave to his foundation at St. Stephen
Greek or Saracen from the fabulously we
he would have marvelled at their intrinsic
skill they displayed.

The magnitude of this achievement is all
when it is remembered that England inherited
tion of the Roman world than any other of the
kingdoms which grew up on the ruins of the Ro
where in western Europe Ostrogoths, Visigoths, and
imperial territories and in varying degrees shared t
previous inhabitants. They were tribal migrations, led
historical figures, at dates which can be narrowly de
they settled in areas which are clearly definable: they esta
kingdoms. They came to settle rather than to destroy, an
as their capacities permitted, to perpetuate a way of life w
knew, admired, and wished to emulate. The barbarian con
southern Britain was totally different. Between the end of
Britain and the Anglo-Saxon conquest occurred a hiatus d
which Roman influences declined and Celtic influences reasse
themselves: this development brought the civilization of the nat
inhabitants of Britain nearer to that of their subsequent master
but it meant that the Roman influence on Anglo-Saxon England was
slight. The newcomers were uninfluenced by Roman administrative
methods, Roman religion, Roman law, or the Latin language: they
had nothing but what they brought with them. Nor did the advent
of the Angles and Saxons remotely resemble a mass migration: the
difficult sea crossing would have made that impossible. They arrived
over a long period of time, some as invited federates, some to conquer
and fight for a settlement, others to occupy lands secured by their
kinsfolk. They came in independent bands each under its own leader
and though the main avenues of ingress were the Humber and its
tributaries, the Wash, and the coasts immediately opposite the Low
Countries, there was no unity of command in any of these areas.
They established independent kingdoms each under its own king or
prince.

The fragmentation of political authority among the invaders goes

kingdoms of southern Britain. By the middle of the ninth century supremacy had passed in turn from Kent to East Anglia, to Northumbria for much of the seventh century, to Mercia for much of the eighth century, and finally to the kings of Wessex. But there seemed no reason why the supremacy of Egbert's descendants should prove more permanent than had been that of Aethelbald and Offa, and everywhere in western Europe established political authority was under challenge from the Vikings. Hindsight reveals that the role of the Vikings in English history was to destroy the kingdoms north of the Thames so that the lone survivor, Wessex, ruled by a succession of distinguished kings, could assume the leadership of all Englishmen against the Danes. Alfred's achievement lay firstly in defending Wessex; secondly, in formulating a concept of kingly power which could appeal to all his subjects and even to the Danes, when they were brought under the rule of his successors. Alfred projected the image of a theocratic king, absolute in power because his authority was derived from God, but whose powers were dedicated to the service of God on earth. Alfred was careful to avoid the appearance of innovation; law was still, in theory, custom enunciated by the ' witan ' but in practice it was powerfully influenced by the will of a ruler whose sanction was God's will. Circumspectly, and slowly at first, the king enlarged the area of his concern for his people, but by the end of the tenth century he had made himself responsible for the peace and good order of his whole kingdom, more than the residuary legatee of justice to whom in the final event appeal might be made. The tenth century saw the mystique of kingship raised to unprecedented heights, powerfully assisted by the efforts of churchmen who realized how completely their own efforts depended on royal support: the effective power of the king was greater than ever before. A product of Edgar's good peace and of his piety was a monastic reformation which brought in its train another great period of achievement in learning and the arts.

Though England had been made by the kings of Wessex no one man, however energetic, could rule England by his unaided efforts. The increasing power of kings was matched, as the boundaries of the kingdom were enlarged, by the increasing importance of those confidants to whom kings entrusted subordinate powers. The old aristocracy of the pre-Danish period had been largely eliminated during the wars and from the time of Alfred aristocracy was the reward for service to West Saxon kings: ealdormen, sheriffs, and thegns were royal officials and strong kings ensured that such they would remain. Kings granted away rights of jurisdiction to their magnates both lay and ecclesiastical: at the same time economic forces operated to encourage lesser men, even thegns, to attach themselves to greater men. In this there was nothing detrimental to royal authority—lords were simply local agents for the maintenance of order who enforced the law promulgated by the king and witan, albeit at considerable profit, both financially and in prestige, to themselves. Such devolution of authority, essential in an age which lacked the resources to create a bureaucracy, could become dangerous; but only if kings relinquished their interest in government. Distance from the centre always favoured local independence but only in the reign of Aethelred did it threaten the fabric of the realm.

No kingdom in Europe could rival the machinery of a tenth century English king for making his wishes known and securing obedience to his orders. From the king's writing-office issued a flow of writs remarkably alike for their number and the regularity of their formulae: written in the vernacular so that they could be read aloud and understood in the local courts they made his will known and publicized his grants of privileges.[1] Despite differences of local custom a uniform system of local courts, each presided over by a royal official, administered a law with which the king himself was being increasingly involved. Alone among kings in western Europe the kings of England controlled a system of direct national taxation and a coinage common to the whole realm. The military arrangements of England had proved equal to the task first of defending Wessex, then of reconquering the Danelaw. If they did not serve to repulse Swein and Cnut the fault lay in the leadership of the armies rather than in their intrinsic deficiencies.

Little of this was changed by the accession of first Swein, then of Cnut, to the English throne. Just as the Germans had swallowed up the Romano-Britons, so, four centuries later they absorbed the new Scandinavian element whose first waves had arrived in the ninth century and were reinforced in the early eleventh century. There may have been fewer Danes than was once supposed and they may have often settled in areas previously only sparsely inhabited, but

---

[1] P. Chaplais, ' The Anglo-Saxon Chancery: from the diploma to the writ ', *Journal of the Society of Archivists*, III (1966) has sounded a warning note against exaggerating the degree of organization in the royal writing office in the late Anglo-Saxon period.

the absorption of the Danelaw into England was a remarkable phenomenon. Of course, the Danelaw long retained customs peculiar to
the Danes but there were marked regional variations in other parts
of England as well and so there continued to be for many centuries
after the Norman Conquest. Not until the thirteenth century did an
English king habitually travel north of the Humber; in the fifteenth
century Northumberland knew no lord but a Percy and in the south-
west the families of Bonville and Courtenay meant more than the
king of England. Despite the influx of Danes and the social and legal
peculiarities they sustained, the inhabitants of England in the
eleventh century were as conscious as they had been in Bede's time
that there was a land called England whose inhabitants could be
described as Englishmen. Regional distinctions did not assume the
guise of political particularism. How deep this went one cannot say
and certainly the horizon of most men must have been limited to the
villages in which they toiled so laboriously; but the versions of the
Anglo-Saxon Chronicle written in the reign of Edward the Confessor,
one at Canterbury and the other somewhere in northern England,
speak with the same voice. They give independent accounts of the
events of Edward's reign and are particularly detailed in their
versions of Godwin's quarrel with the king in 1051. It is the northern
writer whose views are particularly illuminating: he tells us that
the northerners were prepared to fight the army of Earl Godwin if
the king so ordered:

> But some men thought that it would be great folly, were the two sides
> to come together in battle; well nigh all that was most gallant in England
> was in one or other of the hosts.

And when trouble recurred in the next year:

> It was hateful to almost all of them that they should fight against men
> of their own kin, because there were very few who were worth much
> in either army who were not Englishmen. . . . They did not wish that
> by destroying each other, they should put this country at the mercy
> of foreigners.

Whether written in northern or southern England the language
that the chroniclers used was the same—West Saxon, which had
become the common language of England. The northern chronicler
shows that irrespective of their racial origins and their local territorial affiliations men, in a crisis, were conscious that they were
Englishmen, owing a common loyalty to the king.

Cnut did his utmost to rule as a king of England accepting all that he found. In his reign that king was the head of a Scandinavian empire which maintained contacts with all the civilized west: his alliance was coveted by every ruler in western Europe and the range and variety of English contacts with the Continent was more extended than ever before. He ruled a kingdom immediately responsive to his will. In 1042 it would have appeared incredible that within thirty years England would be conquered by the ruler of the duchy of Normandy, which at that time was enduring the wretchedness of a minority, whose nominal duke was under the tutelage of great vassals whose energies were largely occupied with dismembering and appropriating the attributes of ducal authority. Even ten years later the game was not lost. In 1051-52 the rebellion of Godwin suddenly lost its threatening aspect when the king called out the fyrd, and the local thegns who had commended themselves to the earl drifted away from his army. Edward's greatest and only significant failure was his failure to generate an heir.

A SIMPLIFIED GENEALOGY OF NORTHUMBRIAN KINGS,
c. 560–729

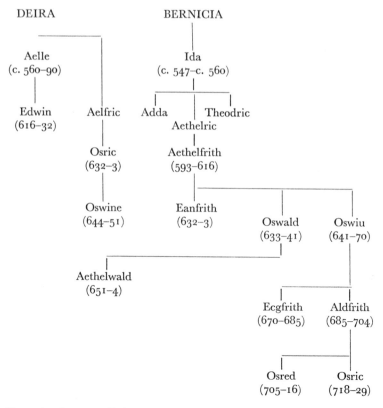

DEIRA   BERNICIA

Aelle   Ida
(c. 560–90)   (c. 547–c. 560)

Edwin   Aelfric   Adda   Theodric
(616–32)   Aethelric

          Osric   Aethelfrith
          (632–3)   (593–616)

          Oswine   Eanfrith
          (644–51)   (632–3)   Oswald   Oswiu
                                   (633–41)   (641–70)

Aethelwald
(651–4)
                                   Ecgfrith   Aldfrith
                                   (670–685)   (685–704)

                                   Osred   Osric
                                   (705–16)   (718–29)

Note: the dates supplied are 'conventional' and may require some revision in the light of current research.

A SIMPLIFIED GENEALOGY OF MERCIAN KINGS, c. 632–823

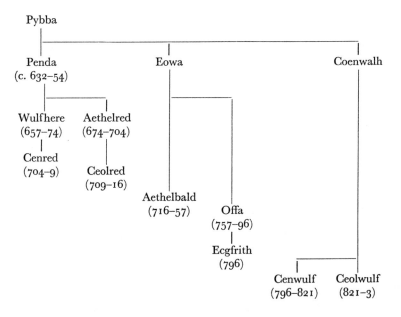

Pybba

Penda (c. 632–54) Eowa Coenwalh

Wulfhere (657–74) Aethelred (674–704)

Cenred (704–9) Ceolred (709–16)

Aethelbald (716–57) Offa (757–96)

Ecgfrith (796)

Cenwulf (796–821) Ceolwulf (821–3)

THE KINGS OF WESSEX AND ENGLAND, c. 802–1042

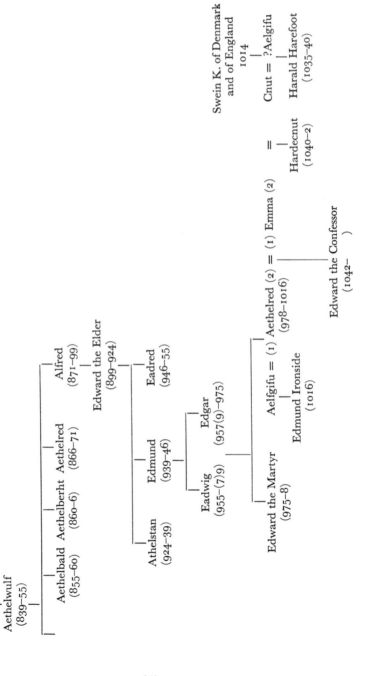

12*

NOTE ON BOOKS

The indispensable companion to serious work on Anglo-Saxon England is D. Whitelock, *English Historical Documents, c. 500-1042* (London, 1955). In a single volume it contains an excellent selection of source materials in translation (including all the Anglo-Saxon Chronicles to 1042) and a general introduction to Anglo-Saxon England, as well as introductions and comprehensive bibliographies arranged under subjects. The *Annual Bulletin of Historical Literature* published by the Historical Association serves to keep Professor Whitelock's book up to date.

An attempt has been made in the footnotes to this volume to indicate source materials published since 1955, but two works call for special mention. The important recent edition of Bede's *Ecclesiastical History of the English People* (Oxford, 1970) contains an excellent text and translation, but the notes to C. Plummer's edition, *Venerabilis Bedae Opera Historica* (2 vols., Oxford, 1896) still make it invaluable to the serious student. P. H. Sawyer, *Anglo-Saxon Charters* (London, 1968) is a catalogue of all known texts which includes references to important discussions of individual charters.

GENERAL HISTORIES

The best short introduction to the Anglo-Saxons is D. Whitelock, *The Beginnings of English Society* (London, 1952). It is difficult to believe that any large-scale general histories of the period will, for a long time, supersede the contributions of J. N. L. Myers in R. G. Collingwood and J. N. L. Myres, *Roman Britain and the English Settlements* (2nd edn, Oxford, 1937), and F. M. Stenton,

Anglo-Saxon England (3rd edn, Oxford, 1971). P. Hunter Blair, *An Introduction to Anglo-Saxon England* (Cambridge, 1959) is a work of acute scholarship conceived on a different plan, and D. L. Kirby, *The Making of England* (London, 1967), though sometimes idiosyncratic contains several outstandingly good chapters. H. R. Loyn, *Anglo-Saxon England and the Norman Conquest* (Oxford, 1962) is a good, and the only, comprehensive account of the social and economic history of the period. The collection of Sir Frank Stenton's essays, *Preparatory to Anglo-Saxon England,* ed. D. M. Stenton (Oxford, 1970) contains his superb series of Presidential Addresses to the Royal Historical Society on ' The Historical Bearing of Place-Name Studies ' in addition to much else of great value.

Standard Secondary Works

No attempt is made here at a comprehensive bibliography, but among older books those mentioned here are still valuable. Three books by H. M. Chadwick, *Studies on Anglo-Saxon Institutions* (Cambridge, 1905), *The Origins of the English Nation* (Cambridge, 1907), and *The Heroic Age* (Cambridge, 1907) reflect an unsurpassed breadth of learning. P. Vinogradoff, *Villeinage in England* (Oxford, 1892), *English History in the Eleventh Century* (Oxford, 1908), *Growth of the Manor* (London, 1911), and F. W. Maitland, *Domesday Book and Beyond* (Cambridge, 1897) were pioneer works of social and economic history. So too, in different fields, were E. T. Leeds, *The Archaeology of the Anglo-Saxon Settlement* (Oxford, 1913), F. Liebermann, *The National Assembly in the Anglo-Saxon Period* (Halle, 1913), and L. M. Larson, *The King's Household in England before the Norman Conquest* (Madison, 1904). W. Bright, *Chapters in English Church History* (Oxford, 1897) and W. Hunt, *History of the English Church* (London, 1907) and, especially, H. Williams, *Christianity in Early Britain* (Oxford, 1912) remain useful accounts of the Church. C. Plummer, *Life and Times of Alfred the Great* (Oxford, 1902) is the best available biography of that king, written by a great scholar. R. H. Hodgkin, *History of the Anglo-Saxons* (3rd edn, Oxford, 1952) ends with the death of Alfred.

The years between the two world wars saw the publication of J. E. A. Jolliffe, *Pre-Feudal England: The Jutes* (Oxford, 1933), and the same scholar's provocative but stimulating, *The Constitutional History of England* (2nd edn, London, 1947), which provoked from

F. E. Harmer the important review article, 'Anglo-Saxon Charters and the Historian' (*Bulletin of the John Rylands Library*, XXII, 1938). Important contributions to our understanding of the Vikings were H. Shetelig and H. Falk, *Scandinavian Archaeology* (Oxford, 1937), and T. D. Kendrick, *A History of the Vikings* (London, 1930). Ecclesiastical history was advanced by J. F. Kenney, *Sources for the Early History of Ireland*, Vol. I: *Ecclesiastical* (Columbia, 1929), J. A. Duke, *The Columban Church* (Oxford, 1932), the volume of essays, *Bede: his Life, Times and Writings*, ed. A. Hamilton Thompson (Oxford, 1935), and J. A. Robinson, *The Times of St. Dunstan* (Oxford, 1923). The most important work to appear during the war years was D. Knowles, *The Monastic Order in England* (2nd edn, Cambridge, 1949); H. M. Cam, *Liberties and Communities in Medieval England* (Cambridge, 1944) contains studies on the early history of the hundred.

Modern Works

It might be supposed that after so much prolonged study there would be general agreement among scholars on most of the important topics of Anglo-Saxon history. This is probably less true of the present time than of thirty years ago; not only are archaeological and numismatic studies constantly increasing the material evidence available but older interpretations are under constant critical scrutiny. Much of the most interesting recent work on the period has appeared in volumes of studies by different authors collected in commemoration of their masters. Such are *The Early Cultures of North-West Europe*, ed. C. Fox and B. Dickins (Cambridge, 1950), *Aspects of Archaeology in Britain and Beyond*, ed. W. F. Grimes (London, 1951); *Dark Age Britain*, ed. D. B. Harden (London, 1956); *The Anglo-Saxons*, ed. P. Clemoes (Cambridge, 1959); *Anglo-Saxon Coins*, ed. R. M. H. Dolley (London, 1961); and *England before the Conquest*, ed. K. Hughes and P. Clemoes (Cambridge, 1971). Other volumes of collected essays are those edited by N. K. Chadwick, *Studies in Early British History* (Cambridge, 1954), *Studies in the Early British Church* (Cambridge, 1958), and *Celt and Saxon* (Cambridge, 1963); see, too, *Christianity in Britain, 300-700*, ed. M. W. Barley and R. P. C. Hanson (Leicester, 1968), *Angles and Britons: O'Donnell Lectures* (Cardiff, 1963), and the papers delivered to the *Fourth Viking Congress*, ed. A. Small (Edinburgh, 1965). Two collections of studies by individual authors, both highly revisionist in their approach are H. P. R. Finberg, *Lucerna* (London, 1964), and E. John *Orbis Britanniae* (Leicester, 1966). The annual Jarrow Lectures, given by a succession of distinguished scholars, have notably increased our understanding of the age of Bede. A few references to contributions in learned periodicals have been noticed in the footnotes to this book: not only are specifically ' historical ' periods important but much of value to the historian will be found in the publications of local societies and in journals primarily devoted to other disciplines; such are *Antiquity, Archaeological Journal, Journal of the British Archaeological Association, Medieval Archaeology, Numismatic Chronicle* and *British Numismatic Journal.*

In view of the importance of non-historical categories of evidence to the historian of Anglo-Saxon England the unpretentious introduction to the problems dealing with such material by F. T. Wainwright, *Archaeology and Place-Names and History* (London, 1962) will be found useful. For place-names A. H. Smith, *English Place-Name Elements* (Two parts, Cambridge, 1956).

A useful introduction to some tendencies of scholarship since the end of the second World War is D. Whitelock, *Changing Currents in Anglo-Saxon Studies* (Cambridge, 1958). The most important monographs to have appeared since 1945 are W. Levison, *England and the Continent in the Eighth Century* (Oxford, 1946), K. H. Jackson, *Language and History in Early Britain* (Edinburgh, 1953) and J. W. Wallace-Hadrill, *Early Anglo-Saxon and Germanic Kingship* (Oxford, 1971). Other valuable publications include S. S. Frere, *Britannia* (London, 1967); J. N. L. Myres, *Anglo-Saxon Pottery and the Settlement of England* (Oxford, 1967); G. J. Copley, *The Conquest of Wessex in the Sixth Century* (London, 1954); C. Green, *Sutton Hoo: the excavation of a royal ship burial* (London, 1963), and D. A. Binchey, *Celtic and Anglo-Saxon Kingship* (Oxford, 1970). F. M. Stenton *The Latin Charters of the Anglo-Saxon Period* (Oxford, 1955) is the only extended discussion of Anglo-Saxon charters that we have. Early Church history has been enriched by K. Hughes, *The Church in Early Irish Society* (London, 1966); H. Mayr-Harting, *The Coming of Christianity to Anglo-Saxon England* (London, 1972), and P. Hunter Blair, *The World of Bede* (London, 1970). M. Deanesley, *The Pre-Conquest Church in England* (2nd edn, London, 1963) is an up-to-date survey of the whole period.

Recent contributions to Viking history are G. Turville Petre, *The*

Heroic Age of Scandinavia (London, 1951), E. O. G. Turville-Petre, *Myth and Religion of the North* (London, 1964), Gwyn Jones, *A History of the Vikings* (London, 1968), and P. H. Sawyer, *The Age of the Vikings* (2nd edn, London, 1971).

Controversial, but stimulating and important, are E. John, *Land Tenure in Early England* (Leicester, 1960), C. W. Hollister, *Anglo-Saxon Institutions on the Eve of the Norman Conquest* (Oxford, 1962), and the relevant chapters in H. G. Richardson and G. O. Sayles, *The Governance of Medieval England* (Edinburgh, 1963) and in their *Law and Legislation in Medieval England* (Edinburgh, 1966). Monographs dealing with topics in late Anglo-Saxon history are F. Barlow, *The English Church 1000-1066: A Constitutional History* (London, 1963), and T. J. Oleson. *The Witanagemot in the Reign of Edward the Confessor* (London, 1955).

Literary studies of importance to the historian are: G. K. Anderson, *The Literature of the Anglo-Saxons* (Princeton, 1949), K. Sisam *Studies in the History of Old English Literature* (Oxford, 1953) D. Whitelock, *The Audience of Beowulf* (Oxford, 1951), R. W. Chambers, *Beowulf: An Introduction* (3rd edn, C. L. Wrenn, Cambridge, 1959). C. E. Wright, *The Cultivation of Saga in Anglo-Saxon England* (Edinburgh, 1939), and R. M. Wilson, *The Lost Literature of Medieval England* (London, 1952), are as instructive as they are interesting. M. Alexander, *The Earliest English Poems* (London, 1966) is a book of translations which though unpretentious in format provides an excellent introduction to Anglo-Saxon poetry. An inexpensive but first-rate translation of the Chronicle is that by G. M. Garmonsway, *The Anglo-Saxon Chronicle* (London, 1953); and of Bede's *Ecclesiastical History* that of L. Sherley-Price (London, 1955). Anglo-Saxon art is faithfully treated by G. Baldwin Brown, *The Arts in Early England* (6 vols., London, 1903-37), and by T. D. Kendrick in *Anglo-Saxon Art to A.D. 900* (London, 1938), and *Late Saxon and Viking Art* (London, 1949); special mention must be made of F. Wormald, *English Drawings of the Tenth and Eleventh Centuries* (London, 1952). A. W. Clapham, *English Romanesque Architecture,* vol. I, *Before the Conquest* (repr. Oxford, 1966) and H. M. and J. Taylor, *Anglo-Saxon Architecture* (2 vols., Cambridge, 1965) are both, in their different ways, excellent.

INDEX

ABERCORN, see of, 92, 93, 104, 142
Abingdon (Berks.), abbey of, 88, 285, 287, 288; see also Aethelwold
Acca, bp. of Hexham, 103, 150, 157, 161
Adamnon, abbot of Iona, 25, 62, 105, 117; his Life of St Columba, 62; his tract on the Holy Places, 144, 179
Aedan, king of Dalriada, 40
Aelfgar, s. of ealdorman Aelfric of Hampshire, 303
Aelfgifu of Northampton, 320, 325-6
Aelfheah the Bald, bp. of Winchester, 283, 285, 286
Aelfheah II, bp. of Winchester, abp. of Canterbury, 314, 332
Aelfheah, ealdorman of Hampshire, 259
Aelfhelm, ealdorman of Northumbria, 302, 303
Aelfhere, ealdorman of Mercia, 259-60, 271, 298-300, 311
Aelflaed, d. of king Offa, 147
Aelfric, abbot of Eynsham, 292, 312
Aelfric, ealdorman of Hampshire, 303, 304
Aelfric, s. of Aelfhere ealdorman of Mercia, 271, 303
Aelfric (Puttoc), abp. of York, 327, 335
Aelfthryth, d. of king Alfred, 197, 266
Aelfthryth, w. of king Edgar, 298, 299, 300
Aelfwald, king of Northumbria, 146, 166, 169
Aelfwine, bp. of Winchester, 335
Aelfwynn, d. of Aethelred ealdorman of Mercia, 246
Aelle, king of Deira, 39
Aelle, king of Northumbria, 148, 215
Aelle, king of the South-Saxons, 19, 31, 45, 113, 114

Aesc (Oisc), king of Kent, 17, 19-20, 120
Aethelbald, king of Mercia, 103, 113, 136, 145, 162-3, 164, 165, 170-2, 193
Aethelbald, king of Wessex, 213, 226
Aethelberg, d. of king Aethelberht, 73, 74
Aethelberht, abp. of York, 152, 161, 189
Aethelberht, king of East Anglia, 164
Aethelberht, king of Kent, 33, 57, 66, 68-73, 113, 114-15
Aethelberht, under-king of Kent, king of Wessex, 213-14, 226
Aethelflaed, d. of king Alfred, 226, 238-40
Aethelfrith, king of Northumbria, 41-2
Aethelheard, abp. of Canterbury 202, 205
Aethelheard, king of Wessex, 120
Aethelhere, king of East Anglia, 118
Aethelmaer, s. of ealdorman Aethelweard, 312, 315
Aethelnoth, abp. of Canterbury, 328, 334, 335
Aethelred, abp. of Canterbury, 204
Aethelred, ealdorman of Mercia 223, 226-7, 238
Aethelred, king of England, 298, 300-11; conduct of war, 302-5; defeat by Swein, 311-18; policy towards Danelaw, 301-2; resilience of administration under, 306-11.
Aethelred, king of Mercia, 87-8, 103, 142, 166
Aethelred, king of Northumbria, 146, 147, 164, 169
Aethelred, king of Wessex, 203, 215, 216
Aethelric, bp. of Dorchester, 335
Aethelric, king of Bernicia, 41
Aethelric, under-king and comes of the Hwicce, 164

359